SECOND EDITION

Data Management at Scale
Modern Data Architecture with
Data Mesh and Data Fabric

Piethein Strengholt

Beijing · Boston · Farnham · Sebastopol · Tokyo

Data Management at Scale

by Piethein Strengholt

Published by O'Reilly Media, Inc., 1005 Gravenstein Highway North, Sebastopol, CA 95472.

O'Reilly books may be purchased for educational, business, or sales promotional use. Online editions are also available for most titles (*http://oreilly.com*). For more information, contact our corporate/institutional sales department: 800-998-9938 or *corporate@oreilly.com*.

Acquisitions Editor: Michelle Smith
Development Editor: Shira Evans
Production Editor: Katherine Tozer
Copyeditor: Rachel Head
Proofreader: Piper Editorial Consulting, LLC

Indexer: nSight, Inc.
Interior Designer: David Futato
Cover Designer: Karen Montgomery
Illustrator: Kate Dullea

April 2023:   Second Edition

Revision History for the Second Edition
2023-04-10:   First Release
2024-01-05:   Second Release

See *https://oreilly.com/catalog/errata.csp?isbn=9781098138868* for release details.

978-1-098-13886-8

[LSI]

Table of Contents

Foreword

Whenever we talk about software, we inevitably end up talking about data—how much there is, where it all lives, what it means, where it came from or needs to go, and what happens when it changes. These questions have stuck with us over the years, while the technology we use to manage our data has changed rapidly. Today's databases provide instantaneous access to vast online datasets; analytics systems answer complex, probing questions; event-streaming platforms not only connect different applications but also provide storage, query processing, and built-in data management tools.

As these technologies have evolved, so have the expectations of our users. A user is often connected to many different backend systems, located in different parts of a company, as they switch from mobile to desktop to call center, change location, or move from one application to another. All the while, they expect a seamless and real-time experience. I think the implications of this are far greater than many may realize. The challenge involves a large estate of software, data, and people that must appear—at least to our users—to be a single joined-up unit.

Managing company-wide systems like this has always been a dark art, something I got a feeling for when I helped build the infrastructure that backs LinkedIn. All of LinkedIn's data is generated continuously, 24 hours a day, by processes that never stop. But when I first arrived at the company, the infrastructure for harnessing that data was often limited to big, slow, batch data dumps at the end of the day and simplistic lookups, jerry-rigged together with homegrown data feeds. The concept of "end-of-the-day batch processing" seemed to me to be some legacy of a bygone era of punch cards and mainframes. Indeed, for a global business, the day doesn't end.

As LinkedIn grew, it too became a sprawling software estate, and it was clear to me that there was no off-the-shelf solution for this kind of problem. Furthermore, having built the NoSQL databases that powered LinkedIn's website, I knew that there was an emerging renaissance of distributed systems techniques, which meant solutions could be built that weren't possible before. This led to Apache Kafka, which combined scalable messaging, storage, and processing over the profile updates, page visits, payments, and other event streams that sat at the core of LinkedIn.

While Kafka streamlined LinkedIn's dataflows, it also affected the way applications were built. Like many Silicon Valley firms at the turn of the last decade, we had been experimenting with microservices, and it took several iterations to come up with something that was both functional and stable. This problem was as much about data and people as it was about software: a complex, interconnected system that had to evolve as the company grew. Handling a problem this big required a new kind of technology, but it also needed a new skill set to go with it.

Of course, there was no manual for navigating this problem back then. We worked it out as we went along, but this book may well have been the missing manual we needed. In it, Piethein provides a comprehensive strategy for managing data not simply in a solitary database or application but across the many databases, applications, microservices, storage layers, and all other types of software that make up today's technology landscapes.

He also takes an opinionated view, with an architecture to match, grounded in a well-thought-out set of principles. These help to bound the decision space with logical guardrails, inside of which a host of practical solutions should fit. I think this approach will be very valuable to architects and engineers as they map their own problem domain to the trade-offs described in this book. Indeed, Piethein takes you on a journey that goes beyond data and applications into the rich fabric of interactions that bind entire companies together.

— Jay Kreps
Cofounder and CEO at Confluent

Preface

Data management is an emerging and disruptive subject. Datafication (*https://oreil.ly/ xtutZ*) is everywhere. This transformation is happening all around us: in smartphones, TV devices, ereaders, industrial machines, self-driving cars, robots, and so on. It's changing our lives at an accelerating speed.

As the amount of data generated skyrockets, so does its complexity. Disruptive trends like cloudification, API and ecosystem connectivity, microservices, open data, software as a service (SaaS), and new software delivery models have a tremendous effect on data management. In parallel, we see an enormous number of new applications transforming our businesses. All these trends are fragmenting the data landscape. As a result, we are seeing more point-to-point interfaces, endless discussions about data quality and ownership, and plenty of ethical and legal dilemmas regarding privacy, safety, and security. Agility, long-term stability, and clear data governance compete with the need to develop new business cases swiftly. We sorely need a clear vision for the future of data management.

This book's perspective on data management is informed by my personal experience driving the data architecture agenda for a large enterprise as chief data architect. Executing that role showed me clearly the impact a good data strategy can have on a large organization. After leaving that company, I started working as the chief data officer for Microsoft Netherlands. In this exciting new position, I've worked with over 50 large customers discussing and attempting to come up with a perfect data solution. Here are some of the common threads I've identified across all enterprises:

- An overarching data strategy is often missing or not connected to the business objectives. Discussions about data management mostly pivot to technology trends and engineering discussions. What is needed is business engagement: a good strategy and well-thought-out data management and analysis plan that includes tangible value in the form of business use cases. To make my point: the focus must be put on usage and turning data into business value.

- Enterprises have difficulties in interpreting new concepts like the data mesh and data fabric, because pragmatic guidance and experiences from the field are missing. In addition to that, the data mesh fully embraces a decentralized approach, which is a transformational change not only for the data architecture and technology, but even more so for organization and processes. This means the transformation cannot only be led by IT; it's a business transformation as well.

- Enterprises find it difficult to comprehend the latest technology trends. They're unable to interpret nuances or make pragmatic choices.

- Enterprises struggle to get started: large ambitions often end with limited action; the execution plan and architecture remain too high-level, too conceptual; top-down commitment from leadership is missing.

These experiences and my observations across a range of enterprises inspired me to write this second edition of *Data Management at Scale*. You may wonder why this book is worth reading, over the first edition—let's take a closer look.

Why I Wrote This Book and Why Now

The first edition was founded on the experience I gained while working at ABN AMRO as chief data architect.[1] In that role, my team and I practiced the approach of federation: shifting activities and responsibilities in response to the need for a faster pace of change. We used governance for balancing the imperatives of centralization and decentralization. This shift was supported by a central data team that started to develop platforms for empowering business units to meet their goals. With platforms, we introduced self-service and aligned analysts to domains, supporting them in implementing their use cases. We experimented with domain-driven design and eventually switched to business architecture for managing the architectural landscape as a whole. I used all these experiences as input for writing the first edition.

The term *data mesh* as a description of a sociotechnical approach to using data at large was coined at around the time the manuscript for the first edition was being finalized. When Zhamak Dehghani's article describing the concept appeared on Martin Fowler's website (*https://oreil.ly/Metdq*), it revealed concrete names for concepts we'd already been using at ABN AMRO for many years. These names became industry terms, and the concept quickly began to resonate with large organizations as a solution to the friction enterprises encounter when scaling up.

So, why write a second edition? To start with, it was the data mesh concept. I love the ideas of bringing data management and software architecture closer together and

---

1 The statements and opinions expressed in this book don't necessarily reflect the positions of ABN AMRO or Microsoft.

businesses taking ownership of their data, but I firmly believe that, with all the fuss, a more nuanced view is needed.

In my previous role as an enterprise architect, we had hundreds of application teams, thousands of services, and many large legacy applications to manage. In such situations, you approach complexity differently. With the data mesh architecture, *artist*, *song*, and *playlist* are often used as data domain examples. This approach of decomposing data into fine-grained domains might work well when designing microservices, but it isn't well suited to (re)structuring large data landscapes. A different viewpoint is needed for scale. Next, a more nuanced and pragmatic view of data products is needed. There are good reasons why data must be managed holistically and end-to-end. Enterprises have reusability and consistency concerns. They're forced by regulation to conform to the same dimensions for group reporting, accounting, financial reporting, and auditing and risk management. I know this might sound controversial, but a data product cannot be advocated to be managed as a container: something that packages data, metadata, code, and infrastructure all together in an architecture as tiny as a microservice. This doesn't reflect how today's big data platforms work. Finally, the data mesh story isn't complete: it focuses only on data that is used for analytical purposes, not operational purposes; it omits master data management;[2] the consumer side must be complemented with an intelligent data fabric; and it doesn't provide much data modeling guidance for building data products.

Another incentive for publishing a second edition was concerns about the book's practicality. The first version was perceived by various readers as too abstract. Some critical reviewers even left comments questioning my hands-on experience. In this second edition I've worked hard to address these concerns, providing many real-world examples and concrete solution diagrams. From time to time, I also refer to blog posts that I've written about how to implement designs. One final note on this: *there are a large number of very complex topics to cover, which are also highly context-sensitive.* It would be impossible to provide examples of everything in a single volume, so I've had to use some discretion.

I'm excited to share my thoughts on best practices and observations from the field, and I hope this book inspires you. Reflecting on my time working at ABN AMRO, there are lots of good lessons to be taken from other enterprises. I've seen a lot of good approaches. There's no right or wrong when building good data architecture; it's all about making the right trade-offs and discovering what works best for your situation.

---

2 The terminology "master/slave" is clearly offensive, and many organizations have switched to alternatives like "source/replica" or "primary/subordinate." We strive to be as inclusive as possible, but will use "master data management" in this book because the industry hasn't yet adopted an alternative.

If you've already read the first edition, you should find this one significantly different and much improved. Structurally it's more or less the same, but every chapter has been revised and enhanced. All the diagrams have also been revised, new content has been added, and it's much more practical. Within each chapter you'll find many tips, starting points, and references to helpful articles.

Who Is This Book For?

This book is intended for large enterprises, though smaller organizations may find much of value in it. It's geared toward:

Executives and architects
> Chief data officers, chief technology officers, chief architects, enterprise architects, and lead data architects

Analytics teams
> Data scientists, data engineers, data analysts, and heads of analytics

Development teams
> Data engineers, data scientists, business intelligence engineers, data modelers and designers, and other data professionals

Compliance and governance teams
> Chief information security officers, data protection officers, information security analysts, regulatory compliance heads, data stewards, and business analysts

How to Read or Use This Book

It's important to say up front that this book touches upon a lot of complex topics that are often interrelated or intertwined with other subjects. So we'll be hopping between different technologies, business methods, frameworks, and architecture patterns. From time to time I bring in my own operational experience when implementing different architectures, so we'll be working at different levels of abstraction. To describe the journey through the book, I'll use the analogy of a helicopter ride.

We'll start with a zoomed-out view, looking at data management, data strategy, and data architecture at an abstract and higher level. From this helicopter view, we'll start to zoom in and first explore what data domains and landing zones are. We'll then fly to the source system side of our landscape, in which applications are managed and data is created, and circle until we have covered most of the areas of data management. Then we'll fly over to the consumer side of the landscape and start learning about the dynamics there. After that, we'll bring everything we've covered together by putting things into practice.

To help you navigate through the book, the following table gives a high-level overview of which subjects will be intensively discussed in each chapter.

Table P-1. Key topics in each chapter

	Ch. 1	Ch. 2	Ch. 3	Ch. 4	Ch. 5	Ch. 6	Ch. 7	Ch. 8	Ch. 9	Ch. 10	Ch. 11	Ch. 12
Data management	X											
Data strategy	X	X	X									X
Data architecture		X	X				X					X
Data integration				X	X	X	X					
Data modeling				X			X		X			
Data governance								X				
Data security								X				
Data quality				X								
Metadata management									X			
MDM										X		
Business intelligence											X	
Advanced analytics											X	
Enterprise architecture							X					X

Chapter 1 introduces the topic of data management. It gives a contextual view of what data management is, how it's changing, and how it affects our digital transformation. It provides an assessment of the state of the field in recent years and guidance for working out a data strategy. In Chapter 2, we'll jump into the details of managing data at large, exploring domain-driven design and business architecture as methodologies for managing a large data landscape using data domains. Next, Chapter 3 focuses on topologies and data landing zones as a way of structuring your data architecture and aligning with your data domains.

The following chapters discuss the specifics of distributing data. Chapter 4 focuses on data products, Command Query Responsibility Segregation (CQRS), and guiding principles, and presents an example solution design. Chapter 5 discusses API management, and Chapter 6 covers event and notification management. Chapter 7 brings it all together for a comprehensive overview, complemented with architecture guidance and experience.

Next, we delve deeper into more advanced aspects of data management. Chapter 8 examines how to approach data governance and security in ways that are practical and sustainable for the long term, even in rapidly changing times. Chapter 9 is a deep dive into the use, significance, and democratizing potential of metadata. Chapter 10 offers guidance on using master data management (MDM) to keep data consistent over distributed, wide-ranging assets, while Chapter 11 addresses turning data into value. Chapter 12 concludes the book with an example of making it real and a vision for the future of data management and enterprise architecture.

Conventions Used in This Book

The following typographical conventions are used in this book:

Italic
> Indicates new terms, URLs, email addresses, filenames, and file extensions.

`Constant width`
> Used for program listings, as well as within paragraphs to refer to program elements such as variable or function names, databases, data types, environment variables, statements, and keywords.

This element signifies a tip or suggestion.

This element signifies a general note.

This element indicates a warning or caution.

O'Reilly Online Learning

For more than 40 years, *O'Reilly Media* has provided technology and business training, knowledge, and insight to help companies succeed.

Our unique network of experts and innovators share their knowledge and expertise through books, articles, and our online learning platform. O'Reilly's online learning platform gives you on-demand access to live training courses, in-depth learning paths, interactive coding environments, and a vast collection of text and video from O'Reilly and 200+ other publishers. For more information, visit *http://oreilly.com*.

How to Contact Us

Please address comments and questions concerning this book to the publisher:

O'Reilly Media, Inc.
1005 Gravenstein Highway North
Sebastopol, CA 95472
800-998-9938 (in the United States or Canada)
707-829-0515 (international or local)
707-829-0104 (fax)

We have a web page for this book, where we list errata, examples, and any additional information. You can access this page at *https://oreil.ly/data-mgmt-at-scale-2e*.

Email *bookquestions@oreilly.com* to comment or ask technical questions about this book.

For more information about our books, courses, conferences, and news, see our website at *http://www.oreilly.com*.

Find us on Facebook: *http://facebook.com/oreilly*.

Follow us on Twitter: *http://twitter.com/oreillymedia*.

Watch us on YouTube: *http://youtube.com/oreillymedia*.

Acknowledgments

I would like to acknowledge Jessica Strengholt-Geitenbeek for allowing me to write this book. She has supported me throughout this journey, taking care of the kids and creating room to allow me to work on this, and she's the love of my life.

I also would like to thank ABN AMRO, and especially Santhosh Pillai for his trust and for guiding me throughout my career at the company. Many of the initial ideas for this project originated in his mind. Without the countless discussions he and I had, this book wouldn't exist. Next, I would like to thank Microsoft for providing the support I needed to write this second edition. In addition, many others provided support and feedback on the book: thanks to Tim Ward (CEO at CluedIn), Batuhan Tuter, Nasim Mehrshid, Rob Worrall, Frank Leisten, and all the others who contributed in various ways.

Thanks also to the book's technical reviewers, John Mallinder and Ole Olesen-Bagneux. Your valuable insights and feedback helped validate the technical content and make this a better book.

Finally, I would like to thank all the fantastic crew members from O'Reilly for their support and trust. Shira, thank you for taking care of me. I enjoyed our conversations, and I'm grateful for your constructive feedback. Katie, thank you for your continuous support and transparency. To my fantastic copyeditor Rachel Head, thank you for your hard work to review and edit all content. You really have done an outstanding job by debugging the content and connecting my sentences.

CHAPTER 1

The Journey to Becoming Data-Driven

The pre-COVID-19 world was already fast and highly data-driven, but the pace of change has accelerated rapidly. Fierce competition, a digital-first era, ever-increasing customer expectations, and rising regulatory scrutiny require organizations to transform themselves into modern data-driven enterprises. This transformation will inevitably result in future organizations being more digital than those of today, and having a different view of data. Tomorrow's organizations will breathe data and embrace a philosophy that places it at the heart of their business. They will manage data as a product, make strategic decisions based on data analysis, and have a culture that acts on data.

Data-driven isn't just a buzzword.[1] Being data-driven provides an organization with a significant competitive advantage over other organizations. It can be proactive, and it can predict what will happen before it does. By using data correctly, organizations can quickly react to changes. Using data leads to greater confidence because decisions are based on facts, not intuition. With data, new industry trends and business opportunities can be spotted sooner. Customer retention and satisfaction are improved as well, because data tells organizations what customers think, how they behave, and what they want. With data, organizations can be more flexible, agile, and cost effective, because data provides insights into measured results, employee loyalty, dependencies, applications, and processes. So, the imperative for organizations to transform themselves into data-driven enterprises is definitively there.

Before we jump into the transformation itself, we'll explore the present-day challenges that require us to reevaluate how data must be managed. We'll establish a common definition of data management, encompassing all the disciplines and

---

1 The data analytics market is surging. It reached $200+ billion in annual spending in 2022, according to IDC (*https://oreil.ly/8OZzk*).

activities related to managing data as an asset. After that, we'll zoom in on several key technology developments and industry trends, and consider their impact on data management. We'll look at some best practices from the last decade of data management, providing insights into why previous-generation architectures are hard to scale. Finally, we'll consider what a next-generation data architecture might look like, and I'll present a set of action points that you will need to address while developing your data strategy.

Recent Technology Developments and Industry Trends

Transforming an organization to become data-driven isn't easy. It's a long-term process that requires patience and fortitude. With more data available, traditional architectures can no longer be scaled up because of their size, complexity, monolithic designs, and centralistic operating models. Enterprises need a new data strategy and cloud-based architecture. A paradigm shift and change of culture are needed, too, because the centralized data and IT operating models that work today will no longer work when applying federated data ownership and self-serve consumption models. This requires organizations to redefine how people, processes, and technology are aligned with data.

Recent technology developments and industry trends force us to reevaluate how data must be managed. We need to shift away from funneling all data into a single silo toward an approach that enables domains, teams, and users to distribute, consume, and use data themselves easily and securely. Platforms, processes, and patterns should simplify the work for others. We need interfaces that are simple, well documented, fast, and easy to consume. We need an architecture that works at scale.

Although there are many positives about evolving into a truly data-driven organization, it's important to be aware of several technology developments and industry trends that are impacting data landscapes. In this chapter, I'll discuss each of these and its influence on data management. Firstly, analytics is fragmenting the data landscape because of use case diversity. Secondly, new software development methodologies are making data harder to manage. Thirdly, cloud computing and faster networks are fragmenting data landscapes. In addition, there are privacy, security, and regulatory concerns to be aware of, and the rapid growth of data and intensive data consumption are making operational systems suffer. Lastly, data monetization requires an ecosystem-to-ecosystem architecture. The impact these trends have on data management is tremendous, and they are forcing the whole industry to rethink how data management must be conducted in the future.

Fortunately, new approaches to data management have emerged over the past few years, including the ideas of a *data mesh* and *data fabric*:

- The data mesh (*https://oreil.ly/kBtUG*) is an exciting new methodology for managing data at large. The concept foresees an architecture in which data is highly distributed and a future in which scalability is achieved by federating responsibilities. It puts an emphasis on the human factor and addressing the challenges of managing the increasing complexity of data architectures.

- The data fabric (*https://oreil.ly/bjl2F*) is an approach that addresses today's data management and scalability challenges by adding intelligence and simplifying data access using self-service. In contrast to the data mesh, it focuses more on the technology layer. It's an architectural vision using unified metadata with an end-to-end integrated layer (fabric) for easily accessing, integrating, provisioning, and using data.

These emerging approaches to data management are complementary and often overlap. Despite popular belief among data practitioners and what commercial vendors say, they shouldn't be seen as rigid or standalone techniques. In fact, I expect these approaches to coexist and complement one another and any existing investments in operational data stores, data warehouses, and data lakes.

In the transition to becoming data-driven, organizations need to make trade-offs to balance the imperatives of *centralization* and *decentralization*. Some prefer a high degree of autonomy for their business teams, while others prioritize quality and control. Some organizations have a relatively simple structure, while others are brutally large and complex. Creating the perfect governance structure and data architecture isn't easy, so while developing your strategy, I encourage you to view these approaches to data management as frameworks. There's no right or wrong. With the data mesh approach, for example, you might like some of the best practices and principles, but not others; you don't necessarily have to apply all of them.

In this book, I'll share my view on data management—one that is based on observations from the field while working closely with many large enterprises, and that helps you to make the right decisions by learning from others. We'll go beyond the concepts of data mesh and data fabric, because I strongly believe that a data strategy should be inclusive of both the operational and analytical planes, and that the decomposition method for both data domains and data products must be altered to fit the scale of large enterprises. To help you in your journey, I'll share my observations on the strategies and architectures different enterprises have designed, why, and what trade-offs they have made.

Before we jump into details, we need to agree on what data management is, and why it's important. Next, we need to determine how to define boundaries and shape our landscape based on various trade-offs. Finally, we'll examine how current enterprise data architectures can be designed and organized for today and tomorrow.

Let me lay my cards out on the table: decentralization is not a desired state, but the inevitable future of data. I therefore have a strong belief that scalability is forcing data management to become more decentrally organized. Managing data at scale requires you to federate key responsibilities, set strong standards, and properly align central and local resources and activities. This change affects multiple areas: people, processes, and technology. It forces you to decompose your architecture, dividing and grouping responsibilities. The shift from centralization to decentralization also contradicts the established best practice from the past decade: building large data silos in which all data is collected and integrated before being served. Although data warehouse and lake architectures are excellent approaches for utilizing data, these centralized models are not suited to a decentralized distributed data architecture.

Now that we've set the scene, I ask that you take a deep breath and put your biases aside. Many of us might be deeply invested in centralized data architectures; this has been a best practice for many years. I acknowledge that the need for data harmonization and for bringing large amounts of data into a particular context remains, and that doing so brings value to organizations, but something we must consider is the *scale* at which we want to apply this discipline. In a highly distributed ecosystem with hundreds or even thousands of applications, is the best way of managing data to apply centralization on all dimensions? Is it best to integrate and harmonize all data?

Data Management

The term *data management* refers to the set of processes and procedures used to manage data. The Data Management Association's Data Management Body of Knowledge (DAMA-DMBOK) (*https://oreil.ly/BKIm6*) has a more extensive explanation of data management, which it defines as "the development, execution, and supervision of plans, policies, programs, and practices that deliver, control, protect, and enhance the value of data and information assets throughout their life cycles."[2] The DAMA-DMBOK identifies 11 functional areas of data management, with data governance at the heart, as shown in Figure 1-1. It's crucial to embed all of these deeply into your organization. Otherwise, you'll lack insight and become ineffective, and your data will get out of control. Becoming data-driven—getting as much value as possible out of your data—will become a challenge. Analytics, for example, is worth nothing if you have low-quality data.

---

2 The Body of Knowledge is developed by the DAMA community. It has a slow update cycle: the first release was in 2008, the second one in 2017.

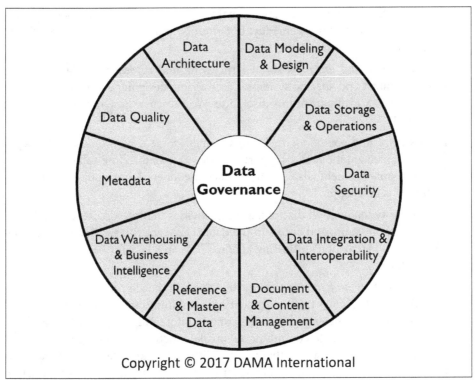

Copyright © 2017 DAMA International

Figure 1-1. The 11 functional areas of data management

The activities and disciplines of data management are wide ranging and cover multiple areas, some closely related to software architecture.[3] In this book, I'll focus on the aspects of data management that are most relevant for managing a modern data architecture at scale. Let's take a closer look at the 11 areas identified in this figure and where they're covered in the book:

- *Data governance,* shown at the heart of Figure 1-1, involves all activities around implementing and enforcing authority and control over the management of data, including all corresponding assets. This area is described in detail in Chapter 8.

- *Data architecture* involves the definition of the master plan for your data, including the blueprints,[4] reference architectures, future state vision, and dependencies.

---

3 *Software architecture* refers to the design and high-level structure of software needed to develop a system that meets business requirements and includes characteristics such as flexibility, scalability, feasibility, reusability, and security. If you want to learn more, read *Fundamentals of Software Architecture* by Mark Richards and Neal Ford (O'Reilly).

4 A blueprint is also known as a *reference implementation*. It consists of the Infrastructure as Code (IaC) definitions to successfully create a set of services for a specific use case.

Managing these helps organizations make decisions. The entire book revolves around data architecture generally, but the discipline and its activities will be covered fully in Chapters 2 and 3.

- *Data modeling and design* is about structuring and representing data within a specific context and specific systems. Discovering, designing, and analyzing data requirements are all part of this discipline. We'll discuss these topics in Chapters 4, 7, and 11.

- *Data storage and operations* refers to the management of the database design, correct implementation, and support in order to maximize the value of the data. Database management also includes database operations management. We'll address this in Chapter 11.

- *Data security* includes all disciplines and activities that provide secure authentication, authorization, and access to the data. These activities include prevention, auditing, and escalation-mitigating actions. This area is described in more detail in Chapter 8.

- *Data integration and interoperability* includes all the disciplines and activities related to moving, collecting, consolidating, combining, and transforming data in order to move it efficiently from one context into another. *Data interoperability* refers to the capability to communicate, invoke functions, or transfer data among various applications in a way that requires little or no knowledge of the application characteristics. *Data integration*, on the other hand, is about consolidating data from different (multiple) sources into a unified view. This process, which I consider most important, is often supported by extra tools, such as replication and ETL (extract, transform, and load) tools. It's described extensively in Chapters 4, 5, and 6.

- *Document and content management* is the process of managing data stored in unstructured (media) and data formats. Some aspects of this will be discussed in Chapters 5 and 6.

- *Reference and master data management* is about managing critical data to make sure the data is accessible, accurate, secure, transparent, and trustworthy. This area is described in more detail in Chapter 10.[5]

- *Data warehousing* and *business intelligence* management includes all the activities that provide business insights and support decision making. This area, including advanced analytics, is described in more depth in Chapter 11.

---

5 We use the term "master data management" (MDM) in this book because it has been widely adopted and has no industry-wide alternative at the time of this writing, but we welcome more inclusive alternatives to "master/slave" terminology.

- *Metadata* management involves managing all data that classifies and describes the data. Metadata can be used to make the data understandable, ready for integration, and secure. It can also be used to ensure the quality of data. This area is described in more detail in Chapter 9.

- *Data quality* management includes all activities related to managing the quality of data to ensure the data can be used. Some aspects of this area are described in Chapters 2 and 3.

The part of the DAMA-DMBOK that needs more work, which inspired me to write the first edition of this book, is the section on *data integration and interoperability*. I believe this section is lacking depth: the relationship to application integration and software architecture is not clear. It doesn't discuss decentralized architectures, and it lacks modern guidance on the interoperability of data, such as observability best practices and modern data pipeline management. In addition, the link to metadata management is weak. Metadata needs integration and interoperability, too, because it is scattered across many tools, applications, platforms, and environments in diverse shapes and forms. The interoperability of metadata—the ability of two or more systems or components to exchange descriptive data about data—gets insufficient treatment: building and managing a large-scale architecture is very much about metadata integration. Interoperability and metadata also aren't well connected to the area of data architecture. If metadata is utilized in the right way, you can see what data passes by, how it can be integrated, distributed, and secured, and how it connects to applications, business capabilities, and so on. There's limited guidance in the DAMA-DMBOK about managing your data as a whole by utilizing and connecting metadata.

Another concern I have is the view DAMA and many organizations have on achieving end-to-end semantic consistency. As of today, attempts to unify semantics to provide enterprise-wide consistency are still taking place. This is called a *single version of the truth*. However, *applications are always unique, and so is data*. Designing applications involves a lot of implicit thinking. The (domain) context of the business problem influences the design of the application and finds its way into the data. We pass through this context when we move from conceptual design into logical application design and physical application design.[6] It's essential to understand this because it frames any future architecture. When data is moved across applications, a data transformation step is always necessary. There's no escape from this data transformation dilemma! In the following chapters, I'll return to this idea.

---

6 If you want to learn more about the different phases of data modeling, see my blog post "Data Integration and Data Modelling Demystified" (*https://oreil.ly/qEuCE*). The conceptual model is sometimes also called the *business model*, the *domain model*, *domain object model*, or *analysis object model*.

Another view I see in many organizations is that data management should be central and must be connected to the strategic goals of the enterprise. Some organizations still believe that operational costs can be reduced by centralizing all data and management activities. There's also a deep assumption that a centralized platform can take away the pain of data integration for its users and consumers. Companies have invested heavily in their enterprise data platforms, which include data warehouses, data lakes, and service buses. The activities of master data management are strongly connected to these platforms because consolidating allows us to simultaneously improve the accuracy of our most critical data.

A centralized platform—and the centralized model that comes with it—will be subject to failure because it won't be able to keep up with the developments and trends that underpin decentralization, such as analytics, cloud computing, new software development methodologies, real-time decision making, and data monetization. While they may be aware of these trends, many companies fail to comprehend the impact they have on data management. Let's examine the most important trends and determine the magnitude of that impact.

Analytics Is Fragmenting the Data Landscape

The most trailblazing trend is *advanced analytics*, which exploits data to make companies more responsive, competitive, and innovative. Why does advanced analytics disrupt the existing data landscape? With more data available, the number of options and opportunities skyrockets. Advanced analytics is about making what-if analyses, projecting future trends and outcomes or events, detecting hidden relations and behaviors, and automating decision making. Because of the recognized value and strategic benefits of advanced analytics, many methodologies, frameworks, and tools have been developed to use it in divergent ways. We've only scratched the surface of what artificial intelligence (AI), machine learning (ML), and natural language processing (NLP) will be capable of in the future.

OpenAI's new ChatGPT (*https://openai.com*) is a mind-blowing example of what AI is capable of. The models behind OpenAI, which include the Generative Pre-trained Transformer (GPT) series, can work on complex tasks such as analyzing math problems, writing code snippets, producing book essays, creating recipes using a list of ingredients, and much more.

These analytical trends force data to be distributed across many analytical applications because every individual use case requires different data. Unique business problems require unique thinking, unique data, and optimized technology to provide the best solution. Take, for example, a marketing business unit whose goal is to identify new sales opportunities for older and younger customers. Targeting these two audiences requires different features—measurable properties for analyzing—in datasets. For example, prospects that are younger will be segmented and clustered differently than prospects that are older. Asking the marketing department to use a single dataset for both target audiences requires many compromises, and you'll probably end up with a feature store that doesn't add any value to each use case.[7] The optimal solution for generating the most value is to give either use case its own unique set of features optimized for each learning algorithm. The increasing popularity of advanced analytics and resulting use case diversity issues lead to two problems: data proliferation and data intensiveness.

With data proliferation, data is distributed and scattered across a myriad of locations, applications, and databases. This is because consuming domains need to process the data to fit it into their unique solutions. This data distribution introduces other problems. For one, when data is repeatedly copied and scattered throughout the organization, it becomes more difficult to find its origin and judge its quality. This requires you to develop a single logical view of the same data that is managed in different locations. Additionally, extensive data distribution makes controlling the data much more difficult because data can be spread even further as soon as it leaves any given application. This requires you to develop a framework for efficiently reusing data, while applying governance and staying compliant with external regulations.

The proliferation of analytical techniques is also accelerating the growth of data intensiveness: the *read-versus-write ratio* is changing significantly. Analytical models that are constantly retrained, for example, constantly read large volumes of data. This impacts application and database designs because we need to optimize for data readability. It might also mean that we need to duplicate data to relieve systems from the pressure of constantly serving it, or to preprocess the data because of the large number of diverse use case variations and their associated read patterns. Additionally, we might need to provide different representations of the same data for many different consumers. Facilitating a high variety of read patterns while duplicating data and staying in control isn't easy. A solution for this problem will be provided in Chapter 4.

The Speed of Software Delivery Is Changing

In today's world, software-based services are at the core of most businesses, which means that new features and functionality must be delivered quickly. In response to the demands for greater agility, new ideologies have emerged at companies like Amazon, Netflix, Meta, Google, and Uber. These companies have advanced their software development practices based on two beliefs.

---

7 A *feature store* is a tool for storing commonly used features (individual measurable properties or characteristics of a phenomenon).

The first belief is that software development (Dev) and information technology operations (Ops) must be combined to shorten the systems development life cycle and provide continuous delivery with high software quality. This methodology, called *DevOps*, requires a new culture that embraces more autonomy, open communication, trust, transparency, and cross-discipline teamwork.

The second belief is about the size at which applications must be developed. Flexibility and speed of development are expected to increase when applications are transformed into smaller decomposed services. This development approach incorporates several buzzwords: *microservices (https://microservices.io), containers, Kubernetes (https://kubernetes.io), domain-driven design, serverless computing*, etc. I won't go into detail on all of these concepts yet, but it's important to recognize that this evolution in software development involves increased complexity and a greater demand to better control data.

The transformation of monolithic applications into distributed applications—for example, microservices—creates many difficulties for data management. When breaking up applications into smaller pieces, the data is spread across different smaller components. Development teams must also transition their (single) unique data stores, where they fully understand the data model and have all the data objects together, to a design where data objects are spread all over the place. This introduces several challenges, including increased network communication, data read replicas that need to be synchronized, difficulties when combining many datasets, data consistency problems, referential integrity issues, and so on.

The recent shift in software development trends requires an architecture that allows more fine-grained applications to distribute their data. It also requires a new *DataOps* (*https://oreil.ly/G8Bt4*) culture and a different design philosophy with more emphasis on data interoperability, the capture of immutable events, and reproducible and loose coupling. We'll discuss this in more detail in Chapter 2.

The Cloud's Impact on Data Management Is Immeasurable

Networks are becoming faster, and bandwidth increases year after year. Large cloud vendors have proven that it's possible to move terabytes of data in the cloud in minutes, which allows for an interesting approach: instead of bringing the computational power to the data—which has been the common best practice because of network limitations—we can turn it around and bring the data to the computational power by distributing it. The network is no longer the bottleneck, so we can move data quickly between environments to allow applications to consume and use it. This model becomes especially interesting as software as a service (SaaS) and machine learning as a service (MLaaS) markets become more popular. Instead of doing all the complex stuff in-house, we can use networks to provide large quantities of data to other parties.

This distribution pattern of copying (duplicating) data and bringing it to the computational power in a different facility, such as a cloud data center, will fragment the data landscape even more, making a clear data management strategy more important than ever. It requires you to provide guidelines, because fragmentation of data can negatively impact performance due to data access lag. It also requires you to organize and model your data differently, because cloud service providers architected separate compute and storage to make them independently scalable.

Privacy and Security Concerns Are a Top Priority

Enterprises need to rethink data security in response to the proliferation of data sources and growing volume of data. Data is inarguably key for organizations looking to optimize, innovate, or differentiate themselves, but there is also a darker side with unfriendly undertones that include data thefts, discrimination, and political harm undermining democratic values. Let's take a look at a few examples to get an idea of the impact of bad data privacy and security.

UpGuard (*https://oreil.ly/TzrsU*) maintains a long list of the biggest data breaches to date, many of which have capitalized on the same mistakes. The Cambridge Analytica breach (*https://oreil.ly/lLZSG*) and 500 million hacked accounts at Marriott (*https://oreil.ly/0zJdf*) are impressive examples of damaging events. Governments are increasingly getting involved in security and privacy because all aspects of our personal and professional lives are now connected to the internet. The COVID-19 pandemic, which forced so many of us to work and socialize from home, accelerated this trend. Enterprises cannot afford to ignore the threats of intellectual property infringements and data privacy scandals.

The trends of massive data, more powerful advanced analytics, and faster distribution of data have triggered a debate around the dangers of data, raising ethical questions and discussions. Let me share an example from my own country. In the Netherlands, the Dutch Tax Administration practiced unlawful and discriminatory activities. They tracked dual nationals in their systems and used racial and ethnic classifications to train models for entitlements to childcare benefits. The result: thousands of families were incorrectly classified as criminals and had their benefits stopped. They were ordered to repay what they already had received, sometimes because of technical transgressions such as failing to correctly sign a form. Some people were forced to sell their homes and possessions after they were denied access to debt restructuring.

This is just one example of improper use of data. As organizations inevitably make mistakes and cross ethical lines, I expect governments to sharpen regulation by demanding more security, control, and insight. We've only scratched the surface of true data privacy and ethical problems. Regulations, such as the new European laws on data governance (*https://oreil.ly/phxAG*) and artificial intelligence (*https://oreil.ly/NiT1T*) will force large companies to be transparent about what data is collected and purchased, what data is combined, how data is used within analytical models, and what data is distributed (sold). Big companies need to start thinking about transparency and privacy-first approaches and how to deal with large regulatory issues now, if they haven't already.

Regulation is a complex subject. Imagine a situation in which several cloud regions and different SaaS services are used and data is scattered. Satisfying regulations, such as the GDPR (*https://gdpr-info.eu*), CCPA (*https://oreil.ly/xzWpY*), BCBS 239 (*https://oreil.ly/zFj8I*), and the new Trans-Atlantic Data Privacy Framework (*https://oreil.ly/qDuto*) is difficult because companies are required to have insight and control over all personal data, regardless of where it is stored. Data governance and correctly handling personal data is at the top of the agenda for many large companies.[8]

These stronger regulatory requirements and data ethics concerns will result in further restrictions, additional processes, and enhanced control. Insights about where data originated, how models are trained, and how data is distributed are crucial. Stronger internal governance is required, but this trend of increased control runs contrary to the methodologies for fast software development, which involve less documentation and fewer internal controls. It requires a different, more defensive viewpoint on how data management is handled, with more integrated processes and better tools. Several of these concerns will be addressed in Chapter 8.

Operational and Analytical Systems Need to Be Integrated

The need to react faster to business events introduces new challenges. Traditionally, there has been a great divide between transactional (operational) applications and analytical applications because transactional systems are generally not sufficient for delivering large amounts of data or constantly pushing out data. The accepted best practice has been to split the data strategy into two parts: operational transactional processing and analytical data warehousing and big data processing.

However, this divide is subject to disruption. *Operational analytics*, which focuses on predicting and improving the existing operational processes, is expected to work closely with both the transactional and analytical systems. The analytical results need to be integrated back into the operational system's core so that insights become relevant in the operational context. I could make the same argument for real-time events: when events carry state, the same events can be used for operational decision making and data distribution.

---

8 *Personal data* is any information related to an identified or identifiable natural person.

This trend requires a different integration architecture, one that better manages both the operational and analytical systems at the same time. It also requires data integration to work at different velocities, as these tend to be different for operational systems and analytical systems. In this book, we'll explore the options for preserving historical data in the original operational context while simultaneously making it available to both operational and analytical systems.

Organizations Operate in Collaborative Ecosystems

Many people think that all business activities take place within the single logical boundary in which the enterprise operates. The reality is different, because many organizations work closely with other organizations. Companies are increasingly integrating their core business capabilities with third-party services. This collaboration aspect influences the design of your architecture because you need to be able to quickly distribute data, incorporate open data,[9] make APIs publicly available, and so on.

These changes mean that data is more often distributed between environments, and thus is more decentralized. When data is shared with other companies, or using cloud or SaaS solutions, it ends up in different places, which makes integration and data management more difficult. In addition, network bandwidth, connectivity, and latency issues inevitably arise when moving data between platforms or environments. Pursuing a single public cloud or single platform strategy won't solve these challenges, because decentralization is the future. This means that if you want APIs and SaaS systems to work well and use the capabilities of the public cloud, you must be skilled at data integration, which this book will teach you how to do.

The trends discussed here are major and will affect the way people use data and the way companies should organize their architectures. Data growth is accelerating, computing power is increasing, and analytical techniques are advancing. Data consumption is increasing, too, which implies that data needs to be distributed quickly. Stronger data governance is required. Data management also must be decentralized due to trends like cloud services, SaaS, and microservices. All of these factors have to be balanced with a short time to market, thanks to strong competition. This risky combination challenges us to manage data in a completely different way.

---

9 *Open data* is data that can be used freely and is made publicly available.

Enterprises Are Saddled with Outdated Data Architectures

One of the biggest problems many enterprises are dealing with is getting value out of their current data architectures.[10] The majority of existing data architectures use a monolithic design—either an enterprise data warehouse (EDW)[11] or a data lake—and manage and distribute data centrally. In a highly distributed and consumer-driven environment, these architectures won't fulfill future needs. Let's look at some of the characteristics of each.

The Enterprise Data Warehouse: A Single Source of Truth

Most enterprises' first-generation data architectures are based on *data warehousing* and *business intelligence*. The philosophy is that centralization is the silver bullet to solve the problem of data management. With this approach there's one central integrated data repository, containing years' worth of detailed and stable data, for the entire organization. But when it comes to distributing data at large, such a monolithic design has several drawbacks.

Enterprise data unification is an incredibly complex undertaking and takes many years to complete. Chances are relatively high that the meaning of data differs across domains,[12] departments, and systems, even if data attributes have similar names. So, we either end up creating many variations or just accepting the differences and inconsistencies. The more data we add, and the more conflicts and inconsistencies that arise, the more difficult it will be to harmonize the data. We will likely end up with a unified context that is meaningless for the end users. In addition, for advanced analytics such as machine learning, leaving context out can be a significant problem because it's impossible to correctly predict the future if the data is meaningless or unrecognizable.

Enterprise data warehouses behave like *integration databases* (*https://oreil.ly/vDCOh*), as illustrated in Figure 1-2. They act as data stores for multiple data-consuming applications. This means that they're a point of coupling between all the applications that want to access the data. It's often assumed that centralization is the solution to data management—this includes centralizing all data and management activities using one central team, building one data platform, using one ETL framework and one canonical model, etc. However, with a centralized architecture, changes need to

---

10 An enterprise's data architecture comprises the infrastructure, the data, and the schemas, integrations, transformations, storage, and workflows required to enable the analytical requirements of the information architecture.

11 For background information on (enterprise) data warehouses and why they don't scale, see my blog post "The Extinction of Enterprise Data Warehousing" (*https://oreil.ly/RO6Hv*).

12 A *domain* is a field of study that defines a set of common requirements, terminology, and functionality for any software program constructed to solve a problem in the area of computer programming.

---

be carried out carefully because of the many cross-dependencies between different applications. Some changes can also trigger a ripple effect of other changes. When you've created such a highly coupled and difficult-to-change design, you've created what some engineers call a "big ball of mud."

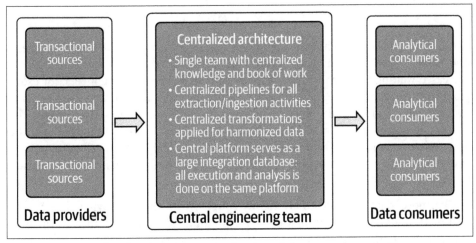

Figure 1-2. Centralized architectures are a bottleneck for many organizations: one team must wait for another team to finish its work

Big Ball of Mud

A big ball of mud (*https://oreil.ly/8bY2t*) is a haphazardly structured, sprawling, sloppy, duct-tape-and-baling-wire, spaghetti-code jungle. The term, introduced by Brian Foote and Joseph Yoder, describes a system architecture that is monolithic, difficult to understand, hard to maintain, and tightly coupled because of its many dependencies. Figure 1-3 shows a dependency diagram (*https://oreil.ly/Fdckr*) that illustrates this. Each line represents a relationship between two software components.

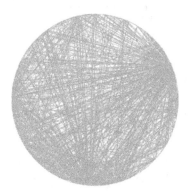

Figure 1-3. Big ball of mud dependency diagram

A big ball of mud, as you can see, has extreme dependencies between all components, which makes it practically impossible to modify one component without affecting others. Data warehouses, with their layers, views, countless tables, relationships, scripts, ETL jobs, and scheduling flows, often result in such a chaotic web of dependencies.

Because of the data warehouse's high degree of complexity and the fact that there's one central team managing it, the lack of agility often becomes a concern. The increased waiting time sparks the creativity of taking shortcuts. Engineers, for example, might bypass the integration layer and directly map data from the staging layer to their data marts, while other developers create workarounds using views that quickly combine data from different layers. The *technical debt* (future rework) that accumulates as a result will cause problems later. The architecture will become more complex, and people will lose insight into the creative solutions crafted to ensure timely delivery.

Furthermore, data warehouses are tightly coupled with the underlying chosen solution or technology, meaning that consumers requiring different read patterns must export data to other environments. As the vendor landscape changes and new types of databases pop up, warehouses are increasingly required to distribute data away from the location where it is managed. This trend undermines the grand vision of efficiently using a single central repository and utilizing the underlying (expensive) hardware.

Life cycle management of historical data is often an issue too. Data warehouses are seen as archives of truth, allowing operational systems to clean up irrelevant data, knowing the data will be retained in the warehouse. For advanced operational analytics—something that emerged after data warehouses made an appearance—this might be a problem. If data has been transformed by a central team that manages all of the organization's data, it may no longer be recognizable to the team that delivered it (or usable for the intended operational use case). Additionally, making the data available quickly may be difficult, given that many warehouses typically process data for many hours before storing it. This is necessary because before being stored, the data must be transformed, combined, and integrated with other data.

Data quality is often a problem as well. Who owns the data in a data warehouse? Who is responsible if source systems deliver corrupted data? What I often see at organizations is that a central engineering team takes care of data quality issues caused by other teams. In one instance, the engineers fixed the data in the staging layer so that it would load properly into the data warehouse. These fixes became permanent, and over time hundreds of additional scripts had to be applied before data processing could start. These scripts aren't part of trustworthy ETL processes and don't allow for data ownership and lineage (*https://oreil.ly/tGbQC*) that can be tracked back.

Regulatory issues can crop up too. Warehouses often lack insight into ad hoc consumption and further distribution, especially when data is carried outside of the boundaries in which it is managed. With new regulations, data ownership and insight into the consumption and distribution of data is important because you need to be able to explain what personal data has been consumed by whom and for what purpose.

Given the total amount of data in a typical data warehouse, the years it took to develop it, the knowledge people have, and intensive business usage, a replacement migration would be a risky and time-consuming activity. Therefore, many enterprises continue to use this architecture and feed their business reports, dashboards,[13] and data-hungry applications from a data warehouse, despite the high maintenance costs and lack of flexibility.

The Data Lake: A Centralized Repository for Structured and Unstructured Data

As data volumes and the need for faster insights grew, engineers started to work on other concepts. *Data lakes* emerged as an alternative for access to raw and larger volumes of data.[14] Providing data as is, without having to structure it first, enables any consumer to decide how to use it and how to transform and integrate it.

Data lakes, like data warehouses, are centralized (monolithic) data repositories, but they differ from warehouses in that they store data before it has been transformed, cleansed, and structured. Schemas therefore are often determined when reading data. This differs from data warehouses, which use a predefined and fixed structure. Data lakes also provide greater variety by supporting multiple data formats: structured, semistructured, and unstructured.

Many data lake implementations collect pure, unmodified, raw data from the original source systems. Dumping in raw application structures—exact copies—is fast and allows data analysts and scientists quick access. However, the complexity with raw data is that use cases always require reworking the data. Data quality problems have to be sorted out, transformations are required, and enrichments with other data are needed to bring the data into context. This introduces a lot of repeatable work and is one reason why data lakes are typically combined with data warehouses. Data warehouses, in this combination, act like high-quality repositories of cleansed and

---

13 Reports tend to be mainly tabular, but they may contain additional charts or chart components. Dashboards are more visual and use a variety of chart types.

14 James Dixon, then chief technology officer at Pentaho, coined the term *data lake* (*https://oreil.ly/4E_WB*).

harmonized data, while data lakes act like (ad hoc) analytical environments, holding a large variety of raw data to facilitate analytics.

Designing data lakes, just like data warehouses, is a challenge. Companies like Gartner, VentureBeat AI, and Deloitte see high failure rates for big data projects—often more than 60%.[15] Data lake implementations typically fail, in part, because of their immense complexity, difficult maintenance, and shared dependencies:

- Data that applications push into a data lake is often raw and likely a complex representation of how the individual applications internally organize their data. When you follow this approach, your data lake quickly becomes a collection that includes tens of thousands of tables, incomprehensible data structures, and technical values that are understood only by the applications themselves. Additionally, there's tight coupling with the providing applications, since the inherited structure is an identical copy. When consumers use this data directly, there's a real risk that data pipelines will break when those providing applications change their data structures.

- Analytical models in data lakes are often trained on both raw and harmonized data. It isn't unthinkable that both data engineers and data scientists are technically data plumbing, creating data and operating these data pipelines and models by hand or in their data science projects. Data lakes therefore carry substantial (operational) risks.

- Data lakes are often a single platform shared by many different use cases. Due to their tight coupling, compatibility challenges, shared libraries, and configurations, these platforms are hard to maintain.

These are just a few reasons why the failure rate of big data projects is so high. Other reasons include management resistance, internal politics, lack of expertise, and security and governance challenges.

The Pain of Centralization

Enterprise data warehouses or central data lakes can be scaled up using techniques like metadata-driven ELT, data virtualization (*https://oreil.ly/g_dve*), cloud services, distributed processing, real-time ingestion, machine learning for enrichments, and so on. But there's a far bigger problem: the centralized thinking behind these architectures. This includes centralized management, centralized data ownership, centrally clustered resources, and central data models that dictate that everybody must use the same terms and definitions. One consequence of this centralization is that removing data professionals from business domains limits creativity and

---

15 Brian T. O'Neill maintains a reference list on failure rates (*https://oreil.ly/oxZ_D*).

business insights. Teams are forced into constant cross-communication and ticket management, because they are at a distance. *It's the central operating model that is the bottleneck*: the central team can't handle all questions and requests quickly enough. It's for good reason that organizations are embracing decentralized methodologies like the data mesh and advocating domain-driven design. A federated model with domain teams can be a superpower: it promotes independence and accountability; it enables scaling because autonomous teams govern, share and consume data in parallel; and it fosters improvements in quality, collaboration, and productivity.

However, there's a caveat to decentralization. Federation of responsibilities always starts with centralization, which involves on an enterprise level defining standards, setting boundaries, and providing expertise and scalability. Without a central authority, decentralized empowerment becomes a huge problem. I've observed situations where teams started to define their own technology, interoperability, and metadata standards; where departments mandated complete control over their own data, so it couldn't be combined with data from other teams; and where teams applied their own data-modeling standards, reference-data standards, granularity levels, and so on, making it impossible to combine or integrate data between domains. To summarize: scalability through decentralization doesn't come without risks, and those risks can be best mitigated by central alignment of organization, governance, technology, and architecture. So, what you need is a *data strategy*: a plan that (re)defines culture, organization and people, architecture, governance and processes, and rules required to turn yourself into a data-driven organization.

Defining a Data Strategy

Now that you understand the importance of data, recent trends, and the challenges that come with centralization and decentralization, what might a strategic path toward a successful data transformation look like? To answer this question, a strategy exercise must be carried out, taking into account the company's business models and the role of data within them. Strategists and architects should consider whether changes to the existing business models are warranted, and whether conditions are right for, for example, applying federation.

It is convention to begin by analyzing the organization and the conditions in which the company operates. From there, an enterprise view must be developed that connects the building blocks of the enterprise to applications and data sources, processes, people, and other technology solutions that are used to realize the strategy. This view enables visualization of the (data) architecture that will allow the company's strategic objectives to be met. In the next chapter, I'll connect back to all of these aspects, but first let's look at the steps for defining a data strategy.

Developing a strategy can be difficult. It often involves a prediction of what business value can be created or what may be true in the future. It requires connecting high-level ambitions to resources, processes, and supporting capabilities. If you don't already have a data strategy or are unsure about your ambitions, please consider the following action points:

- First, focus on your business goals and strategy. Don't get hooked up in the hype about the latest technology changes.

- Embrace the company's vision and adapt it to how data will boost it. Determine how data can play a better role in solving your business problems. Try to quantify the business impact. Next, define what your core business strategy will look like for the next three years and after.

- Determine the correct balance between "defensive" and "offensive." Is full control a top priority? Or do you want to have the flexibility for disruptive innovation? How does regulation impact your strategy? These considerations will influence your initial design and the pace of federating certain responsibilities.

- Establish clear and measurable milestones. Create a plan to determine when your data strategy is successful and provides value. Define metrics and key performance indicators (KPIs) for measuring outcomes.

- Create a communication plan to ensure your strategy is understood and communicated throughout the organization.

- Determine your first focus area. This might be research and development, regulatory compliance, cost reduction, increased revenues, or something else.

- Identify barriers within your organization that might prevent a successful outcome, and look for ways around them.

- Rethink your strategy for talent and determine whether your organization is fit to fully take advantage of data. If not, create a (cultural) transition and hiring plan for aligning your business departments by making them responsible for managing and using data at large.

- Define what your next-gen IT capabilities will look like. Is future IT responsible for all execution? Or does future IT acts as a center of excellence for providing leadership, best practices, training, research, and support?

- Define what a data-driven culture looks like. For example, identify what skills and education are needed. Do you plan to allow full self-service data usage by business users? Is there willingness to share data with others?

- Gather data about your existing environments. For example, does every organizational business unit participate within the same ecosystem boundaries? Or do you see different rules applied within different environments? Start by creating a high-level overview of your data landscape by analyzing the different environments and data sources. Study where data is created, and how that data is distributed and used.

- Determine whether you will need to transform your software development methodology. If so, determine how this might impact your delivery model for building your next-gen architecture.

- Establish what a transition toward the future will look like. Is your transition a radical remodel or an organic evolution?

- Define some first high-level technology choices. For example, do you plan to take advantage of scalable cloud computing for processing data? Do you prefer flexibility and adaptability, so you will be developing your IT capabilities to be vendor-agnostic? Or do you prefer consuming native services, with the risk of vendor lock-in?

- Create an executive presentation with the most important elements, all high-level with sections: why, what, gaps, road maps, and investment cases.

- Create a cost management strategy by aligning your budget with the goals and use cases. Determine a plan for reviewing and willingness to invest in data management. In addition to that, align the budgets with your IT life cycle management process, which entails planning, outsourcing, procurement, deployment, and potential decommissioning.[16]

Addressing these action points should make your high-level ambitions and strategy clear. It's important to do this first, because the strategic direction will provide input for decisions about architecture, processes, ways of working, transition road maps, governance, and so on.

Note that a data-driven strategy will look different for every organization, depending on its ambitions, the size and type of the business, planned funding and investments, the existing culture and level of maturity, and the underlying business objectives. For example, in my previous role at ABN AMRO, we wanted customers to have a bespoke, seamless, and unified experience throughout their digital journey when interacting with our data-driven bank. Therefore, we decided to strongly align and integrate all retail, corporate, and international business units. This meant that all business units had to work within the same data-centric ecosystem, follow the same data literacy program, and adhere to the same architectural principles. To facilitate this, we also had to integrate the different enterprise architecture functions for designing, guiding, and controlling the enterprise as a whole.

In another organization, the data strategy might look completely different. For example, if the business objectives are less closely aligned throughout the organization, there might be fewer needs for standardization and integration. If you've recently experienced the traumatic event of data leakage, then you will probably be strongly focused on data defense. If your primary objective is to monetize data and build

---

16 Technologies are volatile, so at some point you may need to replace or upgrade them.

partnerships, your focus will be on delivering interoperability for economic value and data that is valuable in the sense that it's worth consuming for the purchasing party. The most important point is to align your data strategy with your current and future business needs.

Before we wrap up, I want to acknowledge that some people advocate that an overarching strategy isn't required. For them, it's too much up-front work. Instead of developing a plan, they believe you should just get started and see what happens along the way while implementing use cases. This approach will absolutely deliver immediate value. However, in the long term it will have disastrous consequences for your architecture because there will be no commitment to consistency and standardization. Without a guiding map, the transition could be a long march in the wrong direction, requiring frequent reboots and backpedaling exercises.

Wrapping Up

A strategy is the starting point of every digital transformation. Data undoubtedly is a core ingredient. But how do you ensure that data actually contributes to your long-term goals and ambitions? And how do you facilitate the organizational change that is needed for using data at large? This is where a helicopter view is required, to enable a real understanding of the business from end to end. Planning for success requires you to first get a complete picture. You need to zoom out and get an abstract view of your business, before zooming in to specific problem spaces. After that, you need to define an architecture and organizational structure that will support your transition and align with your overall planning, way of working, and governance model. As we progress further into the book, you'll learn more about these concepts.

Designing an architecture that matches all of your data strategy requirements and ambitions is the hardest part of the transition. First, you must create a holistic picture of your organizational structure, applications, processes, and data landscape. Next, you can work out different potential scenarios by balancing dimensions such as flexibility, openness, control, time, cost of realization, risks, and so on. Each potential scenario might include road maps, transition architectures, and different future states. This process is a dynamic and collaborative exercise and goes far beyond creating simple visualizations. An important note on this: setting out the strategic and future direction starts top-down, from the business. It shouldn't come from only the IT department.

An important aspect of your data strategy is balancing the imperatives of centralization and decentralization. For example, do you federate governance and activities, or architecture and infrastructure, or both? There's a lot of confusion on this subject, as we often see extremes. For example, the data mesh, as a reaction to centralized data organizations, architectures, and governance models, promotes a 180-degree change of direction. It embraces decentralization in all aspects by advocating that all data must be decentrally owned by domains using decentrally managed infrastructure. On paper, decentralization resonates well with business leaders and IT managers, but in practice, things aren't that easy.

Decentralization involves risks, because the more you spread out activities across the organization, the harder it gets to harmonize strategy and align and orchestrate planning, let alone foster the culture and recruit the talent needed to properly manage your data. The resulting fragmentation also raises new questions, like "How many business models or domains do I have?" and "How many data platforms do I need?" What I have observed in practice is that many architects and data practitioners find domain decomposition and setting boundaries the hardest part of decentralization. Often, there's a fundamental lack of understanding of business architecture and domain-driven design. Many data practitioners find the conceptual notions of domain-driven design too difficult to grasp. Others try to project oversimplified or object-oriented programming examples onto their data landscape.

The principles underpinning decentralization are also subject to discussion with regard to how data and platforms must be managed. Among data engineers, there's skepticism because no open interoperability standards for data products exist yet. In addition, there are concerns about the usability of data when individual teams operate in bubbles.

These observations are a nice transition to the following chapters. In the next chapter, we'll fly our helicopter one level lower, taking you close enough to identify your architecture, data domains, and landing zones. I'll help you with this by simplifying the vocabulary of domains and providing you with pragmatic guidance and observations from the field. After that, we'll fly over to the source system side of our landscape and stay there for a few chapters before our journey continues. Bon voyage!

CHAPTER 2

Organizing Data Using Data Domains

The trends discussed in Chapter 1 require us to rethink the way data management is done. We've talked about the tight couplings that arise when making exact copies of application data and the difficulties of operationalizing analytics on raw data. We've also looked at the unification problems, the tremendous effort of building an integrated data warehouse, and its impact on agility. As discussed in Chapter 1, we need to shift toward an approach that enables domains, teams, and users to distribute, consume, and use data themselves easily and securely. We need a strategy and organizational change that moves data closer to the business. We need platforms, processes, patterns, and standard interfaces that simplify the work for others. We need a data management architecture that works at scale. This chapter discusses this further, starting with how to organize the landscape using data domains.

Before we delve into that topic, however, we'll explore a number of generally acknowledged principles of how applications are designed and work together. After that, we'll zoom in on the inner architecture of applications and discover what we can learn from that. Then we'll turn our attention to domains, looking at domain-driven design and business architecture. We'll discuss different characteristics of domains, key data management principles, and domain ownership responsibilities. By the end of this chapter, you'll understand what data domains are and why they are important. This background theory is necessary to understand the core drivers of your new architecture. In subsequent chapters, we'll take a more in-depth look at patterns, designs, diagrams, and workflows, and you'll start to understand how this domain-oriented architecture links all the areas of data management together.

Application Design Starting Points

In preparation for our deep dive, I want to spotlight some key application design principles that are widely acknowledged and will be referred to many times throughout this book.

Each Application Has a Data Store

In the context of data management and moving data between applications, we can assume that each application has some form of data storage. So whenever you run into a data-usage situation, you need to store data in an application database. Yes, there might be stateless applications that store their data elsewhere, applications that share the same database, or applications that do in-memory processing. But this still implies that all applications need to store their data somewhere.

Applications Are Always Unique

Business challenges are never the same. In Chapter 1, I noted that applications are used to solve *specific* problems. Each application's data is unique and unlike the data and context from other applications. This is rooted in how we create applications. There are several stages to the design and development process.[1] We start with conceptual thinking about the business requirements and needs; then we translate our business knowledge to a logical application data model, which is a more formal and concrete representation of the requirements. Finally, we make the physical application data model—the true design of the application—which is based on the nonfunctional requirements from the logical design.

Every context is unique, and we can say the same for applications and the data underpinning the business problems. Each business problem requires a distinctive sphere of knowledge. This ties into the concept of domains, but before we get to that, let's examine what the origin of data means for data management.

Golden Sources

In a fragmented and distributed environment, it can be difficult to determine the authoritative sources of original and unique data. Therefore, it's important to know where the data originated and where it's managed. I use the foundational concept of

---

[1] If you want to get into the fundamentals of data integration and modeling, I encourage you to read my blog post on the topic (*https://oreil.ly/PUT4t*).

the *golden source* throughout this book;[2] this is the authoritative *application* where all authentic data is managed within a particular context.[3]

When you capture only unique data, and always directly from your golden sources, you ensure you have exact, consistent accountability for your data. This is essential for implementing strong data governance, because different domains sometimes try to claim ownership of physical datasets and data designs. Identifying your golden sources therefore should be your starting point. Golden sources are also important for data quality. They're the point where data is either created or first input into a system. By fixing data quality issues at the golden source, you avoid those issues popping up in other places because the data is always distributed from this source.

The Data Integration Dilemma

Because applications have unique contexts, a transformation is always needed when moving data from one application to another. This implies that some form of data integration is always required. Whether you move data using ETL (extract, transform, and load) or ELT (extract, load, and transform), virtual or physical, batch or real-time processes, there's no escape from the data integration dilemma. A data transformation is always required when moving data across applications, regardless of the design or type of architecture.

Application Roles

Applications are either data providers or data consumers, or, as we'll see, sometimes both. For one application to use data, another application must create and provide it. This might seem obvious, but in the context of integrating and distributing data across a large number of applications and systems, it's important for the purposes of accountability.

In the data community, you will encounter terms like *source system–aligned* and *consumer-aligned domains*. These terms refer to the same providing and consuming roles, although they use a different level of granularity: the domain viewpoint versus the application viewpoint.

---

2 Some people use the term *system of record* (SOR), which is the authoritative source for a given data element or piece of information.

3 Identifying the authoritative applications may not be easy. Some authoritative sources can be hidden behind complex patterns that you need to understand in order to find them. For more about golden sources, see Andy Graham's book, *Mastering Your Data* (Koios).

Depending on whether a system or application acts as a provider or consumer, as shown in Figure 2-1, the rules of the game change: different architectural principles are applied.

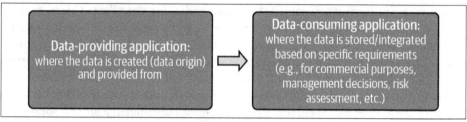

Figure 2-1. The application roles of data provider and data consumer frame our architecture

The data provider and data consumer roles apply for *external parties* as well. External parties, for example third parties, are those that operate outside the logical boundaries of the enterprise's ecosystem. They generally exist in separate, uncontrolled environments. As mentioned in Chapter 1, many companies see the public web as a treasure chest of (open) data they can monetize to create and share reusable services. This new way of collaboration has changed organizational boundaries. The new architecture I am introducing in this book requires the flexibility to allow external parties to be both data providers and data consumers. Additional security measures are usually needed, since external parties aren't always trusted, known, or directly related to the larger context.

 Can you directly consume data from external parties, or should you create another abstraction layer for decoupling? This depends on whether the external party can or is willing to mediate by complying with and conforming to your principles, and whether you need to conform to standards set by the external provider. If mediation by an external party can't be guaranteed, then an additional layer of abstraction and decoupling is required. If mediation is possible, direct consumption may be acceptable.

What else do we need to consider for our architecture, in addition to the unique contexts in which applications operate, the roles of data provider and consumer, and the transformation that always takes place between applications? What makes a good overall architecture? In the next section, we'll zoom in for a closer look at some software architecture patterns to see what inspirations we can draw from them.

Inspirations from Software Architecture

Data integration between applications is about managing the complexity of communication and the interoperability of data. In enterprise architecture we usually look at the bigger picture, but how do the components inside an application work together to distribute and share data, and what can we learn from that? Zhamak Dehghani, who coined the term *data mesh* (*https://oreil.ly/4R2PM*), got her inspiration from microservices,[4] so let's examine that architectural style and its influence.

Microservices, as pictured in Figure 2-2, use an architectural approach to software development where applications are composed of small independent services that communicate using lightweight communication patterns. So instead of building and packaging your application as one big monolith, you split it up into smaller components known as *microservices*.

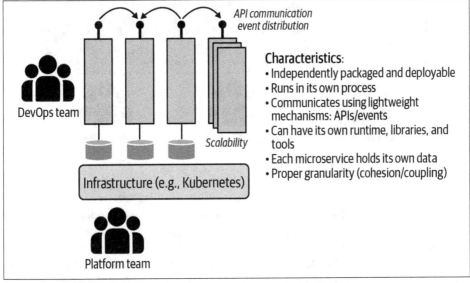

Figure 2-2. High-level representation of a microservices architecture

One of the benefits of using a microservices architecture is that microservices can be developed, tested, and deployed individually and independently. Each microservice manages its own runtime and data and runs in its own dedicated process, which makes your design much more scalable. Instead of scaling your entire application, you can scale individual application components up and down independently

---

4 Prior to founding Nextdata, Dehghani was director of emerging technologies in North America at Thoughtworks. Consultants from Thoughtworks are front-runners in promoting microservices and data mesh architectures.

as needed. The same flexibility holds for programming languages: you can mix languages and choose whatever works best for a given component. For example, you might write your first microservice using C#, your second microservice using NodeJS, your third using Python, and so on.

This all sounds great, but there's a caveat here: the more microservices you add, the harder it gets to manage your microservices architecture. Imagine a situation where an application has grown to a size where three development teams are needed to maintain it, and all the microservices directly communicate with one another, as shown in Figure 2-3.

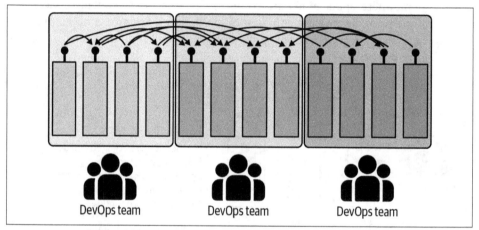

Figure 2-3. Complex communication

The way the microservices communicate within this architecture makes this application a fragile system.[5] If one service fails or starts misbehaving, it could cause a ripple effect across the entire system. To avoid such a disaster, you can use a pattern for controlling the communication between microservices called a *service mesh*. It takes the logic governing service-to-service communication out of the individual services and abstracts it into a layer of its own. A service mesh provides features such as monitoring, discoverability, graceful shutdown, policy enforcement, and so on.

A service mesh can be used for grouping and decoupling microservices. With this architectural pattern, you group microservices together, for example in namespaces (*https://oreil.ly/V40pP*), based on functional cohesion. The microservices within a group (safe boundary) can communicate directly, but to communicate with microservices in another group, they must use the service mesh. The service mesh, in this

---

5 A community term for such an architecture is a *distributed big ball of mud*. A landscape consisting of many microservices communicating with each other acts as a complex state machine, with increasingly unpredictable results as the landscape grows.

pattern, behaves as a safe proxy. Figure 2-4 shows what your revised architecture might look like if you applied the principles of domain-oriented design and added a service mesh.

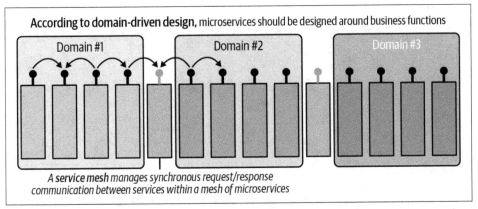

According to domain-driven design, microservices should be designed around business functions

Domain #1   Domain #2   Domain #3

A *service mesh* manages synchronous request/response communication between services within a mesh of microservices

Figure 2-4. Adding a service mesh to manage synchronous request/response communication between services

In the updated architecture design, microservices are grouped together based on cohesion, or the degree to which individual microservices belong and work together. In this configuration, each DevOps team owns and controls a specific part of the architecture. This ownership and functional alignment reduces the risk of the application misbehaving because dependencies are better managed. Another best practice is that whenever a DevOps team want their microservices to communicate with those of another DevOps team, they should use a service mesh to decouple their specific part of the application from other parts.

A service mesh in a microservices architecture provides management, such as security and shared request logic, for synchronous request/reply communications. For asynchronous communications, it can easily be replaced with an event broker—for example, for distributing notifications and events between microservices. Depending on the communication style you need, you can either pick one pattern or use them side by side.

What is missing in this microservices design is an analytical data architecture, providing support for data that is used for analytical purposes. To make the comparison between a service mesh and a data mesh, in a service mesh, service requests are routed between microservices through proxies. The service mesh governs service-to-service communication, abstracting it out of individual services and into another layer. In data mesh, analytical data is served through *data products*. A data product transforms the data, maintains its integrity, governs its policies, and ultimately serves it.

A data product benefits from the same architectural advantages of a service mesh, as you can see in Figure 2-5. Dehghani describes it (*https://oreil.ly/DdUBD*) as "a new architectural quantum…the smallest unit of your architecture that has all of the structural components to do its job."

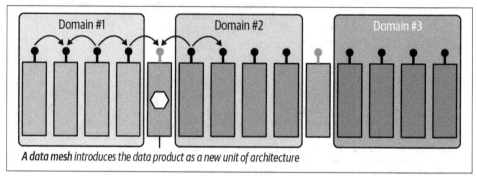

Figure 2-5. Data mesh architecture showing data products: the smallest independently deployable units

Although the idea of making data products the smallest units of your architecture is brilliant, not all architectures are created from only microservices. Today's architectures in enterprises generally consist of many applications, ranging from large legacy systems to commercial off-the-shelf (COTS) products, SaaS, operational data stores, master data management stores, data warehouses, and so on. Many of these applications are often shared between users or organizational units. How do you properly set boundaries in such a large-scale data architecture? Let's try to find the answer by zooming out!

Data Domains

Setting boundaries for defining ownership is one of the most important aspects of designing architectures. There are a lot of trade-offs that determine where those boundaries should lie. A commonly cited best practice is to use a methodology called *domain-driven design* (DDD). In the following section, I'll discuss the essential theory behind DDD (without going into too much detail). After that we switch to business architecture, for revising the definition of a domain.

Domain-Driven Design

DDD is an approach to software development that involves complex systems for larger organizations, originally described by Eric Evans in his book *Domain-Driven Design* (Addison-Wesley). It's popular because many of its high-level practices have had an impact on modern software and application development approaches, such as microservices. Let's take a look at some of the key concepts.

Bounded contexts

The *bounded context* is a central concept in domain-driven design. Bounded contexts are used to set the logical boundaries of a domain's solution space to better manage complexity. These boundaries are typically explicit and enforced on areas with clear and high cohesion. Domain dependencies can sit on different levels, such as specific parts of the application, processes, associated database designs, platforms, etc. These boundaries are typically explicit and enforced on areas with clear and high cohesion. It's important that teams understand which aspects, including data, they can change on their own and which are shared dependencies where they need to coordinate with other teams to avoid breaking things. Setting boundaries, as you saw in the microservices example in the previous section, helps teams and developers manage the dependencies more efficiently.

Bounded contexts are *polymorphic*, which means their size and shape can vary based on one's viewpoint and the surroundings. That is, a bounded context can shift and overlap with other bounded contexts depending on what viewpoint you take. This means you need to be explicit when using bounded contexts; otherwise, others might not understand exactly what you're referring to.

Domains and Bounded Contexts

DDD differentiates between bounded contexts, domains, and subdomains. *Domains* are the problem spaces we're trying to address. This is where knowledge, behavior, laws, and activities come together. They're the areas where we see semantic coupling: behavioral dependencies between components or services. Domains are usually decomposed into subdomains to better manage the complexity. A common example is decomposing a domain in such a way that each subdomain corresponds to a different part of the organization.

Not all subdomains are the same. They can be classified as either core, generic, or supporting. *Core subdomains* are the most important. They're the secret sauce, the ingredients that make the business unique. *Generic subdomains* are nonspecific and typically represent business problems that can easily be solved with off-the-shelf products. *Supporting subdomains* don't offer competitive advantage but are necessary to keep the organization running. Usually, they aren't that complex.

Bounded contexts are the logical (context) boundaries. They focus on the solution space: the design of systems and applications. This can be code, database designs, and so on. There can be alignment between the domains and bounded contexts, but this isn't required. Bounded contexts are technical by nature and thus can span across multiple domains and subdomains.

The idea behind setting logical boundaries, or using bounded contexts, is that responsibilities are clearer and will be better managed. Communication between team members is efficient because the same people are working on similar objectives. Setting logical boundaries on software is similar to dealing with microservices, in a way.

On an enterprise level, we logically group applications with high cohesion or shared interest (that is, applications that perform similar tasks or have similar responsibilities). Some people refer to these as functional domains, logical groups, clusters, or organizational capabilities.

Grouping entities, processes, or applications together isn't a new idea. The big difference between "traditional" grouping and the domain-driven design model are the *enforced, strict boundaries* of DDD. Bounded contexts, Evans argues, can evolve independently but *must* be decoupled. Decoupling is usually achieved by hiding or abstracting the complex internal functionality of the application and making sure the interfaces and layers reach a certain level of stability.

Ubiquitous language

A *ubiquitous language* in DDD is a common, rigorous language built up and shared by developers and users. It's similar to the shared set of definitions, vocabulary, jargon, and terminology people within any particular focus area use. Ubiquitous language helps connect people within large teams or across teams, where it can be difficult to settle on a common vocabulary. To avoid too much cross-communication and inconsistent terminology between teams, ubiquitous languages are used to support the design of the applications or software within a domain. Thus, there isn't necessarily one unified language across the enterprise, although there might be overlap.

I highly recommend reading *Semantic Software Design*, by Eben Hewitt (O'Reilly). This book uses design thinking and draws a parallel between semantics and the design of an architecture.

Bounded contexts and ubiquitous languages have a strong relationship because within DDD each bounded context is expected to have its own ubiquitous language. Applications or application components that belong together and are managed within a bounded context should all use the same language. If a bounded context grows to the extent where understanding it becomes a challenge for the team, the bounded context can be broken up into smaller parts. If the bounded context changes, the ubiquitous language is also expected to change. The rule of thumb is that one bounded context is managed by one team (Agile or DevOps) because it's easier for members of a single team to be aware of the current situation and all of its dependencies.

I often bring up the concept of bounded contexts with culture to make it clear that definitions and terminology often aren't the same between different teams. Context is specific and usually based on what we know. Each bounded context has a different objective, a different background, and, most significantly, a different culture. Culture affects how we think, design, and model. Within a culture, there may be subcultures: smaller groups of people who share a common set of objectives and practices. The same applies in DDD: a bounded context can be divided into multiple subdomains or multiple smaller bounded contexts. As you saw in Chapter 1, there's a strong dependency between (business) context and application design. So, the ubiquitous language that is used to describe the context influences the design of applications as well.

The DDD approach uses bounded contexts for setting the boundaries of independent areas with a high level of cohesion. If we project DDD onto our application landscape on an enterprise level, then the domain boundaries keep not only the application(s) together but also the language, knowledge, team resources, and technologies. However, the difficulty with DDD for data management is that the original use case for DDD was modeling of complex systems in the context of software development (for example, microservices). It was not intended to be used for modeling enterprise data, and data management practitioners often find it too abstract and technical. Let me help you to better understand by providing a metaphor. Think of a domain as an area of common interest, such as the street you live on. The street is a domain, and each house represents a subdomain. Each house stands on its own property, but it doesn't fill the whole property because it's surrounded by a garden and a fence. The fence in this example represents the boundary of the bounded context. In this example, individual homeowners take responsibility for maintaining their houses and can do whatever they want within their boundaries. However, when crossing the boundaries (fences), there are certain rules to adhere to. For example, they should always enter and exit the property via a common driveway and drive along the street or walk on the sidewalk.

If we take, for example, the data mesh as a concept for democratizing data, and implement the principle of domain-oriented data ownership for greater flexibility, how would this work in practice? What might a transition from enterprise data modeling to DDD modeling look like? What learnings can we take from DDD for data management?

Business Architecture

My recommendation, when designing a large-scale architecture, is to start by examining the scope and getting an understanding of the strategic problem spaces you're trying to address. It's important to do this exercise first, before jumping into the details of a technical implementation. As DDD advocates, it helps to set logical boundaries between the problem spaces because this makes responsibilities clearer and ensures they are better managed.

To determine how to group your problem spaces, I encourage you to look at your business architecture. In its Guide to the Business Architecture Body of Knowledge (BIZBOK Guide) (*https://oreil.ly/imfcf*), the Business Architecture Guild describes business architecture as representing "holistic, multidimensional business views of: capabilities, end-to-end value delivery, information, and organizational structure; and the relationships among these business views and strategies, products, policies, initiatives, and stakeholders." Architects use business architecture as the basis for setting principles, guidance, desired outcomes, and the boundaries of the enterprise and its business ecosystem.[6] In other words, we can draw a parallel from bounded contexts to business architecture and business capabilities.

Business capabilities

To solve business problems and satisfy needs, a common technique is to use *business capabilities*. A business capability is a building block used within business architecture. The term was introduced by Ulrich Homann (*https://oreil.ly/JhjPW*),[7] who defined it as follows:

> A business capability is a particular ability, or capacity that a business may possess or exchange to achieve a specific purpose or outcome. A capability describes what the business does (outcomes and service levels) that creates value for customers; for example, pay employee or ship product. A business capability abstracts and encapsulates the people, process/procedures, technology, and information into the essential building blocks needed to facilitate performance improvement and redesign analysis.

Business capabilities are useful because they provide an abstraction of the business reality to help companies meet their strategic business goals and objectives. They capture and describe the relationships between data, processes, people, and technology within a particular context and are used to deliver end-to-end value. To make it clearer how business capabilities are actually used, I'll focus first on *value streams*. Value streams, as the name implies, focus on value-add: they're typically sets of actions that are carried out to deliver value. For example, a value stream might deliver a product, service, or experience to a group of customers.

If you take value streams as a starting point, you'll see that business capabilities are required to provide value in each of the steps. Figure 2-6 illustrates the relationships between value streams, business capabilities, and the underlying business processes,

---

6 James Moore, author of *The Death of Competition* (Harper), defined a business ecosystem as "a collection of companies that work cooperatively and competitively to satisfy customer needs."

7 Chris Richardson, one of the authors for Microservices.io, has also recognized the business capability view (*https://oreil.ly/wBZj2*).

technologies, and information. The relationships between value streams and business capabilities are many-to-many. For example, Figure 2-6 shows a business-to-business (B2B) value stream that is linked to multiple business capabilities. Some of these capabilities may also be used within the retail business value stream.

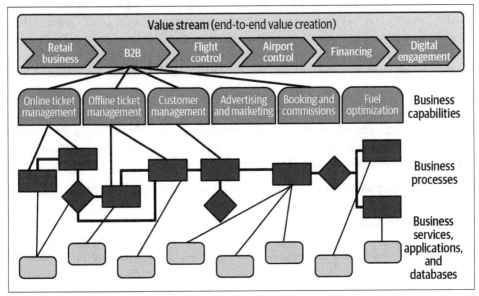

Figure 2-6. Mapping value streams to business capabilities

Managing complexity starts by creating a holistic view. *Business capability models* in that respect help to provide the necessary insights for determining, for example, what applications are shared. A business capability model represents the overall organization's strategic business objectives and activities in a structured visualization. Each business capability is implemented at least once and used within a value stream. Business capabilities are usually described in a *capability map* that is a hierarchical description of what the business does. We usually talk about Level 1, Level 2, and Level 3 business capabilities (or more levels depending on the complexity of the business), where each level is a decomposition of one or more capabilities at a higher level.

 There's a design principle for business capability models. Business capabilities are unique, mutually exclusive, and collectively exhaustive, and ensure that there are no duplicates, overlaps, or gaps.

Good business capability models are relevant to the business and defined in business terms. The importance of a capability can be tied to specific business objectives and metrics. Capability models provide a fairly stable view of the business because the fundamental business objectives rarely change, although the underlying processes, applications, and data do change over time. A business capability model can also be used for mapping to value streams, applications, and processes or plotting dependencies, or perhaps to show what impact a new strategy has on business capabilities. For example, to show the effectiveness of your data management strategy and its impact on the organization, you can plot KPIs onto implemented business capabilities.

In Figure 2-7, I've created a business capability map for a fictional airline company, Oceanic Airlines, which needs to master all the functional areas listed here in order to be successful.[8] For example, Oceanic Airlines must be able to sell tickets, handle baggage and lost items, and maintain its airplanes. The company can outsource some activities, whilst keeping others as the core of its business.[9]

What you will observe in practice is that most of your people are organized around these capabilities. People working on the same business capability share the same vocabulary. The same holds for your applications and processes, which are typically well aligned and tightly connected based on the cohesion of the activities they need to support. Therefore, business capability mapping is a great starting point—but the story doesn't end here.

---

8 Oceanic Airlines is the name of a fictional airline used in several films, television programs, and comic books; for example, the brand is used prominently in the TV series *Lost*.

9 Business capabilities don't tell us anything about organizational structures and organizational boundaries, or whether capabilities are developed in-house or outsourced. They can also move independently within or across organizations. For example, a capability like an online payment service can initially be developed in-house, but later be outsourced to PayPal. This organizational change shouldn't affect the business capability. The specific ability to process online payments, in order to achieve the enterprise goals, remains the same.

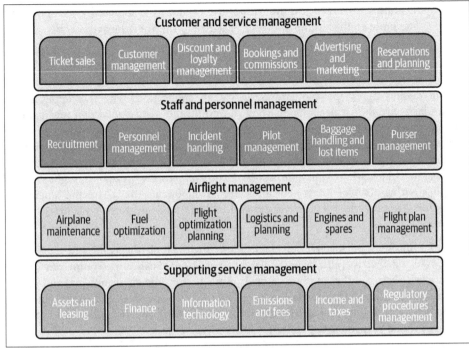

Figure 2-7. Example functional domain decomposition of an airline company—this business capability model represents a high-level breakdown of an organization from the perspective of its business capabilities

Linking business capabilities with applications

To better manage your enterprise architecture, you should make sure that your business capabilities, bounded contexts, and applications are aligned. When doing so, it's important to follow certain ground rules. It's vital that the business capabilities stay on the business level and remain abstract. They represent what an organization does and target the *problem space*. They are your language for communication and strategy.

When a business capability is implemented, a realization or "capability instance" for a specific context is created. Within these boundaries in the *solution space*, multiple applications and components can work together to deliver specific business value. Applications and components that are aligned with a specific business capability stay decoupled from applications aligned with other business capabilities.

It's important to mention that the logical application boundaries are framed: ideally, applications would be linked to only one capability instance. They shouldn't span across or be linked to multiple capability instances at the same time. The whole set of these applications, within the boundaries of the capability instance, forms a bounded context. The same applies to the data and processes—they're cohesive as well.

Application Boundaries

What defines the scope and boundaries of an application? The way application boundaries are drawn depends on your viewpoint; the word *application* means different things to different people. You might define it as how application code and data are bundled, deployed together, and isolated from that of other applications. From another viewpoint, applications can be the virtual address spaces, such as virtual machines, where different processes run. Yet another viewpoint might see an application as a set of integrated application components that share the language runtime system (*https://oreil.ly/NFQjS*) and talk to other integrated code via service layers.

From a business perspective, an application might be all the code and data that are used together to fulfill a particular business need. Such a viewpoint can draw boundaries across different physical environments, runtime environments, and platforms. Boundaries can also be based on (political) ownership and organizational structures within the company. Briefly summarized, what you and others think of as an application very much depends on your point of view.

For data management, we can combine two viewpoints to create a comprehensive breakdown. The concept of an application, in itself, remains abstract. It's a logical boundary in which application components can be built or deployed together. Application components, unlike applications, are tangible: they target the solution space. They have a size and a composition and exist in the context of technology. For example, an application module packaged and deployed as a Docker container or JAR file is a tangible artifact.

Combining these two different viewpoints delivers a lot of value. On the application level, we can connect business capabilities, product owners, DevOps teams, projects, and so on. On the application component level, we can connect IT products, versions, configuration items,[10] contracts, maintenance plans, and more.

Delineating a clear relationship between business capabilities and application architecture gives you many benefits. It makes guidelines for decoupling interfaces and applications much clearer. It helps you better execute data governance; you could argue that all data that is created within a specific context for a particular business capability belongs to a specific product owner. Product ownership and data

---

10 In Information Technology Infrastructure Library (ITIL) terminology, configuration items (CIs) are components of an infrastructure that is under configuration management.

ownership suddenly become much more aligned. You can also draw conclusions on a capability level more easily because applications are explicitly linked to capabilities.

Domain Boundaries and Granularity

Setting exact boundaries and the right level of granularity of these boundaries isn't an exact science. It's an art, one that comes with heuristics. I like to map the domain boundaries to the logical boundaries of the business architecture for the purposes of data management and understanding the scale and complexity of the enterprise. Other people look more at organizational boundaries, business processes, or domain expertise. Another way of determining the domain boundaries is by working out a detailed blueprint of your software architecture and determining what application components should be either more loosely coupled or more strongly connected. This technique is relatively popular, especially within microservices. All of these approaches are valid, and you may choose to apply any of them depending on the scope, size, and context of the business problem(s) you are trying to solve.

If you want to better understand what domain boundaries are about and how to set bounded contexts, I encourage you to look at domain storytelling (*https:// oreil.ly/Imivx*), event storming (*https://oreil.ly/uNizW*), and the bounded context canvas (*https://oreil.ly/cWXvT*). All of these techniques are focused on understanding domain complexity, learning what's happening inside the domain, and learning how to structure or decompose it.

Applications and components that are aligned with a specific business capability stay decoupled from applications and components that are aligned with other business capabilities. This allows for greater flexibility, and it's where domains and bounded contexts come into play, like in our earlier discussion of boundary fences and houses. You can set clear principles: bounded contexts are derived from and exclusively mapped to business capabilities. They represent the boundaries of business capability implementations and behave like domains. If business capabilities change, bounded contexts change. Preferably, you would expect full alignment between domains and corresponding bounded contexts, but reality—as you'll learn in "Domain Characteristics" on page 45—can be different.

To make this more concrete, let's go back to our Oceanic Airlines example. Figure 2-8 shows what some of the bounded context boundaries and domain implementations might look like in this fictional company.

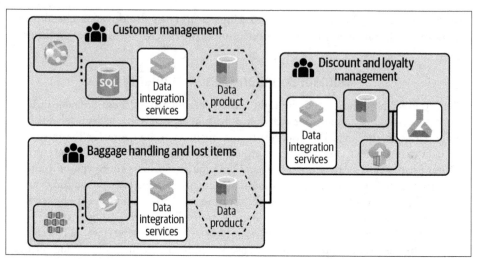

Figure 2-8. How applications and components work together within the solution space

The customer management domain is required to maintain information about customers and their relationships. The team managing this domain has deep expertise. It knows what relevant data exists, and therefore also knows best what data should be served to other domains. This domain's inner architecture is decoupled, so all application components within its boundaries can communicate directly using application-specific interfaces and data models. With this approach, data is aligned with the domain context. Because of that, the data automatically inherits the ubiquitous language: a constructed, formalized language,[11] agreed upon by stakeholders and designers from the same domain, to serve the needs of that domain. The distribution of data to other domains is formalized: it has to leave the property via the common driveway and conform to the rules of the road. In other words, when domains communicate with other domains, they use standardized interfaces.

Capability realizations

When working with a business capability map, it's essential to acknowledge that some business capabilities can be instantiated several times. Figure 2-9 visualizes the relationship between business capabilities and business capability instances.

---

11 A common way to formalize languages is by storing all business terms and definitions in a data catalog.

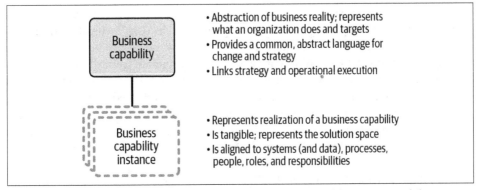

Figure 2-9. *The relationship between a business capability and business capability instances is one-to-many*

For instance, Oceanic Airlines might have multiple localized realizations, or implementations, of the "baggage handling and lost items" capability: one for each region in which the company operates (Asia, Europe, etc.). Each of these implementations might use different technology services, with different teams operating those services. Because the relationship between business capabilities and capability instances (realizations) is one-to-many, you end up with additional (sub)domains when implementing business capabilities several times.

Shared capabilities

More important is how you should handle shared business capabilities. Such capabilities are typically implemented centrally, using an as-a-service model, and provided to different lines of the business. "Customer management" might be one example of such a capability: Oceanic Airlines' Asian and European business lines might use the same system for administrating their customers. So how do you project domain data ownership on a shared capability? There are likely multiple business representatives taking accountability for customers in the same shared administration system and underlying database. To conclude, there's an application domain and a data domain! From a data viewpoint, your domain and application bounded contexts don't always perfectly align. Conversely, you could argue that from a business capability's viewpoint, there's still a single data and application concern.

 Organizations will almost certainly encounter shared business capabilities due to the monolithic nature of enterprise resource planning (ERP), supply chain management (SCM), and customer relationship management (CRM) systems, which traditionally span many domains. So, it's imperative to crack this nut early on.

For shared capabilities such as complex vendor packages, SaaS solutions, and legacy systems, I recommend being consistent in your domain data ownership approach. One technique might be to segregate data ownership via data products. This means multiple data products from different data domains originate from the same application domain. In the example of customer management, different data products could represent different concerns: one data product for all Asia-related customers and one for all Europe-related customers. A different technique for handling shared data is to ask your application domains to design a single data product that encapsulates metadata for distinguishing data ownership inside the data product. You could, for example, use a marked column name for ownership, mapping each row to a single specific data domain. In Chapter 8, I'll provide a diagram and additional guidance when discussing data governance and security.

Figure 2-10 illustrates the difference between a generic business capability and a shared business capability. As you can see, the complexity with shared capabilities is that they have a single provider who determines the realization of the capability in alignment with the different domains that use it.

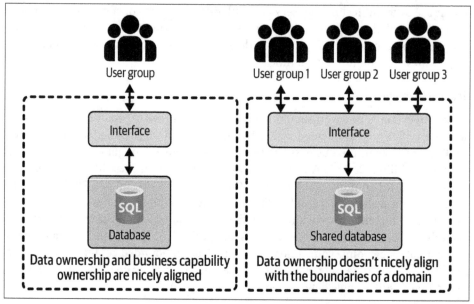

Figure 2-10. Generic (left) versus shared (right) business capabilities

Ideally, your teams owning the business capabilities are aligned with your application domains, so software ownership and data ownership are also aligned. If breaking up your domains isn't possible, you need to differentiate between application ownership and data ownership. So, in the example of customer management, you would have one application owner that is responsible for the underlying technology services, pipelines, and application components, and multiple data owners (business representatives) taking responsibility for different datasets, including metadata registration, privacy, security, and so on.

Complex applications

Another area to pay attention to is applications that cater to multiple business capabilities, which are common in large and traditional enterprises. For example, Oceanic Airlines might use one software package to facilitate both cost management and assets and leasing. Such shared applications are generally large and complex; they might be vendor business suites or legacy monoliths that provide as many features as possible. While this might seem similar to the issue described in the previous section, in this case the complexity is different: it's not that a single business capability is shared between teams, but rather that a single application and database are shared by different business capabilities. This raises the same data ownership issues that we discussed previously.

Domain Characteristics

When mapping domains and applications, you'll learn there are different data distribution patterns, based on the creation, consumption, or redelivery of data. I recommend defining principles, designing architecture blueprints, and aligning these with the characteristics of your domains. At a high level, we can distinguish between two types of domains.

Source system–aligned domains are domains that are aligned with golden source systems, where the data originates. These systems are typically transactional or operational by nature. The principle for sharing data from these domains is to capture the data directly from the golden source systems. In order to facilitate the correct capture of data and ownership information, you can support these domains with standardized services for data transformation and sharing. An example of this type of domain can be seen in Figure 2-11. This domain uses the "common driveway" pattern for distributing data products to other consuming domains.

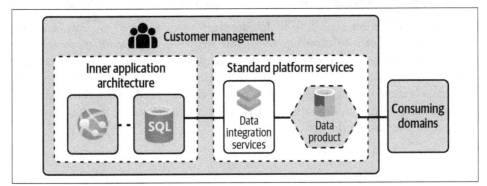

Figure 2-11. The customer management domain is source system aligned

Consumer-aligned domains are domains that consume and use data from other domains. They are the opposite of source system–aligned domains because they're aligned with specific end user use cases that require data from other domains. They consume and transform data to fit their business needs. To cater to these consuming needs, you should support these domains with standardized services for data transformation and consumption. An example of a consuming domain is shown in Figure 2-12. This domain uses standard platform services for turning data into value.

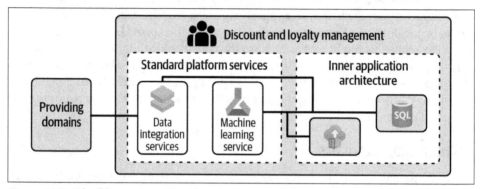

Figure 2-12. The "discount and loyalty management" domain is a consumer-aligned domain

A different and more difficult scenario, which we'll cover in depth in Chapter 10, is when data needs to be reused. Imagine a situation in which multiple downstream consumers are interested in the same combination of data from different domains. To isolate and more effectively manage these overlapping and shared concerns, you might want to bring business logic for building the shared data together in a location where it's managed apart from the places where the data is used. Figure 2-13 shows how this could work in practice. In this example, the "emissions and fees" domain behaves as an aggregate domain by first combining and integrating data, then using this data for itself and sharing it with other domains. This customer/supplier pattern is especially useful when integration requirements between domains overlap.

Another collaboration model is to let domains work together in only a purely upstream/downstream relationship. With this setup, an *aggregate domain* acts as a dedicated supplier of combined data to other domains. Such a supplier domain behaves as a data consumer and provider at the same time. It does this by consuming the data, creating a domain aggregate (a combined data product), and then directly distributing it. In this collaboration model, the newly created data product isn't used as input for use cases of the domain itself.

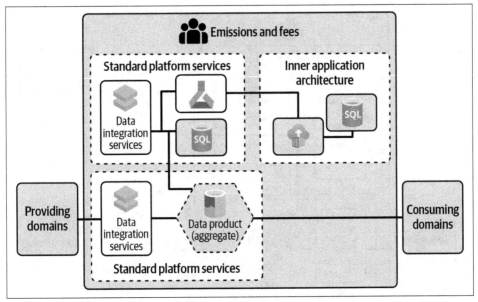

Figure 2-13. Different patterns are blended together in the emissions and fees domain

A *domain aggregate* is a cluster of domain objects that can be treated as a single unit. When you have a collection of objects of the same format and type that are used together, you can model them as a single object, simplifying their usage for other domains. A domain aggregate shouldn't be confused with data aggregation, which is the process of grouping data and expressing it in a summary form.

Another scenario, illustrated in Figure 2-14, is when consumers become providers after creating new data—for example, by making predictions about passengers' travel habits. Before they become providers, these consuming domains use bits of domain logic from other domains combined with their own domain logic to transform the aggregated data into new data products, which might be of interest to other domains as well. Such domains are sometimes called *constructor domains* because they create something new.

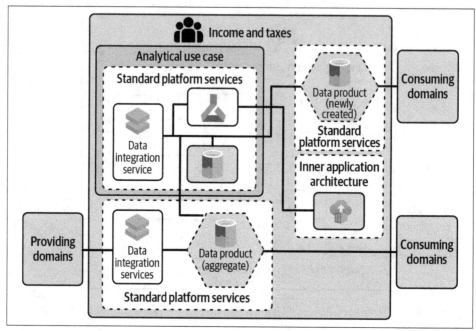

Figure 2-14. The "income and taxes" domain behaves as a constructor domain: it aggregates data to use for its own purposes and exports the newly created data product to other domains

The difference, compared to the previous domain aggregation scenarios, is that the newly created data product contains new business insights. Thus, the data sent to the consumers has not only gone through some structural changes, but has also been enriched with new business insights using a different context.

 For all of these scenarios, it's important to follow the best practice of using a common driveway for data distribution.

As you've seen, domains can be classified by the characteristics of data product usage and distribution. Depending on the situation, the rules of the game may change: for example, different blueprints and architectural patterns may apply. In the next chapters, we'll connect back to the scenarios that we've just discussed.

Patterns for complex integration challenges

When breaking apart your enterprise landscape into a more fine-grained domain structure, you'll encounter complex integration challenges. If we take the example of Oceanic Airlines, customer data from the "customer management" domain may be required in many different domains, and the "flight plan management" domain must know whether a pilot still exists in the "pilot management" domain's administration system before planning a flight. How can you address these complexities?

The best practice is to standardize on several common driveway patterns allowing different styles of integration. For example, when performing data processing at large, domains can serve data products to other domains, allowing them to read data intensively. For strongly consistent reads (and commands), for example, API services are recommended. We'll cover these and related topics in more depth in Chapters 4, 5, and 6.

Strengths of business capability modeling

The benefit of business capability modeling is that it helps you to better recognize and organize your domains in a distributed architecture. It provides a holistic view of how data and applications deliver value to your business. This allows you to prioritize and focus on your data strategy and real business needs. You can also use this model beyond the realm of data. If, for example, scalability is a concern, you can identify your most critical core business capabilities and develop a strategy for those.

Some people may raise the concern that building such a target-state architecture by mapping out everything up front is an intensive exercise. The proposed alternative is identifying your domains organically while onboarding them into your new architecture. With this approach, instead of defining your target state from the top down, you work bottom up, exploring, analyzing, and experimenting as you transition your current state toward the target state. This might save you some time initially, but it can result in the need for complex moving or remodeling operations when things start to break. A more nuanced approach is to work in both directions, mapping things out in broad strokes and adding detail over time.

Operating an enterprise data management architecture requires standardizing patterns, working with clear design principles, and making hard choices. In the next sections, I will start with the basic design choices and gradually reveal the most important patterns and principles.

Principles for Distributed and Domain-Oriented Data Management

Now that you have a clearer understanding of the data sharing and cross-domain collaboration models, I'd like to share some key principles that you should keep in mind to ensure your distributed data management strategy is successful. I'll start with some high-level advice here, then get deeper into specifics for data domains and data providers:

Avoid data silos.

The first design principle is to discourage the use of silos or integration hubs for data distribution. Data silos require additional transformation steps, which makes the chain between provider and consumers longer and much harder to manage. In, for example, the data warehouse model, we have to deal with inconsistencies when integrating all the data because bounded contexts often conflict. Data providers and data consumers in the data warehouse model are tightly coupled, which makes the dependencies much more difficult to manage. Organizations often can't trust data silos because of data quality issues, corrections, and inconsistencies.

By eliminating data silos for data distribution and using newer and more modern forms of data integration and distribution, we avoid teams bypassing the integration obstacles and driving the architecture into an unmanageable point-to-point architecture.

 Connecting your domains using point-to-point interfaces creates exponential complexity and should be avoided at all costs. For example, interconnecting 100 applications results in 5,000 point-to-point connections. For 1,000 applications, there will be roughly 500,000 point-to-point connections. Point-to-point connections can't provide the control and agility enterprises need because the sheer number of communication channels makes it nearly impossible to oversee all dependencies.

Only capture and modify data at the golden source.

The second principle is aimed at increasing trust in data. It's important to ensure you're capturing only unique data from your golden sources before distributing any data to other systems. Changes to original data should be made only at the golden source within the domain, with approval from the owner. For transparency and trust, it's important to make your golden sources publicly known, so I encourage you to set up a central register or catalog that keeps track of all unique golden source systems.

Respect the rules of data ownership.

When applications consume and use data, they can become new golden sources. In this circumstance the data truly has a new context, so there are new facts. This brings us to our next principle: when data has been changed and new facts are created, *new ownership is expected.* Simple "syntactic transformations," such as filters, unions, upper- to lowercase conversions, and field renames do not require new ownership, since all the facts remain the same. This is strongly linked to another foundational principle: *don't distribute any data you don't own.* When distributing data that originates in and is owned by another domain, always ensure your domain gets approval from that domain.

Design Principles for Data Domains

When implementing domain-driven design on an enterprise scale, the biggest change in managing dependencies and separating concerns is that the DDD philosophy and bounded contexts will be used for setting the logical boundaries in the application landscape. Bounded contexts, as we discussed earlier, are about finding the right level of cohesion and ideal size for properly managing a problem area. Once a bounded context has been identified, it must be decoupled and allowed to communicate with other bounded contexts only through formalized endpoints (this is the common driveway pattern we've been discussing).

Using the domain-driven design model on an enterprise level is quite different from using the siloed approach, where all data is centralized in a highly integrated environment using enterprise languages. In DDD, each bounded context uses its own ubiquitous language. When the bounded context changes, the ubiquitous language changes. The enterprise language in our new architecture becomes a collection of many ubiquitous languages.

The DDD model isn't explicit about how to find cohesion and determine the boundaries of a bounded context. Therefore, I recommend also adhering to the following list of design principles when designing a new architecture:

Data is managed by and delivered throughout the domains.

The quality of the data, the data pipeline, and data readability are concerns of the domain. The people who are expected to know the data best are responsible for managing it. The data ownership model will be distributed rather than centralized.

Bounded contexts are linked to instantiated business capabilities.

A bounded context implements—and thus represents an implementation of—a business capability instance, or a specific part of one. The bounded context therefore focuses on the same solution area.

A bounded context can be linked to one or more applications.

A bounded context can be a decomposition of one application or multiple applications. In the case of multiple applications, all are expected to deliver value for the same (business) capability instance.

 There are different ways of decomposing and decoupling a complex architecture. The level of granularity and decoupling can be determined using domains: multiple applications within a domain form a bounded context and are decoupled from other domains. An alternative is to make the level of granularity more fine-grained and decouple applications from applications. This would force domains, which can have a certain degree of autonomy, to always decouple their applications.

The ubiquitous language is shared within the bounded context.

Applications or application components distributing data within their own bounded context use the same ubiquitous language. The terms and definitions don't conflict. Each bounded context has a one-to-one relationship with a conceptual data model.

Bounded contexts are infrastructure-, network-, and organization-agnostic.

The cohesion is about application functionality, processes, and data. From a data management standpoint, the bounded context doesn't change regarding infrastructure, network, or organization.

One bounded context belongs to one team.

Ideally, each bounded context belongs to one Agile or DevOps team, because when there's one team, the number of coupling points is manageable and they're easily understood by all team members.

The boundaries are strict.

The boundaries of the bounded context are strict. Each bounded context is distinct. Business concerns, processes, and data that belong together must stay together and be maintained and managed within the bounded context.

Decouple when crossing the boundaries.

Within a bounded context, tight coupling is allowed; however, when crossing the boundaries, the interfaces must be decoupled.

Any shape of data for a particular bounded context is allowed, as long as the explicit boundaries are respected.

Domain data shouldn't be delivered via additional or intermediate systems.

Additional layers, such as a cross-domain data virtualization layer, will obfuscate golden source systems. Such layers increase complexity, change the data and its quality, and make it difficult to trace the data's lineage back to the origin. Using additional or intermediate systems to pass on data is discouraged.

 The data mesh architecture strongly advocates that there isn't a single data model. The reality is different, because there are clear and shared relationships across the business that are crucial for correctly modeling your data. Ignoring these relationships will result in data that can no longer be integrated across domains. These aspects will be discussed in Chapters 10 and 11.

Generic data services must remain domain-agnostic.
Domain logic and integration complexity should stay in the bounded context and shouldn't be placed in any of the generic data services. This allows domains to do what they do best: focus on delivering value without worrying about hidden domain logic that could spoil interaction with other domains.

The DDD approach significantly increases agility because data providers and data consumers are more loosely coupled. Each business domain within the logical boundaries of the bounded context can change at its own speed because the only dependencies a domain has are with data endpoints, such as data products.

Best Practices for Data Providers

Moving data from one context into another is always difficult because it requires knowledge about both contexts. A problem is that applications in general aren't optimized for intensive data consumption. Schemas are often highly normalized, business logic is hidden inside the data, or documentation is missing. To ease the pain of data integration, we need to observe some additional principles for how data is modeled, exposed, and presented from one bounded context to another:

Hide the application technical details.
Data consumers don't need to become experts on the physical data model and shouldn't be required to rebuild application functionality to use the data. From an application perspective, this means that data providers must filter out any application logic that requires specific knowledge about the application. This principle also touches on the technical data we typically find in applications, such as migration information, logging information, or database schemas. This technical data is specific and probably only of interest to the internal domain. Data providers should filter out any data that won't be of interest to consumers before exposing it.

Optimize for intensive data consumption.

Many applications aren't optimized for intensive data consumption. Allowing domains to easily consume data doesn't mean providing heavily normalized data with endless parent/child structures to other domains. Data should be more denormalized and intuitively grouped together. User-friendly field names will help data consumers find what they're looking for. Inconsistencies and differences in naming conventions and data formats are expected to be solved up front. In this approach, data must be optimized for generic consumption, with the aim of making it as reusable as possible to meet all data consumers' potential needs. This ties back to the increasing read/write ratio, as discussed in Chapter 1.

The ubiquitous language is the language for communication.

Each bounded context acting as a data provider should expose its data using its own ubiquitous language. This implies data providers shouldn't incorporate business logic from other domains into their domain.

Interfaces must have a certain level of maturity and stability.

This principle is about abstracting the pace of change. If domain ranges frequently change, for example, an abstraction to a more stable range is expected. The schema also has to provide a stable level of compatibility.

Data should be consistent across all patterns.

This principle requires consistency in how data is exposed across the different patterns. The element *customer address*, for example, should be consistent across all patterns even if the same data is exposed multiple times.

This approach of pulling in self-describing, user-friendly data is different from data lake implementations in which raw data is directly shared. In a data lake (see "The Data Lake: A Centralized Repository for Structured and Unstructured Data" on page 17), the data is typically pulled straight in as a one-to-one copy from the source and then (directly) used for downstream consumption. The data and interfaces are tightly coupled with the underlying source systems, so any source system change will immediately break the production pipeline. Because of this, enterprises have difficulty operationalizing advanced analytics successfully. So, as a general best practice, don't absorb changes from your application teams. Instead, ask your domain teams to encapsulate their physical data models within their domain boundaries. This means that upstream domain teams build their own domain objects or data products.

What we can conclude from these principles is that data providers should expose their data in a more user-friendly, consumable, and logical way. Performing repeated work on raw data must be avoided. Data should be represented as an abstract version of the logical business model rather than as the pure physical data model from the application. In Chapter 4, I'll give much more concrete guidance on what a good representation of the data is.

Domain Ownership Responsibilities

Federating ownership of your architecture among domains requires respecting some additional principles. In addition to your domains taking ownership of applications and data products from those applications, your domain teams have to take on additional responsibilities, such as:

- Taking ownership of data pipelines, such as ingesting, cleaning, and transforming data, to serve as many data customers' needs as possible

- Improving data quality and respecting service level agreements (SLAs) and quality measures set by data consumers

- Encapsulating metadata or using reserved column names for fine-grained row/column-level filtering and dynamic data masking

- Adhering to metadata management standards, including:
  - Application and source system schema registration
  - Providing metadata for improved discoverability
  - Observing versioning rules
  - Linking data attributes and business terms
  - Ensuring the integrity of metadata information to allow better integration between domains

- Adhering to data interoperability standards, including protocols, data formats, and data types

- Providing lineage, either manually or by linking source systems and integration services to scanners

- Completing data-sharing tasks, including identity and access management reviews and data contract creation

The principles from these sections can be respected strongly or loosely. For ad hoc, exploratory, experimental use cases, interfaces can be more volatile or less optimized for direct consumption. For stable production use cases, the principles should be closely followed. You can even mix these approaches by allowing combinations within a system: for example, one data product can be delivered in a way that strongly follows the design principles outlined here while another data product, probably a less important one, can be delivered more loosely.

Respecting these principles is essential because the new architecture facilitates data distribution and integration in different ways. If you want to become data-driven and foster data consumption, all of your domains must make their data and the way it's provided a first-class concern. Domains must adhere to these principles and apply them to all of the communication patterns presented in the next chapters.

Transitioning Toward Distributed and Domain-Oriented Data Management

At this point, you may be thinking: "OK, these business capabilities and principles make sense, but where do I start?" The prerequisites that you need in order to successfully transition toward domain-oriented data ownership can be summarized as follows:

- Agree on the set of terminology to use when discussing concepts like application, application component, (data) domain, and business capability. The way application and domain boundaries are drawn depends on your viewpoint because these words mean different things to different people. Therefore, it's important to create clear definitions and determine how these concepts are aligned. Guidance and the support of using a metamodel will be discussed in Chapter 9.

- Use business capability mapping to structure your business concerns. In large enterprises, business capabilities are a great way to describe an organization in a holistic way. Note that a business capability is about the what, not the how. The implementation details and alignment with the technology architecture will be discussed in Chapter 3.

- After identifying business capabilities, concretely map what applications and data contribute to what business concerns. Identify and list your golden sources, and identify the owners of the data. I also recommend keeping a list of all your applications using an IT service management solution, a configuration management database like ServiceNow (*https://oreil.ly/RzPgq*), or a homegrown application catalog.

- While listing your business capabilities and applications, ask yourself whether those applications are allocated to only one business capability, shared across multiple business capabilities, or used within a service model. Identify which applications are shared between business capabilities, and which business capabilities are shared between value streams. For large applications that are shared between teams, divide the data into cohesive and self-contained bounded contexts, each with separate ownership. I'll come back to this with additional guidance in Chapter 8.

- Chart your data consumption and map how data consumption aligns to data creation—boundaries can also be defined by consuming demands, such as data processing or data harmonization. During this exercise, it's important to identify any shared or overlapping data concerns. At a later point, you'll need to strike a balance between conformation and autonomy. Guidance for this will be provided in Chapter 10.

- Define your (data) domains. The rule of thumb is that each domain is aligned with the realization of a business capability. In this solution space, multiple applications and components can work together to deliver specific business value. For this exercise, strive to align your bounded contexts, business capabilities, and teams. A bounded context, as you learned, is the encapsulation of a business capability, and each business capability is implemented (instantiated) at least once. For spreading your domain perspectives among your teams, a guiding principle is that each bounded context should be owned by a single team. However, a single team can own several bounded contexts.

- Boundaries shouldn't overlap. If this happens, you might need to align or recalibrate your organizational structure with your domain structure. A traditional company structure with centralized operations and development teams is harder to model around business domains than a flat organization structure with cross-functional teams. Consider whether you prefer virtual team alignment, if you want to move people across teams, and what a step-by-step transition toward the target state could look like.

- A bounded context is an area where policies and standards apply. For oversight purposes, chart your business capabilities using a capability map and use this as input for applying policies and standards. The underlying domains will inherit the policies and standards that you've set on the business capability level. Thus, this map will serve as a guide showing what standards apply in which areas.

- Clearly spell out what must happen when the demarcation lines are crossed— that is, what standards and principles your domains must follow. Distributing data and integrating applications across domain boundaries is difficult, for many reasons: systems designed for operational within-domain usage might not be easily interoperable, the processes might be difficult to synchronize, or it might simply be that the people involved are distant and don't know each other very well. This is the danger zone, with all kinds of hazards to navigate through.

Accurate, comprehensive insights into your current state are the basis for any digital transformation. It's impossible to work toward an optimized future state without having a clear understanding of where you are now. Once the current state is known, you can start planning what organic change could look like.

Wrapping Up

Let's recap what you've learned so far. The critical path to successfully implementing a new design is that everything, absolutely everything, must be built around business capabilities. It's a *business-focused* approach, which ensures real value delivery. Therefore, you must anchor your business capabilities to your key business strategies. The business capabilities themselves define your problem spaces. They're the domains that define your architecture. Systems, databases, applications, processes,

APIs, teams, and data products all map into these domains. The alternative (grains of sand) approach of using DDD, as typically seen within microservices, is mainly useful for digging up complexity and untangling application interfaces.

Next, you learned about setting strong boundaries. By enabling domains or business teams to change and exchange data independently in a federated model, you achieve more flexibility and allow domains to work in parallel. Each domain in a federated model owns and manages a piece of the overall architecture. By logically grouping applications in a bounded context on the level of business capabilities, you ensure that applications that share the same concerns are managed together and have no direct dependencies with applications managed by a different business concern. This approach creates clarity and agility for the organization because teams can fully focus on delivering the value of single business capabilities. Each domain, fenced in by the logical boundaries of the bounded context, maintains a specific part of the overall architecture, including the authoritative, unique datasets. One final note: it's important to remember that this discussion of domains and decoupling is not specifically related to the data mesh architecture. Setting clear demarcation lines is universal for any data management or application integration paradigm.

Reaching the level of a mature domain architecture isn't simple. It starts with enterprise architecture as a discipline. Enterprise architecture leaders should drive the process of change and ensure that the business vision is translated into a solid design. It also starts with setting standards centrally. Transitioning toward being data-driven requires that individual teams give up their mandate to make decisions about how boundaries are drawn and how data is owned, managed, distributed, and consumed. Ownership requires discipline and daily practice. This responsibility shift is likely to spark resistance, and you may have to make political choices. Without strong guidance, the organizational transformation won't happen and the architecture won't fulfill its full potential. Teams that ignore boundaries, deploy the data services themselves, and do point-to-point integration run the risk of data sprawl.[12] Reusability, consistency, and data quality are important aspects of the new architecture. Consistent communication, commitment, and strong governance are required to scale up.

In addition, this data landscape modernization requires a pragmatic approach, since moving away from a tightly coupled landscape is difficult. By starting piecemeal and slowly scaling up, you give your domains and users an opportunity to recognize the benefits, so they want to contribute to new architecture that will give the organization a competitive advantage. Over time, your architecture can be expanded, with more domains, additional integration patterns, and enhanced capabilities. We'll come back to the step-by-step approach in Chapter 12 when we discuss putting theory into practice.

---

12 *Data sprawl* refers to the overwhelming amount and variety of data produced by enterprises every day.

I ended this chapter with a lot of theory about domain-driven design, business architecture, data sharing and cross-domain collaboration models, and so on. If this all seemed a bit too conceptual, don't worry. In the next chapters, we'll get back in our helicopter to get a view of the solution space and learn about landing zones, data products, APIs, and events. We'll fly one level lower, but still stay above the clouds so we have a good vantage point.

CHAPTER 3

Mapping Domains to a Technology Architecture

Now that you know what data domains are and how to recognize them, it's time to discuss how to group and manage them together, and how to plot them in a technology architecture. The decomposition of your functional domains and architecture and the alignment between these two is important because there's a strong correlation between the architecture and how governance standards must be implemented, controls will be set, data products will be managed, and so on.

My experience is that between organizations, there are significant differences in how they decompose and manage their domain architectures. Organizations make trade-offs when designing a large-scale architecture, because it must be shaped to fit their unique organizational requirements and strategy. These trade-offs cover many aspects, such as ownership, organizational size and complexity, security, pace of change, technology, cost management, and cultural and political characteristics. As discussed in Chapter 1, some organizations prefer a high degree of autonomy, while others prefer quality and control. Some organizations have a relatively simple structure, while others are brutally large and complex. It's not easy to balance all of these requirements, so organizations typically pick a common architectural design that matches most of their requirements to use as a base and build on that. As you'll see, choosing the right architectural foundation from the start helps avoid problems later on.

This chapter is divided into two parts. The first part focuses on *domain topologies*: the way in which domains are grouped, interrelated, and arranged. We will study several common architectural designs and discuss what drives organizations and why they might favor one design over another.

In the second part of this chapter, we'll discuss *landing zone topologies*: the way domains can be aligned with the solution space. We'll look at cloud configurations, standard services, approaches for organizing storage, and more. I close this section with a pragmatic example, again using the fictional Oceanic Airlines from Chapter 2. In both sections, I'll bring in my own experience from working with many customers and discuss the trade-offs that must be considered.

Domain Topologies: Managing Problem Spaces

In the previous chapter, you saw that the concept of decentralized data ownership federates responsibilities across different domains. We discussed that before figuring out technology stacks and letting loose your data teams, you should first take a look at the big picture and identify your problem spaces (or more positively formulated, business opportunities). We touched upon business capabilities and that building a business capability map is a great starting point. We also discussed many design principles and guidelines for good data ownership.

But when gluing domains together, how are problem spaces and solution spaces expected to work together? Should you group domains on certain characteristics? If so, which ones, why, and how? Should you give all domains full autonomy to connect themselves to a network of data products, or should there be a central authority involved? How do you deal with cross-domain data concerns? For example, can domains overlap with other domains? If so, how does the data flow? Is the model more a hub-and-spoke or peer-to-peer design? In this section, we'll answer all of these questions by walking through different domain topologies.[1]

Keep in mind that the principles of data ownership and domain boundaries remain the same for all the topologies we'll discuss. Each domain is responsible for its own data, manages data as a product, and uses the common driveway pattern discussed in Chapter 2. The topologies we'll discuss here are about exploring the balance between governance and flexibility, dependence and independence, control and autonomy.

Fully Federated Domain Topology

The first domain topology that we'll discuss is what I call a *fully federated* domain topology. To best explain how this topology organizes data domains, I'll use the example of the data mesh. This is a decentralized approach for managing data at large, which is founded in four principles: domain-driven ownership of data, data as a product, the self-serve data platform, and federated computational governance. In

---

1 These domain topologies are like network topologies. They describe the physical and logical relationship of domains in a network, the schematic arrangement of the links and domains, or some hybrid combination thereof.

---

its purest theoretical form, the data mesh is a fine-grained architectural design that puts a strong emphasis on federation with no central orchestrator. Figure 3-1 shows an abstract example of how domains within a data mesh are organized. This topology strives for fine-grained decoupling and high reusability of data.

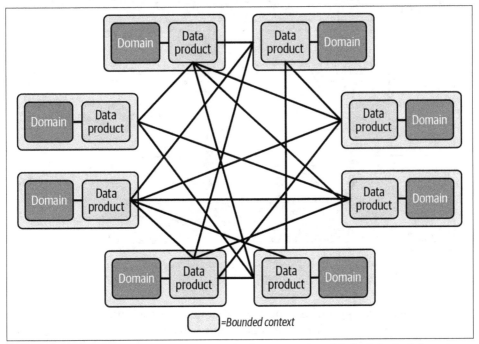

Figure 3-1. The data mesh is an example of a fine-grained and fully federated domain topology

As you can see, the boundaries of autonomy are nicely aligned with individual domains. Each domain has full end-to-end responsibility for its own data. Each domain operates independently, serves data as a product, and has a data sharing responsibility to other domains. This is the same fine-grained decomposition as is generally seen within organizations that have adopted microservices architectures.

What you also see in Figure 3-1 are direct lines between domains. Data distribution in a data mesh happens peer-to-peer: directly, without relying on a dedicated central authority. Domains are flexible and don't rely on a central team for coordination or data distribution. Governance is computational (i.e., automated); compliance is enforced through the platform.

In a data mesh, data products are fine-grained. In simple terms, you instantiate many different small data product architectures for serving and pulling data across domains. In these architectures, data and metadata, infrastructure, and code are combined and deployed together as single unit. An image of how this works conceptually is presented in Figure 3-2.

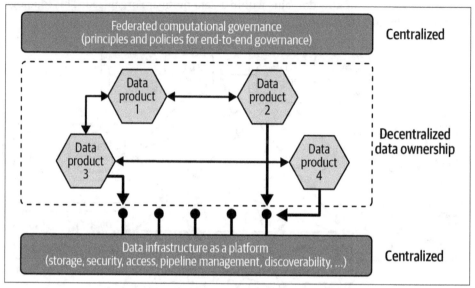

Figure 3-2. Data mesh logical architecture: centralized federated computational governance and self-serve platform capabilities, decentralized data ownership

The data mesh topology enables fine-grained domain specialization. It offers organizational flexibility and fewer dependencies because the interaction is many-to-many. Finally, it promotes intensive reuse of data since there's a high degree of data product creation, each of which is an architectural quantum (*https://oreil.ly/L1Ynv*).

Although the fine-grained and fully federated design appears perfect theoretically, when organizations look at it more deeply, they often raise concerns and identify potential challenges. Let's take a look at what is stopping organizations from implementing architectures like the data mesh.

The elephant in the room

First, a data mesh requires conformation from all domains in terms of data interoperability, metadata, governance, and security standards. This process of standardization doesn't happen spontaneously. It requires the organization to move its architecture and way of working through different stages, from preconceptualization, conceptualization, discussion, and writing, to implementation and control. Because domains in this architecture have almost complete jurisdiction over their applications and data, it's expected to be a difficult exercise to get all domain teams to conform to a common way of working. Domains have conflicting interests: some domains only demand data, while domains that don't consume any data consider building data products to be a costly investment. Besides conflicting interests, domains could also have contradicting preferences with regard to technology and ways of working. Some enthusiasts may even promote full domain autonomy without any enterprise architecture involvement. The bottom line is that aligning all the domains requires you to break political boundaries. You need critical mass and support from the wider community.

Second, organizations fear capability duplication and heavy network utilization. Many fine-grained data product architectures imply a dramatic increase in the sheer number of infrastructure resources. This can make your architecture costly and complex to manage. For example, imagine a large-scale organization that has thousands of applications and footprints on premises and in different clouds. How can you easily and securely manage network connectivity between domains when they communicate peer-to-peer? Peer-to-peer communication grows exponentially when the number of applications increases. This is an especially serious problem for companies that rely on a central team that maintains visibility and security over the network. In this example, it would mean a constant flow of communication between domains and the networking and security team.

Third, the fine-grained granularity of data product architectures poses problems: performance suffers when data needs to be pulled from many and different locations; data lookups, data quality validations, and reconciliation of historical data are difficult when data is siloed; and isolating issues is challenging when data processing is scattered. These issues largely reveal themselves when many domains rely on data from a lot of other domains. For example, financial institutions must ensure consistent reporting across the enterprise. By regulation, it's mandatory to conform accounting, financial and group reporting, and auditing and risk management to use the same dimensions. A typical solution to this reconciliation problem is to bring a lot of data closer together, an approach that heavily contrasts with the data mesh.

Fourth, companies have difficulties attracting and retaining the right talent. Decentralizing data management and establishing a platform to support a data mesh topology—including automatic data product architecture creation, policy enforcement, intelligent routing, decentralized orchestration, cataloging, and delivery—is a complex and risky undertaking. To implement a data mesh, you need a large pool of highly skilled software engineers with knowledge of DataOps, automation, security, platform design, and so on. It's likely that you will require significantly more engineers to get a data mesh started because critical mass is needed for successful adoption. Not all organizations are willing to make such a large investment, let alone able to attract the right talent.

In the final analysis, a fine-grained and fully federated domain topology is an excellent choice, but hard to achieve. I see this topology often at organizations that are born in the cloud, use mainly microservices, pursue multicloud strategies using a limited number of applications, are relatively young, and have many highly skilled software engineers. Adopting this topology also might be a considered decision when there's already a high degree of autonomy within your company.

Governed Domain Topology

Making the producers fully accountable for the data they create, manage, and distribute is one of the things organizations really like about the data mesh architecture. It federates the responsibility of managing data. This alignment makes sense because data producers are experts on their own data. They know how their systems are designed and what data is managed inside these systems. They often work closely with end users or business analysts and therefore know what good data quality means to consumers of data. In addition, federation provides scalability: multiple teams independently develop data pipelines and serve data in parallel. So, it's not surprising that many large enterprises are interested in federating tasks and responsibilities.

To lower the overhead of managing infrastructure, you can adjust the previous topology by adding a central distribution layer. While the resulting *governed domain* topology doesn't exactly implement a data mesh architecture, it does adhere to many data mesh principles: each domain operates within a clear boundary and has autonomous ownership over its own applications and data products, but those data products must be distributed via a centrally managed and shared logical entity, as shown in Figure 3-3.

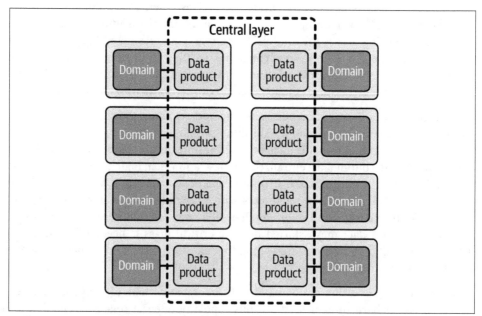

Figure 3-3. A governed domain topology

This topology has similarities with a hub-and-spoke model.[2] By adding a centrally shared data product architecture, it efficiently manages data distribution; it allows data to be delivered once to a centralized logical location and then consumed many times by different consumers.

 Should domains always expose or share all the data they produce? It depends. My recommendation is to build data products using a demand-driven approach—i.e., only when the need is there. Then, as a general best practice, I recommend building data products in such a way that they potentially serve as many (reusable) data consumers as possible. However, I have seen some organizations that require all data to always be made available. Such organizations anticipate becoming data-driven and thus require a fast time to market.

Organizations often feel that central distribution, as seen in Figure 3-4, better targets concerns of conformation in the early stages of development; for example, when automation is absent. You can more easily block data distribution or consumption, enforce metadata delivery, or require a specific way of working when a single platform for data distribution is used. Another benefit of central distribution is that an abundance of network traffic is avoided because there's a central point of connectivity. If all domains distribute their data using peer-to-peer connectivity, you'll see an explosion of incoming and outgoing connectivity points. Distribution to and from a central logical entity solves this problem.

With central distribution, organizations also attempt to make their architectures more cost-effective. Some complement the central distribution layer with shared computational services. You could, for example, take the Apache Spark processing part out of individual data product architectures and share that computation across multiple domains to ensure data is processed more cost-effectively. Having a central layer for distribution also simplifies meeting the *time-variant* and *nonvolatile* requirements that are typical of data warehousing workloads.[3]

---

2 Hub-and-spoke is a well-known architectural pattern in which data transfer and interserver communication travel through a centralized hub.

3 These concepts were introduced by Bill Inmon in his book *Building the Data Warehouse* (Wiley). *Time-variant* means historization takes place, so you can time travel and see older datasets. *Nonvolatile* means that once data is processed, it won't change. So, historical data should never be altered. We'll talk more about historization in Chapter 4.

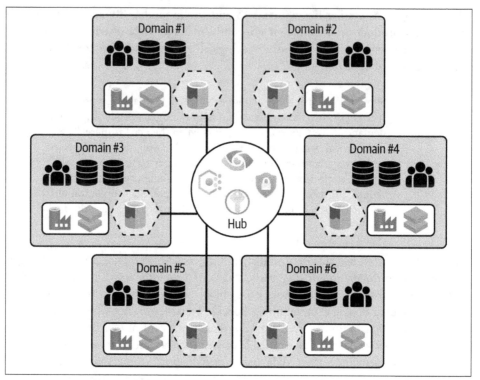

Figure 3-4. An abstract design showing how domains can take ownership over their own applications, data, and data products, with data products routed via a central logical entity

This topology requires conformance from domains, as they have to distribute and route data via a central logical entity. Together with the stronger centralization, this is an important factor to keep in mind. It introduces more coupling between your domains, and may lead to a longer time to market: your central distribution layer can act as a bottleneck, hindering domains from delivering business value when central capabilities aren't ready. This topology can also be more difficult to implement for multicloud deployments because building a central data distribution service that seamlessly moves data across different clouds is difficult, given the lock-in and limited flexibility of some cloud native services.

A governed domain topology is still a shift from central to federated data management. It might be complex to implement, but nevertheless, I see many organizations choosing a governed domain topology in order to have more scalability. This is true of most financial institutions and governments that I've worked with, as well as other large organizations that value control, quality, and compliance over team autonomy.

Partially Federated Domain Topology

Not all organizations have the luxury of having many highly skilled software engineers on staff. Others have constraints or are forced to work with legacy applications that are hard to maintain and extract data from. Organizations that fall into these categories often implement "some" federation, using a topology like the one visualized in Figure 3-5.

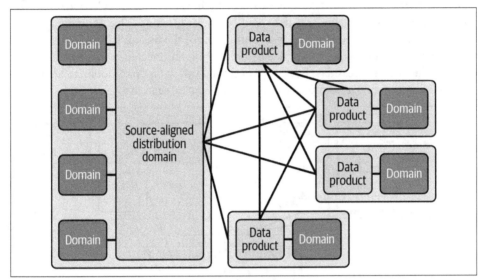

Figure 3-5. Partially federated domain topology: federation on the consuming side, a bit of centralization on the source system–aligned side

What distinguishes this topology from the previous topologies? There's less federation and more centralization. There's a data product management mindset, but data is managed in a central and shared data product architecture. Sometimes, when a domain team lacks the necessary skills or resources, there's even a central engineering team that takes ownership of data. In these kind of situations you see *virtual* alignment: project team members help to resolve issues and onboard data on behalf of a domain.

On the consuming side of this architecture, there's typically a higher degree of autonomy and a mesh style of data distribution. Different domain teams work on use cases and take ownership for their transformed data and analytical applications. The outcome or newly created data is distributed peer-to-peer or pushed back into the central data platform.

A consideration for this topology is increased management overhead for source system–aligned domains, as they're likely to be onboarded by a central team. Organizations that use this architecture are likely to suffer from problems stemming from different operating models, a lack of self-service features, and more complex guidance and principles. There also might be inconsistent rules for data distribution because consuming domains often are also providing domains.

Value Chain–Aligned Domain Topology

Organizations with core competencies in supply chain management, product development, or transportation take great care of their value chains. What characterizes these organizations is value-add delivered by their domains. The domains typically work in a stream-aligned fashion, as an entire slice of the business (thus, end-to-end). Because of this, domains are typically tightly interconnected and operational by nature. They also process data backward and forward, from operational, to analytical, back to operational. An example of this topology can be seen in Figure 3-6.

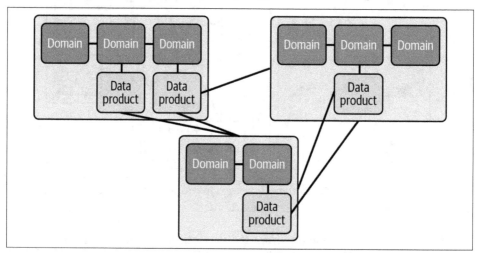

Figure 3-6. Value chain–aligned domain topology: tight domain alignment around a chain of business activities

A *value chain* in this context is a small group of domains that work closely together to achieve a common value-add. Value chains themselves require higher levels of autonomy and can be seen as larger domains. Within these larger domains, you typically see different patterns: there's internal value chain data distribution as well as cross–value chain data distribution. Within the boundaries of the value chain itself there may be less or limited adherence to central standards, but when data crosses the boundaries of the value chain, those standards must be observed.

When applying a value chain–aligned domain topology, you can mix different types of governance models: you might require strict adherence in one domain, but allow relaxed controls in other domains. Another consideration with this topology is that it requires stronger guidance from architects because boundaries might not always be that explicit (for example, when business capabilities are shared between different value streams). A final consideration for adopting this topology is that you become less data-driven because only data that crosses a value chain boundary finds its way to a data product.

Coarse-Grained Domain Topology

Some organizations gained scale by growing organically, through mergers and acquisitions. These organizations generally have complex landscapes with sometimes hundreds, or even thousands, of applications and systems. Within these complex structures, there are different levels of governance, alignments, and decompositions. Some structures might stand on their own and operate autonomously, while others are more integrated with the holding group structures of the organization.

The structures observed within these organizations are typically large. Individual domains might hold dozens or hundreds of applications. This *coarse-grained* topology is abstractly visualized in Figure 3-7.

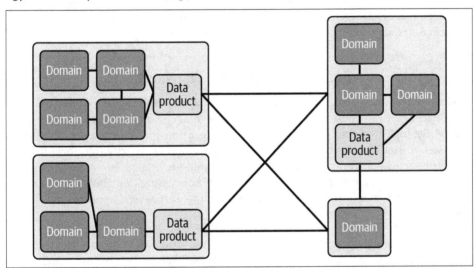

Figure 3-7. Coarse-grained domain topology: domains are coarsely aligned around, for example, business units, regions, or business capabilities

The difficulty with a coarse-grained domain topology is that boundaries aren't always explicit. Domains may overlap with other domains, or sit in larger domains. In addition, applications and data aren't always aligned with the business objectives. More often, domain boundaries are based on relatively broad organizational or regional viewpoints. Such groupings might create political infighting over who controls data and what governance rules should be applied to correctly manage it.

Another challenge is that a coarse-grained approach to managing applications and data introduces capability duplication. It's likely that each coarse-grained domain uses its own data platform for onboarding, transforming, and distributing data. Such an approach of implementing many platforms leads to duplication. For example, data quality management and master data management are likely to be needed across the enterprise. A federated platform approach might lead to many implementations of data quality and MDM on the various data platforms. Ensuring consistent implementation of these services across all platforms requires strong collaboration and guidance. The larger your organization is, the harder it gets.

This multiplatform approach often raises many questions: how do you calibrate data platforms and domains? Are larger domains that are connected to the same data platform allowed to share data directly? How do you deal with overlapping data requirements when the same data is needed on different platforms? How can you efficiently distribute data between domains and platform instances? A good starting point, before implementing any platform services, is to make a proper domain decomposition of your organization using business capability modeling, discussed in Chapter 2. Next, establish application and data ownership, then formulate strong guidance on data product creation and distribution.

Domain-Oriented Data Warehouses

Some organizations envision domain orientation by implementing large, coarse-grained data warehouses using canonical data models, or *supermodels*, with one language used to connect all parties within a larger domain. In this approach, warehouses or data lakes capture and retain raw data, and then directly transform it into a harmonized domain model. After harmonization, the original domain serves data directly to operational applications and to other consuming domains. When a data warehouse acts as a store for numerous domains, there are several important things to keep in mind:

- Implementing specific logic for one set of use cases while directly serving out generic data to other domains is extremely difficult. These are two contrasting concerns, which can't easily be combined into one design. For example, you may need to abstract data for consumers, while adding extra complexity for other use cases. The end result, when implementing this in the same data model, is usually a design that is hard to work with.

- Retaining only raw data and directly harmonizing it means you can no longer easily facilitate operational reporting or analytics. You either have incoming data that is raw, tightly coupled, and too complex to work with, or harmonized data that is meaningless for the operational use cases.

- The risks involved when carrying out changes are significantly increased because all use cases are coupled to the same underlying structure. That is, consumers that are only interested in data from a single source are coupled to other systems and may be affected by them, because the data first is combined in a harmonized layer, and then served out.

A shared database model, such as a large domain data warehouse for multiple domains with different business concerns, will eventually lead to serious problems and must be avoided at all costs.

When an organization is considering a coarse-grained domain topology as a starting point, they should plan a transition toward a more fine-grained and decentralized model. A coarse-grained approach implies a high level of autonomy, and therefore requires stronger governance policies and self-service data platform capabilities. For example, specific guidance might be needed for registering and making a data product discoverable, depending on the technology and interoperability choices made by the domains. Otherwise, a proliferation of approaches across domains can lead to poor visibility and increased costs.

The coarse-grained domain topology described here is a long way from a data mesh implementation. Usually, the demarcation lines for domains aren't set. This risks creating larger silos, with extra coupling between systems. Coarse-grained boundaries also introduce data ownership obfuscation because data products are distributed via intermediary systems, silos, or point-to-point interfaces, which makes it harder to determine the actual origin. To mitigate these risks, set clear demarcation lines, and strongly standardize on technology services, metadata, and interoperability standards. Also, observe principles such as only capturing unique data and capturing data directly from the original source using its unique domain context.

Coarse-Grained and Partially Governed Domain Topology

Some large, complex organizations aim to overcome issues of complexity, peer-to-peer distribution, and interoperability deviation by building a central layer of distribution that sits between these coarse-grained boundaries. An abstract visualization of such a topology is shown in Figure 3-8.

In this topology, teams or organizational structures agree on a distribution platform or marketplace through which data can be published and consumed. It incorporates some of the characteristics of the governed domain topology, but it allows for more relaxed controls within these larger boundaries.

All of the coarse-grained topologies require a high degree of maturity in the data platform team. All components need to be self-service and must integrate well between the central layer of distribution and the domain platforms. Metadata management, governance standards, and policies are crucial. If the central architecture and governance team has no strong mandate, these architectures are subject to fail.

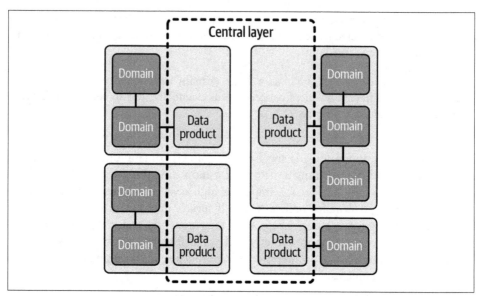

Figure 3-8. Coarse-grained and partially governed domain topology: coarse-grained alignment, while governing cross-boundary distribution of data

Centralized Domain Topology

Some organizations are resistant to decentralization. Not all organizations are able to equip all their teams with engineering tools for performing the tasks of data product creation. Not all organizations have 500+ data engineers. Not all organizational teams are familiar with complex data modeling techniques, change data capture, Kubernetes, and Python notebooks. Companies demand different approaches depending on their size, business needs, and existing architecture.

Many organizations that I've worked with have implemented hub-and-spoke network topology architectures with centralized platform teams for managing all common infrastructure, including data platforms. For generic data services, organizations often use central teams that work closely with other teams for onboarding or consuming data. The data product mindset is envisioned by requiring teams to take ownership of data, which implies support when troubleshooting, fixing data quality problems, or addressing ingestion issues. But when it comes to complex engineering there's a maturity curve, so central teams also often help with onboarding data, pipeline configuration, training, and guiding teams on best practices. These enabling teams may also take ownership of data in situations where another team lacks the necessary skills.

The same maturity curve typically also arises on the data-consuming side. In many cases, teams rely on a shared pool of resources for providing knowledge and help on configuration, ingestion, and transformation of their data. They use the lessons learned to make improvements to enhance services, such as the framework for data pipelines and ingestion, and make these more dynamic and configurable. It's a constant calibration between addressing inefficiency and enabling self-service versus time spent helping to onboard new data.

To address capability duplication concerns, enterprises often choose one central (domain-oriented) data platform over many deployed components that are all managed by individual teams. This is also where I see many overlaps with, for example, data lakehouse architectures.[4] In such a scenario, there's a central and shared data platform that handles all data ingestion, storage, transformation, and output of data in one logical data lake. Data organization and alignment with source systems or domains happens within the central platform. A reference model showing such an architecture with a single platform instance and domain-aligned data ownership is provided in Figure 3-9.

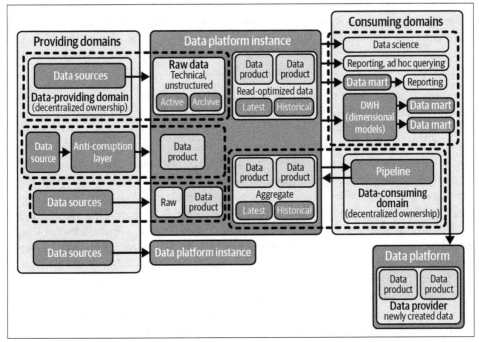

Figure 3-9. A reference model showing how domains can collaborate on a shared platform instance using a centralized domain topology

---

4 A *data lakehouse* (*https://oreil.ly/I1dqO*) is an architecture design that combines the flexibility, cost-efficiency, and scale of data lakes with the data management and ACID transactions of data warehouses, enabling business intelligence (BI) and machine learning (ML) on all data.

In this design, there's one logical storage layer for distributing data between domains. This layer, which is called a *data platform instance* in Figure 3-9, acts as a decoupling point between all teams. For the providing domains side, segmentation and isolation typically are achieved by physically segregating data in the platform by using storage accounts, buckets, containers, or folders. During data onboarding, data is often layered and processed through several stages, such as raw and curated. The end result (often called a data product) is an enriched and cleansed version of the data that originated from the source system. Organizations often try to accelerate this process by enabling self-service and applying techniques like metadata-driven ingestion.

On the consuming domains side, you may find different consumption patterns based on the needs of the consumers. Some use cases (for example, data science and reporting) will directly consume data, while other use cases push data into a newly created data mart or data warehouse. Semantic layers and data virtualization are often applied to bring data together in virtual or logical groups of data. These newly created datasets are often also called data products, and are aligned with the use cases of different data consumers. Like on the providing side, on the consuming side you often see self-service models. Organizations use catalogs to let end users request data and provide tools to consume and republish data.

The centralized domain topology typically contrasts with all other topologies when it comes to using enterprise-wide data models or enterprise-wide data harmonization. Although enterprise data modeling has a negative reputation because of its complexity and the length of time needed to develop it, I see still many organizations applying some enterprise-wide data modeling for addressing concerns about data reusability and standardization. Newly modeled datasets in such a scenario sit in a separately managed zone apart from where source system– and consumer-aligned is managed. Data in this zone is typically owned by a central team. This enterprise data is highly governed and well documented. The amount of enterprise standardization differs between organizations. Most organizations only model some data—for example, only their most important and most often used dimensions—while some attempt to model all data. The principles for consumption of these "enterprise data products" also differ: some organizations mandate that the team always consume these data products, while others take a more flexible approach with domains allowed to choose what data they consume. The concerns of addressing enterprise consistency will be discussed in Chapter 10.

The higher degree of centralization in this topology helps smaller organizations to address concerns like traveling through large historical datasets without the need to move data from one domain to another, data coherence (the degree to which the data is logically connected and mutually consistent), efficiency of MDM, and reducing costs by sharing compute resources between different teams. At the same time, it carries over some best practices from the data mesh architecture, such as data product thinking, domain-oriented and -aligned data ownership, self-serve functionality, and data governance.

Picking the Right Topology

Finding a good balance between centralization and decentralization remains a dilemma for many organizations. A shift from managing data centrally to decentrally completely redefines what data management means for an organization. Instead of centrally executing all areas of data management, your central team becomes responsible for defining what constitutes strong data governance. The domain topologies laid out in this chapter will help you to understand what level of centralization or decentralization you can apply, how demarcation lines can be set, and how domains within your architecture will interact and connect.

It's a misconception that enterprises must implement only one of these domain topologies. Organizations can combine or mix different topologies, depending on what trade-offs they would like to make. For example, in Figure 3-10, a relatively flexible governance model is combined with a stricter and more centralized model. Several domains operate in a fully federated manner, while others are organized in hub-and-spoke and centralized models.

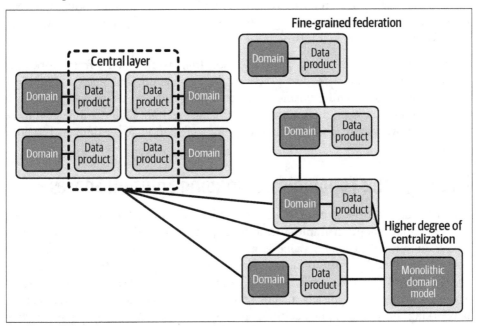

Figure 3-10. Combining different domain topologies in a single organization

It's also a misconception that the initial topology you select will be the final topology you end up with. There's no perfect equilibrium in which domains are grouped and interconnected. Consider the universe: in the beginning, we had collisions, mergers, and crashes. At a later stage, the universe entered a state with more harmony and a better view of what causes gravity. This led to a calmer state with less change. Designing a large-scale architecture is similar: you'll go through all these different phases, so don't strive for a perfect initial design because you'll set yourself up for failure. Instead, "Start small and fail fast, fail fast to succeed faster."

To summarize and conclude: when choosing a domain topology, I recommend setting fine-grained domain boundaries where possible because becoming data-driven is all about making data available for intensive (re)use. If you make your domain boundaries too coarse-grained, you'll force undesired couplings between many applications, and data reusability will suffer. Each time data crosses the boundaries of business capabilities or functional concerns, strive for decoupling. This best practice means that within a domain's inner architecture, tight coupling is allowed. However, when crossing boundaries, domains must stay decoupled and distribute read-optimized data for sharing data with other domains.

When you define your domain topology structure, you must also design and implement the underlying technology architecture. So far, we haven't touched on the solution space, but consider what these topologies will look like when they're implemented as a technology architecture. Can you apply isolation and modularity? Can, for example, domains be logically grouped together, and if so, what are good candidates for sharing platform infrastructure?

A recommendation is to use a cloud adoption framework. Such a framework provides prescriptive guidance, best practices, documentation, and open source blueprints. It helps by aligning business and technology objectives, thereby making it easier to choose the right route forward. In the next section, we'll examine how these frameworks work and what a technology implementation for a domain topology might look like.

Landing Zone Topologies: Managing Solution Spaces

When building a large-scale architecture on cloud infrastructure, it's recommended to use a cloud adoption framework and adopt the methodology of using landing zones. Simply put, a *landing zone* is a set of standard building blocks that allow you to automatically create projects, infrastructure, and environments that are preconfigured in line with security policies, compliance guidelines, and best practices. These building blocks typically include services for security, governance, automation, networking, storage, compute, auditing and logging, and data management. Landing zones come in different flavors and can be adjusted via configuration. Some organizations make them generic in order to facilitate as many scenarios as possible. Others make them specific, which means you have, for example, landing zones that are optimized for data-related scenarios.

Landing zones provide preconfigured environments for your domains and are provisioned through code. Open source blueprints and best practices are provided by all major cloud providers and include the following:

- The AWS Cloud Adoption Framework (*https://oreil.ly/FIeR4*) by Amazon
- The Microsoft Cloud Adoption Framework for Azure (*https://oreil.ly/MuL4F*)
- The Google Cloud Adoption Framework for GCP (*https://oreil.ly/1Hj6J*)

A best practice for data landing zone blueprints is to host these in an open and central repository. Providing transparency will encourage your domain teams to contribute and participate. At the same time, a central team will be responsible for oversight and ensure standardization across all implementations.

Landing zones accelerate the implementation of large-scale architectures, because they allow you to standardize on what services are offered to your teams. They offer ease of deployment, consistency in naming, policy enforcement, scaling, security, backup and disaster recovery, and regulatory compliance. They also ensure that when new workloads land in your architecture, the proper infrastructure is already in place.

Generally the cloud adoption frameworks are composed of two building blocks, which are fundamental for all deployment choices:

A data management landing zone
> This is the foundation of your architecture. It contains all the supervision capabilities for overseeing and managing your workloads, such as security components, firewalls, monitoring solutions, and services for end-to-end data management; these include the data catalog, data lineage, the API catalog, MDM services, central metadata repositories, and so on. By principle, this zone is always domain-agnostic.

Data landing zones or landing zones
> These are accounts or subscriptions that host your domain workloads or use cases. They include key capabilities for your domains, so they can develop specific applications. For data-related use cases, landing zones must provide services for things like integration, reporting, machine learning, databases, storage solutions, runtimes, or compute pools for analytical processing, orchestration, and so on.

Cloud adoption frameworks aren't always explicit about the exact type of data architecture you must implement. If you study the different cloud providers' documentation and best practices, you'll learn that these frameworks can be used for any common data management and analytics solutions, including (enterprise) data warehouses, data lakes, data lakehouses, data fabrics, and data meshes. So, they can be used for any of the previously discussed domain topologies. Let's carry on and discover how these frameworks support an architecture design. We'll do this by studying different deployment options and discussing considerations for each design. At the end of this section, I'll make things more concrete by showing how blueprints can support the deployment of the architecture from Oceanic Airlines.

 Landing zones come in different flavors. When a landing zone is called a *landing zone* or *application landing zone*, it tends to be more generic, used for a wide range of applications and workloads. When a landing zone is called a *data landing zone*, it focuses on data and analytical processing. The focus of a *control zone*, *management zone*, or *platform zone* is on managing centralized or shared services.

Single Data Landing Zone

The simplest deployment design for building a data architecture involves using one (data) management landing zone and one data landing zone, as shown in Figure 3-11. This type of minimalistic setup is recommended for scenarios in which strong control and standardization are desired, you're at the start of a new implementation, and/or simplicity is preferred. All data–management related services are centralized within the management landing zone. The same centralization applies for all data-related domains: they reside in the same single data landing zone, where a landing zone represents a single subscription or account that contains standard sets of services.

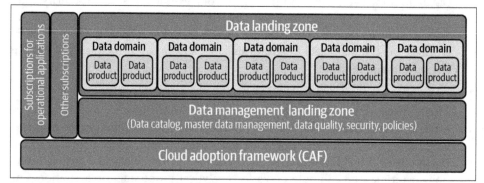

Figure 3-11. The minimal recommended setup consists of a single data management landing zone and a single data landing zone

The following objectives generally serve as the basis for such a design:

- The goal is to set a foundation for domains to organize their data end-to-end, including strong and consistent governance for lineage, data quality, security, data cataloging and sharing, and so on.
- Each providing domain owns and operates multiple data products with its own data and technology services, which are independent from those of other domains. Similarly, each consuming domain operates its own set of tools to perform analytics and reporting.
- Data domains may play the role of a provider, a consumer, or both. Depending on what roles they play, more or less services are mapped.
- A data lakehouse approach is considered a best practice for enabling teams to build data products. Data domain providers ingest data into their respective data lake services through a set of pipelines that they manage, own, and operate.

What might this architecture look like in the solution space? To demonstrate, let's return to the Oceanic Airlines example from Chapter 2. In Figure 3-12, you can see how different domains within the company collaborate and use data. Each area in the design is a repeatable blueprint that provides a set of standardized services.

On the left and right, you see operational applications that are provisioned through regular landing zones. Each domain has its own landing zone, for reasons of autonomy, flexibility requirements, geographical location, and security requirements.

In the middle, you see data-related services that are provisioned through a single data landing zone. The services that are provided from this zone are generic for all domains, although they are aligned to either a data provider or a data consumer: data-providing services empower domains to ingest, store, transform, and serve data, while consuming services empower domains to build analytical applications and perform analytics for data-driven decisions.

At the bottom is a data management landing zone. This zone manages all the central or domain-agnostic services, such as the data catalog, for managing data end-to-end.

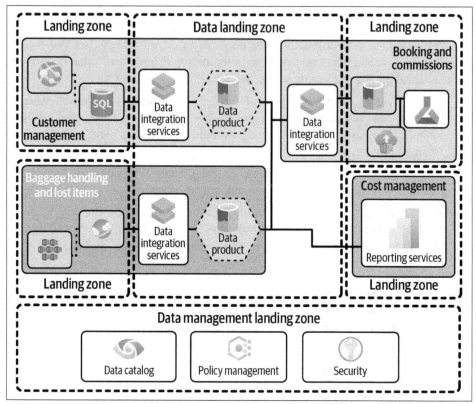

Figure 3-12. How different domains within Oceanic Airlines might operate

Some organizations ask me the question: "Could we just use one single landing zone for our architecture?" Yes, it's technically possible to combine all data management and data-related services within one giant landing zone, but then you would lose the ability to scale at a later point in time. Therefore, the best practice is to always start with (at minimum) one data management zone and a separate data landing zone.

In Figure 3-12, you'll see that I've decided to position the reporting services within a generic landing zone, not within the data landing zone. This is a design decision that we'll come back to in Chapters 4 and 11. You'll also see that some of the domain boundaries span across regular landing zones and the (shared) data landing zone. This is another design decision.

An alternative configuration could be to provision a generic landing zone for each domain that holds both application and data services together. Such a design would be more appropriate for enabling stronger domain autonomy, with all services aligned to the respective domains. The downside, however, is that it is hard to standardize landing zones and blueprints because business domains and their applications, as you've learned, are always unique and different.

Let's leave the practical example for now and zoom out to the point where we started discussing the topology. When provisioning a single landing zone, you may wonder how to best organize services within the landing zone itself. The generic best practice when deploying a set of services is to group them together logically, for example using tags or resource groups. With this approach, each domain team uses such a resource group for managing its data solutions end-to-end. The motivation of grouping and mapping services this way is that all services share a common life cycle of being provisioned, updated, and decommissioned. In addition to that, the grouped services inherit the same security controls, as they all belong to the same domain.

The alignment of services and domains can also be done differently: instead of exclusively mapping services to domains, you can share services between domains. Sharing services is primarily done for the purposes of security, process simplification, and cost savings. For instance, imagine a situation in which you use a high-performing database and transformation framework for processing data. Instead of provisioning many (expensive) services for all your domains, you could choose to share the same set of services between domains. In some cases this may lead to a cost reduction or more uniform way of working that is easier to control and manage.

When sharing services, it's important to understand that the segregation and security generally happens one level deeper, within the service itself. My recommendation for deciding whether to share services is to categorize the services and determine the operating model for each category or type. You'll often need to make trade-offs between cost efficiency, implementation costs, flexibility, security, and management overhead.

Organizing data products

The same trade-offs must be considered for data products. Storage accounts, data lake services, or databases are often used for storing and managing these. When using any of these services, each domain is mapped to an instance, and each instance hosts a set of data products from a single domain. You can see a reflection of this design in Figure 3-13.

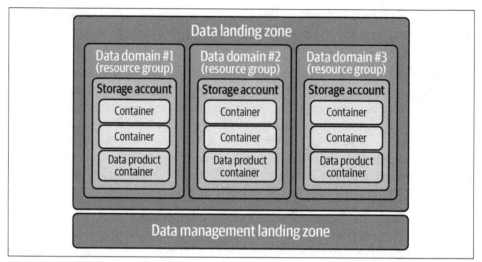

Figure 3-13. All data products are hosted within a container that is aligned with the resources of a domain

This configuration gives domains more freedom and flexibility in terms of how they manage their data products—for example, each domain can choose how to stage or layer its data. This design also allows for different security models, feature specialization, quotas, and service tags per domain. Additionally, performance is more predictable because each domain has its own performance limitations.

 AWS, Azure, and GCP manage their resources using different types of hierarchies. AWS uses four levels: organization, organizational unit, account, and resource. Azure uses five levels: root, management group, subscription, resource group, and resource. GCP uses four levels as well: organization, folder, project, and resource. For more information on this topic, see Petteri Kivimäki's blog post (*https://oreil.ly/oPdAL*).

However, you can also change the design in such a way that a single instance of a storage service is shared between different domains. In this case, data product segregation is generally done at a deeper level, within the service itself, via containers, buckets, folders, or logical databases. You can see an example of such a design in Figure 3-14.

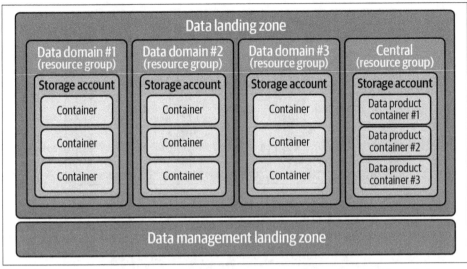

Figure 3-14. Data products are segregated via containers using a central shared storage account instance that is provisioned within the data landing zone

This approach is sometimes a better choice, for several reasons. First, it eases security responsibilities for domains and provides greater efficiency in managing services, because a consistent hierarchical structure can be more easily enforced for all domains. Second, it handles large data processing tasks better because all data products are stored centrally and closely together. It may also be preferable when a uniform security or stricter governance model with central services is required. For instance, a data contract service that automatically assigns user access rights to data products is easier to develop when different data products share the same underlying storage layer. I'll come back to this and provide more considerations in Chapter 4.

There are also drawbacks to sharing a storage service across domains. For example, there could be performance and configuration limitations because items and bandwidth are shared between domains. Also, you don't have the flexibility to turn on or off specific features for individual domains because only one instance is used, and there's more coupling and more conformance required from your domains.

A slight variant of the centralized design is seen in Figure 3-15. The difference, compared to the previous design, is that we've moved the central management of data products into the data management landing zone.

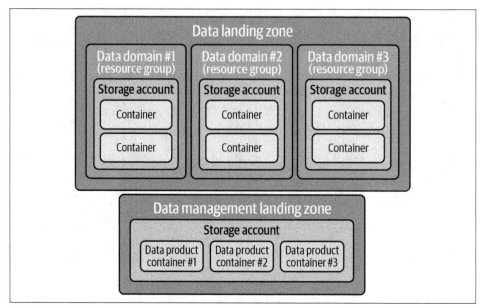

Figure 3-15. Data products are segregated via containers using a central shared storage account instance that is provisioned within the data management landing zone

This scenario of using a data management landing zone for data product management might be preferable when moving data closer to centrally managed services, such as MDM or data quality services. In these cases, it sometimes might be better to have data closer to where it is processed.

 You do not need to make an explicit choice for how you would like to manage your data products for all domains. You can combine any or all of the previously discussed approaches and blend them within the single landing zone topology or any other topology discussed in this chapter. For example, you could provide dedicated storage accounts for the majority of your domains, while sharing resources for some other domains. In the end, it's all about making the right trade-offs.

Scaling a single landing zone

Let's leave data product management for now and go back to the data landing zone. The rationale for using a single data landing zone is to apply standardization and keep things simple. It's appropriate in cases where you use only one cloud provider and provision all resources in a single region, you don't have complex billing or account structure requirements, and you want or need to baseline all services and policies across all domains. When applying this form of simplification and standardization, there should be no (or few) contrasting requirements between domain teams.

All involved teams must be well aligned on your release plan for making changes to the overall blueprint.

Note that using a single data landing zone doesn't mean you can't scale. If more domains or data products need to be onboarded into your architecture, you can quickly add more resource groups with predefined services. You can scale even further by enabling self-service and automation. An attention point for scaling is that your data domains should follow the data management principles outlined in the previous chapter.

The single data landing zone topology can be useful for smaller organizations, greenfield projects, or situations in which strong standardization is desirable. It can also be a good starting point for an organization that plans to build something more complex. In this case, you envision a future transition to a more fine-grained and fully federated implementation, using multiple landing zones.

Source- and Consumer-Aligned Landing Zones

In our discussion of the previous topology, we didn't take into consideration any other cloud service accounts or on-premises applications. This is because with a single landing zone, it will be difficult to manage their sometimes contrasting concerns simultaneously. Let's study a design that is better equipped to deal with these challenges.

Data onboarding remains one of the most difficult aspects of using data at large. It often requires extra services for addressing complicated integration challenges. Integration for onboarding differs from integration for data consumption because source systems can be incredibly complex. To accommodate this, you can slightly alter the previous design by using two landing zones: one for managing complex services for the source system side, and another with more standardization applied for the consuming side. Figure 3-16 demonstrates this topology.

On the left is a landing zone that provides data services to facilitate sourcing data and building data products. These services, for example, can be change data capture services, API services, or specialized connectors for legacy systems. They typically pull data from various locations: on premises, other cloud-based environments, external APIs, or SaaS vendors. This landing zone typically also involves more overhead because services are shared between domains, as well more coupled with underlying operational applications. The landing zone on the right is optimized for consumption and provides services focused on turning data into value. These services may include, for example, machine learning and reporting.

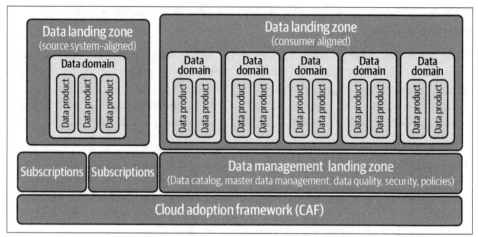

Figure 3-16. A topology with separate source system– and consumer-aligned landing zones might better address complex integration challenges

When segregating the concerns of providing and consuming data, I encourage you to ensure your data domains follow all the principles of domain-oriented data ownership. Domains should take ownership of data and are allowed to directly distribute data to other domains. The deployment model of this architecture can be perfectly aligned with the hybrid or partially federated topology discussed earlier, as well as with the fine-grained and fully federated model. In the latter case, you examine the domains' roles, which can be either providing or consuming. If domains play both roles, you would expect to see them on both sides of the architecture.

Hub Data Landing Zone

The next topology we'll consider uses a hub that sits between the other landing zones and acts as a central point of connectivity and distribution. The hub isolates domains by preventing them from directly distributing data themselves. Instead, all data flows through this central location. To a degree, the hub is a scaled-out version of the centrally managed storage services that we discussed in "Organizing data products" on page 83. The difference is that these storage services are grouped in a dedicated landing zone.

The benefit of using a hub is that you're aware of every data movement. In addition, a hub-and-spoke architecture more effectively uses the network: data products are only copied once, and then distributed from the hub to the consuming domains. This approach, as seen in Figure 3-17, naturally follows a governed domain topology: data is distributed via a central logical entity or authority.

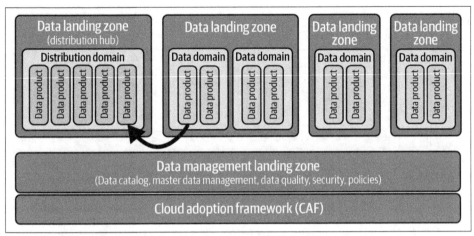

Figure 3-17. In this model, the hub acts a central distribution point

The design of the hub is usually different from other data landing zones. It's domain-agnostic and owned by a central team responsible for overseeing which data is distributed to which other domains. Inside the hub, you typically see mainly central storage services. Inside these, data is logically organized per domain, isolated, and not integrated. The hub typically also carries (self-service) services to facilitate providing or consuming data.

With a hub, you can also apply data virtualization. So, instead of duplicating data or always provisioning data products in the hub, domains use standard services for serving out virtualized data products. Such virtualization could simplify the overall data access management or could camouflage the underlying technical complexity of a diverse landscape, if your domains are using different services.

This topology is a good option if your organization needs to control what data is distributed and consumed by different domains. It's also a useful option for managing large quantities of historical data for many large data consumers, because a hub is more efficient when sharing data across many customers. The hub model is commonly seen within the financial industry, regulated environments, and organizations that operate on a global scale and are required to have full control of all cross-regional data movements.

Multiple Data Landing Zones

On a larger scale, multiple data landing zones are better for separating duties or concerns. Figure 3-18 shows an example of what this data architecture might look like.

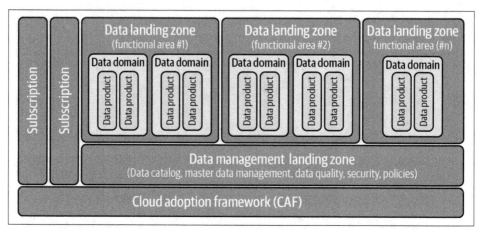

Figure 3-18. Multiple data landing zones better allow for separation of concerns

Multiple aspects determine which functional data domains you should logically group together and make candidates for sharing a data landing zone. Let's take a look at some of the main factors:

Security controls
Different applications might have different security profiles, requiring different control policies and mechanisms around them.

Cohesion and efficiency in sharing data
You should consider how large data processing tasks will be managed within landing zones, because these types of workloads often require data to be stored close together.

Regions
Regional or geographical boundaries could result in the implementation of the same business capabilities and blueprints. Multiple regions should always result in multiple landing zones.

Isolation
A landing zone becomes a unit of security protection. Potential risks and security threats should be contained within a landing zone without affecting others. There could be different security needs that require you to isolate one landing zone from another. The same applies for data isolation. Isolating data stores to a landing zone limits the number of people that can access and manage that data store. This contains the exposure of private data and helps with, for example, GDPR compliance.

Flexibility and pace of change
There can be differences in the velocity of innovation within domains. These disruptive changes might contrast with other domains that strongly value stability over agility.

Value streams and business processes
Different business units or products might have different purposes and processes. You should establish different landing zones to serve business-specific needs.

Selling off
If there's a chance that you might want to sell off or separate out some capabilities, it wouldn't be wise to integrate them tightly with shared services from other domains.

Differences between teams
Different teams have different responsibilities and resource needs. Highly skilled and mature teams typically want to operate their own services and infrastructure.

Cost management
Some enterprises want to implement chargeback/showback models in their cloud infrastructure to split and manage costs based on capacity that has been used.

Limit allocation
Certain clouds have limits per subscription or account. Separating workloads into different landing zones allows you to set limits more accurately, and avoids preventing applications with different resource needs from working as intended.

Experiments and learning
Experiments can fail, so it's better to manage these apart from other workloads.

Politics
Unfortunately, political boundaries can be a driving force as well.

Service level agreements
Contrasting availability and continuity requirements could result in the usage of extra services.

Let me provide an example of how these items may influence your landing zone design. Imagine a situation where you build a new architecture in the cloud. When you deploy your first resources, you must make an explicit choice about the cloud region in which your applications will be deployed. For example, if you are based within the United States, your first landing zone and applications will be deployed in the USA region. Now imagine that after some time you need to expand your business to Europe. Because of the geographic boundary (data residency), you need to provision a second data landing zone within the European cloud region. After you've expanded to Europe, you land a substantial investment for innovation for the European market. Due to the nature of these disruptive and risky activities, you decide to provision a third data landing zone in which these resources will be managed apart from all your other resources. With this investment, you decide to further expand your business. This time you intend to set up a partnership structure with another company, which has a different level of trust. You decided to not integrate this partner with your existing business activities. Consequently, you set up a fourth data landing zone.

Provisioning multiple data landing zones in this manner can help you group functional domains based on cohesion and efficiency. When doing so, ensure that all your data landing zones adhere to the same auditing and controls for data management. The linking pin for all the landing zones is your management landing zone. This central logical entity should oversee what domains sit where and what data they create, distribute, and use.

Different landing zones don't stand alone. They can be connected to hubs or other landing zones with shared data lakes or storage services. This pattern allows domains to collaborate across your enterprise. For example, you can apply shared storage services or data virtualization to allow your domains to directly read data from other domains without duplicating it.

When deploying multiple data landing zones, realize that there's management overhead attached to each one. A typical landing zone requires configuration for accounts, linking services, linking landing zones to other zones, and so on. If you define the number of data landing zones as n, then you might end up with n network connectivity points for at least all the storage accounts and potentially other services within these zones. This could lead to an exponential increase in the number of configuration items you need to manage. The bottom line is that there is a strong relationship between the number of landing zones and the amount of configuration management overhead.

Multiple Data Management Landing Zones

The last topology we'll consider is for large enterprises operating on a global scale—for example, organizations that have many highly specialized departments using hundreds or thousands of applications. In such a scenario, there could be contrasting data management requirements between different parts of the organization. To tackle this, you can deploy multiple management landing zones and data landing zones together in one architecture. Such a design is visualized in Figure 3-19.

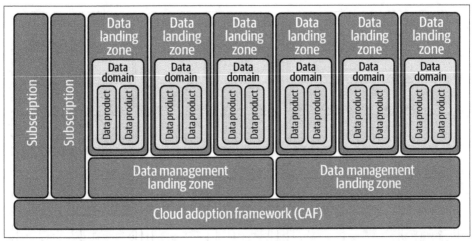

Figure 3-19. Large-scale enterprises may require different management landing zones

Each landing zone introduces management and integration overhead, so you should make a conscious decision about whether the extra complexity is warranted. For example, adding another management landing zone might make sense for situations where your organization's (meta)data must not be seen by anyone outside the organization, or where different parts of the organization manage different parts of the infrastructure using their own unique ways of working, policies, security standards, data management methods, and so on. You might also want to use this topology when you have different MDM services that manage data from different parts of the organization.

If you decide to use the scaling mechanisms described in these sections, your architecture and organization can grow progressively without limitation. You can scale by adding more landing zones or domains, and you can manage complexity and costs by providing multiple blueprints. Let's discover how this works through a concrete example.

Practical Landing Zones Example

In Chapter 2, we discussed business capabilities and domains. We used the fictional company Oceanic Airlines as an example for learning how to organize capabilities and set boundaries. Knowing how we can use domain topologies and data landing zones to design a large-scale architecture, what would a potential architecture using landing zones look like for this hypothetical company? Let's discover this by unpacking the design shown in Figure 3-20.

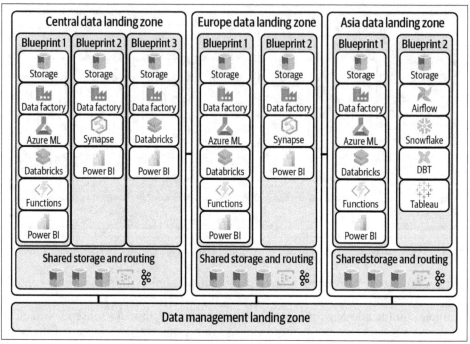

Figure 3-20. Oceanic Airlines architecture with multiple landing zones

As you can see, we have three data landing zones and one data management landing zone. The motivation for implementing multiple data landing zones is that Oceanic Airlines has decided to cluster its domains using a geographical logical grouping. Domains are clustered in different regions across the globe, and in order to guarantee low latency and stability, each domain wants to have its data as close as possible to its geographical location. Therefore, the company has established three landing zones: one for the US (the "Central") data landing zone, one for Europe, and another for Asia.

Figure 3-20 is inspired by a real-world implementation of the data architecture at Amadeus (*https://amadeus.com*). This enterprise has extended its architecture with an infrastructure provisioning plane via which domains can do self-service provisioning of the required infrastructure for sharing or using data. The whole process of adding a new data domain just takes a few minutes and involves filling in a simple form. More information can be found in the Microsoft customer story (*https://oreil.ly/UmNQj*).

In this architecture, each data landing zone is complemented with a central layer with shared storage services. The rationale for centralization over decentralization here is that Oceanic Airlines values cost control and stronger data consistency over flexibility and agility. Many domains within the regions in which the company operates perform cross-domain activities, such as data lookups and data quality validations. It's often necessary to exchange large and historical datasets between domains. In addition, these datasets sometimes need to be distributed between geographical locations. Having a central logical entity for distributing data between domains addresses these distribution concerns.

To cater for the various and complex needs of its domains, Oceanic Airlines has decided to develop several blueprints for each of the individual landing zones. Each time a new domain lands in a data landing zone, a blueprint is chosen and a new architecture is created. Each blueprint acts as a reference design that can be used as a baseline for the initial requirements. Services that domains don't require will be disabled. In addition, blueprints can be enhanced by the central team depending on specific domain requirements. For example, if a specific service or component is missing, it may be added to the blueprint used for creating that specific instance. All blueprints are hosted within a code repository that is managed by the central platform team. This team oversees what blueprints are used by what domains for what purposes.

Each blueprint delivers a repeatable set of custom services. Between these blueprints, there are differences. For example, in Asia, there are teams that are trained for different services. To cater for these needs, a blueprint 2 is created, using different services and tools than the rest of the organization.

Finally, Oceanic Airlines uses a common architecture to advocate consistent governance. All blueprint instances use policies for monitoring, cost management, security, and control. The same types of policies apply for all data landing zones, and they're all connected to the underpinning data management landing zone. This means domain teams automatically adhere to the same auditing, controls, and data governance standards. For example, computational governance is automatically enforced by connecting all data services to the central data catalog.

Wrapping Up

A data journey is as much an organizational journey as it is a technological one. Ideally, you start building your strategy, including a governance model for your domains, well before the first workloads and use cases are rolled out. The topologies discussed in this chapter offer starting points for you to kick-start your data ambitions. But before you start implementing, there are considerations to be made. The right one for you will depend on the conditions at your organization. For smaller or less mature organizations, a centralized approach to data management is often more appropriate, given the level of complexity that you need to manage. In such a situation, I recommend starting with a simpler, more centralized approach and preparing for more federation and decentralization in the future. For larger organizations that have the engineering capacity, it's valuable to study the different domain topologies outlined in this chapter.

For your company's journey, remember that a transition toward a fully domain-oriented architecture is a cultural shift that involves many nuances, trade-offs and considerations. This transition also requires you to establish a new culture. There are far too few genuinely great data engineers out there, so you'll need to start your search for "data champions," "data cheerleaders," and "inspiring leaders" with a proven track record early. To accelerate your data landing zone program, look for people with experience in this particular area.

You need to invest internally, and train your existing talent pool to become data professionals with both IT and business knowledge. You'll need "evangelists" to build relationships with C-level management and find top-level sponsors. Look for ambassadors who can be key communicators to other stakeholders. Changing your organizational culture requires that you build the case for change. Start preparing your organization for changes in the world of data and the impact those changes will have on data management. This means a lot of campaigning and "saving souls," but it also means putting your foot down when things go in the wrong direction.

Federation doesn't mean that you need to overprovision services and resources. You can share services between domains to make your architecture more cost-efficient or enforce a standard way of working across domains. Implementing the data management architecture will require working closely with your organization's (cloud) infrastructure team. Many companies go through long and expensive processes that fail to deliver anything of value, sometimes after years of effort. It doesn't have to be this way! Consider a step-by-step approach using blueprints and landing zones, as provided by all major cloud providers. This will enable you to onboard new data domains in a quick, secure, effective, and standardized manner. Align your data platform and cloud teams, or create a virtual team when starting your journey. This avoids constant cross-communication between different teams.

For your first landing zone, identify a small-scale but big-picture project to prove the concept. Aim to get it delivered within 8 to 16 weeks. It doesn't have to be perfect or production-ready. Invite critical stakeholders and ambassadors to demonstrate progress and conduct reviews. Regularly get their feedback to avoid big surprises. Don't try to predict everything in advance, but learn lessons as progress is made. Feed those back into the iterative and evolving design, and don't be afraid to step back and change direction if that is what the feedback is saying.

Your data landing zone(s) and corresponding blueprints will be constantly evolving. Create broad and holistic design goals and have the landing zone design be a living entity rather than a fixed artifact. It's important to be clear and transparent about what consumers get out of the box. Be vigilant about what constitutes the core and careful when reviewing and adding new requirements. Also provide foundational guardrails for security and compliance. Landing zones can be used for isolation: setting boundaries in which data will be managed using standardized services. I recommend to start using a baseline environment and not build an environment from scratch. Don't introduce too many customizations at the beginning of your journey. To keep your architecture scalable, strive for simplicity and standardization. Put a strong emphasis on automation. If you can't automate it, consider not using it.

In the next chapter, we'll get back in our helicopter and take it down to the level of the applications and systems in which data is created. We'll take a closer look at the concept of data products, as you may encounter different definitions in the data community, and learn about data product management. See you there!

CHAPTER 4

Data Product Management

You may be wondering about the term *data product*—is it just another buzzword? In this chapter, we'll be cutting through the confusion to discuss what data products really are. I'll cover all the essential information you need to have for serving large quantities of data to other domains. We'll start with a disambiguation of the term because practitioners have many different interpretations and definitions. Next, we'll examine the pattern of Command Query Responsibility Segregation (CQRS) and why it should influence the design of your data product architectures. We'll discuss various design principles for data products, and you'll learn why a well-designed, integrable, and read-optimized data model is essential for your consumers. Then we'll look at data product architectures: what they are, how they can be engineered, what capabilities are typically needed, and the role of metadata. I'll try to make this as concrete as I can by using a practical example. By the end of this chapter, you'll have a good understanding of how data product architectures can help make vast amounts of data available to data consumers.

What Are Data Products?

Making the producers of data accountable for it and decentralizing the way data is served is a great way to achieve scalability. Dehghani uses the phrase "data as a product" (*https://oreil.ly/IsjlH*) and introduces the concept of "data products," but there's a big difference between the two. *Data as a product* describes the thinking: data owners and application teams must treat data as a fully contained product they're responsible for, rather than a byproduct of some process that others manage. It's about how data providers should treat data consumers as customers and provide experiences that delight; how data should be defined and shaped to provide the best possible customer experience.

A *data product* differs from data as product thinking because it addresses the architecture. Within the data community, you see different expectations and interpretations of how data products relate to architecture. Some practitioners say a data product isn't just a dataset containing relevant data from a specific bounded context; it also contains all the necessary components to collect and serve data, as well as metadata and code that transforms the data. This interpretation aligns with Dehghani's description of a data product as an architectural quantum (*https://oreil.ly/yvZpx*), a "node on the mesh that encapsulates three structural components required for its function, providing access to [the] domain's analytical data as a product." Those three components, according to Dehghani, are code, data and metadata, and infrastructure. So, her focus is clearly on the solution architecture, which may include all the components needed for obtaining, transforming, storing, managing, and sharing data.

Some practitioners have different views on data products. For example, Accenture (*https://oreil.ly/noV4B*) refers to datasets, analytical models, and dashboard reports as data products. Such a view differs significantly from Dehghani's because it focuses on the physical representation of data, and doesn't necessarily include any metadata, code, or infrastructure. So, before we can design an architecture, we first need to align on a common terminology for data products and determine what must be included or not.

Problems with Combining Code, Data, Metadata, and Infrastructure

In an ideal world, data and metadata are packaged and shipped together as data products. Ferd Scheepers, chief information architect at ING Tech Group Services, gave a presentation at Domain-Driven Design Europe 2022 on the subject of metadata management. During this presentation, he explained that metadata is critical for data management because "metadata is data that provides information about other data." To reinforce the importance, he draws an analogy to how flowers are distributed within the Netherlands.

The Aalsmeer Flower Auction is the largest flower auction in the world. From Monday to Friday, some 43 million flowers and 5 million plants are sold every day. Traders from all over the world participate in the auction each working day. On arrival, flowers are labeled and sent to designated facilities. For buyers, the entire process is seamless: you digitally place orders, submit quantities, and provide a price and a destination. The great part of the story is that the auction is fully metadata-driven. All flower boxes are equipped with barcodes that include essential information about their contents, such as country and city of origin, quantities, starting bid price, weight, production and expiration dates, producer's name, and so forth. When flowers are sold, another barcode is added with information for shipping: buyer ownership details, destination, shipping instructions, and so forth. Without metadata, the flower auction wouldn't be able to function.

Within the flower auction, flowers and metadata are always managed and distributed together because the physical objects are connected to each other. However, in the digital world, it doesn't work that way! Let me provide some examples to make this clearer. If you use a central data catalog for managing and describing all your data, then data and metadata are managed apart from each other. In this example, all the metadata sits in your data catalog and all the physical data is stored elsewhere, likely in many other locations. The same separation applies, for example, for a metadata-driven ingestion framework that manages the extract and load process of data. Such a framework doesn't crawl metadata from hundreds of data product containers before it starts processing data. A metadata-driven ingestion framework, as an architectural component, generally manages metadata in a stand-alone database, which is separated from the data itself. It uses this metadata to control the process and dependencies through which data is extracted, combined, transformed, and loaded.

The same goes for lineage and data quality information. If the associated metadata were to be packed within the data product container itself, you would need to perform complex federated queries across all data products to oversee lineage or data quality from end to end. Alternatively, you could replicate all the metadata to another central location, but that would dramatically overcomplicate your overall architecture. And how would you handle security, privacy classifications, sensitivity labels, or ownership information for the same semantic data that has several physical representations? If you were to strongly glue metadata and data together, the metadata would be duplicated when data products are copied because both sit in the same architecture. All metadata updates would then need to be carried out simultaneously over several data product containers. This would be a complex undertaking, requiring all of these containers to be always available and accessible. You could implement an overlay architecture to carry out these updates asynchronously, but this would again dramatically overcomplicate your overall architecture.

To conclude, viewing a data product as a container gluing code, data and metadata, and infrastructure together is actually far too naive. The definition of a data product needs a revision that better reflects the reality of how data platforms work these days.

Data Products as Logical Entities

If the previous definition isn't a good one, how should we define a data product? I firmly believe that managing data and technology should be done from different architectural viewpoints: one that addresses the concerns of managing data, and another that addresses the concerns of managing the underlying technology architecture. Figure 4-1 shows what this might look like.

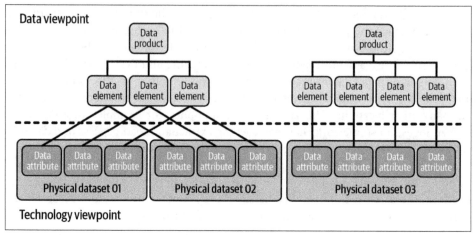

Figure 4-1. Separate viewpoints for managing the data and the technology

Why would you separate the concerns of managing data and technology? First, because you can make the architecture more cost-effective and reduce the overhead of managing infrastructure complexity. You enable scenarios of using "data product architectures" in which multiple "data products" are managed.

Second, a separation of data and architecture better facilitates scenarios in which the same (semantic) data must be distributed. Distributing data might be needed, for example, when performing cross-domain data validation or enrichment. Duplicating and preprocessing data is also sometimes required for facilitating multiple use cases at the same time; for example, when storing the exact same data in Parquet and Delta Lake file formats. When you do this, you duplicate data without changing the underlying semantics. This scenario is reflected in Figure 4-1: physical datasets 01 and 02 share the same semantics, and the individual physical data attributes link to the same elements.

Third, you avoid tight coupling between data and metadata. Imagine a situation in which data and metadata are always stored together in the same container. If, for example, owners, business entities, or classifications change, then all corresponding metadata within all data product architectures will have to change as well. In addition to that, how do you ensure consistent data ownership? If you duplicate metadata, there's a potential risk of data ownership changing as well. This shouldn't be possible for the same semantic data that has different physical representations in different locations.

Separating data and metadata changes the definition of a data product: *a data product is an autonomous logical entity that describes data that is meant for consumption.* From this logical entity you draw relationships to the underlying technology architecture— that is, to the physical locations where read-optimized and consumer-ready physical data assets are stored. The data product itself includes a logical dataset name; a description of the relationships to the originating domain, the unique data elements, and business terms; the owner of the dataset; and references to physical data assets (the actual data itself). It's semantically consistent for the business, but it could have multiple different shapes and representations on a physical level. These changes require a data product to be defined as technology-agnostic. This metadata is kept abstract for the sake of flexibility.

In Chapter 9, I'll make the logical viewpoint of a data product concrete by showing screenshots of a metamodel for data product management. If you don't want to wait to learn how this works, I encourage you to read "The Enterprise Metadata Model" on page 266, then come back and continue reading here.

When you define data products as logical entities, you're able to describe, classify, label, or link data (e.g., to domains, data owners, organizational metadata, process information, and other metadata) without being specific on the implementation details. One level below a data product, there are data elements: atomic units of information that act as linking pins to physical data, interface metadata, application metadata, and data-modeling metadata. To describe the physical data, you need technical metadata, which includes schema information, data types, and so on.

Now that we have a clear idea of what data products are, let's continue by examining what impacts their design and architecture. We'll start with CQRS, then look at read-optimized modeling and other design principles. After all this, we'll zoom out a bit to examine the data product architecture.

Data Product Design Patterns

Changing the definition of a data product doesn't mean we should abandon the concept of managing data as a product. Application owners and application teams must treat data as self-contained products that they're responsible for, rather than a byproduct of some process that others manage. Data products are specifically created for data consumers. They have defined shapes, interfaces, and maintenance and refresh cycles, all of which are documented. Data products contain processed domain data shared with downstream processes through interfaces in a service level objective (SLO). Unless otherwise required, your (technical) application data should be processed, shaped, cleansed, aggregated, and (de)normalized to meet agreed-upon quality standards before you make it available for consumption.

In Chapter 1, you learned about the engineering problems of limiting data transfers, designing transactional systems, and handling heavily increased data consumption. Taking out large volumes of data from a busy operational system can be risky because systems under too much load can crash or become unpredictable, unavailable, or, even worse, corrupted. This is why it's smart to make a read-only and read-optimized version of the data, which can then be made available for consumption. Let's take a look at a common design pattern for this: CQRS.

What Is CQRS?

CQRS (*https://oreil.ly/qmeLE*) is an application design pattern based on making a copy of the data for intensive reads.

Operational commands and analytical queries (often referred to as *writes* and *reads*) are very different operations and are treated separately in the CQRS pattern (as shown in Figure 4-2). When you examine the load of a busy system, you'll likely discover that the command side is using most of the computing resources. This is logical because for a successful (that is, durable) write, update, or delete operation, the database typically needs to perform a series of steps:

1. Check the amount of available storage.
2. Allocate additional storage for the write.
3. Retrieve the table/column metadata (types, constraints, default values, etc.).
4. Find the records (in case of an update or delete).
5. Lock the table or records.
6. Write the new records.
7. Verify the inserted values (e.g., unique, correct types, etc.).
8. Perform the commit.
9. Release the lock.
10. Update the indexes.

Reading the database, compared to writing, takes a smaller amount of computing resources because fewer of those tasks have to be performed. For optimization, CQRS separates writes (commands) from reads (queries) by using two models, as illustrated in this figure. Once separated, they must be kept in sync, which is typically done by publishing events with changes. This is illustrated by the "events arrow" (the lightning bolt icon) in Figure 4-2.

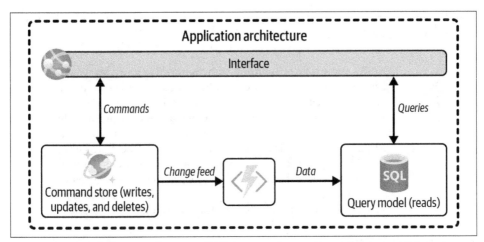

Figure 4-2. An application that uses CQRS separates queries and commands by using two different data models: a command model for the transactions and a query model for the reads

A benefit of CQRS is that you aren't tied to the same type of database for both writes and reads.[1] You can leave the write database objectively complex but optimize the read database for read performance. If you have different requirements for different use cases, you can even create more than one read database, each with an optimized read model for the specific use case being implemented. Different requirements also allow you to have different consistency models between read stores, even though the write data store remains the same.

Another benefit of CQRS is that there's no need to scale both the read and write operations simultaneously. When you're running out of resources, you can scale one or the other. The last major benefit of not having a single model to serve both writes and reads is technology flexibility. If you need reading to be executed very quickly or need different data structures, you can choose a different technology for the read store while still respecting the ACID database properties (atomicity, consistency, isolation, and durability), which are needed for the command store.

Although CQRS is a software engineering design pattern that can help improve the design process for specific (and possibly larger) systems, it should greatly inspire the design and vision of your data product architecture. *The future model of an architecture must be that at least one read data store per application is created or used whenever other applications want to read the data intensively.* This approach will

---

1 A drawback of CQRS is that it makes things more complex—you'll need to keep the two models in sync with an extra layer. This could also generate some additional latency.

simplify the future design and implementation of the architecture. It also improves scalability for intensive data consumption.

 CQRS has a strong relationship with *materialized views*.[2] A materialized view inside a database is a physical copy of the data that is constantly updated by the underlying tables. Materialized views are often used for performance optimizations. Instead of querying the data from underlying tables, the query is executed against the precomputed and optimized subset that lives inside the materialized view. This segregation of the underlying tables (used for writes) and materialized subset (used for reads) is the same segregation seen within CQRS, with the subtle difference that both collections of data live in the same database instead of two different databases.

Read Replicas as Data Products

Using replicas as a source for reading data isn't new. In fact, every read from a replica, copy, data warehouse, or data lake can be seen as some form of CQRS. Splitting commands and queries between online transaction processing (OLTP) systems, which typically facilitate and manage transaction-oriented applications, and an operational data store (ODS, used for operational reporting) is similar. The ODS, in this example, is a replicated version of the data from the OLTP system. All these patterns follow the philosophy behind CQRS: building up read databases from operational databases.

 Martin Kleppmann uses the "turning the database inside-out" pattern (*https://oreil.ly/YToL6*), another incarnation of CQRS that emphasizes collecting facts via event streaming. We'll look at this pattern in Chapter 6.

Data product architectures should follow the CQRS philosophy too. They take the position of a replicated copy of the data and are used to allow data consumers to read intensively. They're highly governed and inherit their context from the domains and underlying applications. At a high level, this means that whenever data providers and data consumers want to exchange data, as shown in Figure 4-3, a data product architecture must be used.

---

2 TechDifferences (*https://oreil.ly/PAoPD*) has an overview of the differences between a database view and materialized view.

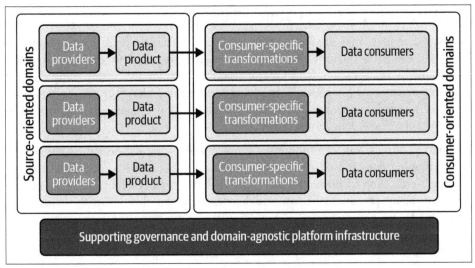

Figure 4-3. Decentralized collaboration of data providers and data consumers

Notice that data products are positioned on the left, near data providers, and transformation steps are near data consumers. This positioning originates from the unified approach of serving data to consumers. Instead of using a single unified data model, the design is changed to provide cleaned and readily consumable versions of the domain data to all consuming applications. This data isn't meant to deliver behavior or functionality. The nature of the data, compared to the operational data, is therefore different: it's optimized for intensive readability, empowering everyone to quickly turn data into value!

Design Principles for Data Products

Creating read-optimized and user-friendly data is the way forward. This sounds simple, but in practice it's often more difficult than expected. Specifically, you need to consider how the data should be captured, structured and modeled. The difficulties arise when you have to build data products repeatedly and in parallel with many teams. You want to do this efficiently, avoiding situations where each new data consumer leads to a newly developed data product, or a long cycle of studying complex data structures and working out data quality issues. You want maximum reusability and easy data to work with! This section presents a set of design principles that are helpful considerations when developing data products. Be warned, it's a long list.

Resource-Oriented Read-Optimized Design

Analytical models that are constantly retrained constantly read large volumes of data. This impacts data product designs because we need to optimize for data readability. A best practice is to look at resource orientation for designing APIs. A resource-oriented API is generally modeled as a resource hierarchy, where each node is either a simple resource or a collection resource. For convenience, they're often called resources and collections, respectively.

For data products, you can follow the same resource-orientation approach by logically grouping data and clustering it around subject areas, with each dataset representing a collection of homogeneous data. Such a design results in the data in data products being precomputed, denormalized, and materialized. On the consuming side, this leads to simpler and faster downstream consumption because there's no need to perform computationally expensive joins. It also reduces the time it takes to find the right data because data that belongs together is logically grouped together.

When applying a resource-oriented design to your data products, then, consequently, heavily normalized or too technical physical data models must be translated into more reusable and logically ordered datasets. The result is more denormalized and read-optimized data models, similar to a Kimball star schema or Inmon data mart. This also means that complex application logic must be abstracted away. Data must be served to other domains with an adequate level of granularity to satisfy as many consumers as possible. For any linked data products, this implies that cross-references and foreign key relationships must be consistent throughout the entire set of data products. Consuming domains, for example, shouldn't have to manipulate keys for joining different datasets! Building data products using this approach consequently means that domains own the semantic logic and are responsible for how data is transformed for improved readability. Enough about this, though—let's take a look at some other best practices and design principles.

Data Products and Data Vaults

You might be wondering whether you can design your data products using a Data Vault model. The Data Vault is a data modeling design pattern used for building a data warehouse.[3] It aims to provide flexibility, maintainability, and scalability by decoupling entities with additional relationships. Due to its considerable complexity, it makes data difficult to understand by "outsiders" who haven't been trained in the technique. Additionally, it will make your architecture slower and more expensive because the methodology of fine-grained data modeling often contradicts with the

---

3 Morris's article on Data Vault 2.0 (*https://oreil.ly/XxYgg*) describes "the good, the bad and the downright confusing" about this design pattern.

underlying distributed storage architectures of large cloud vendors. It requires many consumers to go through the iterations of joining and integrating data.

Figure 4-4 compares a Data Vault schema to a simple star schema. In short, the Data Vault methodology replaces entities with hubs, links, and satellites to support constantly evolving business requirements.

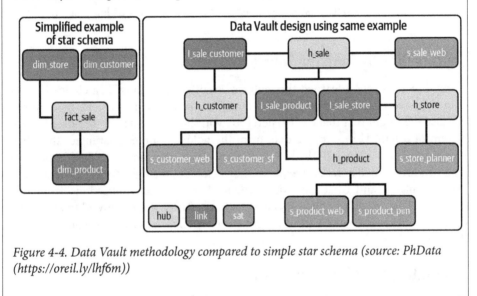

Figure 4-4. Data Vault methodology compared to simple star schema (source: PhData (https://oreil.ly/lhf6m))

Data Product Data Is Immutable

Data product data is *immutable* and therefore *read-only*. Why must your read(-only) data stores be immutable? This property guarantees that we can regenerate the same data over and over again. If we use a read-only design, no different versions of the truth will exist for the same domain data. Data product architectures that follow this principle don't create new semantic data. The truth can be modified only in the golden source application.

Using the Ubiquitous Language

It's essential to understand the context of how the data has been created. This is where the ubiquitous language comes in: a constructed, formalized language, agreed upon by stakeholders and designers, to serve the needs of the design. The ubiquitous language should be aligned with the domain—that is, the business functions and goals. The context of the domain determines the design of the data products. A common implementation is to have a data catalog in which all of this information is stored, along with information from the domains. Publishing context and transparently making definitions clear to domains enables everybody to see and agree on the origin and meaning of data.

Some organizations require domains to use human-friendly column names in their data product physical datasets. This isn't essential, as long the mapping from the physical data model to the conceptual data model is provided. This linkage enables your domains to translate business concepts from the ubiquitous language to physical data.

Capture Directly from the Source

In my previous role, I learned that enterprises often have long data chains in which data is passed from system to system. For data management, this can be a problem because the origin isn't that clear. Therefore, you should always capture data from the system of origin. Using unique data from the golden sources guarantees that there's one source of truth for both data access and data management. This implies that data products are distinct and explicit: they belong to a single domain, which means they're isolated and can't have direct dependencies with applications from other domains. This design principle also means that domains aren't allowed to encapsulate data from other domains with different data owners, because that would obfuscate data ownership.

Clear Interoperability Standards

It's important to define how data products are served to other domains. A data product could be served as a database, a standardized file format, a graph, an API endpoint, an event stream, or something else. In all cases, you should standardize the interface specifications. If all of your domains define their own set of standards, data consumption becomes terribly difficult. Therefore, standardization is critical. This requires you to clearly define your different distribution types (e.g., batch-, API-, and event-oriented), metadata standards, and so on. Be specific about what a data product architecture looks like; for example, batch data products are published in Delta format and must be registered in a data catalog.

No Raw Data

A data product is the opposite of raw data because exposing raw data requires rework by all consuming domains. So, in every case, you should encapsulate legacy or complex systems and hide away technical application data. If you insist on making raw data available, for example for research analysis, make sure it's flagged and temporary by default. Raw or unaltered data comes without guarantees.

The principle of no raw data, as discussed in Chapter 2, also applies for external data providers: external parties who operate outside the logical boundaries of your enterprise's ecosystem. They generally operate in separate, uncontrolled network locations. Ask your ecosystem partners to conform to your standard or apply mediation via an intermediate domain: a consuming domain that acts as an intermediate by abstracting complexity and guaranteeing stable and safe consumption.

Don't Conform to Consumers

It's likely that the same data products will be used repeatedly by different domain teams for a wide range of use cases. So your teams shouldn't conform their data products to specific needs of (individual) data consumers. The primary design principle should be to maximize domain productivity and promote consumption and reuse.

On the other hand, data products can and do evolve based on user feedback. You should be careful here! It can be tempting for teams to incorporate specific requirements from consumers. But if consumers push business logic into a producing domain's data products, it creates a strict dependency with the provider for making changes. This can trigger intense cross-coordination and backlog negotiation between domain teams. A recommendation here is to introduce a governance body that oversees that data products aren't created for specific consumers. This body can step in to guide domain teams, organize walk-in and knowledge-sharing sessions, provide practical feedback, and resolve issues between teams.

it belongs. For IFRS, this means asking other domains to deliver to the accounting department the information it needs to make its calculations correctly. That information should preserve the original context of the providing domain, allowing other domains to consume the data as well.

Missing Values, Defaults, and Data Types

I've experienced heated debates over how missing, low-quality, or default data should be interpreted. For example, suppose the web form of an operational system requires a value for the user's birth date, but the user doesn't supply this data. If no guidance is provided, employees might fill in a random value. This behavior could make it difficult for consumers to tell whether the data is accurate or contains default values. Providing clear guidance, such as always defaulting missing birth dates to absurd or future values, such as 9999-12-31, enables customers to identify that data is truly missing.

You may also want to introduce guidance on data types or data that must be formatted consistently throughout the entire dataset. Specifying the correct decimal precision, for example, ensures that data consumers don't have to apply complex application logic to use the data. You could set these principles at the system or domain level, but I also see large enterprises providing generic guidance on what data formats and types must be used across all data products.

Semantic Consistency

Data products must be semantically consistent across all delivery methods: batch, event-driven, and API-based. To me this sounds obvious, but I still see organizations today providing separate guidance for batch-, event-, and API-oriented data. Since the origin of the data is the same for all distribution patterns, I encourage you to make the guidance consistent for all patterns. I'll come back to this point in Chapter 7.

Atomicity

Data product attributes must be atomic. They represent the lowest level of granularity and have precise meaning or semantics. That is, it should not be possible to decompose them into meaningful other components. In an ideal state, data attributes are linked one-to-one with the business items within your data catalog. The benefit here is that data consumers aren't forced to split or concatenate data.[4] Another benefit of using atomic data is that any policy rules can be decoupled from the data. If

---

4 Believe it or not, I once saw a legacy application in which multiple customer values were concatenated into a single field using double pipe operators, like Firstname||Middlename||Lastname.

regulation forces you to reconsider sensitive labels, for example, you don't have to relabel all your physical data. With a good metadata model and atomic data, any changes should be automatically inherited from your business metadata.

Compatibility

Data products should remain stable and be decoupled from the operational/transactional applications. This requires a mechanism for detecting schema drift, and avoiding disruptive changes. It also requires versioning and, in some cases, independent pipelines to run in parallel, giving your data consumers time to migrate from one version to another.

The process of keeping data products compatible isn't as simple as it may sound. It might involve moving historical data between old and new data products. This exercise can be a complex undertaking as it involves ETL tasks such as mapping, cleaning up, and providing defaulting logic.

Abstract Volatile Reference Data

You might want to provide guidance on how complex reference values are mapped to more abstract data product–friendly reference values. This requires nuance for agility mismatches: if the pace of change is high on the consuming side, your guiding principle must be that complex mapping tables are maintained on the consuming side; if the pace of change is faster on the providing side, the guiding principle is that data product owners should be asked to abstract or roll up detailed local reference values to more generic (less granular) consumer-agnostic reference values. This guidance also implies that the consumer might perform additional work, such as mapping the more generic reference values to consumer-specific reference values.

New Data Means New Ownership

Any data that is created because of a business transformation (a semantic change using business logic) and distributed is considered new, and falls under the ownership of the creating domain. The data distribution principles discussed in this chapter should be enforced for any newly created data that is shared.

It's fundamentally wrong to classify use case–based, integrated data as (consumer-aligned) data products. If you allow use case–specific data to be directly consumed by other domains, those domains will be highly dependent on the implementation details of the underlying consuming use case. So instead, always create an additional layer of abstraction and decouple your use case from other consumers. This approach to taking consumer-specific data and turning it into a new data product allows your domains to evolve independently from other domains.

A concern when distributing newly created data is traceability: knowing what happens with the data. To mitigate the risks of transparency, ask data consumers to catalog their acquisitions and the sequences of actions and transformations they apply to the data. This lineage metadata should be published centrally. I'll come back to this in Chapters 10 and 11.

Data Security Patterns

For data security, you need to define guidance for data providers. This should include the following:

- Guidance on encapsulating metadata for filtering and row-level access. By providing metadata along with the data, you can create policies or views to hide or display certain rows of data, depending on whether a consumer has permission to view those rows.

- Guidance on tags or classifications for column-level access and dynamic data masking. These tags or classifications are used as input for policies or views.

- Guidance on efficiently storing data in separate tables for providing coarse-grained security, enhancing performance, and facilitating maintenance.

We'll talk more about these topics in Chapter 8.

Establish a Metamodel

For properly managing data products and their corresponding metadata, I highly encourage you to create a consistent metamodel in which you define how entities (such as data domains, data products, data owners, business terms, physical data, and other metadata) relate to each other.[5] When working on your metamodel, it's best to use a data catalog to enforce capture of all the necessary metadata. For example, each time you instantiate a new data product in your catalog, it can trigger a workflow that begins by asking the data provider to provide a description and connect the data product to a data owner, originating application, data domain, and so on. Next, the catalog might ask the provider to link all of the data product elements to business terms and technical (physical) data attributes. It might then run automated tests to check whether these physical locations are addressable, and ask for classifications and usage restriction information.

---

5 A metamodel is a framework for understanding what metadata needs to be captured when describing data.

Allow Self-Service

Data products are about data democratization. To improve the data product creation experience, consider building a data marketplace and offering self-service capabilities for discoverability, management, sharing, and observability. For example, allow engineers to use the data catalog's REST interface so data product registration can be automated. If done properly, engineers can register their data products as part of their continuous integration/continuous delivery (CI/CD) pipelines. More guidance on this subject will be provided in Chapter 9.

Cross-Domain Relationships

In the operational world, systems are often intertwined or strongly connected. Imagine an order system through which customers can place orders. It's likely that such a system will hold data from the customer database. Otherwise, it wouldn't be able to link orders to customers.

If domains develop data products independently from other domains, how do consumers recognize that certain data belongs together or is related? To manage these dependencies, consider using a catalog or knowledge graph that describes the relationships between the datasets and references the join keys or foreign keys across data products.

When providing guidance on managing cross-domain relationships, it's important that data always remain domain-oriented. The alignment between data and data ownership must be strong, so no cross-domain integration should be performed before any data is delivered to other domains.

Enterprise Consistency

Strong decentralization causes data to be siloed within individual domains. This causes concerns over the accessibility and usability of the data, because if all domains start to individually serve data, it becomes harder to integrate and combine data on the consuming side. To overcome these concerns, you may want to introduce some enterprise consistency by providing guidance for including enterprise reference values (currency codes, country codes, product codes, client segmentation codes, and so on). If applicable, you can ask your data product owners to map their local reference values to values from the enterprise lists.

Some data practitioners will argue that the use of enterprise reference values doesn't conform to a true data mesh implementation. This is true to some degree, but without any referential integrity you'll see duplicated efforts for harmonization and integration across all domains. Note that I'm not suggesting you build a canonical enterprise-wide data model, as seen in most enterprise data warehouse architectures, but simply provide some reference data as guidance. The resulting consistency can be helpful in a large-scale organization in which many domains rely on the same reference values.

The same guidance applies for master identification numbers, which link master data and data from the local systems together. These data elements are critical for tracking down what data has been mastered and what belongs together, so you might ask your local domains to include these master identifiers within their data products. More best practices in this area will be provided in Chapter 10.

Historization, Redeliveries, and Overwrites

To meet the needs of consumers, data providers often need to keep historical data in their original context. For example, consumers may need this data to perform retrospective trend analyses and predict what will happen next. To do this well, I recommend formulating guidance based on the design of the system, the type of data, and how it should be historized for later analysis. For example, datasets with master data should always be transformed into slowly changing dimensions. We'll look at processing historical data in more detail in "Data Historization" on page 122.

Business Capabilities with Multiple Owners

When business capabilities are shared, I recommend defining a methodology for handling shared data. This may involve using reserved column names within your data products to define ownership, physically creating multiple data products, or embedding metadata within your data products.

Operating Model

Success in data product development requires an operating model that ensures effective data management, the establishment of standards and best practices, performance tracking, and quality assurance. A typical data product team usually comprises a supporting architect, data engineers, data modelers, and data scientists. This team must be adequately supported and funded to build and continually improve their data products. Additionally, there must be an organizational body that institutes and oversees standards and best practices for building data products across the entire organization. I find organizations are most successful when they develop playbooks: documents that describe all of the company's objectives, processes, workflows, trade-offs, checklists, roles, and responsibilities. Such playbooks are often hosted in open repositories, allowing everyone to contribute.

Establishing good standards and best practices includes defining how teams can measure performance and quality, as well as designing how the necessary services must fit together for each consumption pattern so they can be reused across all data products. To ensure that data products meet consumers' needs and are continually improving, teams should measure the value and success of their activities. Relevant metrics may include the number of consumers of a given data product, outstanding and open quality issues, satisfaction scores, return on investment, or use cases enabled.

Now that we've explored the foundations for the necessary mindset shift of managing data as products, let's tackle the questions that architects get most often: What is a good strategy for creating data products? Should it be facilitated with a centrally provided platform, or must domains cater to their own needs?

Data Product Architecture

To significantly reduce the complexity of your architecture, you need to find the right balance between centralization and decentralization. At one end of the spectrum is a fully federated and autonomous approach, allowing every domain to host its own architecture and choose its own technology stack. However, this can lead to a proliferation of data products, interface protocols, metadata information, and so on. It also makes data governance and control much harder because every domain must precisely implement central disciplines such as archiving, lineage, data quality, and data security. Working out all these competences in the domains themselves would be a challenge and would lead to fragmented, siloed complexity.

At the other end is a federated and centrally governed approach, not with a single silo, but with multiple platform instances or landing zone blueprints sharing the same standard infrastructure services. Standardized components and shared infrastructure reduce costs, lower the number of interfaces, and improve control. Ideally, multiple data product architectures would be hosted on the same platform infrastructure, but they're logically isolated from each other.

High-Level Platform Design

Let's unpack the architecture and components that are needed for building data products. Exposing data as a product enables data consumers to easily discover, find, understand, and securely access data across many domains. Having said that, the main focus of the common platform capabilities for data product distribution should be on capturing data, transforming data into read-optimized versions, and securely serving data to other domains. Any analytical or reporting capabilities for developing use cases for data-driven decision making will be added to the architecture later; those are discussed in Chapter 11.

In a little more depth, at a minimum your data product architecture should have the following capabilities:

- Capabilities for capturing, ingesting, and onboarding data via your input ports
- Capabilities for serving or providing data to diverse domains via your output ports

- Metadata capabilities for documenting, discovering, monitoring, securing, and governing data
- Data engineering capabilities for developing, deploying, and running the data product's code
- Data quality and master data management capabilities
- Data marketplace capabilities for delivering a unified data shopping experience

Figure 4-5 is a logical design of a data product architecture, demonstrating how data is captured, transformed, and served to other domains. We'll go into more detail on each individual component, but first I'll provide a high-level overview. At the top, there's a metadata layer that provides insights into the available data, its properties, and relationships to other data management areas. Within this layer there are metadata repositories for orchestration, observability, contract management, and so on. These are the linking pins between your data marketplace and data product architecture.

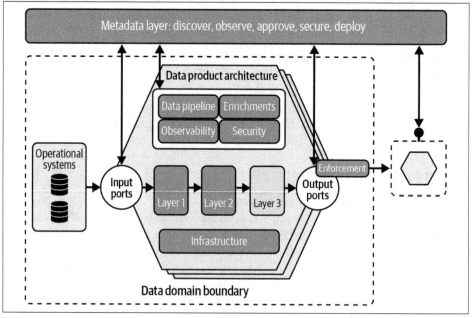

Figure 4-5. Example data product architecture

When you use shared infrastructure, different data product architectures are isolated and not directly shared between domains. Each data product architecture, and accountability, remains with the data provider. A data provider, and thus a domain, has its own data product architecture instance and its own pipeline and takes ownership of the quality and integrity of the data.

The key to engineering shared platforms and data product architectures is to provide a set of central foundational and domain-agnostic components and make various design decisions in order to abstract repetitive problems from the domains and make data management less of a challenge. In the next sections, I'll highlight the most important considerations, based on observations from the field.

Capabilities for Capturing and Onboarding Data

Data onboarding is the critical first step for successfully building a data architecture. However, the process of extracting source system data also remains one of the most challenging problems when using data at large. It requires several considerations.

Ingestion method

First, you should determine the speed at which data must be delivered or synchronized. Roughly speaking, there are two scenarios to choose from:

Batch processing
> Consumers that require data only periodically can be facilitated with batch processing, which refers to the process of transferring a large volume of data at once. The batch is typically a dataset with millions of records stored as a file. Why do we still need batch processing? In many cases, this is the only way to collect our data. Most significant relational database management systems (RDBMSs) have batch components to support movement of data in batches. *Data reconciliation,* the process of verifying data during this movement, is often a concern.[6] Verifying that you have all of the data is essential, especially within financial processes. In addition, many systems are complex, with tremendous numbers of tables, and Structured Query Language (SQL) is the only proper way to select and extract their data.

Real-time data ingestion
> Consumers that desire incremental or near-real-time data updates can be best facilitated with *event-driven* or *API-based ingestion.* Such processing allows us to collect and process data relatively quickly and works well for use cases where the amounts of data are relatively small, the computations performed on the data are relatively simple, and there's a need for near-real-time latencies. Many use cases can be handled with event-driven ingestion, but if completeness and large data are a major concern, most teams will fall back on the traditional batches. We'll pay more attention to this in Chapter 6.

---

6 *Reconciliation* can be implemented in many different ways. For example, you can compare row counts, use column checksums (*https://oreil.ly/NqCeO*), slice large tables and reprocess them, or use data comparisons tools such as Redgate (*https://www.red-gate.com*).

Although real-time data ingestion has started to gain popularity, a streaming-only (Kappa) architecture will never fully replace batch processing for all use cases. Within most enterprises, I expect both ingestion methods to be used side by side.

Complex software packages

For all data onboarding, it's important to acknowledge the diversity of specialized software packages. Many are extremely difficult to interpret or access. Database schemas are often terribly complex, and referential integrity is typically maintained programmatically through the application instead of the database. Some vendors even protect their data, so it can only be extracted with support from a third-party solution.

In all of these complex situations, I recommend you evaluate for each source system whether you need to complement your architecture with additional services that allow extracting data. Such services might hide these complex source system structures and protect you from lengthy and expensive mapping exercises. They also protect you from tight coupling because typically the data schema of a complex vendor product isn't directly controlled by you. If the vendor releases a product version upgrade and the data structures change, then all your data pipelines break. Bottom line, a third-party component is worth the investment.

External APIs and SaaS providers

External API or SaaS providers typically require special attention too. I have examined situations where a full dataset was required, but the SaaS provider only provided a relatively small amount of data via an API. Other providers might apply throttling: a quota or a limit for the number of requests. There are also providers with expensive payment plans for every call you make. In all of these situations, I recommend either obtaining a tool that supports extraction from APIs or building a custom component that periodically fetches data.

A correctly designed custom implementation might route all API calls to your data product architecture first. If the same request has been made recently, the results are directly served from the data product architecture. If not, the SaaS provider's API is triggered and the results are returned and also stored in your data product architecture for any subsequent calls. With this pattern, a full collection of data can eventually be populated for serving consumers.

Lineage and metadata

For all of your data extraction and onboarding components, it's important to pay close attention to data lineage extraction. Organizations find it important to know what data has been extracted and what transformations were applied on the data. Standardization and determining how connectors would integrate with your data lineage repository is an important exercise. You should do this investigation up front, so you know what will integrate and what will not. Lineage can be hard to add retrospectively, given its tight dependence on transformation frameworks and ETL tools; it's best to select, test, validate, and standardize before starting the actual implementation.

Data Quality

Data quality is another important design consideration. When datasets are ingested into the data product architecture, their quality should be validated. There are two aspects to this.

First, you should validate the integrity of your data, comparing it to the published schemas. You do this because you want to ensure new data is of high quality and conforms to your standards and expectations, and take action otherwise. This first line of defense is the responsibility of the data owners, data stewards, and data engineers. These are the team members who create and source the data. It's up to them to ensure that the data meets the data quality requirements stipulated by regulators or by the data consumers.

Second, there are quality checks that are more federated by nature. This validation relies less on individual data product teams because other teams define what constitutes good data quality. These kinds of data quality checks are typically run asynchronously and flag or/and notify respective parties. The federated controls are usually functional checks: completeness, accuracy, consistency, plausibility, etc. Data integrity and federated data quality are two different disciplines that sometimes have their own metadata repository in which schema metadata or functional validation rules are stored. In this case, each has its own standard platform services.

For your platform design, a benefit when using shared infrastructure for data product architectures is that you can leverage the power of big data for data quality processing. For instance, Apache Spark (*https://spark.apache.org*) provides the distributed processing power to process hundreds of millions of rows of data. To use it efficiently, you can use a framework to document, test, and profile data for data quality. Great Expectations (*https://greatexpectations.io*) and Soda (*https://www.soda.io*), for example, are open standards for data quality that are used by many large organizations. Another advantage of managing data quality on shared infrastructure is that you can perform cross-domain referential integrity checks. Source systems often refer to data from other applications or systems. By cross-checking the integrity of the references and comparing and contrasting different datasets, you'll find errors and correlations you didn't know existed.

When data quality monitoring is implemented properly, it not only detects and observes data quality issues but becomes part of the overall data quality control framework that checks and adds new data to the existing data.[7] If for whatever reason quality drops below a specified threshold, the framework can park the data and ask the data owners to take a look and either vouch for, remove, or redeliver the data. Having a control framework for data quality means that there's a closed feedback loop that continuously corrects quality issues and prevents them from occurring again. Data quality is continuously monitored; variations in the level of quality are addressed immediately. Bear in mind that data quality issues must be resolved in the source systems, not within your data product architecture. Fixing data quality issues at the source ensures they won't pop up in other places.

The impact of data quality shouldn't be underestimated. If the quality of the data is bad, consumers will be confronted with the repetitive work of cleaning up and correcting the data. I also want to stress the importance of standardization. If individual teams decide on their own data quality frameworks, it will be impossible to compare metrics and results between domains.

Data Historization

Correctly managing historical data is critical for a business, because without this they're unable to see trends over time and make predictions for the future. Standards should also be considered for managing historical data. This section provides some background and explores a few different representations and approaches for managing this data.

Organizing historical data is a key aspect of data warehousing. In this context, you often hear the terms *nonvolatile* and *time-variant*. Nonvolatile means the previous data isn't erased when new data is added to it. Time-variant implies that the data is consistent within a certain period; for example, data is loaded daily or on some other periodic basis, and doesn't change within that period.

Data products play an important role in storing and managing large quantities of historical data. But how would you address this in a decentralized architecture? A difference from data warehousing is that data products preserve data in its original context. No transformation to an enterprise data model is expected because data products are aligned with domains; the original (domain) context isn't lost. This is a major benefit: it means domains can "dogfood" their own data products for their own operational use cases, such as machine learning, while serving data to other domains at the same time. As a consequence, domains have an intrinsic need to care about the data they own. Ultimately, this practice of using one's own data products will improve both their quality and customer satisfaction.

---

7 For a discussion of how Azure Synapse Analytics and Microsoft Purview can be integrated together to intelligently process and validate data using Great Expectations, see my blog post "Modern Data Pipelines with Azure Synapse Analytics and Azure Purview" (*https://oreil.ly/QFMXn*).

Although a data product architecture is a technology-agnostic concept, it's likely that many of these architectures will be engineered with lower-cost distributed filesystems, such as data lake services. This means different ways of data processing are required for updating and overwriting master, transactional, and reference data. Therefore, I recommend considering one or a combination of the following approaches, each of which involves a trade-off between investing in and managing incoming data and the ease of data consumption. Each approach has pros and cons.

Point-in-time

The first approach for managing historical data is storing the original data as a historical reference, usually immutable. Think of a reservoir into which data is ingested using a copy activity. In this insert-only approach, it's recommended to partition the data logically, for example, using a date/time logical separation (see Figure 4-6).[8]

data partitioned per delivery date			
ID	Name	Email	Delivery_date
1	John Snow	john.snow@example.com	1-1-2019
2	Brian Stark	brian.stark@example.com	1-1-2019
1	John Snow	john.snow@example.com	2-1-2019
2	Brian Stark	brian.stark@example.com	2-1-2019
3	Elis Smith	elis.smith@example.com	2-1-2019
1	John Snow	john.snow@example.com	3-1-2019
2	Brian Stark		3-1-2019
3	Elis Smith	elis.smith@example.com	3-1-2019

Data is processed and stored into slowly changing dimensions (type 2), allowing users to select specific vales			
ID	Name	Email	Start_date	End_date
1	John Snow	john.snow@example.com	1-1-2019	
2	Brian Stark	brian.stark@example.com	2-1-2019	2-1-2019
3	Brian Stark		3-1-2019	
3	Elis Smith	elis.smith@example.com	2-1-2019	

Figure 4-6. Examples of how data looks when partitioned with full-dimensional snapshots or slowly changing dimensions (type 2)

---

8 Partitioning is a common technique for organizing files or tables into distinct groups (partitions) to improve manageability, performance, or availability. It's usually executed on data attributes, such as geographical (city, country), value-based (unique identifiers, segment codes), or time-based attributes (delivery date, time).

Managing only full snapshots is easy to implement. At each ETL cycle, the entire output is stored as an immutable snapshot. After that, table schemas can be replaced using the location in which the new data is stored. The container is a collection of all of these point-in-time snapshots. Some practitioners might argue that this approach results in data duplication. I don't consider this a problem, because cloud storage is relatively cheap these days. Full snapshots also facilitate redelivery, or rebuilding an integrated dataset that holds all the changes made over time. If a source system discovers that incorrect data was delivered, the data can be submitted again, and it will overwrite the partition.

> Only using a point-in-time representation approach might be appropriate when the data that is provided already contains all the needed historical data—for example, if data is provided in such a way that it already contains start and end dates for all records.

A drawback of snapshotting full datasets is that (retrospective) data analysis is more difficult. Comparisons between specific time periods are problematic if start and end dates are not available, because consumers will need to process and store all the historical data. Processing three years' worth of historical data, for instance, might require processing over a thousand files in sequence. Data processing can take up a lot of time and compute capacity, depending on the size of the data. Therefore, it's recommended to also consider an interval approach.

Interval

Another approach for managing and presenting historical data is building up historical datasets in which all data is compared and processed. For example, you might create datasets using *slowly changing dimensions* (SCDs),[9] which show all changes over time. This process requires ETL because you need to take the existing data delivery and compare that data with any previous deliveries. After comparison, records are opened and/or closed. Within this process, typically an end date is assigned to values that are updated and a start date to the new values. For the comparison, it is recommended to exclude all nonfunctional data.[10]

---

9 A slowly changing dimension is a dimension that stores and manages both current and historical data over time in a data warehouse. Dimensional tables in data management and data warehousing can be maintained via several methodologies, referred to as type 0 through 6. The different methodologies are described by the Kimball Group (*https://oreil.ly/NUUW1*).

10 For example, within your processing framework you can use the `exclude_from_delta_processing` parameter on an attribute level to exclude data from being compared.

Can I Design My Data Products Using Data Virtualization?

I waited until the historization discussion to bring up data virtualization. Data virtualization and data product creation aren't a great combination for several reasons:

- Data virtualization isn't complementary to data life cycle management. It can't move irrelevant data out of the underlying systems. It requires all historical data to stay in the OLTP systems, which in the long term makes data virtualization an expensive solution.
- The data virtualization layer leads to tighter coupling.[11] If source systems change, changes to the data virtualization layer are immediately required as well. Views or additional layers can help, but any change still requires coordination between the source system owners and engineers maintaining the data virtualization layer.
- Data virtualization relies on the network. In a distributed environment with a lot of networks and hops (passing through additional network devices), latency is expected to increase. Additionally, there's coupling, so if the network is down, the virtualization layer is broken.
- Data virtualization is limited by the underlying supportive technology, which is typically an RDBMS. Although data virtualization can read many database systems, in general it doesn't allow you to create document, key/value, columnar, and graph database endpoints.
- For intensive and repeatable queries data virtualization uses more computing power, because transformations are performed in real time when data is queried. Caching techniques can reduce this effect, but the amount of computing power required will always be greater when using data after it has been preprocessed for consumption.

Bottom line: access to data products can be virtualized, but you shouldn't design and develop your data products using only a data virtualization engine.

The approach of comparing intervals and building up historical data has the benefit of storing data more efficiently because it's processed, deduplicated, and combined. As you can see in Figure 4-6, the slowly changing dimension on the right side takes up half the number of rows. Querying the data, for example using a relational database, is consequently easier and faster. Cleaning the data or removing individual records, as you might need to for GDPR compliance, will be easier as well, since you won't have to crunch all the previously delivered datasets.

---

11 Some database vendors provide a database (virtual) query layer, which is also called a data virtualization layer. This layer abstracts the database and optimizes the data for better read performance. Another reason to abstract is to intercept queries for better security.

The downside, however, is that building up slowly changing dimensions requires more management. All the data needs to be processed. Changes in the underlying source data need to be detected as soon as they occur and then processed. This detection requires additional code and compute capacity. Another consideration is that data consumers typically have different historization requirements. For example, if data is processed on a daily basis, but a consumer requires representation by month, then they will still need to do an additional processing step.

In addition, the redelivery process can be painful and difficult to manage because incorrect data might be processed and become part of the dimensions. This can be fixed with reprocessing logic, additional versions, or validity dates, but additional management is still required. The pitfall here is that managing the data correctly can become the responsibility of a central team, so this scalability requires a great deal of intelligent self-service functionality.

Another drawback of building up historical data for generic consumption by all consumers is that consumers might still need to do some processing whenever they leave out columns in their selections. For instance, if a consumer makes a more narrow selection, they might end up with duplicate records and thus need to process the data again to deduplicate it. For scalability and to help consumers, you can also consider mixing the two approaches, keeping full-dimensional snapshots and providing "historical data as a service." In this scenario, a small computation framework is offered to all consumer domains, by which they can schedule historical data to be created based on the scope (daily, weekly, or monthly), time span, attributes, and datasets they need. With short-lived processing instances on the public cloud, you can even make this cost-effective. The big benefit with this approach is that you retain flexibility for redeliveries but don't require an engineering team to manage and prepare datasets. Another benefit is that you can tailor the time spans, scopes, and attributes to everyone's needs.

Append-only

Some data delivery styles can be best facilitated with an append-only approach. With this method, you load only new or changed records from the application database and append them to the existing set of records. This works for transactional data as well as event-based data, which we'll discuss in Chapter 6. The append-only approach is often combined with change data capture, where you set up a stream of changes by identifying and capturing changes made in standard tables, directory tables, and views.

Historization and Streaming Ingestion

Real-time data ingestion is typically handled in two different ways. In the first scenario, transformations happen on the fly as data comes in, and the result is directly appended in, for example, a NoSQL database. This whole process usually takes a couple of seconds or minutes. The main objective is to serve the data as soon as it arrives. In the second scenario, real-time data is processed periodically, for example as microbatches. The main goal here is to merge and historize all the data so data can be consumed downstream at a faster interval. A consideration when merging data is the latency of processing because processing takes time.

Defining your historization strategy

The right historization approach for a data product depends on the data types, consumer requirements, and regulations. All of the approaches for historizing and building up data products can be combined, and you may use different approaches for different kinds of data. Master data, for example, can be delivered from an application and built up using the slowly changing dimensions style. Reference data can be easily processed using snapshotting, while you might want to handle transactional data for the same system via append-only delivery. You can retain full snapshots of all deliveries while also building up slowly changed dimensions.

To be successful in data product development and design, a comprehensive strategy is the key. Best practices should focus on how to layer data and build up history within each of your domains. This layering strategy may include the development and maintenance of scripts and standard services, such as change data capture services.[12]

The best practices outlined here are meant to provide insights, but are also shared to show that data product management is a heavy undertaking. In the next section, we'll dive more deeply into some of the solution design aspects when developing an architecture. We'll do this using a real-world example while taking into consideration what we've already discussed.

Solution Design

Now that you're familiar with some best practices and design principles, it's time for something more practical: building read-optimized abstractions over your complex application data using solutions and services. The technologies and methodologies that organizations apply for developing data products typically differ significantly from enterprise to enterprise. This is also a difficult subject to address because there

---

12 One of my blog posts (*https://oreil.ly/srK-Z*) has a simple sample script for processing SCD tables in Delta format using Spark pools.

are no platforms or products to manage the full data product life cycle. It would take another book to describe all the different ways to implement an end-to-end data product architecture, so instead I'll focus on the key consideration points before discussing a concrete example:

- The cloud has become the default infrastructure for processing data at large because it offers significant advantages over on-premises environments. All the popular cloud platforms provide a set of self-serve data services that are sufficient to kick-start any implementation.

- Data lake services are a popular choice among all types of organizations. With data volumes increasing on a daily basis, placing data in, for example, an HDFS-compatible cloud object storage is a great way to make your architecture cost-effective. The benefits of these types of services include separation of storage and compute and the reduction of data duplication by using lightweight query services.[13]

- A popular stack is processing data with Spark, Python, and notebooks. Motivations for this pattern include a wide and active community, the benefits of open source and strong interoperability, and wide-ranging support for varying use cases, from data engineering to data science. While Spark is an excellent choice for ETL and machine learning, it isn't optimized for performing low-latency and interactive queries. Another consideration when using notebooks is to pay attention to repetitive activities, such as data historization, technical data transformations, and schema validation. A common best practice when using notebooks is to design common procedures and a metadata-driven framework using configurable procedures for destinations, validations, security, and so on.[14]

- For data transformation and modeling, many organizations complement their architecture with extra services, like dbt (*https://www.getdbt.com*). Although Spark with custom code can be used for data transformation, companies often feel larger projects can be better streamlined by templating and writing configurations. Both templating tools and notebooks are viable options, and can also complement each other. I see lots of companies that first handle data validation, technical transformation, and historization with notebooks, then integrate their data with tools like dbt.

- Orchestration and workflow automation are needed to manage the process from ingestion all the way to serving data. Although standardization is key for observability, it's a best practice to give each team freedom to develop its own local knowledge, and to pursue local priorities. Another best practice is to integrate

---

13 By separating storage from compute, you can automatically scale infrastructure to match elastic workloads.

14 See my blog post "Designing a Metadata-Driven Processing Framework for Azure Synapse and Azure Purview" (*https://oreil.ly/ZSpWX*) for details on this concept.

your CI/CD and workflow processes, but keep your pipelines independent for each application or data product.

- When selecting any tools, I recommend searching for *modern data stack*. There are many popular options to choose from, varying from open source to closed source solutions.

- Metadata management services, such as data catalogs and data lineage tools, often sit outside data product architectures. These services are offered as generic services by a central authority. Considerations will be discussed in great depth in Chapter 9.

A common question with regard to data product design is how the concepts of a data lake and data mesh relate. While at first glance they might seem contradictory, the underlying technology of data lakes complements the vision of data product design. So, there's nothing wrong with using data lake technologies in a data mesh.

Another frequently asked question is whether each domain has autonomy to select its own modern data stack. Enthusiasts quickly draw a parallel between microservices and data mesh architectures, and argue that full autonomy enables each domain to make its own optimal technology choices. However, many organizations fail because domain teams make contrasting decisions. Imagine you have 25 "autonomous" teams, all implementing their data product architectures using their own tools and ways of working. If all the tools differ, how will you collect lineage, data quality metrics, monitoring statistics, and results from master data management? How can you achieve interoperability between platforms when each team uses its own standard? I'll address these questions at the end of this chapter, but it's important to note that identity, governance, and interoperability are the cornerstones of any federated pattern. Sacrifice any one of these pillars, and you quickly end up with many point-to-point solutions, which get architecturally expensive and difficult to govern. Autonomy starts with enterprise architecture, at a central level, and requires standardization. Flexibility is about loose coupling and removing dependencies. Autonomy shouldn't end up in organizational chaos, uncontrolled technology proliferation, an explosion of costs, or a combination of all these.

Real-World Example

In this section, I'll walk you through a real-world example of creating a data product architecture. This example won't be that complex, although it contains the essential ingredients for later discussion and evaluation. Let's assume the data product architecture is being designed for an organization where roughly half of the domains are operational and transactional by nature. These systems are marked as golden sources and are the starting point for data ingestion. The other domains are consumer-driven; data must be served to them.

For an extensive walkthrough of this example, including screen-shots and step-by-step instructions, see my blog post "Using DBT for Building a Medallion Lakehouse Architecture" (*https://oreil.ly/PNhEt*).

If I were tasked to design a data product architecture for this organization on Azure, I might propose the solution seen in Figure 4-7. My starting point would be to provision a data landing zone (*https://oreil.ly/J5Mbb*) and some resource groups with a standardized set of services for my first domain: Azure Data Factory (ADF), Azure Data Lake Storage (ALDS), and Azure Databricks. Subsequently, I would collect and harvest data using a service like ADF (*https://oreil.ly/mSyb7*). Where possible, I would use prebuilt connectors. Alternatively, I would ask application owners to export and stage their data in intermediary locations. These could be, for example, Blob Storage accounts (*https://oreil.ly/MFBg2*), from which the data will be picked up for later processing.

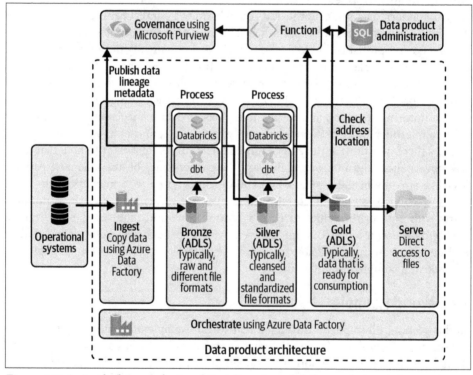

Figure 4-7. A simple data product architecture using a lakehouse design: it features services for data ingestion, data product creation, and data governance

I would use ADLS (*https://oreil.ly/RNly0*) to store data in my data product architecture. A common design pattern for grouping data is using three containers:[15]

Bronze
> Raw data that might be in multiple formats and structures.

Silver
> Filtered and cleaned data, stored using a standardized column-oriented data file format.

Gold
> Read-optimized data that is ready for consumption by other domains. Some organizations call these read-optimized or consumer-friendly datasets data products.

After configuring my data lake, I would continue the exercise by creating my first data pipeline. First, I would use the copy activity (*https://oreil.ly/PIY2k*) for copying data into the Bronze layer. Data in this layer is stored using Parquet format because no versioning is required. For historizing data, a *YYYYMMDD* partitioning scheme is used. Older versions of data are kept for ad hoc analysis or debugging purposes.

Next, I would add another pipeline activity to execute notebooks and pass parameters (*https://oreil.ly/T3nd3*) to Databricks.[16] Databricks will use a dynamic notebook to validate data, then drop any existing schemas and create new ones using the *YYYYMMDD* partition locations.

For the Silver layer, my preferred file format is Delta, which offers fast performance and protection from corruption. Retention (*https://oreil.ly/RN182*) is enabled for the cases where you need to roll back changes and restore data to a previous version—for each operation that modifies data, Databricks creates a new table version, storing 30 days of history by default. For selecting data from the Bronze layer and transforming it using a type 2 SCD table design, I prefer dbt. I apply limited transformations when moving data to Silver, selecting only functional data. Before I select any data, I perform a set of tests to ensure the data is of high quality and meets integrity standards. One last note for this layer: if I have different sources, I treat these as separate data feeds. The integration and combination of all the data is handled in the next layers.

---

15 If you plan to set up a data lake, the "Hitchhiker's Guide to the Data Lake" (*https://oreil.ly/RVWEb*) is a great resource with guidance and best practices.

16 Microsoft has developed a solution accelerator together with the OpenLineage project. This open source connector transfers lineage metadata from Spark operations in Azure Databricks to Microsoft Purview, allowing you to see a table-level lineage graph. The project is hosted on GitHub (*https://oreil.ly/uKwN4*).

For moving data into the Gold layer, where it is integrated and made consumer-ready, I need to write business logic to map all the objects into user-friendly and consumable datasets. Again, I use dbt templates for this, creating a template and YML model (*https://oreil.ly/cO1JP*) for each logical data entity. Each template defines the selects, joins, and transformations that need to be applied, and writes to a unique folder (e.g., customer data, order data, sales data, and so on). Each output logically clusters data around a subject area. The data is materialized, and the file format is again Delta.

Finally, I would save and schedule my pipeline within ADF. For all individual steps, I would add additional steps for capturing the load date/time, process ID, number of records processed, error or success messages, and so on.

For each additional domain, I would repeat all of these steps. So, each domain would store its data products in its own domain-specific data product architecture, manage its own data pipeline, and use the same layering for building data products. Once I had the ability to do this in a controlled way at scale, I would start adding variations to this design. For example, I might have several output ports utilizing the same semantic data for different representations for different consumers.

For the governance, self-service, and security pieces of the architecture, I'd propose using a combination of an Azure SQL database (*https://oreil.ly/nuZK3*), Azure Functions (*https://oreil.ly/oWukr*), and Microsoft Purview (*https://oreil.ly/fPmLs*), a unified data governance service. These components can be deployed in the data management landing zone and used to catalog and oversee all data products.

For publishing data products, I would ask all domains to publish their data products via a declarative function, as part of their CI/CD pipelines. This function could, for example, take the dbt YML specifications from the Gold layer as input and store these specifications in a SQL database. Next, the function would validate that the provided location and schema information represent the universal resource identifier (URI) and structure of the data product. If so, it will make another call to publish all the information into the catalog. This final call makes the data publicly available for other consumers.

For providing data access to my consumers, I would propose using self-service data discovery and access (*https://oreil.ly/zjeeW*). In the background, this will create access control lists (ACLs) (*https://oreil.ly/bsl22*) for individual data products. ACLs aren't great for fine-grained column-level or row-level filtering, but for the purpose of this real-world example, they're fine. More complex scenarios will be discussed in Chapter 8.

This real-world example has been simplified for teaching purposes. In reality, data product management is more complex because of the need to take into account factors like security, profiling, complex lookups, data ingestion and serving variations, and different enrichment scenarios. For example, there might be specific restrictions for archiving data, tokenization, or accessing data within a certain time frame.

Let's quickly recap the key points from this example. First, we quickly laid out the foundation for data product creation. We made the domain accountable for the life cycle of the data under its control, and for transforming data from the raw form captured by applications to a form that is suitable for consumption by external parties. Second, the architecture can be easily scaled by adding more domains with additional data product architectures. Third, we applied several data mesh principles, such as domain-oriented data ownership, data-as-a-product thinking, self-service data platforms, and federated computational governance. In the next section, we'll turn our attention to the numerous considerations you must make when scaling up.

Alignment with Storage Accounts

It's important to pay attention to the alignment of data product data and storage accounts. In the example design in the previous section, I decided to share a data product architecture with multiple data product datasets from a single domain. An alternative would have been to align each dataset with a dedicated storage account and Spark pool for data processing. Such a setup will tie together data, code, metadata, and the necessary infrastructure, and would be closer to the data product concept within a data mesh. It simplifies access management and enables automation so that you can provision processing clusters and storage accounts on the fly. If, for example, your Silver layer is temporal, you can wipe it out once it's no longer required. On the other hand, closely linking data products and infrastructure dramatically increases infrastructure overhead and the number of pipelines that you need to manage. For example, it may result in a large number of permissions and network and service endpoints that need to be managed, secured, scanned, and monitored, or generate a complex web of storage accounts because data products are often derived from the same underlying data. So, you'll need to weigh how closely you want to align your data products with your infrastructure.

What about having multiple domains share the same storage account? This is also possible, but having multiple domains share the underlying storage infrastructure requires a different container and folder structure. This is a pattern I often see at smaller organizations, because centrally managed storage eases the management burden and other issues commonly seen when moving and securing data. On the other hand, it requires all domains to share the same limits and configuration items, such as ACLs and IP address rules. It's probably also not the best approach if you need georedundancy and flexible performance.[17] Again, you'll need to consider the trade-offs.

Alternatively, you could strike a balance between locally and centrally aligned data by implementing a hybrid approach of using both domain-local and central storage accounts. In this case, each domain uses an internal, dedicated storage account in which all domain-specific processing is done (for example, in the Bronze and Silver layers). Such an account is meant for internal use only and won't be exposed to any other domains. Next to these domain-local storage accounts, there's a centrally shared storage account, which is meant for distributing the final data of the data products (created in the Gold layer) to other domains. This shared storage account is often managed by a central department. The rationale for such a design is to provide flexibility for domains while maintaining oversight of all the data products' data exchanges.

Alignment with Data Pipelines

Another important consideration is the alignment of data pipelines and data products. As you saw earlier, a data pipeline is a series of steps for moving and transforming data. It generally uses metadata and code, just like in a metadata-driven ingestion framework, to determine what operations to execute on what data. In the previous example, we used the same pipeline for all the data products, but some practitioners advocate using a dedicated pipeline for each one. So the question is, which approach is better for your situation?

To answer this question, consider the granularity of your data products and the corresponding data pipelines. Suppose you batch process the data from one application and build several coarse-grained data products (datasets) from it, each using its own data pipeline. It's likely that multiple pipelines will be processing the same underlying source system data because input data for data products often overlaps. This means some processing steps may be repeated, which makes maintenance harder. Additionally, moving specific parts of the data through different pipelines at different intervals causes integrity issues, which makes it hard for consumers to combine data later.

Having too fine-grained a setup for your data products and data pipelines is challenging as well. If an underlying source system generates hundreds of small data products each having their own data pipeline, it will be hard to troubleshoot issues and oversee dependencies: a complex web of repeated processing steps may be observed. Additionally, it will be hard for consumers to use the data, as they will have to

---

17 Georedundancy is achieved by distributing critical components or infrastructures (e.g., servers) across multiple data centers in different geographic locations. For example, for cloud storage you can choose between conventional hard disks and faster solid state drives

integrate many small datasets. Referential integrity is also a big concern here because many pipelines are expected run at slightly different intervals.

To conclude, having a dedicated pipeline for each data product is usually not the ideal solution. The recommended best practice is to create one pipeline using the appropriate series of steps that takes the entire application state, copies it, and then transforms the data into user-friendly datasets.

Capabilities for Serving Data

Let's switch to the serving side of the data product architecture and see what components and services we need to provide there. For serving the data from the output ports,[18] there are different dimensions of data processing that impact how the data product architectures can be engineered. The data product architecture's design largely depends on the use cases and requirements of the consuming domains. In many cases, you're processing data that isn't time-critical. Sometimes answering the question or fulfilling the business need can wait a few hours or even a few days. However, there are also use cases in which the data needs to be delivered within a few seconds.

Data product management shouldn't be confused with data value creation, such as through business intelligence and machine learning applications. Despite the overlap, on the consumer side you generally see heavy diversification in the way data is used. Hence, data product creation must be managed apart from data value creation.

In recent years, the variety of storage and database services available have vastly increased. Traditionally, transactional and operational systems are designed for high integrity and thus use an ACID-compliant and relational database. But non-ACID-compliant schemaless databases (such as document or key/value stores) are also trending because they relax the stronger integrity controls in favor of faster performance and allow for more flexible data types, such as data originating from mobile devices, gaming, social media channels, sensors, etc. The size of the data can make a difference: some applications store relatively small amounts of data, while other applications might rely on terabytes of data.

---

18 The recommendation for a data mesh is to share data products using highly standardized interfaces, providing read-only and read-optimized access to data. These interfaces are also known as *output ports*.

Why Are There So Many Different Databases?

When choosing a database, there are many factors and trade-offs to consider. In addition to the structure of the data, you'll need to evaluate your needs with regard to consistency, availability, partition tolerance, and caching and indexing for better performance. There are different ways to store data and retrieve it: small chunks, big chunks, chunks that are sorted, etc. There are distributability and consistency trade-offs that can affect performance, as can features such as continued monitoring and analytics. Finally, there are nonfunctional requirements to consider, such as vendor lock-in, support, compatibility, and query languages. The bottom line is that no database can excel in all dimensions at the same time. Select the solution that best matches your requirements.

The advantage of using a data product architecture is that you can add multiple designs for the specific read patterns of the various use cases.[19] You can duplicate data to support different data structures, velocities, and volumes, or to serve different representations of the same data. You could offer a file-based endpoint for ad hoc, exploratory, or analytical use cases, a relational-based endpoint to facilitate the more complex and unpredictable queries, a columnar-based endpoint for data consumers requiring heavy aggregations, or a document-based endpoint for data consumers that require a higher velocity and a semistructured data format (JSON). You could even model your data products with nodes and relationships using a graph database.

When providing different endpoints or output ports, all must be managed under the same data governance umbrella. Accountability lies with the same providing domain. The principles for reusable and read-optimized data also apply to all data product variations. Additionally, the context and semantics are expected to be the same; for example, the notion of "customer" or "customer name" should be consistent for all data that is served. The same ubiquitous language must be used for all the data products that belong to the same data provider. We'll look at how semantic consistency is ensured across all endpoints and other integration patterns in Chapter 7.

Data Serving Services

When zooming in on the user and application interactions with the data product architectures, you'll typically find that there are a large variety of data access patterns to provide. These patterns might include ad hoc querying, direct reporting, building up semantic layers or cubes, providing Open Database Connectivity (ODBC) to other

---

19 When using an enterprise data warehouse for data distribution, it's often difficult to facilitate various forms and dimensions of the data. Enterprise data warehouses are generally engineered with a single type of technology (the RDBMS database engine) and thus don't allow much room for variations.

applications, processing with ETL tools, data wrangling, or data science processing. In order to support these, it's essential to give your data product architecture sufficient performance and security functions.

 For all data-consuming services, you want to be consistent on data access and life cycle management. This is what data contracts are for; we'll discuss these in Chapter 8.

Distributed filesystems, such as cloud-based object storage, are cost-effective when it comes to storing large quantities of data but aren't generally fast enough for ad hoc and interactive queries. Many vendors have recognized this problem and offer SQL query engines or lightweight virtualization layers to solve it. The benefit of allowing queries to be executed directly against data products is that data doesn't have to be duplicated, which makes the architecture cheaper. These tools also offer fine-grained access to data, and they make the operational data store obsolete. The data that sits in a product architecture becomes a candidate for operational reporting and ad hoc analysis. Data virtualization options are good solutions, but only fit for simple reporting use cases. If this isn't sufficient, consider alternatives such as duplicating data.

File Manipulation Service

While we're discussing data duplication and the consumption of data, some domains have use cases or applications that accept only flat files (for example, CSV files) as input. For these situations, consider building a file manipulation service that automatically masks or strips out sensitive data that consumers aren't allowed to see. This service, just like all other consumption endpoints, must be hooked up to the central security model, which dictates that all data consumption must respect the data contracts (see "Data Contracts" on page 236). It also prescribes that filters must be applied automatically and are always based on metadata classifications and attributes. We'll discuss this in more detail in Chapter 8.

De-Identification Service

When directly using data products for data exploration, data science, machine learning, and sharing data with third parties, it's important to protect sensitive data from consumers. Thanks to security methods like tokenization, hashing, scrambling, and encryption, you can use rules and classifications to protect your data. Depending on how you engineer the data product architecture, you can apply the following methods:

- Protect data at runtime during consumption. This technique protects sensitive data without making any changes to the data stored, but only when data is queried. Databricks, for example, uses a feature called *dynamic view functions* (*https://oreil.ly/HYm6T*) to hide or mask data when it's being accessed.

- Obfuscate or mask sensitive data before it ever lands in a data product architecture (for example, by using tokenization). The de-identified matching then happens at the stage of consumption.

- Duplicate and process data for every project. You can customize your protection by defining which classifications and masking and filtering rules you use.

Data security relies on data governance. These two disciplines will be discussed in depth in Chapter 8.

Distributed Orchestration

The last aspect that requires design considerations and standardization is supporting teams as they implement, test, and orchestrate their data pipelines. Building and automating these data pipelines is an iterative process that involves a series of steps such as data extraction, preparation, and transformation. You should allow teams to test and monitor the quality of all their data pipelines and artifacts, and support them with code changes during the deployment process. This end-to-end delivery approach is a lot like DataOps, in that it comes with plenty of automation, technical practices, workflows, architectural patterns, and tools.

When standardizing tools and best practices, I recommend that organizations set up a centralized or platform team that supports other teams by providing capabilities for tasks like scheduling, metadata curation, logging metrics, and so on. This team should also be responsible for overseeing end-to-end monitoring, and it should step in when pipelines are broken for too long. In order to abstract away the complexity of dependencies and time interval differences from different data providers, this team can also set up an extra processing framework that can, for example, inform consumers when multiple sources with dependency relationships can be combined.

Intelligent Consumption Services

Building on all of these different capabilities, you could also extend the data product architecture with a layer (fabric) for applying intelligent data transformations upon data consumption, such as automatic profiling, filtering, aligning schemas, combining, and so on. This would enable data consumers to define the data they need and receive it already modeled into the shape they want to have it in. This type of intelligent service typically is also used to deploy a semantic layer that hides complex logic and then presents user-friendly representations to business users. It heavily utilizes metadata, including many other services that are specific to data governance.

A visionary approach would be to fuel your fabric with upcoming technologies such as semantic knowledge graphs and machine learning. Although this trend is relatively new, I give several recommendations for preparing to implement this approach in Chapter 9.

Direct Usage Considerations

A tough design consideration is whether data products should be able to act as direct sources for consuming domains, or if those domains need to extract and duplicate them. I'm talking here about persistent data transformations, which refer to the process by which data is written and stored in a new (data lake or database) location, outside the boundaries of the data product architecture. Avoiding the creation of uncontrolled data copies is preferred, but there may be situations where it's better to have a copy available nearby or inside the consuming application. For example:

- If the data product is used to create new data, logically this data needs to be stored in a new location and requires a different owner.

- If you want to reduce overall latency, it might be better to duplicate data so it's available locally, closer to the consuming application's destination. We'll take a closer look at this in Chapter 6, where you'll learn how to make fully controlled, distributed, materialized views.

- Direct and real-time data transformations might be so heavy that they degrade the user experience. For example, queries on data products might take so long that users become frustrated. Extracting, restructuring, and preprocessing data or using a faster database engine can alleviate this frustration.

- When the consuming application is of such high importance that decoupling is required to avoid data product architecture failure, it might make sense to duplicate the data.

In all of these cases, I recommend implementing a form of enterprise architecture control that dictates which approach is taken for each data product. Be aware that duplicated data is harder to clean, and it can be difficult to get insights on how the data is used. If the data can be copied without restrictions or management, it may be possible for it to be distributed further. Another potential problem is compliance with regulations such as the GDPR or CCPA; we'll discuss this in greater detail in Chapter 11.

Getting Started

A transition toward data ownership and data product development can be a cultural and technical challenge for many teams. For example, not all teams have the necessary knowledge, see the value of data, or are willing to invest in data. If you want to follow a natural evolution to data product development, consider the following best practices:

- Start small. Generate some excitement, and start with one or a few domains whose teams have bought in to the concept of data product development. Show success first, before scaling up.

- Create a consistent definition of what a data product means for your organization. Align this with the metamodel that is being used for metadata management.

- Governance is important, but take it slow. Keep a delicate balance to encourage productivity. Focus on foundational elements, such as ownership, metadata, and interoperability standards. Align with industry standards and best practices wherever possible.

- Your first data products should set an example for the rest of your domains. Put acceptance quality and design criteria in place and focus on dataset design. Resource-oriented API design is a great starting point for building high-quality data products.

- Don't try to build a platform for supporting all use cases at once. At the start, your platform will typically only support one type of data ingestion and consumption: for example, batch data movements and Parquet files as a consumption format.

- Allow centralization, next to decentralization. Your initial data product deployment doesn't have to immediately disrupt your organizational structure. Keep things central for a while before you align engineers with domains, or apply soft alignment to get engineers to work with subject matter experts. At the beginning, domain-specific datasets can be created with support from the central team.

When you're starting out, take it slow. Learn and iterate before moving on to the next stage. Centralization versus decentralization isn't all or nothing; instead, it is a constant calibration that includes nuances and periodic evaluations.

Wrapping Up

Data products are a big change in the way dependencies between domains and applications are managed. Anytime the boundaries of a functional concern or bounded context are crossed, teams should conform to the unified way of distributing data: serving data as data products to other teams. This way of working is important because fewer shared dependencies means less coordination between teams is needed.

At the beginning of this chapter, I drew a distinction between the concepts of "data as a product" and "data products." To recap, data as a product is the mindset that you apply when managing data at large. It's about creating trust, establishing governance, and applying product thinking; it's taking care of the data you value most and putting principles into practice. It's a mindset that your domain teams need to have. They must take ownership of their data, fix data-quality issues at the source, and serve data in such a way that it is useful for a large audience. Instead of a central team absorbing all the changes and integrating data, your domain teams should encapsulate the physical data model within their domain boundaries. This the opposite of throwing raw data over the fence and letting consumers work out data quality and modeling issues. Your domain teams should model and serve data in such a way that it offers a best-in-class user experience.

A data product is a concept you need to demystify for yourself. My recommendation is to begin by standardizing the way you talk about data product management in your organization, as there may be variations in the language and definitions used. Consider defining data products as logical constructs, rather than using a viewpoint that purely focuses on physical representations or the underlying technology architecture. At some point you may introduce a semantic model for your organization, so your data products become graphical representations from which you draw relationships to domains, data owners, originating applications, and physical representations. This may sound a bit too conceptual, but the benefits of managing your data products like this will become clearer when you read Chapter 9.

There's a caveat with data products. They are likely to suffer from similar issues to those seen in microservices architectures, where data is too fine-grained and disjointed, and must be pulled from hundreds of different locations. The solution to these problems is establishing good standards and a central authority that oversees all data product creation activities. Interoperability standards for data exchanges must be set. Coordination is required on changes and how data is modeled and served. Unfortunately, these activities aren't easy. As you learned, data product development has a strong relationship with data warehousing, which consists of many disciplines, such as data modeling (making data consistent, readable, discoverable, addressable, trustworthy, and secure). Some of these activities might be complex, like the historization aspects that we discussed in this chapter.

Data products and the data-as-a-product mindset are about *providing data. Consuming data* is the next stage. While certain activities and disciplines might overlap, as you'll learn in Chapter 11, the concerns of providing data and consuming data aren't the same. By managing data as products and providing the data products as domain interfaces, you eliminate dependencies and better isolate applications with contrasting concerns. This is important because fewer shared dependencies means less coordination between teams is needed.

The data product architecture should be designed collaboratively and based on the organization's needs. Provide generic blueprints to domain teams. Allow other teams to contribute or temporarily join the platform team(s). If, for example, a new consumption pattern is required, deliver it sustainably as a reusable pattern or component. The same applies for capturing and onboarding data. When scaling up and building a modern data platform, many extra self-service application components will be required: these will likely include centrally managed ETL frameworks, change data capture services, and real-time ingestion tooling.

One final and important note: data products, as discussed in this chapter, are meant for making data available. We haven't yet discussed how to make the data usable and turn it into real value. This aspect has different dynamics than data product creation and will have to wait until Chapter 11.

In the next chapter, we'll look at API architecture, which is used for service communication and for distributing smaller amounts of data for real-time and low-latency use cases.

CHAPTER 5

Services and API Management

Most organizations don't want a data mesh. Instead, they want a *data and integration mesh*: a unified approach to holistically manage both the analytical and operational planes. Why? Because there are significant benefits to gain from aligning the two planes. The operational data architecture contrasts with the analytical data architecture because the operational plane processes commands and requires predictability and real-time processing of small datasets, while the analytical plane focuses on data reads and requires complex data analysis, which uses large datasets and isn't that time-critical. However, there's a large amount of overlap in the domain model, how APIs (like data) should be treated as products, and how the boundaries between applications and domains should be set. Your business capabilities are the same when looking at your architecture through an operational or analytical lens. The applications that provide these capabilities have teams behind them that manage them and ensure they stay up and running. The language that the team uses for development is the same. Ultimately, the unique context that influenced the application design matches the context that influences the design of your data products and APIs. In addition, the shift toward loosely coupled applications and autonomous, agile teams within API management is similar to what underpins the shift toward a data mesh architecture. It therefore makes sense to apply similar best practices for data management and API management.

This chapter covers API management, service-oriented architecture (SOA), and many other real-time integration and data patterns. Not all data practitioners are familiar with API management, so in the first sections, I'll bring you up to speed on what SOA and APIs are all about. There's a whole lot that the field of data management can learn from API management! Next, we'll look at some best practices from the past decade and the scalability problems that arise when building complex layers of integration. Finally, I'll draw a parallel between domain-driven design and the management of data products, and explore how APIs must be managed in that light. By the end of this chapter, you'll have a solid grasp of the modern service-oriented architectures used to build scalability in distributed and real-time software systems. You'll also understand how this architecture fits into the bigger picture and relates to the data product architecture, which we discussed in Chapter 4.

Before we start discussing API management, you might be wondering what a chapter on API and service management is doing in book on data management. First, APIs are essential for providing access to the most accurate and up-to-date data. APIs are different from data products in that data products are copies of data, which are always asynchronous by nature. Another important reason why APIs are essential is that they're the operational interfaces to real-time analytical services, such as machine learning services. They're also used for integrating operational and analytical systems, a topic we discussed in Chapter 1. Finally, API and integration patterns play an important role when designing complex data management ecosystems (for example, integrating a data catalog or submitting data contract information).

Introducing API Management

Before we dive deeper into APIs, let's first discuss the basics of APIs and SOA, and some of the integration challenges.

APIs, or *application programming interfaces*, are what allow applications, software components, and services to communicate directly. Operational, transactional, and analytical systems that need to access each other's data or initiate processes in real time are good examples of API patterns; so is interaction with cloud companies, external companies, and social networks. APIs can also play a role when companies want to offer a rich user experience for digital channels. For example, a travel agency might want users of its website to be able to see real-time information on available flights and schedules for airline operators.

Most API communication is synchronous and uses a *request/response pattern*, in which the (service) requestor sends a request to a replier system, which receives and processes the request, ultimately returning a message in response. The requestor waits for this reply before continuing its operations. The amount of data exchanged is typically small, which makes possible the real-time communication necessary for low-latency use cases. The opposite pattern is asynchronous data communication, in which no immediate response is required to continue processing. Data that is transmitted can be delivered at different unsynchronized or intermittent intervals. APIs can also be used asynchronously and combined with event-driven processing. For example, messages that are sent by making HTTP calls to APIs can be parked in a message queue to be processed later. This subscription model is known as *publish and subscribe*, or pub/sub for short.

In this chapter, I focus on synchronous request/response communication. In Chapter 6, I'll discuss event-driven processing, queuing, and asynchronous communication, and how these patterns overlap with SOA and APIs.

API management has a strong relationship with service-oriented architecture. SOA is a modern approach to software development and application connectivity; the concept emerged over a decade ago, and it's widely used today. Although some architects and engineers say it's outdated and claim that "SOA is dead," it's actually more active than ever because of trends such as microservices, machine learning and real-time decision making, business process management, cloud APIs, open APIs (*https://oreil.ly/QEqiD*), and SaaS.

What Is Service-Oriented Architecture?

When you start reading about SOA, you'll come across many different opinions about what it is. Indeed, the author and developer Martin Fowler has said that he finds it impossible to describe SOA (*https://oreil.ly/cAN9H*) because the term means so many different things to different people.

To me, SOA is a design pattern that enables communication between applications through (web-based) services. It's about exposing *business functionality* in the form of *services* or *APIs*. SOA is also used for abstracting and hiding application complexity because with this approach, the applications (and their complexity) disappear into the background. Business functionality is provided instead.

> The Open Group introduced the term *service-oriented architecture* in 2009, in a white paper that eventually became the *SOA Source Book* (*https://oreil.ly/VdrB4*). The Open Group defines SOA as "an architectural style that supports service-orientation. Service-orientation is a way of thinking in terms of services and service-based development and the outcomes of services."

Within SOA, application communication is done via standardized protocols, such as SOAP (*https://oreil.ly/QbkfU*) or JSON (*https://oreil.ly/k4LHu*), and common software architectural styles, such as REST (introduced in the following sidebar). SOA enables real-time synchronous communication (waiting for the reply in order to continue) and asynchronous communication (not waiting).

SOA also decouples and sets clear boundaries between applications and domains. It allows applications to change independently, without the need to change other applications as well. SOA thus can be used as a strategy to develop applications faster and maintain complex application landscapes.

Resources and Operations

Representational State Transfer (REST) is an architectural style that defines a set of constraints and abstraction principles to be used for creating web services.[1] A key concept in REST is *resources* (*https://oreil.ly/lk2oo*), meaning anything that's important enough to be abstracted and referenced as a thing in itself. Resources can be any object or source of information that can be uniquely identified, such as a customer, contract, account, order, or product. For RESTful APIs, the HTTP protocol has set operations for interacting with these resources that mirror the CRUD (create, read, update, delete) database operations:

POST
> A *create* method for creating a new resource.

GET
> A *read* method for retrieving one or multiple or all resources.

PUT
> A method to *update* or replace any existing resource. For updating only specific fields within a resource, *PATCH* is more commonly used.

DELETE
> A method to *delete* a specific resource.

Where REST is the architectural style for APIs, CRUD is the interaction style for manipulating data.

Some architects and engineers argue that SOA is about supplying business functionality or processes and not so much about the data. In a way this is valid, but it's important to realize that the core element is always data. If network packages don't carry any information, communication can never be established. SOA, for this reason, is very much about the data.

Other architects and engineers argue that SOA is used only within the sphere of operational and transactional systems. I don't consider this accurate because SOA is the architecture that connects applications from the operational and analytical worlds in real time. Take, for example, a machine learning model that is trained and served to consumers as a real-time endpoint. For this you need service-to-service and, thus, API connectivity.

Another breakthrough of SOA is the abstraction: how functionality and data are encapsulated by services. Instead of applications invoking or calling each other

---

1 Roy Fielding defined REST in his 2000 PhD dissertation, "Architectural Styles and the Design of Network-Based Software Architectures" (*https://oreil.ly/J7B1r*).

directly, they exchange data or offer functionality via well-defined service interfaces using standard interoperability patterns, as illustrated in Figure 5-1. The complexity and data inside the service provider's applications stay hidden and are no longer a concern to service consumers.[2]

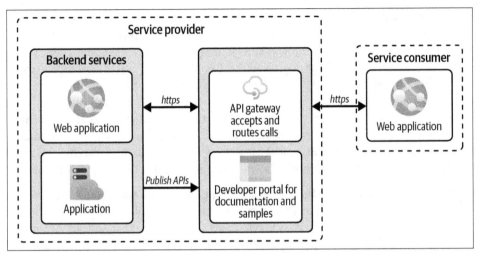

Figure 5-1. Summary of concepts relating to the creation and use of APIs

Instead of invoking the application directly, the integration of applications in SOA is managed by API management services. API calls, in this example, go via an API gateway. The API interface usually has a different structure and hides the complexity of the inner application. Data, therefore, is transformed.

SOA Terminology

The roles of service provider and consumer within SOA are similar to the data provider and consumer roles used in the previous chapters:

- The *service provider* is the application that provides a service to expose functionality and data.
- The *service consumer* is the application that consumes the service and to which the requested data is transferred.

For the sake of simplicity, I'll use *service provider* and *service consumer* in this chapter, but in future chapters, I'll switch back to *data provider* and *data consumer*.

---

2 For more on this topic, see Pat Helland's paper "Data on the Outside Versus Data on the Inside" (*https://oreil.ly/oOH6r*).

The initial aim of SOA was to make IT landscapes more flexible and provide real-time communication between applications. Prior to SOA, most enterprise application communication took place via direct client/server calls, such as remote procedure calls (RPC).[3]

The drawback of direct application-to-application communication is that it involves coupling with the underlying application runtime environment. Applications that want to communicate, for example, via RPC methods require the same client/server libraries and protocols. This doesn't allow for great application diversity because not all libraries and protocols may be available for all languages. Another drawback is compatibility. Versioning is more difficult to manage; if an application method changes, the other application also needs to change immediately because otherwise it might break. The last drawback is scalability: as the number of applications increases, the number of interfaces quickly becomes unmanageable. Typically, the same problems are seen when building point-to-point interfaces between applications.

These drawbacks are the main reasons why engineers and architects started working on a new software architecture based on higher-level abstractions and the key concepts of application frontends, services, service repositories, and service buses. Applications and their application-specific protocols in this model are hidden and expose their functionality and data via services using standard web protocols, such as HTTP. The communication and integration between applications is handled via service buses. The implementation of technologies and methodologies to facilitate this form of communication between (enterprise) applications is known as *enterprise application integration* (EAI).

Enterprise Application Integration

In the early 2000s, with use of the web growing, the *enterprise service bus* (ESB) emerged as a new enterprise application integration platform, part of SOA, to handle integration between different applications and software packages. It added new features above and beyond traditional message-oriented middleware (MOM)[4] and client/server models, such as:

---

3 RPC is similar to the client/server model; it's a pattern that lets one program use and request application functionality from another program located on another system on the network. Rather than using messages, RPC uses an interface description language (IDL) for communication between the client and server. The IDL interpreter must be implemented on both sides.

4 *Middleware*, or *message-oriented middleware* (*https://oreil.ly/Bli92*), is an umbrella term for technologies and products that support sending and receiving messages between distributed systems. The ESB can be considered middleware: it's used to route messages and support reliable processing of these messages.

Orchestrating services
> Composing several fine-grained services into a single higher-order composite service

Rule-based routing
> Receiving and distributing messages based on specified conditions

Transformation to standard message formats
> Transforming one specific data format to another (this also includes data-interchange format transformations, such as SOAP/XML to JSON)

Mediating for flexibility
> Supporting multiple versions of the same interface for compatibility

Adapting for connectivity
> Supporting a wide range of systems for communicating with the backend application and transforming data from the application format to the bus format

The ESB promotes agility and flexibility because it enables companies to more quickly deliver services using buses and adapters. It turns traditional applications into modern applications with easy interfaces. The ESB also decouples applications by providing abstractions and taking care of mediation. The adapter connects the applications and the ESB, and handles the protocol conversions between them.

To facilitate the implementation of the ESB, many software vendors began making their applications and platforms ready for SOA by modernizing their application designs. Standards-based service interfaces emerged based on World Wide Web Consortium (W3C) standards, such as Simple Object Access Protocol (SOAP) with Extensible Markup Language (XML) as the default messaging format.

What Are WSDL, XSD, and Service Repositories?

XML-based communication is typically supported by WSDL, XSD, and a service repository. Web Services Description Language (WSDL), also written in XML, is a standard used to describe a web service and its operations. It specifies the methods, location, data types, and transport protocol. It eases the work of integration and software development because a developer can develop a web service completely by just having the WSDL provided.

WSDL documents are associated with another XML-based document, called an XSD (XML Schema Definition) document. XSD documents describe the schema, which is a definition of how XML documents are structured. They can be used to ensure that a given XML document is valid and follows the rules laid out in the schema.

> XML documents are generally stored in a service repo. This is typically an XML-based registry that publishes information about what web services are available and accessible. The service repo also keeps track of versions, docs, and policies.

SOAP became popular because it uses the Hypertext Transfer Protocol (HTTP) for network communication and has a similar solid structure to HyperText Markup Language (HTML), which is used to build websites. These same HTML and HTTP standards were and still are the foundation for today's internet communication. Based on these communication standards, the ESB acts as a transformation and integration broker, providing universal connectivity between the service providers and service consumers.

 ESBs, within SOA, can become complex monoliths. I'll come back to this in "Parallels with Enterprise Data Warehousing Architecture" on page 155, in reference to making the comparison with enterprise data warehousing.

Besides transforming message formats and giving applications a modern communication jacket, the ESB also provides variations of communication in cases where more complex collaboration is required. Two of them are service orchestration and service choreography. I'll discuss these in detail in the next sections because they make SOA more complex and challenging.

Service Orchestration

Within SOA, the roles of the service provider and service consumer are sometimes obscured when multiple services are combined, which may be done for efficiency, maintainability, or coordination. Integration is often complex and can occur in different ways. The first pattern we'll look at is *service aggregation*, in which multiple services are combined, wrapped together, and exposed as a single, larger service. This can be useful to reduce the pain of management and satisfy the needs of (one or multiple) service consumers. The aggregator in this scenario is responsible for coordinating, invoking, and combining the different services.

Service aggregation requires *service orchestration*, the coordination and execution of tasks to combine and integrate different services.[5] This is commonly done for technical reasons, such as combining, splitting, transforming, inspecting, and discarding

---

5 Some people also use the term *service composition*. Service composability principles encourage designing services in such a way that they can be easily reused in multiple solutions, meaning that existing services can be used to create new services. While service composition denotes the fact that services are combined, it doesn't elaborate on how this is done.

data. The service orchestration process can be short-running, making fairly straight-forward combinations, in cases where a simple service flow across services is needed.[6] For example, in order to get all of a customer's contracts, another customer's product service has to be called first. It can also be long-running, combining services into a more complex flow that requires decision logic and different execution paths. Although service orchestration isn't explicit about the duration, people predominantly use the term in the context of long(er)-running services. Service orchestration requires some disambiguation because it can be done for different reasons.

Should You Orchestrate Using the ESB or on the Consuming Side?

There are two approaches to combining and integrating services. The first is to use the aggregation services of the ESB, which allow consumers to retrieve all the data with a single call. The ESB plays the role of the orchestrator and does all the heavy lifting that comes with it. Consequently, in this scenario the ESB becomes the single point of failure.

The alternative approach is to let the consuming application play the role of orchestrator. In this case, the application must manage the order of calls and combine (integrate) the results.

Both approaches have pros and cons. The benefit of letting the ESB take care of the orchestration is that it promotes reusability of orchestration or business logic and makes data consumption easier. One drawback is that the ESB has to offer adequate performance in combining all the logic. A far bigger drawback is that the role of the service provider becomes more obscure because service aggregation acts as a facade over the different services. Aggregated services typically combine different services from different owners, so no one true owner can guarantee the integrity of the aggregation service.

Having the consuming application handle the orchestration has the advantage of flexibility, but it's less efficient because every consumer needs to implement this itself.

Another common reason for orchestration is business process management (BPM). The processes in this situation contain business logic and are typically long-running. The coordination needed to manage the series of steps requires the process status (state) of every step to be stored, and thus persisted in a database. Long-running business processes are interruptible and can wait for other processes (or human tasks) to finish. They are, in general, asynchronous, so for these types of processes

---

6 *Service flows*, also called *microflows*, are noninterruptible and generally run in a single thread and in only one transaction. They're short in duration and typically use synchronous services only. The process state usually isn't persisted.

the service orchestration pattern is typically accommodated with visual and intuitive BPM software for managing complex workflows and longer-running processes.

 The process layer of the BPM software holds all the information about the data exchange flow between applications and services: the sequence information, dependencies, status, tasks, rules, waiting times, etc. You should *never* store application data in such a process layer; this is a common mistake. BPM software isn't meant for managing application data. Use the BPM API to start processes and retrieve information about the status of the workflow. Don't use it for storing data about customers, products, or contracts because it hasn't been designed for this purpose.

BPM is typically used when you need to orchestrate (long-running) processes across different applications from various domains. It helps domains to separate their business processes from their business application logic. However, when orchestrating processes and data within the application boundaries, it's better to do it individually, within the application itself.

When BPM is managing long-running processes, the nature of processing is typically asynchronous. BPM manages all the dependencies, keeps track of the individual state of each process, and knows when to trigger, retrieve, and store data. The APIs that are used to invoke or call the processes are therefore sometimes called *process APIs*.

Service orchestration is often incorrectly mixed with other types of orchestration. In the context of service-oriented architecture, orchestration is about invoking and executing operational and functional processes needed to deliver an end-to-end service. Typically, this form of orchestration uses application APIs and can be managed by BPM software.

Here are some examples of other forms of orchestration, which include scheduling, automated configuration, and coordination:

- Scheduling processes in operating systems (e.g., cron in Unix-like systems).
- Scheduling processes and tasks within the application boundaries (e.g., internal/native application schedulers).
- Data orchestration for automating data processing (e.g., data movements, data preparation, and ETL processes). Apache Airflow is a common tool for these types of activities.
- Scheduling and orchestrating infrastructure (e.g., provisioning virtual machines, shutting down systems, etc.).

Another form of orchestration is continuous integration/continuous delivery (CI/CD): the automated process of monitoring, building, testing, releasing, and integrating software. This form of orchestration typically uses and combines other forms of orchestration.

Service Choreography

Another pattern that obscures the roles of service providers and consumers is *service choreography*, which refers to the global distribution of process interaction and business logic to independent parties collaborating to achieve some business end. With service choreography, the decision logic is distributed; each service observes the environment and acts autonomously. There's no centralized orchestrator, like with BPM, and no party has total control over the other parties' processes. Each party is responsible for its own part of the overall process. With service choreography, as you can see in Figure 5-2, requests go back and forth in a sort of ping-pong fashion between different service providers and consumers. The logic that controls the interactions between the services sits outside the central platform. The services themselves decide who to call next and in what specific order.

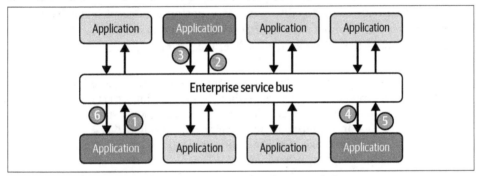

Figure 5-2. Service choreography is a decentralized approach for service participation and communication

Service choreography, aggregation, and orchestration can also be combined. Several services and processes can be managed centrally, while others can independently trigger workflows in other aggregated services. In all situations the roles of the service provider and consumer are obscured, since no domain can guarantee the overall integrity of the interaction.

 Martin Fowler suggests an interesting pattern for applications that communicate and depend on information from other applications in his post "Event Collaboration" (*https://oreil.ly/ajRx-*). Instead of making requests when data is needed, applications raise events when things change. Other applications listen to these events and react appropriately. This is very much in line with the event-driven architecture, which we'll discuss in Chapter 6.

In the last couple of sections, I've mainly focused on services through the lens of process interaction and aggregation. In the next section, we'll explore another way of distinguishing services, by observing the context in which they operate.

Public Services and Private Services

Services target many different objectives. Therefore, a lot of people classify SOA services into types, such as public and private.[7] *Public services*, sometimes referred to as *business services*, deliver specific business functionality. They're required and contribute to solving a specific business problem. These services often group data or logic and represent that in a way that is meaningful to the business. Other services, sometimes called *process services*, initiate a process, trigger a business workflow, or touch on behavioral aspects. Business services tend to be abstract, are the authority for specific business functionality, and operate across application boundaries.

Private services, or *technical services*, are services that don't necessarily represent business functionalities. They're used as part of the internal logic and provide technical data or infrastructure functionality, such as exposing a table of a database as is. Private services can be input for public services. In that case, they're often wrapped into another service that will eventually deliver the business functionality.

> Some people use the terms *infrastructure services* or *platform services*, which are services that abstract the infrastructure concerns from the domains. These services are typically standardized across an organization and involve functionalities that apply to all domains, such as authentication, authorization, monitoring, logging, debugging, or auditing.

Private services in general have a higher degree of coupling since they're less agnostic and don't abstract to a business problem. Some argue that these services shouldn't be published in the central repository or shared between domains because they aren't suited to a wide audience and operate only within application boundaries.

Service Models and Canonical Data Models

When connecting different applications, engineers and developers need a common understanding of the data models and business functionality that different services provide. This is what service models and canonical data models are for. A *service model* describes what the service interface looks like and how the data and its entities, relationships, and attributes are modeled. Depending on its richness, it may

---

7 OpenAPIHub (*https://oreil.ly/xiHZ2*), for example, uses the classifications Public API, Private API, and Partner API.

also include definitions, dependencies with other services, version numbers, syntax, protocols, and other information, such as the application owners, production status, and so on.

The goal of a service model is to provide information that makes it easier to use and integrate services. It's typically platform-agnostic and doesn't try to describe the system. Service models are used in different scopes and exist in different formats. Some exist only in documentation and describe the most used context; others live in tools as code and describe the data and all its attributes and protocols.

Canonical data models differ from service models in that they aim to define services and languages in a standard and unified manner. While service models stay closer to the application, canonical models are used to align and standardize the various service models. Some people desire to apply unification across all services, using a global schema. As a result, canonical models tend to be large and complex.

Parallels with Enterprise Data Warehousing Architecture

The combination of the ESB, aggregation, layering of services, and central canonical data model make traditional SOA implementations more complicated than necessary. Indeed, they face many of the same challenges as enterprise data warehousing architectures.

Canonical model size

The first similarity is the scale at which canonical models are used. Many organizations try to use one single enterprise canonical model to describe *all* services. The enterprise canonical model requires cross-coordination between all the different teams and parties involved. Services in this approach typically end up with tons of optional attributes because everyone insists on seeing their unique requirements reflected. The end result is a monster interface model that compromises to include everybody's needs but isn't specific to anyone; it's so generic that nobody can tell what exactly the services deliver or do. A similar problem is observed with enterprise data warehouses, as discussed in "The Enterprise Data Warehouse: A Single Source of Truth" on page 14.

ESB as wrapper for legacy middleware

The next similarity is the layering and aggregating of services, commonly seen within large legacy middleware platforms and ESBs. Many of these architectures still exist today; they do a large part of the message routing, integration, transformation, and process orchestration, including managing and persisting process state. Some enterprises encapsulate these legacy middleware systems with more modern technologies. The complexity is abstracted, opening the way for more modern communication, such as using JSON instead of RPC. Providing the ancient middleware with a new jacket increases complexity, however, because you've created layers on top of layers (Figure 5-3). This could potentially mean that even a small change leads to a cascading effect of other changes.

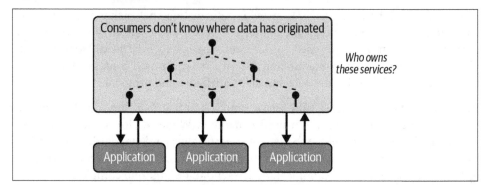

Figure 5-3. Layering services on top of other services decreases transparency

Before you know it, there's a complex flow of service calls. Services are called without knowing exactly where data is coming from or what other services or processes are being initiated, and often no one is willing to take ownership of these services. The same often happens with BPM: technical orchestration and process orchestration are mixed, or all domain and process logic is brought together centrally, making it hard to oversee what processes belong together.

ESB managing application state

The last similarity I want to point out is that the ESB has become a state (data) store for multiple applications.[8] Rather than taking care of the state in the application or a business process management capability, the ESB is used to orchestrate long-running business processes or, even worse, to persist the state that belongs to applications. The ESB becomes a database. The risk of this approach is tight coupling. If the ESB goes down for whatever reason, the state is lost, and all the processes might lose their actual status. Another potential risk is when applications change: if a change is required to the state as well and all applications rely on the state persisted in the ESB, careful cross-coordination is required to safely make all of the changes. The ESB, in principle, should be stateless, except for temporary session management and caching.

---

8 *State management* refers to the management of the state of applications, such as user inputs, process statuses, and so on.

A Modern View of API Management

ESB integration platforms made SOA more complex than it should be. Enterprises took the "E" in ESB literally and implemented monoliths to take care of all the service integration. Central teams dictated what good reusability and design of services would be, and the heavy cross-communication impeded innovation and team agility.

Meanwhile, the modularity of applications and design has been changing with the rise of microservices, and today it's incredibly fast and easy to build APIs using modern services. Thinking about the digital ecosystem, the cloud, SaaS, and the API economy spread APIs outside boundaries of enterprises. Modern databases and applications support RESTful APIs out of the box. Not surprisingly, a new view on SOA is needed.

Federated Responsibility Model

Based on these trends and the need to break up the centralized ESB-based architecture, what should our new API architecture look like? Instead of using the central model, the responsibility of building and exposing services will be given back to the underlying domains. Just like with data product management, you should follow a federated model: domains can then evolve at their own speed without holding up other domains.

In this federated operating model, responsibility for business logic, executing processes, persisting data, and validating context also goes back to the domains. Use of the ESB as a (centralized) integration platform must be discouraged; aggregation and orchestration should be allowed only within the boundaries of a domain. The federated model also impacts the design of APIs: the same user-friendly design principles from data product creation will apply here. Similarly, APIs, just like data products, must be developed using the domain language.

For API management, we can establish some additional principles:

- Expose business functionality or data using the REST resource model (described in the following sidebar) instead of complex systems. This requires a lot of work and focuses on understanding business concepts and their properties, naming relationships properly, designing schemas accordingly, getting the identities and uniqueness right, and so on.

- Optimize as close as possible to the data and avoid heavy orchestration in the API layer. For example, use self-hosted API gateway instances if applications and APIs are hosted on-premises.[9]

---

9 The Azure API Management documentation (*https://oreil.ly/XdCJo*) outlines some additional considerations for managing self-hosted instances.

- Keep domain logic in the domain.

- Build services for consumers using the right level of granularity.[10]

- Simplify and use modern community standards.

- Allow service orchestration (combining multiple API endpoints into one) only within the boundaries of the domain (bounded context).

- Use domain identifiers consistently so that domains can identify the interconnections between resources.

Resource-Oriented Architecture

Within software engineering there's a pattern called *resource-oriented architecture* (ROA) (*https://oreil.ly/N2L88*). ROA is a specific set of guidelines for a RESTful architecture. Data is modeled into collections of homogeneous subject areas or resources, so what logically belongs together is grouped together into a collection or resource. Each resource is an entity that can be identified using a URI. For example, the resource *customers* is used to return all relevant information about customers, which might include names, addresses, and contact information. The data resources in this pattern are noun-oriented and should be self-discoverable and self-explainable as well. (SOA, by contrast, is typically verb-oriented.)

Following these guidelines will help make your API architecture scalable. It allows domains to stay decoupled while leveraging other services without performing too much repeatable work. To facilitate this way of working, a more lightweight integration service must be considered.

API Gateway

With RESTful APIs and the modernization trends in applications, communication and service integration between applications started to change. REST (*https://oreil.ly/9RKWZ*), introduced in "Resources and Operations" on page 146, is an architectural pattern used in modern web-based applications to communicate statelessness. It's based on simplicity: resources—simple represented chunks of related information—are identified by uniform resource identifiers (URIs) and can be connected with hypermedia links.[11] It also uses HTTP with uniform interface methods. RESTful APIs

---

10 Filipe Ximenes and Flávio Juvenal have written a blog post (*https://oreil.ly/sEEyW*) about how RESTful APIs can represent resources that are correctly formatted, linked, and versioned.

11 HATEOAS (Hypermedia as the Engine of Application State) is used to link REST resources. You can find a tutorial on this on the REST API Tutorial website (*https://oreil.ly/BnfAg*).

became popular due to their interoperability and flexibility and are used in websites, mobile apps, games, and more.

 RESTful APIs commonly use CRUD (create, read, update, delete) actions that map to the primitive operations to be performed in a database or data repository. You typically directly handle records or data objects. *REST*, on the other hand, operates on resource representations, each one identified by a URL. These are typically not data objects but complex high-level abstractions.

For example, a resource can be a customer's contract. This resource isn't only a record in a "contract" table but also encompasses the relationships with the "customer" resource, the "agreement" that contract is attached to, and perhaps some other content.

As RESTful APIs became popular, the message formats and protocols started to change as well. The SOAP protocol, with its relatively large XML message format, changed to JSON, which is faster because of its minimal, lightweight syntax. Additionally, JSON messages can be easily cached or stored, for example, in a key/value database. This means API and integration platforms can store data that has been previously requested, then serve that data on demand.

 RESTful APIs, in some cases, can be obfuscated with additional layers or intermediaries for carrying out instructions without exposing their position in the hierarchy to the consumer. This is typically a requirement for providing enhanced scalability (caching and load balancing) and security.

Modern applications and changes in protocols and message designs also started to influence the API architecture. A more lightweight integration component emerged, known as the *API gateway*. An API gateway doesn't have the overhead of adapters or the complex integration functionality of the ESB but still allows encapsulation and provides the management capabilities to control, secure, manage, and report on API usage. It's usually part of API management software that has two components: a developer portal for giving developers access to documentation, code samples, and the list of available APIs, and an API gateway component for accepting HTTP calls and routing these to the underlying services or applications. For the deployment of the API gateway itself, different approaches can be used. Smaller organizations typically deploy a single API gateway instance, at the edge of a data center or in the cloud. Larger organizations typically deploy multiple instances at various locations (within domain teams, organizational departments, or regions).

API as a Product

With the new decoupling patterns clarified, we can take a critical look at the role of the ESB. Only in cases of heavy lifting will the ESB be required; for all other use cases, the API gateway is better positioned. Consequently, the ESB will be used solely to solve the problem of legacy system modernization and heavy technical integration. By discouraging usage of a central integration layer, we force the domains to take a more critical look at their applications and the way services and data are exposed. Domains are encouraged to see and manage their APIs as their products. This implies several considerations, which we'll examine in the next sections.

Composite Services

When managing APIs as products within the boundaries of a domain, special attention must be given to designing composite or aggregation services.[12] Composite APIs, as seen in Figure 5-4, are APIs that often execute a series of REST API requests in a single call. These might be required, for example, when a consumer needs combined data from two systems: say, customers and orders. When building composite services that aggregate, strive to push as much of the integration and transformation logic as possible to the consumers. This forces consuming domains to take ownership of any consumer-specific business and integration logic. For example, when composite services involve complex business logic, you can handle this by deploying additional components or microservices within the boundaries of the domain. So, the party that owns the business logic and corresponding context is also the the party that must own the component and corresponding API. The API gateway, in this collaboration model, has a limited role in the flow of routing API calls. It only validates whether the request and origin are valid.

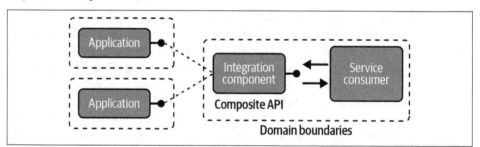

Figure 5-4. With composite services, integration and transformation logic is pushed to the consuming side

---

12 The Azure documentation (*https://oreil.ly/qvafu*) contains a concrete and simple example of a gateway aggregation NGINX service using Lua.

When multiple domains are involved in composite services, careful attention must be paid to consistency, integrity, and security. It's important to register each underlying service in a central repository so domains know what dependencies they might have with other domains. Speaking of that, I don't encourage building composite services on top of other composite services because the orchestration might end up in a chaotic web of calls from one API to another. With respect to security, keep the rule structure and decision logic as close as possible to the originating domain. Other domains shouldn't be able to overrule it or give a higher priority to local rules.

API Contracts

When multiple teams are working on the same API, it's crucial for all of them to agree on the specifications and design. This is where API or service contracts come in.[13]

An API or service contract is a document that captures how the API is designed (structure, protocol, version, methods, etc.) and can be used for setting up agreements between service providers and service consumers.[14] A common standard for creating API contracts is the *OpenAPI Specification* (*https://oreil.ly/elI7o*) (formerly known as the *Swagger Specification*). The benefit of documenting these contracts in code is that both humans and systems can interpret the specifications. Service providers can also receive test procedures from the service consumers, so any changes can be tested to validate whether the service breaks.

API Discoverability

Just like a catalog for data products, I recommend keeping track of services by using a service registry or developer portal. A *service registry* is a tool that stores all critical API information in a central repository. It promotes reuse of services and provides essential information about ownership, versioning, changes, usage, and so on.

Microservices

Now that we've broken up our complex and tightly integrated service-oriented architecture by promoting the decoupling of services from domains, we're ready for a new trend: microservices. We touched on this in Chapter 2, but it's a useful pattern for breaking down applications into smaller, more manageable parts. Some people like to use the term *loosely coupled services*, which immediately shows you the overlap with SOA.

---

13 The Azure API Management DevOps Resource Kit (*https://oreil.ly/uOK71*) is a great repository with examples of setting up API DevOps with Azure API Management.

14 Martin Fowler goes in depth about what advantages consumer-driven contracts offer (*https://oreil.ly/Qcn-3*).

Functions

Function as a service (FaaS), or just *functions*, is another model of how microservices architectures can be designed. It's a relatively new category of cloud computing services via which individual functions—actions, or pieces of business logic—are deployed and executed. FaaS allows engineers to develop, run, and manage application functionalities without the complexity of building and maintaining the infrastructure typically associated with this process. In this compute model, functions are spun up on demand, with a pay-per-use license. This model of hiding infrastructure is also known as *serverless*.[15]

Each function typically has an API that corresponds to that function. The APIs in this model are needed to invoke or wake functions up. The guiding principles for these functions and corresponding APIs are the same as for other APIs. When used internally, within the domain boundaries, functions are allowed to be consumed directly. When domain boundaries are crossed, serverless APIs must be owned, contracted, and registered in the API repository.

Although the functions are often camouflaged by the API gateway, there's significant overlap with event-driven architectures (which we'll discuss in Chapter 6). Serverless functions typically run asynchronously because they can be slow. In cloud computing, the majority of the fast resources are reserved for expensive, or compute-intensive, applications. The remaining "cheap" compute resources are allocated to the serverless functions. Consequently, they don't have very predictable response times. Asynchronous functions can use message queues to store their results and wait for other processes (functions) to pick them up.

Service Mesh

In Chapter 2, we discussed using a service mesh for communication between microservices. Abstractly, a service mesh works similarly to an API gateway, although there are some subtle differences. Both handle decoupling, monitoring, discovery, routing, authentication, and throttling. The main difference is in internal service-to-service communication. Communication within the service mesh isn't routed externally but stays within the internal service boundaries in the environment in which the microservices operate.

Just like an API gateway, a service mesh is implemented using two services: a control plane and a data plane. The *control plane* is the service in which you define routing,

---

15 *Serverless* doesn't mean that there aren't any servers. It's a cloud computing execution model. With serverless, all the infrastructure details are masked from the user. Martin Fowler describes this well (*https://oreil.ly/y2PnK*).

policies, security, and so on. The *data plane* is the service in which the routing occurs and policies and security are enforced.

To see how the microservices architecture fits into the more comprehensive API architecture, take a look at Figure 5-5. In this figure, we see three different API patterns:

- At the top sit the modern applications, which can be exposed directly via the API gateway. In this pattern the application uses modern communication protocols, such as REST/JSON.

- In the middle are the legacy applications, which require additional decoupling via the ESB. The ESB service can be wrapped into the API gateway.

- At the bottom sit the microservices. Microservices communicate internally via the service mesh. APIs, which need to be exposed externally, are decoupled via the API gateway.

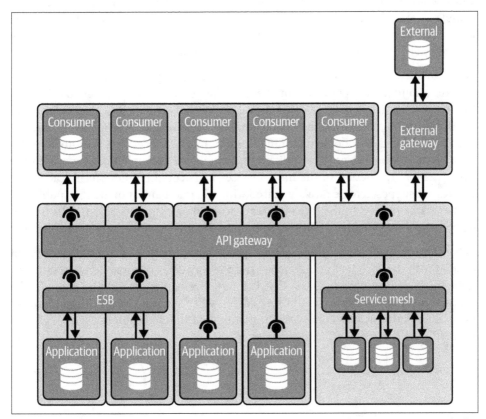

Figure 5-5. API architecture doesn't exclude microservices, nor do microservices exclude API architecture

You might wonder if you always need both a service mesh and an API gateway. As of today, the best practice is to use them side by side because of the architectural differences between the two. A service mesh is a dedicated infrastructure layer that manages service-to-service communication within only microservice-based architectures. It is typically implemented as a microservice. You could use it for enterprise decoupling, but I wouldn't recommend it as your only option because not all domains use microservices. A pragmatic solution for decoupling a microservices-based domain from a domain that doesn't use microservices is to deploy an API gateway, which runs as a standalone component.

Microservice Domain Boundaries

Another concern when managing microservices is the logical boundaries placed around the microservices of the service providers and consumers. If many microservices are running on the same platform, it's important to draw logical lines. Scoping and decomposing services is important because this helps domains manage their complexity and dependencies with other domains. The domain-driven design model is used for setting the boundaries on the services. If the bounded context changes, the boundary changes as well, and services must be decoupled.

When following this logic, you could end up decoupling a microservice twice. The first decoupling takes place within the boundaries of the domain, on the level of the internal service-to-service communication: one microservice is decoupled from another microservice within the same domain. The second decoupling takes place on the level of domain-to-domain communication: microservices that want to communicate with microservices from a different domain are decoupled once more. In the first situation, the design of the microservices APIs could be more technical. These APIs aren't supposed to be directly shared with other domains, nor are they published in the service catalog. In the case of domain-to-domain communication, APIs have to be optimized for consumers, so read-optimized design principles have to be followed.

When setting these domain boundaries, you might observe that there is significant overlap with data product management and the way data is shared between different domains. Business logic and data that is internal remains internal and shouldn't be exposed to other domains. In all other cases—when crossing domain boundaries—many different principles come into the picture and should be applied with regard to how APIs are designed and registered.

Ecosystem Communication

In Chapter 1, I mentioned that many organizations are exploring new API- and web-based business models. Companies across industries have concluded that they have to work closely together with other digital companies to expand, innovate, disrupt, or just be competitive. This trend is expected to continue and will force your architecture to make a clear split between *internal* (service) communication with consumers and *external* (service) communication with consumers.[16] There are three important reasons for this:

- The language organizations use internally is under control of the company, but externally, this isn't often the case. The format and structure of how APIs are designed is often dictated by other parties or by regulation. The revised Payment Services Directive (PSD2), for example, forces banks in the European banking sector to strictly organize their APIs by accounts, counterparties, transactions, etc. As a consequence, additional translation is often required when reusing existing internal services.

- APIs that are exposed to the public web require additional attention because external parties aren't always trusted or known. To secure your APIs safely, they need to be monitored and throttled and have identity service providers for safe access.

- You might want to throttle (limit the number of calls) based on the commercial agreements you make. Commercially provided external APIs often have a consumption plan and are billed based on the number of API calls. API monitoring can be different because you need to distinguish between different API users.

The external and public web service communication might require an additional API layer in your architecture that sits between internal services and external consumers. It's needed to perform two types of mediation: mediation between the external service provider and internal corporate environment, and mediation within the corporate environment itself.

Can the internal and external abstraction be implemented within the same API layer? Technically, you could use a single API to route both the internal and external traffic. However, an important consideration here is your API business strategy. The success of open APIs depends on their ability to attract external developers. The goal of using them is to develop valuable applications that developers and users actually want to use. An additional layer of abstraction would allow for faster innovation because it would decrease the coupling with the internal environment.

---

16 Here, internal doesn't refer to *internal* application APIs. In this case, *internal* means within the organizational or enterprise boundaries.

Another reason to separate internal corporate communication from external traffic is the different security controls on the external environment. External traffic usually requires additional logging, DDoS protection (*https://oreil.ly/OjLEU*), different identity providers, and so on.

External APIs and ecosystem communication are expected to have a great impact on your API strategy because they require you to distinguish between internal and external service communication. Another objective that will impact your architecture is channel communication, which is about delivering a rich customer experience. We'll look at that next.

Experience APIs

APIs are also used to deliver a rich customer experience via web-based or omni-channels (*https://oreil.ly/5vu6g*), where communication happens with customers and content is provided to other business parties. APIs in such a scenario can be distinguished from other APIs because they're used for direct communication with end users, and therefore should be treated differently. In this case, it's more about human interaction than system-to-system interaction. This interaction can take place via websites, mobile devices, chatbots, games, videos, and speech recognition systems. Because the online channels are often the trademark of the company, it's important to offer a great user interface and experience, which requires additional components in the architecture for entitlement checks, request handling and validation, state management, caching, web security, and so on. These components are typically part of a "digital experience" domain.

The reason for managing these components in a different domain, close to the end user, is that improving the user experience is a dedicated activity in itself. Web application security, such as form validation, is different from API security. The user experience also needs to be fast, which can drastically change the way API interaction and caching is done. Making lots of API calls to server-side resources can significantly slow down the user experience. A simple pick list of countries is better stored in a dedicated (cached) component, close to the end users, than retrieved over the network via the API gateway every time it's needed. You want to make fewer calls and be more efficient in what you retrieve. This means that you need to extend your architecture with an additional set of features.

GraphQL

A typical component for providing a uniform API experience is a GraphQL service (*https://oreil.ly/JB4OA*). GraphQL works as an additional layer over existing APIs. It uses a query language for selecting exactly the fields you want to have from multiple APIs. GraphQL can be a good solution for real-time extraction of vast amounts of data from different systems.

GraphQL allows *schema federation* (*https://oreil.ly/zeyJy*), or organizing your schemas as a single data graph to provide a unified interface for querying all of your backing data sources. Again, don't fall into the trap of creating an enterprise data model or a central gateway model. If you want to know more about this, I encourage you to read *Visual Design of GraphQL Data: A Practical Introduction with Legacy Data and Neo4j* by Thomas Frisendal (Apress).

The GraphQL services in an API architecture can be deployed only within a domain, or as a capability for domain-to-domain communication. In the latter setup, all of the principles discussed in Chapter 2 should be followed: all GraphQL endpoints should follow the same design and governance principles.

Backend for Frontend

Another way to improve the user experience and meet frontend clients' needs is to handle user interface– and experience-related logic processing with an additional layer or additional components.[17] You can optimize this layer for specific frontends. Mobile or single-page applications, for example, could have different optimizations and require different components than desktop-based web traffic. You may want to utilize GraphQL in this layer.

As you've seen, there are various patterns and considerations for letting domains interact via APIs. To help you along and show how several aspects come together, in th next section I'll present a high-level API architecture that illustrates how different domains interact. After we've walked through this example, we take a brief look at the role of metadata within API management.

Practical Example

In the next few years, enterprises will deliver innumerable new applications. APIs are at the heart of these. APIs allow for modern "front doors" and enable rich integration between applications. To ensure scalability, you should apply domain-oriented design to your architecture. Ideally, each team takes ownership of its application(s) and delivers a set of APIs for enabling seamless consumption by other domains.

The architecture that you see in Figure 5-6 uses several patterns that we've discussed throughout this chapter. For domains A, B, and C, the principles are the same. They each use an API gateway for publishing their APIs. These API gateways are under the

---

17 Sam Newman describes the design philosophy of leveraging services and applying optimizations and abstractions without the services having a common representation or being bound to each other as "backends for frontends" (*https://oreil.ly/cxfW6*).

control of API governance, ensuring all security standards and other principles are followed.

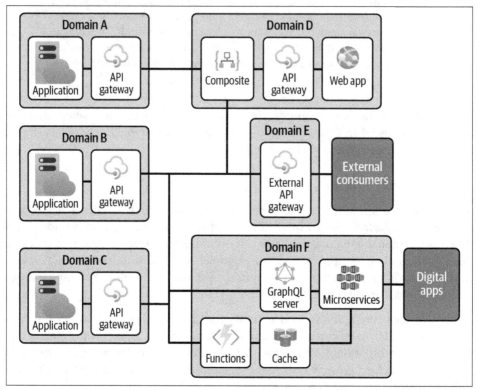

Figure 5-6. Example API architecture showing how different domains are offering and utilizing APIs from other domains

 The architecture described here has been simplified for this explanation. In reality, there will be firewalls, load balancers, application gateways, virtual networks, and so on.

Domains D, E, and F are consuming domains. They use APIs to deliver value or foster collaborative innovation with other parties. As you can see in Figure 5-6, each domain utilizes APIs in a different way. For instance, domain D has developed a composite API to execute a series of requests as a single request. The newly created endpoint is used within a web-based application by the domain itself. Domain E uses an external API gateway pattern. This additional layer is needed for translating and securing APIs for external consumers. Domain F is a larger domain that delivers a rich experience to online customers. It may provide features like virtual agents, chatbots, analytical services, and so on. The architecture of domain F applies a microservices design with a cache for storing session state information. The same store is used for enriching data with information from other domains. There are functions that call other APIs and then store the results in the caching store. This approach allows for an even richer customer experience. Finally, a GraphQL service is used for narrowing down the requests to other domains.

Although the architecture looks simple, it's critically important that all the architecture principles and guidelines laid out so far are followed. For example, all domain boundaries must be clearly set and complex logic must be hidden away behind the API gateway. The same applies for managing the logic where it belongs. In the case of the composite API, logic is needed for building up the sequence of API calls. Since this involves particular business knowledge, it's best to manage this composite component within the domain boundaries of the domain that takes ownership of this knowledge. The same principles must also be applied for publishing and registering APIs; this accelerates adoption and simplifies learning.

Metadata Management

Metadata management is an important aspect of API management. As your number of APIs grows, it's essential to support your domains with finding services, which improves reusability. A best practice is to publish all APIs, including attributes and descriptions, in a central repository or development portal. Commercial API management platforms typically have such a repository, but if you don't want to use a commercial vendor, an open source API management solution also works. OpenAPI.Tools (*https://openapi.tools*) maintains a long list of high-quality, modern open source tooling. It's also a good idea to use the OpenAPI Initiative's (*https://www.openapis.org*) vendor-neutral format for describing APIs. Many organizations use this standard for building, documenting, versioning, and testing APIs.

Microservices and Metadata

Do you need metadata for providing insights about your microservices? Absolutely! Thousands of microservices can run on a large-scale platform. It's important to know who owns what service, what it does, and what data it produces. To let microservices announce themselves, you might want to consider adding metadata labels to the runtime, or invoke an API call after a microservice is deployed. To make it easier for the teams, you can make the API call part of the container base images. Another way to help teams is to provide code snippets or skeleton templates.

It's especially important to keep track of all APIs in a distributed environment where multiple API gateways, ESBs, and service meshes are deployed. This only works if each integration capability is connected to the central repository. Doing so lets you know which services belong to which domains and which domains are interacting. Having this insight is a great advantage for managing the overall landscape.

Read-Oriented APIs Serving Data Products

APIs don't stand alone; they can be used within a data product architecture as well. For example, you can use them to provide real-time access to read-only data, implementing the CQRS (see "What Is CQRS?" on page 104) pattern for real-time communication. You could even separate strongly consistent data reads from eventually consistent data reads within the same boundary. Let me explain how this works. The API gateway in such a design acts a router by distributing API calls to the operational system or data product architecture. To make this concrete, in such a design all the eventually consistent read requests, such as "GET rest/v1/resources/1," will be routed to the read store. All commands, such as "POST rest/v1/resources," will be routed to the command store. Your consumers, when using such a design, won't notice the difference. All they need to know is the endpoint for communication. The intelligent routing happens inside the providing domain.

An alternative data product design is to deploy read-oriented microservices that act as caches from which data is directly consumed. Each microservice in such a design holds a particular data product in its own data store and serves it from an API endpoint. You can draw a parallel with resource-oriented architecture, in which each microservice caches data for one particular resource. Again, the API gateway does the segregation between all commands and queries. Such a design of using read-oriented microservices is close to how the data mesh architecture envisions a data product.

As you learned in Chapter 4, with CQRS you can greatly improve the scalability and performance of your architecture, optimizing to handle queries more efficiently. This also works in a distributed environment, where the operational system sits on one side of the network and the query part on the other side. When the query load is very high, CQRS is the only way to tackle read-intensive data challenges.

Wrapping Up

In a rapidly changing enterprise landscape, you can think of API management and the best practices described in this chapter as a way to refresh your API strategy. The fundamentals of service-oriented architecture remain, but with clearer responsibilities, modern patterns and principles, stronger alignment with data management, and a more flexible architecture. When you plan on transitioning to an API-first strategy, consider adopting the following best practices:

- Build an API strategy and align this with your business architecture. Review the usage within each business capability and show which business capabilities integrate with which other business capabilities.

- Developing the design and structure of your APIs is an important architectural activity. Align your API design with data product design when defining APIs for collaboration with other domains. Remember that the underlying application database for APIs and data products is always the same!

- Separate guidance for APIs meant for internal-application development from APIs meant for collaboration with other domains. Internal APIs, for example, can be technical, while APIs offered to other domains should stable, self-explanatory, and easy to consume.

- Set standards for platforms and services and align these with the scope and roles the APIs play. For example, APIs facing external service consumers must be published on a different API gateway that better matches the increased security requirements.

- Publish guidelines and best practices for API design. Make your API community the owner of this content.

- Pay attention to microservices architectures. Consider adding boundaries rather than leaving teams to face the complexity of hundreds of services.

- Pay great attention to composite APIs because they can make your architecture complex and tightly coupled.

Because of their REST design, using APIs is also a great way to go distributed with all of your data. You can deploy multiple API gateways and service meshes at the same time, potentially with each team or domain using its own API gateway for providing its services. You can stay in control by using metadata repositories that hold information about which services are available and how they're consumed.

The modularity and request/response model of the API architecture also allow highly modular microsolutions for specific use cases. This makes the architecture highly scalable. The caveat here is that you must follow the same design principles discussed in Chapter 2 for the domain architecture. APIs should be seen as products used to generate, send, and receive data in real time. They must be owned and optimized for readability and easy consumption. They should use the domain's ubiquitous language and shouldn't incorporate business logic from other domains.

In the next chapter, we'll focus on asynchronous messaging and event-driven communication and see what lessons we can learn from that. See you there!

CHAPTER 6

Event and Notification Management

Event-driven data architectures are the new paradigm. With these, organizations can transform their businesses into real-time, data-driven experiences. But while they're powerful, they're also overly complex. They require many services, additional components, and frameworks. They are also not a solution for every type of problem. It's worth discussing these considerations when implementing any type of event-driven communication.

In this chapter, we'll concentrate on event and notification management. These are complex areas because they overlap with API management and data product architecture design. We'll look at things like asynchronous communication, event-driven architectures, modern cloud technologies, consistency models, event types, and more. By the end of this chapter, you'll have a good understanding of what event-driven architectures can bring to your organization, and of the trade-offs involved.

There are a few things I'd like to mention up front. First, not all data practitioners are familiar with event-driven architectures. I'll explain some basics and concentrate on event distribution in the context of data management. Second, event-driven architectures can become complex; a complete discussion of this topic could easily fill a whole book.[1] I'll focus on the key aspects and use a reference example to demonstrate the governance model and the most important considerations to keep in mind.

---

1 *Designing Event-Driven Systems* by Ben Stopford (O'Reilly) is a great resource if you want to learn more about event-driven architectures.

Introduction to Events

Before we discuss architecture and governance, I want to examine event data, what it looks like, and why asynchronous communication makes a difference. Event data is information about a change that occurs at a point in time (an *event*). Event data provides a competitive advantage: faster results make insights more relevant, and greater responsiveness leads to higher customer satisfaction. Instead of waiting minutes or hours, you can react immediately. Fraud can be detected the moment it happens. You can see where your web visitors are coming from, interact with them, and improve their customer experience as they navigate your website. Data delivered in a stream of events can be of enormous value to organizations, and its sources can vary hugely, from Internet of Things (IoT) devices to smartphone clicks, in-game player activity, social networks, and changes to traditional operational systems.

Unlike data delivered in offline batches or in response to API requests (in real time), event data focuses on interacting with and reacting to events. It's about *asynchronously* connecting applications and systems. Event data emphasizes high throughput and can be either stateless or stateful. It allows you to exchange information about changes that occur at specific points in time and to move the application state between locations, which enables distributed, up-to-date, materialized views.

Event-driven architectures often use event streaming platforms, which process the inbound events in flight, as the data is streaming through the platform. These software platforms have different "faces" and support various capabilities. For example, they allow you to:

- Manipulate the stream of events by performing real-time ETL and data integration processes
- Run real-time analytics by performing an analysis of a window of events to detect patterns or correlations
- Store data and move it between storage locations in real time
- Trigger functions and issue updates to other systems

There's some overlap with the way data products are stored and APIs are used. Because of that, these event-driven patterns require very good data management. For example, one event may trigger a slew of messages or calls to many different services. From a data management standpoint, you want to be able to track the replies to all of those.

Notifications Versus Carried State

Events come in different shapes, some of which have more overlap with data distribution and data management. One method of distributing events is called *event-carried state transfer*. With this approach, the event itself carries the full state related to the change, so the consumer has all the information it needs and doesn't have to make a separate request for the state after being notified of the event. The consumer can even use these events to build up its own local copy of the data. Example 6-1 shows what this might look like for an "add customer" event. An event can also be shaped in such a way that it contains both old and new data, so, for example, for an "update customer" event, consumers can see exactly what information has been changed.

Example 6-1. Example of an event that carries the full state relating to a customer change

```
{
    "id": "321125215",
    "firstName": "Adolfo",
    "lastName": "Prosacco",
    "gender": "male",
    "birthday": "1997-05-01",
    "address":
    {
        "streetAddress": "17795 Louisiana 182",
        "city": "Baldwin",
        "state": "Louisiana",
        "postalCode": "70514",
        "country": "United States"
    },
    "phoneNumber":
    [
        {
          "type": "home",
          "number": "(813) 872-1350"
        },
        {
          "type": "mobile",
          "number": "(202) 555-0154"
        }
    ]
}
```

An alternative approach is to just send a notification about the event, without the full state. In this case, the event will only contain the bare minimum information: a reference to the state that was changed. Although Example 6-2 has been oversimplified, it's obvious that a consumer of such an event will need to make a call back to the producer to retrieve more information about the change.

Example 6-2. Example of an event that represents a notification of a customer change

```
{
    "id": "321125215"
}
```

The intent with notifications is to get the consumer to react and perform some action. You could argue that these types of events are less interesting from a data management standpoint. However, from an enterprise integration perspective you will certainly want to set standards to follow whenever events cross domain boundaries.

The Asynchronous Communication Model

The key difference between request/response and event-driven communication is the inverted conversational nature of data transmission. With events, you listen instead of talk. This is also where the complexity lies because most users aren't familiar with this way of thinking. Many of us expect an instant response when we put something into action. If we select a link, we expect the new page to show up immediately. If we pick up the phone and start to talk, we expect the person on the other end of the line to hear us. Synchronous communication, where a request is made and a response is given, feels more natural.

Streaming clients typically open connections with the platform and wait for content to be pushed and delivered. The connection in this communication model has a limited life span in which the data can be exchanged. At the end of this period, all connections must be closed and resources cleaned up. A more efficient form of communication than repeatedly opening and closing connections is to keep the connection open for as long as possible. This technique is called *long polling* (*https://oreil.ly/7Bwfw*).

Reactive communication requires a different mindset: you wait for someone to contact you and then take action. Applications and integration platforms can do the same with events, sending an event or message to a message queue and waiting for another application to pick it up. This loose coupling takes away the dependency of waiting for the other party to react immediately. Asynchronous communication thus makes your architecture more resilient, in situations where waiting is feasible.

Next, we'll explore what event-driven architectures look like and examine some different patterns for generating, distributing, and consuming events.

What Do Modern Event-Driven Architectures Look Like?

Event-driven architectures (EDAs), in which events are distributed between applications, can be implemented differently depending on your requirements.[2] Additionally, many platforms and services offer different sets of features. Some services hyperspecialize and exclude certain functionality, while other services try to be as comprehensive as possible. Let's discuss some variations; they'll help you understand how event-driven messaging and data distribution works.

Message Queues

One well-known approach to sharing events across applications is using message queues.[3] A *message queue*, as the name suggests, is simply a queue in which events or messages can reside until they're processed. They've been used in message processing for many years and can be used to facilitate different communication styles. A common example is the *point-to-point consumption model*, where a *publisher* sends messages to the queue and a *subscriber* pulls them from the queue. Message queues, sometimes also called message brokers, can work at high velocities. To ensure that messages are processed once and only once, they are deleted or flagged after the consumer confirms receipt.

Message queues are typically used for transactional or high-integrity event processing—for example, when it's important that each message is processed only once or in a specific sequence (typically first in, first out), or when features like delivery guarantees and dead letter queues for storing undelivered messages are required.

Event Brokers

Another method of sharing events across applications is by using *event brokers*. An event broker is a lightweight piece of middleware that allows direct communication between applications, even if they were written in different languages or implemented using different protocols. Event brokers typically validate, store, route, and directly deliver events to other destinations, acting as intermediaries between applications. As you can see in Figure 6-1, they come in different flavors.

---

2 Clemens Vasters hosts a great repository on the subject of asynchronous messaging and eventing (*https://oreil.ly/UOM8Y*) with lots of presentations, examples, links, and documentation.

3 Message queues can be used to implement a *mediator topology model*: an architecture design that uses central coordination in order to manage the event processing.

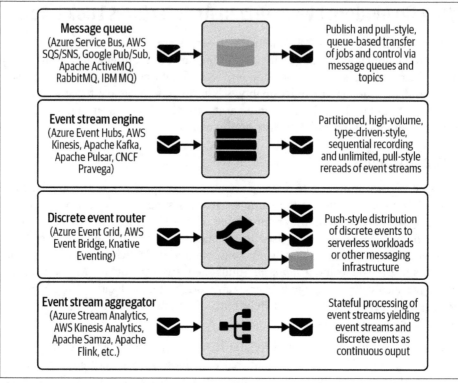

Message queue (Azure Service Bus, AWS SQS/SNS, Google Pub/Sub, Apache ActiveMQ, RabbitMQ, IBM MQ)		Publish and pull-style, queue-based transfer of jobs and control via message queues and topics
Event stream engine (Azure Event Hubs, AWS Kinesis, Apache Kafka, Apache Pulsar, CNCF Pravega)		Partitioned, high-volume, type-driven-style, sequential recording and unlimited, pull-style rereads of event streams
Discrete event router (Azure Event Grid, AWS Event Bridge, Knative Eventing)		Push-style distribution of discrete events to serverless workloads or other messaging infrastructure
Event stream aggregator (Azure Stream Analytics, AWS Kinesis Analytics, Apache Samza, Apache Flink, etc.)		Stateful processing of event streams yielding event streams and discrete events as continuous ouput

Figure 6-1. Different event delivery patterns

Event-driven platforms and services like the ones mentioned in Figure 6-1 organize events together, similarly to how files are organized in a folder within a filesystem. They each use different names for the structures events are grouped into. Apache Kafka, for example, uses the word *topic*. Azure Event Hubs uses the word *event hub*. Amazon Kinesis uses the word *stream*. Abstractly, these names all refer to the same pattern. It's about grouping together events that logically belong together.

Most types of event brokers differ from message queues in that they provide a direct data pipeline or stream of events between applications. Some simply route events between services, while others may aggregate and learn from events that pass by. Unlike event stream routers, event stream aggregators inspect the content of events. A third kind of event broker is the event stream engine, which captures a constant flow of data by using distributed storage capabilities. In order to provide reliable and guaranteed message delivery, some engines rely on a message queue that stores and orders the events until the consuming applications can process them.

Event Processing Styles

Different EDA topologies have different styles of processing events, depending on their complexity and use cases. Multiple styles may be combined in the same architecture.

Simple event processing (SEP) is the simplest style of processing because it concerns processing events that are directly related to specific, measurable changes of condition. Past events won't influence the processing of the current event. No complex workflows are triggered. A practical example is a sensor that submits events as changes occur.

Event stream processing (ESP) processes multiple events (messages) at the same time. The difference, compared to SEP, is that the state of the past events may influence the way future events are processed. A practical example would be stock trading, where you analyze a stream of pricing data and decide whether to buy or sell a stock.

Complex event processing (CEP) is the most complicated form of event processing because an analysis is performed to find patterns to determine whether a more complex event has occurred. The events that are taken into consideration may be evaluated over a long period of time and could even come from multiple sources. For example, you can join multiple streams together to produce a single stream, then apply aggregate operations on the stream to calculate a running count, average, or sum. You can also perform advanced windowing operations, like sliding and tumbling window functions. Practical examples include real-time fraud detection, infrastructure monitoring and alerting, updating low-latency dashboards, etc.

Service-Oriented Architecture Versus Event-Driven Architecture

How does SOA differ from EDA? Or are these architecture styles the same? Both aim for higher agility and advocate the design principles of service agreements, service discoverability, service reusability, service abstraction, and service composability. The significant difference is that EDA allows a level of data inconsistency by allowing data replication, while within SOA, inconsistency is avoided through service isolation. SOA advocates a loose coupling principle, which means that each service is an isolated entity with limited dependencies on other shared resources, such as databases, legacy applications, or APIs. SOA also puts more emphasis on commands, while EDA emphasizes events.

Implementing an event-driven architecture is complex and involves much more than deploying message queues or event brokers. A comprehensive EDA requires many other services and components for creating, collecting, transforming, storing, and consuming events. To understand better how an event-driven architecture works, we'll dive deeper into different areas in the following sections. First, we'll discuss the provider side and learn how events are generated. Next, we'll switch to the consuming side. Finally, we'll connect the two sides and learn how to manage events at scale.

Event Producers

Source systems on the event provider (often called *event producer* or *publisher*) side often don't stream data or generate events by themselves. In many scenarios, additional integration components are required for collecting data from data sources and performing protocol transformation or another integration, such as transforming messages into the right format or filtering, aggregating, or enriching them. The event creation may happen at two different levels: in the application or the database. There are a couple of scenarios and options to choose from. Let's look at some that are well known and their best practices.

Application-generated events

In most cases, applications don't generate events and notifications automatically. So, in order to distribute events, you (as a developer) are required to make modifications to the application architecture yourself. Depending on the situation and application you're dealing with, these modifications can be straightforward or complex. Let me provide a few examples.

For generating or sending events, extra client libraries are typically needed. For instance, if I were developing a Node.js application written in Express that has to submit events to Kafka, the most logical option would be to use the KafkaJS client library. But if I had to connect my application to Azure Event Hubs, then I would probably use a different client library: the Azure Event Hubs client library for Java-Script. To summarize, there are dependencies between the languages, frameworks, and middleware you work with.

Another way of emitting or collecting events is by directly capturing traffic between services. Modern applications or web services can be designed in such a way that events are directly generated by the frontends, user interfaces, or underlying application components: for example, in-browser events like viewing web pages and adding products to the shopping cart can be directly collected via APIs.[4]

Events can also be produced by parsing logs, such as access and server logs. In this case, any anomaly results in an event. In many cases, just like with the Node.js example, you'll rely on extra components to get event publishing up and running.

Bear in mind that, for complex or legacy applications that have been developed without any APIs, event collection might be problematic. Suppose you're working

---

4 Events generated by frontends and user interfaces are typically one-way (fire-and-forget) mechanisms because the message recipients usually aren't required to produce replies.

with an application written in, for example, Visual Basic 6. You'll either need to modernize the application or use the underlying database as an integration point.

Database-generated events

Generating events by reading changes made to the application database is an alternative to using APIs or services.[5] Reading changes can be done via polling, triggers, or change data capture (CDC). This model of distributing events, as you can imagine, has a stronger relationship with event-carried state transfer. Just like in the scenario in which applications generate events, more components and further work may be required.

The first method is a polling-based approach (*https://oreil.ly/3lxkV*) using database connectors. Database tables are mapped to message queues or event streams by repeatedly running queries (typically via Open Database Connectivity or Java Database Connectivity). Each time a new record is inserted into a table, or a row is updated, it's fetched from the table and transferred to either a message queue or an event stream. The polling-based method is relatively easy to set up but might generate a higher load on the database because of the constant querying. Another drawback of polling is that you might need to implement changes to the application and underlying database design. A prerequisite, for example, could be an extra updated_at column that is required in order to detect what new rows need to be fetched from the database.

An alternative to polling is to generate events using a trigger-based approach. A *trigger* is a piece of procedural code, like a stored procedure or database hook, that is only executed when a given event happens. For example, you might have a trigger that is executed each time data is added to a table. This trigger then would either move the records to an events table or change feed, or invoke a function to send the data to another component. A problem with triggers is that they can run slowly when a database is under heavy load. Another drawback is that not all databases support triggers.

Another method for capturing the state is to use CDC.[6] This works by using specialized database tooling and reading every single change from the database transaction or audit log. CDC-based tools utilize the database less because they don't query the database directly, but in many cases they require other commercial or third-party components.

---

5 This form of state is also known as *resource state*, or the current state of a resource on a server at any point in time. Some engineers distinguish between application state, which lives on the client, and resource state, which lives on the server.

6 An example of using CDC with Azure SQL and Debezium can be found in the Microsoft documentation (*https://oreil.ly/qz4tE*).

Capturing data directly from application databases isn't easy. Many applications are designed for operational workloads. They work with complex and heavily normalized data structures to guarantee integrity. In these cases, more transformations or abstractions may be required. A best practice that you may apply is to either use a view or write a processed version of the data to another (temporary) table. You can then read the data from this new location. When following this approach, you prohibit yourself from performing complex data operations in real time at a later stage.

What conclusions can we draw from these different examples? Each application has unique characteristics and may require a custom solution or third-party components. For data management, therefore, it's important that application integration teams and developers work closely with central platform teams on setting standards and best practices. If, for example, a connector is not available, then the central platform team should offer support by building a connector and providing it to other domain teams.

Event Consumers

Now let's switch to the event consumer's side. Here, the variations are dictated by the use case requirements. Consumption patterns are important because they directly affect the experience of other domains. I'll discuss several (though by no means all) scenarios in this section.

The number one reason to use a message queue or event broker, and the simplest use case by far, is to decouple one provider from one consumer via an intermediate layer of communication. A producer publishes messages, and the consumer consumes the messages for the consuming workload. A practical example would be a website activity tracking use case that emits events to a marketing application for keeping track of which customers visited which websites.

A simple variation is where multiple consumers consume from the same stream of events from a single producer. In this scenario, each consumer maintains its own message offset. This pattern is known as *fanout exchange*. A practical example would be a customer administration system that distributes all customer changes to several downstream applications.

A more complex situation would be an operational system that wants to strengthen its inner architecture by using some cloud capabilities. For this, a function-based service might be deployed in the cloud, invoked via events. The function processes the messages, stores the results (perhaps enriching them by calling other services), and then sends them back to the operational system. This pattern is also known as the *strangler pattern*. The supporting function, or application component, in this example can be considered a (serverless) microservice.

An advanced scenario would be to use a stream processing engine or analytical platform to analyze and look for patterns in an aggregated event stream from multiple event providers. Events are inspected, and the occurrence of certain events within a specific time window or matches within a dataset can trigger another event (perhaps initiating an automated action, or informing one or more other systems of this occurrence). As mentioned previously, this pattern of querying and analyzing data before storing it in a database is known as *complex event processing*. Many advanced streaming platforms allow you to perform analytics by providing support for windowing functions (tumbling, hopping, sliding, session, etc.).[7]

Event Stream Processing Versus Complex Event Processing

The differences between event stream processing and complex event processing have been well explained by Srinath Perera on Quora (*https://oreil.ly/YkNwa*). CEP is considered to be a subset of ESP (see Figure 6-2). It may be preferable, depending on the problem and use case you're dealing with.

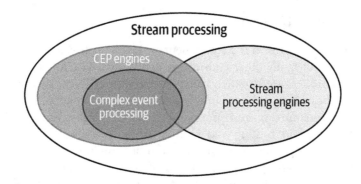

Figure 6-2. Complex event processing is a subset of stream processing

If you need to analyze a single sequence of events ordered by time, or you need to create a processing graph, you use ESP. However, if you need to analyze events in parallel, using a higher-level query language, you use CEP. Stream processing engines focus more on querying the data (filtering, validating the order, etc.) CEP engines place more emphasis on complex analysis, such as comparing the time windows, comparing and looking for correlations between different events, etc.

As the overlap in the center of the figure suggests, however, these differences are starting to fade away as more stream processing engines are borrowing features of CEP.

---

7 Microsoft has a good introduction to Azure Stream Analytics windowing functions (*https://oreil.ly/BV-gN*).

Another scenario, and a different way to use a streaming platform, is not to react or listen to events but to transfer the application state. With state transfer, the primary goal is to keep data in sync, not to take action on events. The two objectives can also be mixed; for example, the pattern of event-carried state transfer is often combined with CQRS, which we looked at in Chapter 4.

What conclusions can we draw from these different examples? First, events may be communicated between applications, or internally within a single application. Thus, you'll need to consider issues like domain boundaries and reusability. Second, events can be used for analytical or operational purposes. An analytical event or a prediction made by a machine learning model may find its way back to a transactional system for operational decision making. Third, each use case has unique characteristics and may require a custom solution. So, you may need to complement your architecture with extra components and create guidance for that.

Now, let's zoom out a bit and examine how event producers and consumers can best be facilitated.

Event Streaming Platforms

The event streaming platform is a component of the event-driven architecture, which can be composed of many other (sub)components (such as CEP engines and event brokers). Event brokers are essential, as they manage the different styles of interaction between event providers and consumers. The core components of event streaming platforms focus on moving and processing event or data streams. This includes receiving messages and routing and sending them to multiple consumers. What makes event streaming platforms different from, for example, API platforms is that they are capable of storing large quantities of data (state) and prevent data loss with their distributed capabilities. As streams of data come in, the platform can transform, combine, filter, or aggregate them. Some platforms also offer complex event processing functions, so you can do the analysis on the consumer side or within the streaming platform.

As you see, there are numerous complexities to take care of. In this section, I'll unpack what's typically inside an event-driven architecture for connecting different domains together. We'll start with a simple example and expand on it gradually.

EDA reference architecture

For simply distributing events between producers and consumers, I propose a light-weight architecture using stream processing services. Figure 6-3 is an example design that shows a serverless, event-driven architecture that receives streams of events, processes them using functions, and routes the final results to other brokers for downstream consumption.

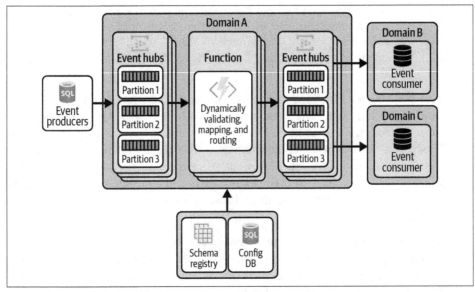

Figure 6-3. A reference architecture connecting event producers and consumers, using Azure Event Hubs and Azure Functions

Looking at this design, the first question you might have is why there are two stream processing services and a function sitting between the event producers and consumers. First and foremost, I recommend decoupling providers from consumers with a set of event brokers because not all event producers might be able to guarantee stable delivery and deliver user-friendly events. Imagine a situation in which you capture messages directly from a web app. In such a scenario, there might be cases where domains make disruptive changes to their application designs. Those domains will need to map the events back to the original structure in order to guarantee stable consumption, or provide a way to call different versions of the same product. With additional stream processing services, domains can evolve and make breaking changes without the need to test compatibility with all the existing consumers. Additionally, you might encounter situations in which events come in a format that is too raw or technical for the consumer. This extra layer allows providers to decouple themselves from consumers. Including an extra set of event brokers also enables a future scenario in which consumers are more distributed, perhaps in multiple regions. Instead of requiring all the consumers to cross the network to collect events, you can bring the data closer to your consumers by having an event broker in each region.

For architectures that use Kafka and require transformation services, I encourage you to look at Decodable (*https://www.decodable.co*) or ksqlDB (*https://oreil.ly/GRzsU*), which provide SQL interfaces for transforming data in a Kafka pipeline.

In Figure 6-3, you see functions that receive, inspect, and route events. These functions don't maintain state. The benefit of this pattern is that you can implement additional validations. For example, you might want to functionally validate the event body and detect any potential duplicates (using components that we haven't discussed yet). Additionally, you may want to restructure messages for improved readability or map them back to their original form if the producers make disruptive changes. Functions allow you to do this without the need of provisioning additional infrastructure.

To make your architecture more self-service, you could think of a design where routing and mapping are metadata-driven. This could be accomplished, for example, by adding a config store that holds metadata indicating which event streams relate to which other event streams. The functions then will read from this store while processing events. You could even extend this approach by implementing a small control framework for deciding what messages or attributes consumers are allowed to see. Additionally, you may want to complement your architecture with a schema registry (*https://oreil.ly/01hPO*) for governance. Such registries allow you to technically validate messages or logically group similar schemas based on certain business criteria, such as domain boundaries.

Data product creation

Let's iterate on our initial reference architecture by allowing events to be persisted so they can be combined (later) with batch data processing. In Figure 6-4, we've added a data product architecture for persisting data over longer periods. The motivation for this is to allow real-time data ingestion for data product creation.

There are two patterns you can implement using this design. The first option is to capture events directly at the moment of ingestion. This may be useful when you want to integrate the events with other data that arrives at different velocities, or if you plan on performing ad hoc analysis or want to debug this data for future analysis. In this situation, the events are aligned with the inner architecture of the providing application. You'll want to put principles in place that avoid directly distributing this data to other domains because the structure is likely to be too raw/technical for the downstream consumers.

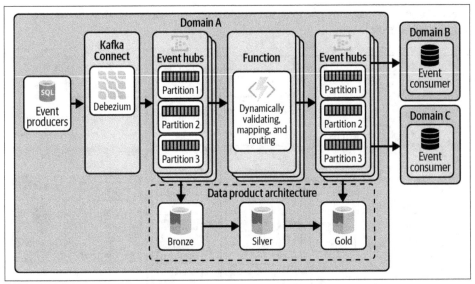

Figure 6-4. Adding a data product architecture to enable persistence of events

To keep things simple, I'll remove the data product architecture in the next iteration. However, in practice, I expect modern and comprehensive architectures to have a combination of all the features discussed in this chapter.

The second option for historizing real-time event data is tapping into the consumption layer. Logically, at this point the data has already been modeled into a user-friendly shape for downstream consumption by other domains. Combining streaming with the consumption layer of the data product architecture enables domains to more quickly see data product changes. Thus, instead of daily (as with batches), domains are able to update their data products, for example, hourly or quarter-hourly.[8]

Event stores

In the next iteration we'll add event stores to our architecture, as shown in Figure 6-5. An *event store* is just a database that stores events in an event-driven architecture. This component is helpful when performing lookups or executing complex queries. Imagine, for example, a situation in which messages must be enriched with other data

---

8 Joe Plumb has written a blog post (*https://oreil.ly/Xn51N*) on how to process data once every minute using a data pipeline with SQL, Azure Functions, Data Factory, and Event Grid.

(e.g., reference data). An event store would be the perfect location to retrieve this other data from.

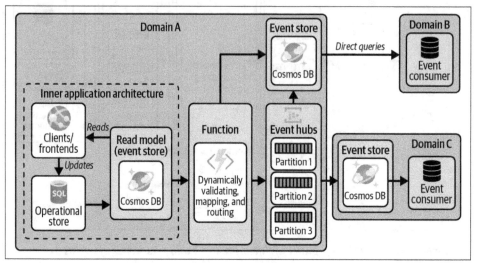

Figure 6-5. Adding event stores to our architecture

Event stores deliver flexibility for querying data and enable information to be stored for much longer. They can either be positioned on the providing side, playing the role of read or command stores, or on the consuming side, playing the role of queryable databases.

Messages in an event store are not deleted after consumption. In effect, the event store is just a list of messages that can be read from the beginning at any time—any consumer can decide what item to process next. This mechanism enables a scenario where multiple consumers can each process the messages at their own speed. If certain consumers would like to start over or reprocess certain messages, this is also possible thanks to the event store. While replaying events, you can repair, manipulate, or enrich them. For example, if you find an error, you can apply a retroactive fix, then replay all the events as new events. This rewind pattern can also be used to combine different streams of events.

A good choice for an event store is a NoSQL database like Azure Cosmos DB (*https:// oreil.ly/KRO4K*), as shown in Figure 6-5. NoSQL databases, especially document stores, are more flexible in the way they handle, process, and store unstructured data. They are schemaless, meaning data structures aren't enforced on any data entering the database. You could use a relational database, but this would require you to define a relational data model up front, before any data can enter the database. You can also use different kinds of event stores for different needs. For example, your architecture might incorporate relational, NoSQL, and graph databases, catering for diverse needs.

Event stores, just like the data product architecture we looked at in the previous section, can be positioned on different sides of the architecture. Let's find out why.

When we position event stores on the data-producing side of the architecture, they retain data in a shape that is closer to the inner application architecture of a domain. We can even make the event stores part of the operational architecture, for example, using them as read stores for CQRS. In this case, the event store would play the role of read replica and can be optimized for reading data much faster—so, instead of reading data from the operational database, you would read from the event store. Such an application design will make your application faster and more flexible; for example, you can independently scale the read or command store, without scaling both.

You can also use event stores as command stores within your operational architecture. This enables *command sourcing*, where you first persist any command before it's processed. Doing this enables you to replay the whole state of your system. It allows you to audit messages and see a trail of what has happened, and set controls on commands before they get processed.

When positioning event stores on the data-consuming side of the architecture, you enable consumers to directly interact with data from another domain without making calls back to the operational application. For example, this can allow consumers to perform complex queries without the need to send them over the network. You can also allow domains to shape events to suit their own needs, transforming them and storing them in their own event stores.

An important feature that modern NoSQL databases like Cosmos DB offer is *change feed (https://oreil.ly/blJmK)*. This feature is a key enabler of event-driven architectures as it enables more design patterns; for example, you can trigger a function each time data enters the database. This means that instead of using a worker process to read new data from the database, you can validate or parse it on the fly as it enters the database. This mechanism is analogous to using ksqlDB with Apache Kafka.

Using a cloud native NoSQL database as your event store has pros and cons. On the one hand, you strengthen your architecture with reactive capabilities. You can more easily process events and have queryable event stores. This is an important advantage as it helps in maintaining the overall simplicity of the architecture. On the other hand, these high-performing databases are often expensive. This can be a blocker for many use cases.

Could we replace the cloud native NoSQL database with, for example, Kafka? Yes, but Kafka wasn't intended to store messages forever. Like Azure Event Hubs, it works better for use cases that need to deal with high data ingestion throughput and distribution to multiple consumer groups that want to consume these messages at their own pace.

In the next section, we'll look at some more complex use cases that depend on fast data ingestion and processing capabilities with analytical features.

Streaming analytics

To support analytical use cases (complex event processing), you'll need to add extra components to your architecture. Depending on the use case requirements, these may include components for real-time analytics, visualization, and more. Some of these components have a distributed processing architecture as well, to enable them to process lots of data. Here are a few example scenarios:[9]

- You analyze and push events directly into a reporting dataset in order to provide a real-time dashboarding experience. A practical example might be a real-time report showing all employees who attempt to log in from different geographical regions within a four-hour time frame.

- You analyze events to complement them with additional data. For example, you might first route events to a fraud detection model that enriches each one with a score, then route these events back into the event-driven architecture for downstream consumption.

- You analyze events by reading information from other databases. For example, when a customer requests a new credit card, you might look up whether their provided identification is still valid.

- You process millions of sensor data records in a time series database, but before doing so, you first want to clean up and correctly timestamp the messages.

- You process traffic data using a geospatial algorithm. For that you push all events into a high-performing processing platform, such as Databricks.

A revised solution design including components to enable streaming analytics might look like Figure 6-6. Streaming services can deliver great value for both event producers and consumers. The possibilities are endless!

To manage your architecture better, I recommend making your services and platforms domain-agnostic. Such a principle means that all analytical components, and the corresponding business logic that comes with them, must be positioned on either the providing or the consuming side of the architecture. You might complement your architecture with extra analytical services, but only for domain-agnostic features, such as generic data quality profiling services.

---

9 Azure Samples (*https://oreil.ly/Jz6a7*) provides several example solutions showing how to stream at scale.

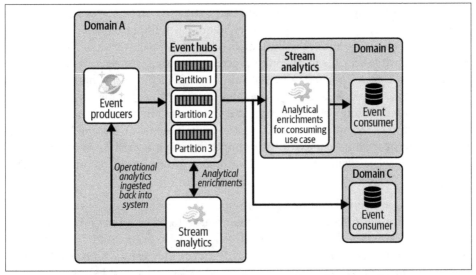

Figure 6-6. Adding streaming analytics components to the reference architecture

What conclusions can we draw from this discussion of event-driven architecture? First, there are many things you need to manage: event brokers for distributing events, event stores for querying data or for queueing, ingestion pipelines for data products, and analytical components for turning data into value. You'll need to provide your domains with guidance on all of these components, if you include them in your architecture. Second, you saw that there are two types of boundaries: there are inner-application event streams between application components, and there's communication between applications in different domains. For both, you need to have governance.

Governance Model

Let's take a step back and look at the governance model for event providers and consumers. Your event-driven architecture should follow the same model used for serving data products and APIs to other domains. All streams of events, such as event streams and queues, must be owned by event providers (data providers). When sharing services between domains and using them for both application-internal and domain-to-domain communication, things can quickly become tricky because we don't want consumers from other domains to pick up internal communication channels. To avoid this, I recommend strong segregation between inner-application event streams and domain-to-domain event streams. You'll recall that from our discussion of ingesting data into your data product architecture using localized storage solutions.

Inner-application and domain-to-domain event streams can be segregated by several methods. A best practice is applying segregation via multiple services: for example, services in the landing zone remain domain-agnostic and are for domain-to-domain distribution, while services in operational accounts or subscriptions are for the inner architecture of an application. Alternatively, you can deploy and share a dedicated platform, for example, in a data management landing zone. In this case, segregation works differently. Using dedicated event streams or event hubs is one method, or you can use naming conventions (embedding the domain name or making it part of the queue or event stream's name by, for example, by using a prefix). Another, stricter method is to isolate event streams using consumers groups, certifications, or multiple clusters.

Events used for internal communication (such as between two application components) are allowed to be technical; they don't have to be adapted (yet) for business use. The streams for these events are called *internal streams* and are considered part of the application or domain logic. This means they can be consumed only by the producing application domain, and aren't directly consumed by other domains, although the events that go into the internal streams can be used as input for meaningful business streams. You can be less strict with metadata policies for these streams as well. For example, internal streams can be listed in the queue or event stream registry with less richness.[10]

Domain-to-domain streams, by contrast, are only allowed to be consumed by other domains. These streams, also called *business streams*, are ready for business consumption and thus are read-optimized. They're decoupled, which means they remain compatible with previous versions, and they're listed in the registry with more details for data consumers than the internal streams. They should follow all the data management principles from Chapter 2.

In the next sections, I'll touch on some additional best practices for moving to an event-driven architecture.

Event Stores as Data Product Stores

Can a streaming platform be used as a database and play the role of a data product store if data is stored longer-term? Absolutely. With event sourcing, state stores, and the rewind capabilities of modern streaming platforms, it's possible to create federated data products that are continuously filled with fresh data. Consumers can generate a copy of the data by using the rewind method, where all events are read again, from the beginning (first message) to the end (last message). After rewinding, they can use streaming to keep their copies of the data up-to-date in real time. This

---

10 The *registry* is a central location for registering all queues and event streams, including ownership, versioning, schema metadata, and life cycle management.

method can be facilitated with CDC by reading all the changes from the application transaction logs.

When persisting data for longer periods, you should determine under what conditions streams can have long-term or infinite (permanent) data retention. One risk of implementing longer retention periods without monitoring is that your architecture can become costly. You might also violate retention and data life cycle management policies, such as the GDPR. Thus, a form of control is required. One principle you could set is to allow for retaining only the latest or unique messages. As an alternative, you can offload the messages to the data product architecture, using less expensive storage options.

Event Stores as Application Backends

Can the central streaming platform be used as an application backend? For example, can Kafka be used as an application data store? Theoretically this is possible, but I generally wouldn't advise it.

There are a few reasons for this. First, streaming is asynchronous by nature. For applications that don't have latency requirements, this won't be a problem, but it will still require removing the retention limits; otherwise, application data may be lost. Second, you create tight coupling between the application and the purpose of enterprise data distribution. These are two different concerns, and their governance shouldn't be mixed.

If you do decide to use a streaming platform as a backend for your applications, I recommend creating clear governance regarding how to deal with such situations. One approach could be to clearly scope this pattern for each domain. Another could be to spin up more platforms for specific domains. The biggest risk of using the streaming platform as a backend is the creation of an integration database (*https://oreil.ly/SHDrh*).

The same principle applies for streams that are derived from other streams. Allowing other consumers to directly consume these event streams could result in a chaotic web of event streams on top of event streams pointing back and forth. These spaghetti trails often result from a lack of control and policy guiding the teams in the usage of the platform. A good principle would be to force consumers to first ingest events into their applications before immediately ingesting them back into the streaming platform.

Streaming as the Operational Backbone

In Chapter 1, I discussed the trend of transactional and analytical systems working more closely together. An event streaming platform is the solution for connecting both kinds of systems. Its components enable the following:

- Extending an operational system with an in-memory system that keeps track of all historical data. Whenever the operational system needs more historical context for its decisions, the streaming platform provides that historical data.

- Extending an operational system with real-time decision logic. When customers buy new products, for example, the financial system is consulted to check any outstanding balances; streaming is used to facilitate this.

- Using command sourcing to persist commands and replay the whole state of the system. This allows missing orders, for example, to be added back into the list and executed at a later time.

 When building operational asynchronous messaging systems at scale, you're likely to enter a situation where the systems are receiving data at a higher rate than they can process it during a temporary load spike. This problem is called *backpressure* (*https://oreil.ly/ 8wbF5*) and can, if not dealt with correctly, lead to exhaustion of resources or even, in the worst case, data loss. There are different strategies for dealing with this problem. Adding additional resources is one solution. Another solution is to set limits on your queues and drop or store messages that exceed the limit elsewhere.

The same architecture can be used to engineer an operational system with a backend consisting of multiple technologies. Streaming here can support keeping data in sync between the different databases or combining and integrating data. Microservices-based architectures often rely on the event-driven architecture as well. Event streaming is one of the patterns that allow microservices to communicate with one another.

Guarantees and Consistency

Stream processing is more complex than batch processing. If something goes wrong in batch processing, you can solve the issue by redelivering all the data and rerunning the batch process. Dealing with failures and inconsistencies in streaming requires keeping some additional considerations in mind.

Consistency Level

The first consideration is the level of consistency (completeness and accuracy of the data) that you want to apply within applications. There are two types of consistency in streaming:

Eventual consistency
> This model guarantees that all data will eventually be reflected in the platform, though it may take some time to propagate. Eventual consistency is a weak guarantee and can work for data that isn't critical.

Strong consistency
> This model guarantees that all events are processed in order. The platform confirms propagation of any update to all copies of the data; once any entity or node makes an update, all replicas are locked until they have been updated.

Providing strong consistency can be difficult. If the velocity of events is so high that the streaming platform can barely keep up, it can be challenging, if not impossible, to design the system in such a way that all messages will be received correctly. The design constraints imposed by strong consistency are therefore unacceptable for various use cases, making eventual consistency the only possible approach. In these cases, you may need to take additional measures to ensure it is correct. For example, you could use an extra database to persist all the data and reconcile occasionally to ensure all data has been correctly synchronized. You can also use additional tooling, such as CDC, to ensure all changes are correctly delivered, or you could build an extra service to ensure consistency by reading, validating, and redelivering missing messages.

Processing Methods

There are different processing methods within the eventual and strong consistency models. *At-least-once processing* ensures that messages don't get lost, but doesn't guarantee that all messages are unique and delivered only once. It's acceptable to have duplicates and for events to be processed multiple times.

Exactly-once processing, also called the *delivered-only-once* model, guarantees that each event is delivered exactly and only once. No messages are lost, nor are there duplicates. Implementing this model might require additional redelivery patterns. Some engineers use additional identifiers to validate the uniqueness of every message.

The last model is called *at-most-once* or *no-guarantee processing*. In this scenario, no guarantees are given that all messages will be delivered correctly. Messages are allowed to get lost or can be delivered multiple times.

You can combine different models, depending on the requirements of your use case and other constraints. An eventual consistency model, for example, can be used to initially deliver messages without acknowledging receipts, and occasionally all messages can be compared, with duplicates removed and missing messages redelivered to ensure that they've been delivered exactly and only once.

Message Order

Another typical challenge with streaming is the message order. In some cases messages are required to be strictly ordered, for example, by order of creation. Kafka allows you to do this, but only using one partition. If you need more partitions for scalability, the ordering must be based on an additional property in the message, such as the row_no. This might require the delivering party to make some adjustments in the delivery. Another approach is to consume all messages and reorder them on the consuming side.

Dead Letter Queue

Some streaming platforms have a *dead letter queue*, which is an additional queue for messages that aren't delivered successfully. These might include messages that exceed the size limit, use an incorrect message format, are sent to an event stream that doesn't exist, or aren't processed within a set time frame. In these cases, messages aren't removed from the system, but rather are placed in the dead letter queue. Typically, a developer needs to manually examine what went wrong. Often, the problem is a change to the providing application that wasn't thoroughly tested; in such a scenario, the problematic messages need to be moved or submitted again to the original queue.[11]

Streaming Interoperability

For interfaces between publishers and subscribers, you'll have to make some technology and design decisions. Some platforms dictate how the providing applications must connect to the platform and what protocol they must use. Other platforms are more open and support a wider range of message protocols to allow transparent interaction between multiple programming languages. A neutral way and popular choice is to use a protocol that encodes messages using an interface description language (IDL) (*https://oreil.ly/2CLeH*) for data format and type validations.

Another option is to look at a framework that supports data serialization. Data serialization frameworks play an important role in compatibility, versioning, and portability when moving data around interfaces. From these standpoints, these frameworks take care of consistent translation to a standardized data format. After translation, many systems, programming languages, and other frameworks can start to use the data. These serialization frameworks also improve data processing with features such as compressing and security (encryption). This makes serialization ideal for distributing

---

11 For more on this topic, see Ning Xia's blog post "Building Reliable Reprocessing and Dead Letter Queues with Apache Kafka" (*https://oreil.ly/-4Z0J*).

data to the data product architecture. Popular serialization framework and protocol options include Apache Avro, Protocol Buffers, Apache Thrift, MQTT, and AMQP.

Another way to produce and consume messages from streaming platforms is to use RESTful APIs that support JSON and XML messages.[12] This is a good choice for online channels or web environments. JSON has the advantage of being schemaless and flexible, but it has one major drawback: it doesn't enforce compatibility as it doesn't enforce schema encoding. So, there's a trade-off to be made between message flexibility and enforcement.

Governance and Self-Service

An event-driven architecture comes with additional metadata capabilities and requirements. The most important of these are the event stream registry (or schema registry), which is used for purposes such as:

Ownership registration
> Events are always owned. The registry keeps track of event ownership, and can also be used to classify message queues and event streams as internal or domain-to-domain.

Schema document management
> It's recommended to manage the schema layout and documentation of all of your messages. For XML and JSON, these are logically the XML or JSON schemas. Serialization formats, like Avro, use their own IDLs. A recommendation for documenting and maintaining events is to look at AsyncAPI (*https://www.asyncapi.com*), which is an open source initiative that seeks to improve the current state of event-driven architectures. For managing all your schemas and documentation together, the preferred approach is to use a tool like a registry.

Version management
> Schemas must be versioned. If they aren't versioned, there will be breaking changes that can directly affect event consumers. For managing schema versions, a registry is the preferred solution.

Lineage
> Unfortunately, lineage for events can be complex and depends on the stream processing engine that is being used. Depending on your situation, you may need to do some custom coding or implementation; for example, invoking the APIs as part of your catalog or data governance solution.

---

12 Kafka doesn't support this form of communication without a REST proxy (*https://oreil.ly/vkjNc*) installed.

EDA's metadata becomes essential when improving the target operating model through self-service. For example, you might want to allow domains to reset their offsets or provision queues and event streams themselves, and have those requests approved automatically. Or you might want domains to design their own REST proxy templates and automatically deploy them using the right security policies. You can also enable domains to apply data filtering before passing messages on to different consumers. My recommendation is to enable these patterns one by one, keeping self-service in mind.

Wrapping Up

Wow, that was a lot of content on events! I hope you now recognize their power, but also see the complexity that comes with them. With events, we can connect applications, federate data, digitalize processes, and improve internal and external communication. They allow us to understand how systems react to each other, which helps us improve our daily business operations.

Stream processing, as you've seen, is complex. To continuously capture data and ingest streams into a platform, you need to enrich your architecture with many additional components. Given the complexity and diversity of the landscape, you can end up using many different toolsets, frameworks, and additional services to, for example, ensure exactly-once processing. My recommendation is to build up slowly and set several ground rules:

- Standardize on services and platforms you offer to your domain teams. Strike a good balance; some tools and services are more specialized, while others try to be as comprehensive as possible. A good architecture is mutually exclusive and collectively exhaustive, so it's comprehensive without too much overlap between what features services offer.

- Set standards for event processing: events are immutable by definition, as they represent things that have already happened.

- Make event producers responsible for the data ingestion: their role is to guarantee "at least once" delivery. Consumers, on the other side, should guarantee "at most once" delivery.

- Segregate event streams: each service must own its event stream from a particular domain.

- Advocate eventual consistency when moving data across domain boundaries.

- Be careful about business logic. Keep your platforms and services for domain-to-domain communication as agnostic as possible.

- Strive for clear separation between internal application and domain-to-domain distribution. Apply all the principles from the previous chapters when crossing borders. For example, when crossing borders, your messages should be based on the ubiquitous language of the domain.

- Focus on automation from the start. Assuming that event distribution becomes successful, there will be hundreds, or even thousands, of event streams that you will need to manage. To make your architecture scalable, define schemas for all events and adopt a contract-first approach.

- Segregate events, notifications, queries, and commands. You might want to formulate principles for each of these: for example, queries must leave the state of the system unchanged, or commands must create, update, or delete some data. Commands must explicitly stay within the transactional boundaries. One of the biggest risks of distributing the concerns of processing commands across multiple applications is that consistency or transactional integrity can no longer be guaranteed. Additionally, commands might be rejected or may land in a dead letter queue. If this happens, you might want to be informed about it.

- Consider building wrappers on top of services for making complex tasks for engineers easier.

When looking at these principles, there's a final note that you have to consider: event-based architectures are complex and only useful when they deliver significant value to your organization. I've experienced many situations in which event-driven communication was used, but no need for speed was required. So, as an organization you might want to set some principles around validating that streaming isn't a false requirement. The business value should justify the added complexity.

In this chapter, you learned a lot about connecting applications and how to distribute data between them. In the next chapter, we'll get back in our helicopter and climb up a level higher, to a viewpoint from which we can oversee all data distribution and application integration patterns. We'll start with a short recap of the past three chapters, connecting various aspects. After that, we'll look at enterprise architecture when architecting for change. Note that we'll be hopping quickly between subjects. This might cause turbulence. Have a safe flight, and enjoy the trip!

CHAPTER 7

Connecting the Dots

It's time for a short intermezzo. The previous three chapters were long, dense reads. You learned about data distribution and integration patterns for connecting applications. We went deep into the rabbit hole and discussed various patterns and considerations for managing different architectures. You also learned about taking a more unified or holistic approach for managing both data and integration.

Now, I'll connect the dots and discuss managing your architecture as a whole, beginning with a quick recap of cross-domain interoperability, data distribution, and application integration. From there, we'll hop between different subjects: the criteria to evaluate when choosing one integration pattern over another, what combinations you can make, and what works best in certain scenarios. You'll see that there's great overlap in best practices for documentation, design, governance, metadata management, security, and the like. Next, we'll shift gears and explore how to inspire, motivate, and guide for change. We'll start with how to correctly manage cross-domain boundaries, discussing a concrete solution design. Then we'll look at how to strive for discovery and semantic consistency, and how to properly guide your teams in such an architectural transition. Finally, we'll examine organizational transformation: how domain teams and platform teams should interact and what lessons you can learn from that. By the end of this chapter, you should have a solid understanding of what managing a large-scale data distribution and integration landscape means. This knowledge will be important as we start extending the landscape by adding more areas of data management.

As we progress through this chapter, I'll include more personal knowledge about the role that enterprise architecture should play when architecting for change. As a lead architect, I was responsible for defining technical design standards, guidelines, and future state architectures. I also headed the Architecture Review Board (ARB) for managing the process of enterprise architecture governance. My experiences taught me that you can use this body for connecting to stakeholders and creating enthusiasm for the work that must be done. Additionally, I had a good overview of all the forces and surroundings within the organizational environment. So, expect more examples as you continue reading!

Cross-Domain Interoperability

In the past, the categorization of data and integration was easy: a clear distinction was made between the operational and analytical sides. The operational side focuses on transaction processing, integrating processes, and sharing functionality (business logic). The analytical side focuses on sharing the same application data among different (analytical) applications. Each side has its own architecture, resulting in differences in patterns, use cases, guidance, personas, and technology. I consider this difference a problem because the people maintaining an application are usually the same people building data products and APIs. To make my point clear, take a look at Figure 7-1. The underlying architecture from which data products originate is the same architecture from which APIs access the resources.

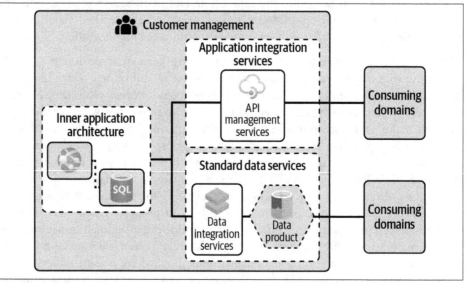

Figure 7-1. The underlying internal application architecture for data products and APIs is the same

The same thing goes for the context or ubiquitous language that served as input for application development. Data products, APIs, and events inherit their language from this same domain context. So, considering the overlap, does it still make sense to manage the operational plane apart from the analytical plane? I advocate a more holistic approach for managing both, which starts with aligning the concerns of managing data and integration. Before we dive more deeply into the notion of managing data products, APIs, and events together, let's do a quick recap of what you've learned so far.

Quick Recap

In Chapter 2, we started with a high-level overview of how domains communicate with other domains. You learned that internal domain and application complexity must be hidden from other domains and that domains should expose standard interfaces that simplify the work for others. In Chapter 3, you learned about domain topologies and discovered how domains can be supported with landing zones and blueprints.

In Chapter 4, you learned about today's data-driven world and the strong demand for read-optimized data. This is where data products come in: they can be used to efficiently read the same data over and over again. You also learned about CQRS and making a copy of the data just for reads, which is synchronously updated. This implies you won't be serving the most accurate data as it is found in transactional applications, but it allows data consumers to read intensively.

Next, in Chapter 5, you learned about API management. APIs are meant for real-time synchronous communication and can be used for communication between legacy systems and modern applications. This is the pattern you'll need to use for transactional queries or strongly consistent (accurate) data.

Finally, in Chapter 6, we looked at event-driven architectures, through which you can transform data in real time and notify other applications of the changes. Event streaming isn't a conversation, but a one-way communication channel that sends data to listeners. Instead of asking, "What data can I request or pull out of an application?" the model is "What data passing by is useful to me?" With streaming, you can react to data quickly.

Although the underlying architectures for data products, APIs, and events are different and, largely speaking, built for different purposes, they also overlap and can be combined. On the one hand, this is great because it offers flexibility, but on the other hand, it makes developing a design for engineers and architects more difficult because there are many trade-offs and considerations to weigh. In the next section, I'll propose a design that provides best practices for developing effective solution designs. After that, I'll share some of the lessons I learned about this while working as a lead architect for a large enterprise.

Data Distribution Versus Application Integration

When aligning data platforms and integration services to your domains, I recommend putting architecture guidance in place regarding the situations in which different patterns should be considered. For that, I propose creating a tactical blueprint, as shown in Figure 7-2, for both data and integration projects. The diagram consolidates all the major patterns discussed in the previous chapters. Different patterns complement one another; we'll talk more about this shortly.

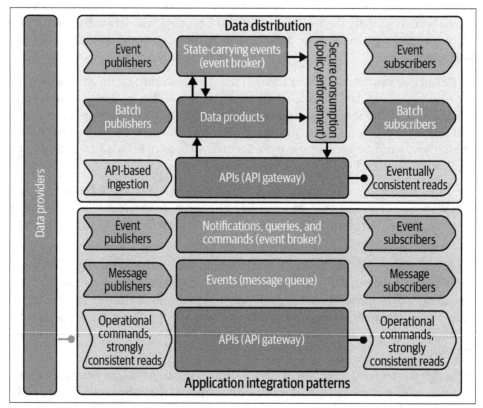

Figure 7-2. Each enterprise integration middleware implementation provides a set of design patterns to address complex data and integration challenges

As you can see, there's an architecture for data distribution and another one for application integration. This is because the two architectures traditionally focus on different concerns. Data distribution is about making data available, moving it between applications. Application integration, on the other hand, is about integrating and connecting applications, including application components. Data distribution and application integration differ in how they're managed organizationally. Application integration is managed as part of DevOps, which concentrates on enterprise software development. Data integration is tackled by DataOps, which focuses more on the management and orchestration of data.

When zooming deeper into data distribution and application integration, there are different patterns to be considered depending on the characteristics of your use case or workload. In the next sections, I'll elaborate further on Figure 7-2 by discussing more deeply how data distribution and application integration patterns work together. We'll start with data distribution, then look at application integration. After that, we'll explore how the overlap between data distribution and application integration can best be managed.

Data Distribution Patterns

Generally speaking, data distribution patterns are used when you need to combine and analyze data—for example, when developing data-intensive applications, performing data visualization or ad hoc querying, developing machine learning models, building data mining applications, and so on. These patterns may also be used for moving batches of data for transactional processing, such as when applications need to process a series of orders or invoices. The common denominator of all these use cases is that they can be scaled up by using eventually consistent reads. This means you work with a copy of the application data (the so-called data products).

When considering data distribution patterns for your use cases, there are two issues to consider. First, you should evaluate the acceptable delay between making operational changes and having them reflected in reads. For example, an application that needs end-of-day data has different requirements than an application that requires data to be delivered within a one-minute time window. Second, you should evaluate the need for periodic (say, end-of-month) reconciliation or auditing. If this process is required, I recommend using a batch-oriented data processing pattern (pattern 2 in Figure 7-3) because it is generally cheaper and easier to implement. Batch data processing is efficient when processing large amounts of data that are collected over a period of time.

When there's a need for speed—for example, when changes made to the operational system and distributed data must be reflected to consumers within a few minutes or seconds—then near-real-time patterns should be considered. You can use API-based or event-based ingestion and consumption for these use cases. The choice is nuanced, as there may be dependencies with the underlying design of the application from which you want to collect the data. API-based patterns (pattern 1 in Figure 7-3) may be the right solution when the provider or consumer wants to initiate the ingestion or consumption. Event-based patterns (pattern 3 in Figure 7-3) might be a good choice when the state transfer is reactive; for example, when using change data capture.

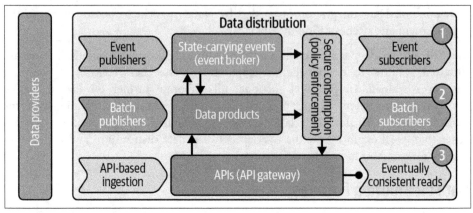

Figure 7-3. Data distribution patterns

API-based and event-based ingestion, as shown in Figure 7-3, can also complement data product creation and batch-based consumption. Imagine, for example, a scenario in which you use a streaming platform to transfer the application state for populating multiple data products at the same time. This pattern is useful when building up distributed data product architectures that span across multiple network or cloud locations. You might also combine data products and events when distributing the updates made to slowly changing dimensions (SCDs). When processing SCDs, you can, for example, use change feed to detect what changes were made to the data and generate events for these. Another combination of patterns you learned about is blending data products and APIs to route query traffic to data products and command traffic to operational systems. This CQRS pattern is useful for lowering the load caused by API calls on operational systems. The key takeaway here is that different data distribution patterns can be combined to complement each other, creating a comprehensive toolkit for data consumption.

Application Integration Patterns

Now let's switch the application integration architecture, which is for situations where speed and stronger consistency are essential. Application integration patterns, as mentioned previously, are focused on enabling individual applications—each designed for its own specific purpose—to work closely together for a specific use case or business problem, such as executing transactions, ordering products, or validating customer accuracy within an operational process. In these cases, you want to retrieve the information directly from the system of record. This is where APIs (pattern 6 in Figure 7-4) excel. They're a good choice for strongly consistent reads and directly invoking commands (i.e., synchronous communication). This pattern enables direct communication between two applications, with an API gateway sitting between these applications as a thin layer for mediation.

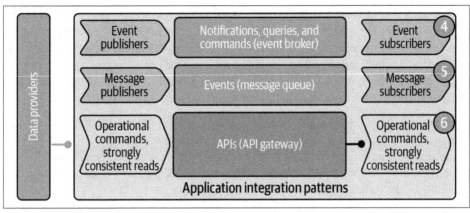

Figure 7-4. Application integration patterns

For asynchronous use cases, consider different patterns: event brokers and message queues (numbered 4 and 5 in Figure 7-4). Why would you prefer asynchronous over synchronous communication? Because it makes your architecture more resilient and cost-effective. Asynchronous communication won't work in every scenario, but when there's no time criticality, it has several benefits over synchronous communication:

- Network issues, such as high latency and low throughput, have no or minimal impact on asynchronous communication.

- Asynchronous communication is elastic; it can more easily be scaled up if there is increased load.

- Asynchronous communication makes application communication more robust against temporary network failures.

- With asynchronous communication, you can implement important features for better resilience, such as retry mechanisms, fallback scenarios, and circuit breakers that stop cascading effects.[1]

Asynchronous communication also has several drawbacks. Because communication isn't happening in real time, it's more difficult to debug and investigate if something goes wrong. When a request/response call fails, you typically notice that immediately. What's more, if an asynchronous system is broken for a long time, it may generate its own set of new problems. Asynchronous communication also may require extra application components. For example, you might want to protect your asynchronous message flows and avoid the risk of losing messages with dead letter queues or circuit breakers.

---

1 A *circuit breaker* (*https://oreil.ly/XFYvP*) is a design pattern used to detect failures. It encapsulates the logic of preventing a failure from constantly recurring.

APIs and events can also be combined for application integration purposes; for example, in a situation in which APIs are flooded with too many concurrent requests. This can result in services failing because the overload prevents them from responding to requests in a timely manner. To solve this problem, you can combine APIs and events to create a queue that acts as a buffer holding the requests to the API gateway. This pattern is also known as *queue-based load leveling* (*https://oreil.ly/y2IjE*).

Designing a good application integration solution is a complex task, given that there may be multiple possible "right" and complementary solutions. It's often a trade-off between different dimensions: performance, maintainability, flexibility, cost, resilience, and so on. These considerations may require you to have a deep understanding of the business problem you're trying to solve.

Although data products, APIs, and events are used to facilitate different scenarios and use cases, there's overlap in the domain context when using all of these patterns within the same boundaries. We already discovered this when reviewing Figure 7-1, where the same application is used for both data distribution and API connectivity. This observation is a nice transition to the topic of semantic consistency and discoverability.

Consistency and Discoverability

When aligning of all your integration and data services, you also want to safeguard data and application integration consistency. This requires all domains to document their application data and interface models. Not only must they be well described but, most importantly, all data attributes *must* be connected to the same set of elements within your business data dictionary.

Capturing context and meaning is important because there can be semantic confusion around the data and integration services between different domains. Terms can have different meanings, so it's crucial to correlate each data element with the right domain and understand what it means, where it originated, and where it's physically stored. In this section, I'll share some best practices for doing this. But first, I want to remind you how the different models relate.

In Chapter 1, I introduced the three phases of design, each represented by a data model: conceptual, logical, and physical. The conceptual design represents the entities and elements of the business; the logical application data model is a representation of the whole application, including its data store, that includes entities, entity names, relationships and properties; and the physical application data model describes the actual implemented design. In an ideal situation, each layer inherits from the previous one, forming a linkage model, so everybody understands how business concepts translate into real-world implementations.

In practice, many engineers bypass the logical modeling step. Some engineers see it as counterproductive, since most models today use either NoSQL schema designs or denormalized data structures. Despite this decline in their popularity, logical models are resurfacing as part of a "modern" data modeling practice. To learn more about logical modeling, read *Fundamentals of Data Engineering* by Joe Reis and Matt Housley (O'Reilly).

When projecting the three-model approach onto data providers and consumers, as illustrated in Figure 7-5, the conceptual models are the first (top) models: they're used to organize the business context. A business glossary can be a starting point for such a model. The logical models are derived from the conceptual models. They represent the logical designs; for example, database designs and interface models.

On the provider's side, you can see that both applications and interfaces are based on the conceptual data model of the domain. The context (such as business terms) doesn't change as data distribution takes place. The only difference when serving data to other domains is that what is exposed is typically a subset of the total business context. The subset of the context that is shared is expected to be the same in all of the data provider's underlying layers, as shown in Figure 7-5.

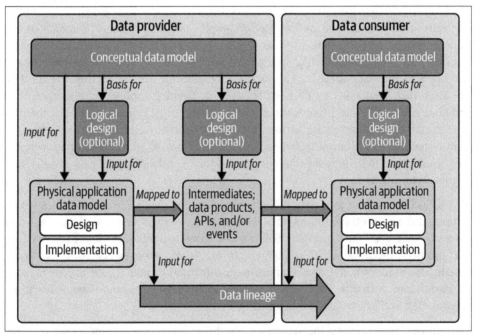

Figure 7-5. Ideally the conceptual, logical, and physical data models' attributes are all connected; because data in data products originates on the provider's side, its attributes will be linked to the provider's conceptual data model as well

If present, logical models are typically stored in a data modeling or design tool. Preferably, the linkage to the conceptual data model's entities or business terms would be provided for each implementation. Physical application models and interface models, which describe the actual implemented designs, should be stored in the environments in which these designs are created. If the designs are missing, I recommend you scan your data sources and capture technical metadata like names, file sizes, columns, and so on. You can store all of this information, for example, in a data catalog.

When connecting data models, you must pay attention to the fact that the same semantic data can have multiple representations. If this occurs, domains should map all technical attributes to the same corresponding business elements. An example could be a data product that stores the same semantic data in different file formats.

On the consuming side, you also have conceptual, logical, and physical models. A difference from the providing side is that no interface models exist, because data is directly transformed and integrated into the target application design. Another difference is that the context has been changed, so the various types of models are expected to have updated and enriched objects when compared to those on the providing side.

In an ideal state, all the models are connected. My recommendation is to capture and store all the business concepts and relationships from the conceptual data models centrally in a data catalog or knowledge graph, link them to the elements of the logical entities of your data products, APIs, and events (which can be stored in another repository), and finally validate everything against the (schema) metadata of the physical interface models. There's no easy solution for connecting the models. To reach that ideal state, you'll need to select or develop tooling, and combine and integrate metadata. You might want to start with a catalog, repository, or documentation portal; when progressing further, aim for consistency and look for insights into commonalities and differences between contexts across all architectural patterns. For this, you'll need to bring data modeling repositories and catalogs for data, APIs, and events closer together.

If you find integrating metadata too complex, you can make a pragmatic start with a data catalog and continue linking the elements from your catalog directly to attributes on a physical level. This approach will provide some insights into what business context has been input for which implementations. As you progress, consider designing a semantic model for the data management information you would like to manage in correlation with the metadata you already manage. Chapter 9 provides more information and examples on this topic.

Data discovery and capturing semantics, as you've learned, are complex subjects. To avoid the pitfalls, consider the following recommendations:

- Choosing the right data modeling methodology is paramount for metadata collection and end-to-end insights. Therefore, consider setting data product modeling and metadata standards jointly with your data product and integration teams. Part of this exercise is selecting corresponding tooling. Also, consider building up an internal community for sharing experiences and tips on how data modeling should be practiced.

- For achieving consistency between the models, consider implementing data quality controls on your metadata. For example, depending on the amount of control and data governance applied, you can validate that all physical attributes are mapped to business terms. If this is not the case, you might want to stop providers from publishing the data or interfaces. Additionally, you might want to report on the amount of coverage to show which domains have done their jobs well or badly.

- Don't wait too long to design your data management metamodel. This will help you understand how entities should be grouped and relate to each other. It will also help you select the right tooling. For example, some companies fully rely on logical designs for metadata-driven and automated deployments of their application designs. Such organizations might require more advanced tooling or better integration with other metadata services.

- Take into account security and privacy concerns. For regulatory reasons, you may need to classify and tag sensitive data, as well do policy-driven enforcement. More considerations on these subjects will be provided in Chapter 8.

- Communicate and be transparent about your data modeling and discovery capabilities. It's important to provide education about how data discovery works and how it helps other domains to more quickly find and use data. Demos and training sessions are essential. Guidelines and implementation workbooks are also critical to success.

- Consider a well-defined taxonomy for the elements of your data management information model. If the definitions of often-used terms such as *entity* or *attribute* are ambiguous, this doesn't foster consistency and makes communication between team members difficult.

The problem often is not the availability of the data itself, but issues with data quality and structure, missing contextual information, etc., which can affect your domain teams' ability to deliver real business value. To avoid these pitfalls, define strategies and best practices for data modeling, data discovery, and semantic consistency ahead of time; develop clear governance with a delineation of who is responsible for maintaining what metadata; establish control processes for validating metadata on data quality; and establish a process to ensure all data modeling metadata is up-to-date.

As the preceding recommendations make and clear, standardization, enterprise guidance, and consistent communication to domain teams are important aspects of your architecture. This leads us nicely into the second part of this chapter, in which I'll share my best practices gleaned from working as an enterprise architect.

Inspiring, Motivating, and Guiding for Change

Implementing change and choosing the right patterns aren't easy. So, in order to support your domain teams in their quest to develop solutions for their problems, I recommend the following best practices:

- Consider supporting your domain architects with design sessions in which they can ask questions and fine-tune their designs. Organize these sessions in close collaboration with other participants, such as enterprise, solution, and technical architects and business representatives. Data and integration are complex subjects, and not everyone might be able to do an accurate assessment of the existing and future situation. Organize walk-in sessions to guide, train, and coach architects on their skills.

- Consider developing a playbook with patterns that architects and developers can choose from. For each pattern, describe the characteristics, maturity stage, recommended technology services, considerations, and advantages and disadvantages. You might want to develop different versions of the playbook for different personas as well. For example, an application developer might have different needs than an enterprise architect who must oversee a larger part of the landscape.

- Publish an official list of approved technology services and products that are available. Link each of these services and products to the patterns in your playbook.

- Consider adjusting your enterprise architecture control process for ensuring your architects do the right things. As an enterprise architect, I proposed changing the solution intent template by adding an extra section for data and integration.[2] With this adjustment, all domain architects had to describe their patterns for data and integration as part of their solution proposals. These proposals were then submitted to the architecture design authority, a body of experts with relevant skills and experience to either approve them or steer the architects in the right direction.

---

2 The solution intent is part of the Scaled Agile Framework (*https://oreil.ly/DjG5l*); it describes the current and evolving requirements, the design, and the intent (or larger purpose) of the solution.

- Set up a competence center to share design decisions and implementation instructions. Such a competence center should focus on coaching and implementation activities, as well providing clear documentation, use case examples, instructions, and code examples. For example, Zalando's API guideline documentation (*https://oreil.ly/bqGm5*) is a living open source document that guides developers and makes it easier for them to work together.

When architecting for change, you'll run into situations where platforms and services aren't yet ready for (stable) consumption and usage. In such cases, it's important to consider the long-term effects of short-term decisions. For example, a new solution that is simple might be easier to migrate later than a solution that is large and complex. Try to make decisions you won't regret later. You may also run into situations that require exceptions or aren't clear-cut. We'll take a look at some of these in the next section.

Setting Domain Boundaries

When trying to decide which data distribution and application integration patterns best fit your needs, it's important that the domain boundaries are clearly set, as discussed in Chapter 2. Setting precise boundaries isn't an easy task, however, as it requires consensus. Deciding where to place certain business logic and abstractions can also be difficult because some functionalities and data transformations don't fit clearly into either the provider or consumer category. Your decisions should be based on knowledge, experience, and common sense.

Let's start with the obvious principles you must set. In Chapter 2, you learned about decoupling business capabilities: within a bounded context, tight coupling is allowed, but when crossing domain boundaries, all interfaces must be decoupled. Figure 7-6 shows a solution design that puts everything you've learned into practice. In this figure, you see four domains distributing data. Two of them are source system–aligned and two of them are consumer-aligned. Observe that we're using generic blueprints from data landing zones for providing standardized services. This gives consistency in the way data is layered and how data products are organized. This design layers data in such a way that domains have flexibility in how they manage local data that is input for data product creation. The data products themselves, however, are distributed via centrally managed storage services.

Let's zoom in a little further to see what other observations we can make.

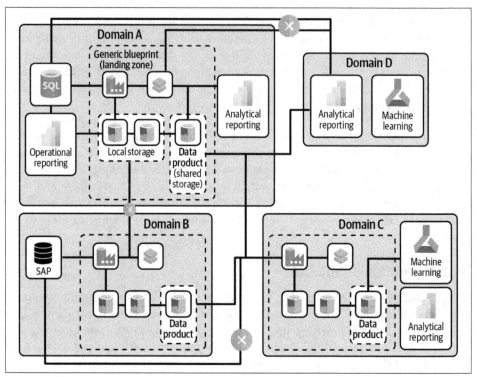

Figure 7-6. Solution example showing domain boundaries, what integration is allowed, and what must be forbidden

For domains A and B, notice that other domains aren't allowed to directly tap into the inner architecture of the operational application. No distribution of raw input data from a data product architecture is allowed. Next, notice that there are two types of reporting: operational and analytical. Operational reporting directly uses the operational system to get insights into the latest and most accurate data. It's typically low-latency and doesn't comprise too much data; the system's main objective is to be operational. Analytical reporting, on the other hand, can combine and query data more intensively, since the data has already been copied.

Domain C is a consumer: it uses data products from two other domains. It also uses data services from the generic blueprint. This is because an extra transformation step is required. Data products from the data providers don't meet the exact requirements of domain C, so the data first lands in this domain's data product architecture, where it is made consumer-specific. Domain D is another consumer that directly uses data products. Its architecture looks simple because it has virtualized data access to incorporate data without making a copy of the data.

When discussing provider- or consumer-specific transformations, a difficult choice is how to manage business logic or reference data that must be mapped to reference data on the other side. If, for example, referential values are detailed and change often, it will be difficult for data consumers to catch up with the changes. Every change to the reference data will affect data consumers. Providers and consumers will therefore have to agree on the right level of granularity. Data providers might need to abstract or roll up the granularly detailed local reference data into a more generic and consumer-agnostic version that is more stable and doesn't change as often.

When setting boundaries, also pay attention to what services and platforms you provide to your domain teams. Guidance will differ for boundaries within a domain and across domains. Let me give two examples. First, an API gateway can be used to facilitate communication between application components, as well as cross-domain communication. The gateway can even be the same product or API management platform. However, when crossing domain boundaries the interoperability differs. Within the boundaries of an application, you can ease your principles because dependencies are clearly scoped. You may, for example, allow APIs to be technical, lack a version, and not use proper response codes. When crossing the boundaries of domains, on the other hand, your interfaces must be decoupled and optimized for easy consumption because cross-domain dependencies are harder to manage. Second, you may allow greater flexibility and more technology choices (e.g., additional services and products) for inner-architecture design and development. For example, you may allow the API gateway product that comes as part of a particular software suite to be used for internal application communication, but not when interfacing to other applications.

Exception Handling

Are there situations where you shouldn't use the standardized integration services for domains or applications? Yes, but just one. The only exception to the rule about using point-to-point interfaces for cross-domain interoperability is for latency-critical applications, which won't meet latency requirements if they're decoupled via an intermediate integration component such as an API gateway. For example, within banking, there are strict requirements for how quickly a payment needs to be processed. The total amount of processing time generally has to be below 100 ms. Within this time frame, numerous things need to be checked: Is the payment unique? Are we processing the same payment twice? Is the account holder eligible to submit the payment? Might the payment be fraudulent? Is the receiving party allowed to receive this payment? If the communicating applications were decoupled via, for example, an API gateway, the latency between domains would increase and the 100-ms time limit would likely be exceeded. Point-to-point connections solve this problem. However, even if you need to break this one rule, I recommend you follow all the other standards you have set. So, if lineage metadata is required, don't allow point-to-point solutions to deviate from this principle. The same applies for the API designs and documentation; even though the API gateway isn't there, domains still have to do their data management duty.

Transitioning to a comprehensive integration and data architecture isn't easy. It requires many different teams to collaborate closely and make the right choices. In the next section, I'll review the actors that are involved and how they interact.

Organizational Transformation

A digital transformation is difficult because it requires changes to technology, processes, culture, and organizational alignment. It's an evolutionary process with people and practices at its core, and with technology as a catalyst for enabling change. The same goes for implementing data management capabilities. It starts with a vision, a comprehensive picture that embraces a more complete and total approach for enacting change. For developing this vision and the overall abstract design, it is usually your chief data officer who should be in the lead. Once the design is complete, the implementation can be put into motion, beginning as a formal project or program.

At the project level, where the data management capabilities are actually put into place, three actors are typically involved:

Domain teams
> Domain teams normally consist of a business owner (data, domain, or product owner), application owner(s), software developers, and data engineers. These teams should clearly communicate with each other about their requirements. Depending on the size of the organization and its level of technical expertise, the teams might vary in their level of autonomy. With some exceptions, domain teams are responsible for maintaining their business applications, databases, and data pipelines, and for delivering or consuming correct datasets.

Central data platform team
> The central data platform team is focused on developing core data competencies. It is usually both a development team and an operations/site reliability team. The main role of the central data platform team is to provide data-driven capabilities to domain teams. It is also expected to deliver best practices, support, CI/CD capabilities, automated testing capabilities, provisioning tools, and pipeline tools such as ETL components.

Central infrastructure (cloud) team
> The central infrastructure team is responsible for managing the physical hardware and assessing all the technology services that support the various organizational units. In the transition to the cloud, this team's role changes: it's the main enabler, assessing services and making them available to other teams. In addition,

this team is responsible for ensuring that all solutions are compliant by design by setting enterprise policies.

Figure 7-7 examines the relationships between these three actors. At the bottom, you see the central infrastructure team. To recap, its role is to offer a broad set of generic infrastructure-related services to all actors of the organization. When the data platform team starts building a data platform, it will work closely with the infrastructure team to enable data-related services. The infrastructure team will focus on aspects such as cost, auditing, control, maintainability, and so on,[3] while the data platform team focuses on turning the vanilla services into easy-to-use, self-service data management capabilities. It sometimes plays the role of a broker and redelivers these services as is, but more often the platform team integrates, modifies, or combines services with the aim of providing a better experience.

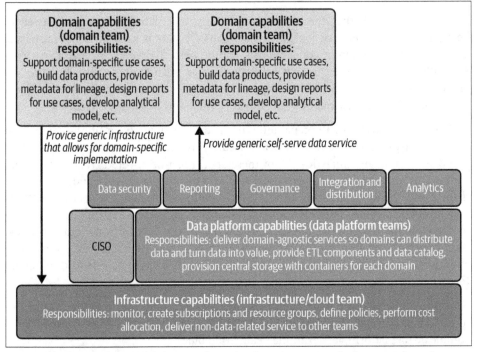

Figure 7-7. Operating model showing how the domain teams, platform team, and infrastructure team work together

At the top of Figure 7-7 are the domain teams. Their role is to deliver expertise in their domain and build services that support the processes and goals of the

---

3 The infrastructure team may also use services itself, for example, for overseeing and controlling all of the IT services. Services used by this team are sometimes referred to as *IT4IT services*.

business, based on their domain expertise. Domain teams may interact with both the central infrastructure team (for generic IT requests, such as when they need a virtual machine provisioned) and the central data team (when they require data services, such as machine learning, for their business solutions).

 Enterprise architects are the driving force in cross-team interactions: they know how to "ride the elevator";[4] they keep the penthouse (where business strategy is defined) and engine rooms (where software is built) connected, and they spot and remove potential obstacles. Whereas the role of a domain architect is to lead the domain team by bringing in relevant domain experience, enterprise architects usually have a wider scope: they connect the dots of business and technology.

I'm often asked whether the infrastructure team and data platform team need to be separate departments or logical units. I don't feel this is necessary. Infrastructure and data are two different concerns that can be perfectly well managed apart from each other. However, the speed of delivery often goes up dramatically when the two teams work together closely. You might even consider creating a virtual team that is composed of resources from both the infrastructure and data platform teams.

As Figure 7-7 also shows, the capabilities of the data platform team (in the center) can be decomposed into several categories: security, reporting, governance, integration and distribution, and analytics. All of these areas must be covered. When scaling up further, I recommend managing these disciplines by putting some boundaries around them. Each one might become a business capability (or domain) of its own, with its own product owners, resources, applications, and processes. You might even want to decouple them using the patterns and principles discussed throughout this book. As a final note on this figure, it's important to be aware that some functions, such as security and operations, cross all layers, because it's everyone's role to think about these.

Now you know who the main actors are. But how do they work together in practice to build a next-generation data architecture? To zoom in on the delivery model for a complex data platform, let's examine Team Topologies.

Team Topologies

Team Topologies (*https://teamtopologies.com*) is "the leading approach to organizing business and technology teams for fast flow, providing a practical, step-by-step, adaptive model for organizational design and team interaction." In their book by

---

4 *The Software Architect Elevator* by Gregor Hohpe (O'Reilly) is a must-read for every architect!

the same name, Matthew Skelton and Manuel Pais share insights on how to build complex solutions using four different Team Topologies:[5]

- A *stream-aligned team* is aligned to a flow of work, typically from a segment of the business domain. These teams frequently interact with and are supported by the other types of teams.
- An *enabling team* helps a stream-aligned team overcome obstacles, providing consultancy services and detecting when capabilities are missing.
- A *complicated subsystem team* assists other teams by dealing with complex tasks, usually in situations where significant mathematics/calculation/technical expertise is needed.
- A *platform team* is a grouping of other team types that provides an internal product to accelerate delivery by stream-aligned teams.

How might we map these Team Topologies to the model that we discussed in the previous section? In Figure 7-8, you see how the collaboration works.

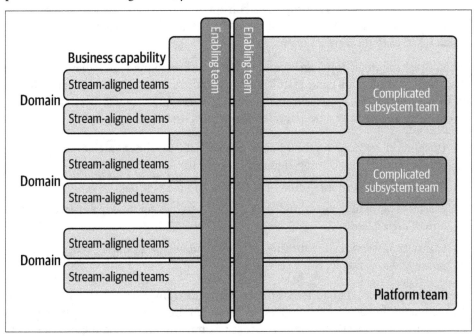

Figure 7-8. Team Topologies approach showing how domain (stream-aligned) teams, enabling teams, complicated subsystem teams, and the platform team work together

---

5 Thoughtworks also recommends Team Topologies for delivering a data mesh.

Let's start with the domain teams. In Team Topologies, domain teams are stream-aligned teams. As you have learned, they focus on business value by turning data into data products, and data products into value. For this, they use, for example, data management services for integrating data or developing pipelines. These services are provided by the data platform and infrastructure teams, which correspond roughly to the platform team in Team Topologies. Simply put, this team's goal is to deliver great services to empower other teams to achieve more with data. Ideally, stream-aligned teams should be able to work independently from one another, in parallel, with each one focusing on a specific business capability.

The mapping of the other two actors to Team Topologies is less clear-cut, and depends more on your perspective. The central data platform team can be viewed as both a stream-aligned team and a platform team. From a data management or infrastructure standpoint, the data platform team acts like a stream-aligned team. It consumes services from the (cloud) infrastructure team and uses these services to develop data management capabilities. However, when looking at it through the lens of a domain (stream-aligned) team, the data platform team is more of a platform team. Initially, the data platform team consumes generic infrastructure services. It adds some secret sauce to these and turns them into data management capabilities, which it serves to the domain teams.

What about the other topologies? Figure 7-8 shows enabling teams that traverse the stream-aligned (domain) and platform teams, and complex subsystem teams that sit off to the side. This is because in the context of data management, there are typically several areas that require a deep level of expertise. These include:

- Integration services for building complex data pipelines, maintaining scripts, executing code, performing engineering activities, and so on
- Security and governance services to protect and manage data
- Master data management and data quality services for making data consistent and of high quality
- Consuming services for turning data into value (for example, business intelligence and machine learning services)

If either the stream-aligned teams or the platform team were to attempt to handle these complex subjects by themselves, it would require them to put in a tremendous amount of work. For efficiency, therefore, I recommend offloading these concerns to an enabling team: a group made up of individuals with a high level of expertise in the area, and with a strong collaborative nature. Enabling teams support and provide training and guidance for other teams. They're also the linking pin between the stream-aligned and platform teams. Not including these teams in your organization could result, for example, in situations where your platform team needs to be present at every meeting about data governance.

Including complicated subsystem teams in your organization often also becomes necessary as the data platform grows. Larger systems, such as complex data management platforms, are likely to include complex subsystems (for example, a data onboarding system that uses machine learning) that require experts with deep knowledge and experience to build and operate. Having these teams available allows stream-aligned teams to delegate activities that they don't have the expertise or capabilities to handle.

Finally, note that between the different types of teams there are no hard resourcing boundaries. It's likely that you will run into situations where one team depends on another team for delivering value. For example, to effectively build its data products, a domain team might need a data modeling service from another team that isn't available yet. In such a situation, your teams can either wait or rotate team members. This model of rotating or borrowing resources, also referred to as *inner sourcing*, is based on the model of open source development. It can help to speed up delivery and also makes knowledge more resilient across the organization.

Organizational Planning

For aligning all your activities, it's important that the planning is correctly tuned. For this, there are typically two cadences.

First, there are *sprints* and *sprint reviews*. Sprints are part of the Scrum framework (*https://oreil.ly/qhnJN*). A sprint is a fixed period of a few weeks in which the teams focus on achieving their goals. At the end of each sprint is a sprint review session where each team reviews its results and revises the planning and objectives for the next sprints. During this exercise, teams can ask for support from other teams, setting up collaborations and partnerships to ensure their goals will be met for the next sprint. The interaction between teams in this cadence is typically one-to-one.

Second, there are larger sessions in which the interaction is many-to-many. After a series of sprints, there's another event, often called *Program Increment* (PI) *planning*.[6] During this face-to-face event, all teams come together to share their goals and ambitions for the next series of sprints. This activity can sometimes last all day. During this event, teams often demonstrate their work to others and give and receive feedback. In a way it's also a social construct that is personally and collectively rewarding, so don't be surprised when more than one hundred people are attending and cake is being served! In my previous role, when working as a lead architect, I also used these PI planning meetings as a forum for pitching future architectures, influencing my audience, and collecting feedback on architecture designs.

The delivery of a new architecture isn't easy. It involves planning, execution, coordination, and organizational change. Future state architectures and diagrams matter,

---

6 More information about PI planning can be found in the Scaled Agile Framework (*https://oreil.ly/R7Sd7*).

but they're supportive to change. When it comes to organizational decomposition and delivery methodologies, such as topologies and Scrum, architects must be seen as leaders who guide and facilitate teams through their implementations. They must oversee and support; they must be pragmatic and realistic, yet set the vision. Most importantly, they must inspire everyone to follow.

Wrapping Up

Shifting from a centralized to a decentralized model is a massive change for today's data-driven enterprises. The new ways of working needed to support federation are expected to cause friction. This means that there are risks involved in the implementation and delivery of your new architecture. I recommend starting with the foundational activities. Begin with business capabilities: delineate your domain (stream-aligned) teams, and align them with your organization. Decentralization requires having a good overview of your domains. Next, you can get started with building the architecture. For this, your central infrastructure and data platform teams must work hand in hand. Approach it piecemeal; pay great attention to metadata management from the beginning, and implement an adequate level of automation and self-service capabilities. During these early phases, your enterprise architects have a crucial role to play. They are responsible for overseeing, communicating with, guiding, and connecting different parts of the organization. The maturity and success of the first phases will determine whether you can move forward or not.

After the foundation is in place, your program can grow as more domains are baked into the offering. Consider what patterns you would like to provide first by examining the demand. Next, determine how you may facilitate this by using the many technologies you can choose from. Strive for standardization, but try to be flexible at the same time. Keep your services under the control of the infrastructure and platform teams to avoid technology proliferation and explosion of costs. Use your community sessions to stay connected with your teams, demonstrate success, and receive feedback.

This chapter provided a high-altitude flyover of data distribution and application integration patterns, as well as an overview of the different elements and actors involved in the organizational transformation described in this book. In the following chapters, we'll stay at a relatively high level, although from time to time we will dive more deeply into some complex subjects. We'll start with data governance and data security. Metadata management and master data management come next. After that, we'll fly our helicopter over the consuming side of the architecture. Fasten your seatbelts and get ready for takeoff!

CHAPTER 8

Data Governance and Data Security

This chapter focuses on data governance and data security. Why discuss these topics together? Because they overlap and share a common goal: data governance determines what the data represents and what it can be used for, and data security then ensures that only authorized parties can access the data (in line with its intended uses).

Uniformly applying security in all areas of your architecture requires standardization and metadata management. There are data owners to be assigned, classifications to be set, and contracts between parties to be maintained. All of this information should be stored centrally in a uniform model. We'll address many of these issues in this chapter, and the remainder in Chapter 9.

Data Governance

You might be wondering why you even need data governance. It is often perceived as a restrictive, bureaucratic, and controlling process. Won't it slow down your data ambitions? These are valid questions, and indeed within small companies or start-ups, there typically isn't any formal data governance; it's done implicitly during the day-to-day activities. In small-scale organizations, most applications and data are owned and managed by a few individuals. Data volumes and varieties are relatively limited, so finding the data you need and getting your questions answered takes little time. Often all you need to do is question the colleague sitting next to you, and if they don't know the answer, it's probably a few desks away.

Trouble arises when companies start to grow. Travel time between departments increases, more people have different focus points, knowledge is scattered, decisions take longer, responsibilities become unclear, data quality issues aren't followed up on, and so on. Organization, accountability, and transparency become more urgent as levels of data consumption and usage increase. Additionally, companies are confronted with new regulations, such as the GDPR and CCPA. These regulations demand total control of data usage, insight into how and where it is distributed, and clearly defined responsibilities. These laws require you to identify and clearly document where data has been stored, where it originated, what it's used for, how it's used, and by whom it is managed. Ensuring compliance while operating thousands of applications and databases is clearly a complex undertaking. Bottom line: the need for data governance is obvious.

The problem with data governance, however, is that most programs and processes are totally ineffective. Data governance solutions often consist of a large set of complex policies and guidance that focuses on controlling, rather than using, data. When these policies are implemented, no one is allowed to see or use the data until it has been "governed" or "brought under control."

Organizations often try to implement data governance with complex tooling. These tools tend to be complicated to configure and hard to integrate with other solutions. What's more, implementing rules-based workflows and audit trails and retroactively uploading the necessary documentation are lengthy processes. There's often limited enthusiasm for data governance; people simply don't see the value. So, knowing the challenges, what should we do differently, and how can we make data governance more pragmatic and effective? Let's find out.

The Governance Framework

Developing an effective data governance approach starts with rethinking the organizational culture, design, operating model, and roles. So far we've been using abstract concepts, like data domains, but now we're going to define a more concrete framework including specific roles and responsibilities, policies and standards, and working instructions to ensure the availability, usability, integrity, and security of your data. Let's start with the roles.

Roles

It's essential to understand that data governance is unique to each organization. Governance should be crafted to meet your specific demands. Therefore, the names and key activities within the overall data governance framework can vary between enterprises; each organization structures and titles these roles a little differently. That said, here's a high-level look at the most common roles and responsibilities of a data governance organization:

Chief data officer
    A chief data officer is responsible for the overall data strategy and data management practices. This person sets the vision, direction, and standards. This role might also be called *data governance leader* or *head of data management*.

Data owner

A data owner, sometimes called a *data trustee* or *process owner*, is an individual employee within the organization who is accountable for the data in question, and for properly managing the corresponding metadata. This includes overseeing data quality, definitions, classifications, purposes for which the data can be used, labels, and so on. Accountability in a distributed ecosystem isn't limited to only corporate data. Data owners are sometimes also product owners and thus can also be accountable for managing the priorities and backlog within a team.

Business user

A business user is a higher-level decision maker, typically a product owner or business representative, who collaborates with business teams on requirements and governance teams on data management policies, processes, and requirements. A business user can also be seen as a strategist whose role is to translate business requirements into a high-level solution.

Application owner

An application owner, sometimes called a *data custodian*, maintains the core of the application and its interfaces. The application owner is responsible for business delivery, functioning, and services, as well as the maintenance of application information and access control.

Data user

A data user is an individual employee within the organization who intends to use data for a specific purpose and is accountable for setting requirements.

Data creator

A data creator is an internal or external party who creates the data in agreement with the application and data owner(s).

Data steward

A data steward makes sure that the data policies and data standards are adhered to. They're often subject matter experts for a specific type of data.

Defined data governance roles are essential to every data governance program, and it is essential to assign ownership on the corresponding levels. This ensures that everyone's responsibilities are clear, yielding the best results.

When studying these roles, you might wonder why there is both a data owner and an application owner. Why not have just one owner? There are many good reasons for separating these roles and not making it one composite role (as the data mesh theory suggests). First, applications might be shared and used by different domains. In Chapter 2, you also learned about shared business capabilities, which are typically implemented centrally, using an as-a-service model, and provided to different parts of the organization. This requires more fine-grained ownership because the ownership activities must be carried out by different people. Second, the person responsible for correcting or overseeing data quality often isn't the person building the data pipelines. These are two different areas of expertise: owning data typically requires deep understanding of the business context, while owning an application requires technical engineering skills.

Creating the framework

In large enterprises, the roles highlighted in the previous section are usually federated: each domain has a formal data owner and supporting roles such as application owners and data stewards. The implementation of these roles, and the process of democratizing data and federating responsibilities, involves a massive organizational shift for enterprises. To support this transition, I recommend bringing all of the roles together in a formal artifact: a framework that serves as the foundation for all data governance activities. This framework must be reviewed and updated regularly, and should be aligned with the roles outlined earlier.

Of course, as mentioned previously, the framework will contain much more than roles. You should extend it with responsibilities, standards, and procedures. Figure 8-1 shows a high-level view of how the different governance roles can be grouped and managed together within the spirit of a domain-oriented way of working: using federated data domain teams and a centralized data governance team. For each role, you see a list of activities and responsibilities.

At the top of Figure 8-1, you see that the diagram is broken down into domains: cross-functional teams focusing on particular parts of the business. Within these domains, different roles interact to achieve the goals of value creation. For these activities, different stakeholders are working together: data owners, application owners, data creators, data stewards, and so on.

Below the domains, roles focus on delivering enabling (central) services and guiding the organization. On this level you'll find architects, advisors, and engineers developing platforms and defining global policies, such as interoperability, metadata, security, and documentation standards.

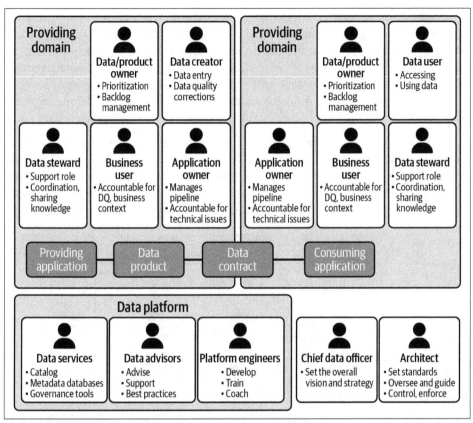

Figure 8-1. A high-level data governance framework that breaks the organization down into domain teams using different roles

The different roles, as defined in this governance framework, don't stand on their own. Close collaboration is often required. For example, a business user in one domain may reach out to a data owner in another domain to request data. If that data isn't generally available as a data product, the data owner is expected to validate whether it can be made available or not. If so, they should reach out to their corresponding application owners to start building the interfaces and initiate the process of making the data available. After that, the different team members should reach a common understanding about what purpose that data will be used for, and this agreement should be captured in a data contract.

To facilitate assigning activities to roles and ensure everyone in the organization is on the same page, it's recommended to formally describe all activities and responsibilities in the framework as well. For example, the framework may include detailed instructions on data quality requirements and procedures for monitoring data, correcting data, and follow-up time.

How should you structure the framework itself? I've seen lots of different representations while working with different organizations. For example, the framework could be a formal Word document broken into sections (executive summary, governance structure, role descriptions, and procedures for data quality, privacy management, security, compliance, and so on), or a series of wiki pages with descriptions and diagrams corresponding to the different activities in the data creation and management life cycle (validating and fixing data quality issues, reporting data lineage, etc.).

In Figure 8-2, you can see an example from one of the customers I've worked with. This framework captures the activities each role is responsible for across the different stages of managing data end-to-end. The responsibilities and activities are described at a high level here, but in order to ensure all roles follow the right processes, I recommend supporting each role with more detailed playbooks and/or guidelines.

	Data creation	Data product creation	Data publish	Data request	Data usage
Data owner	• Coordinate addressing data quality issues • Fix (functional) data gaps	• Coordinate data needs with data consumers	• Provide policies and restrictions of usage • Remediate constraints	• Approve data usage • Conduct periodic review (quarterly) data contracts and sign off	• Collect and coordinate feedback on usage
Application owner	• Maintain and describe application data models • Process application changes	• Develop data pipeline in close collaboration with data engineers • Deliver technical metadata	• Deliver metadata for data product creation • Implement controls for meeting SLAs • Deliver lineage	• Collaborate wth data consumer application owners on technical requirements • Remediate issues	• Collect feedback on usage • Remediate application issues
Data steward	• Coordinate addressing data quality issues • Fix data gaps	• Submit business terms and definintions • Link business terms to technical attributes • Classify sensitive data	• Improve documentation • Share knowledge • Define policies with data owner	• Accomplish consistent data usage by providing feedback to data owner	• Coach, train data users on data-consuming side
Data user	• Support on closing gaps and data quality issues • Share requirements	• Provide feedback	• Provide feedback	• Deliver data usage information for data contact • Coordinate constraints on data usage	• Provide feedback • Share knowledge with data owners and other data users

Figure 8-2. Example framework

You might want to introduce a maturity model with different levels indicating performance and maturity in the various stages of your data life cycle. For example, level 0 might mean no domain team members have received training and no data governance activities are taking place. Level 1 could indicate that team members have received some training and are aware of the basics, but limited governance activities are being performed. Levels 2 and up could indicate increasing degrees of maturity, with level 5 corresponding to all team members having a strong commitment to managing data correctly and doing so efficiently.

You should customize your governance framework to fit the specific needs of your organization. You can make it as complex or simple as you want, as long as it is effective. One final tip: focus on the organizational side, not the technical side, of data management.

Governance body

For data governance to be successful, you need to have a governing body (sometimes called a *data governance team*) that ensures the framework is implemented correctly. Members of this team are typically responsible for the following activities:

- Overseeing that procedures and standards are followed
- Ensuring procedures and documentation are up-to-date
- Establishing training and awareness programs
- Providing transparency about the overall current maturity level of all data governance areas across all domains
- Assigning roles to new individuals
- Performing regular reviews
- Compiling audit reports for ensuring compliancy
- Identifying areas for improvement
- Defining new standards and policies
- Defining the architecture requirements needed for data management

In addition to data owners and stewards, the governance body usually also includes more senior representatives, such as data architects or managers from other business departments. The members of the body typically report to the chief data officer.

When the data governance body assigns different roles, it's important that their associated responsibilities and tasks are described carefully in the framework. Data owners, data users, application owners, and data stewards in particular should be aware of their responsibilities and those of their counterparts. These sets of tasks also include a range of processes (which I'll cover next). The overall responsibilities are typically outlined in a *responsibility assignment* (RACI) matrix (*https://oreil.ly/KgNs7*) that maps out all of the different tasks, roles, and responsibilities and who is accountable for each.

The roles, framework, and governance body serve as the foundation for data governance, balancing between central oversight and proper assignment of responsibilities and activities and ensuring that responsibilities are clear and don't overlap. What else is needed to make data governance more effective?

Processes: Data Governance Activities

Data management is the practical work of carrying out all the activities identified in the governance framework, in accordance with the provided guidelines. In that respect, the governance body has to ensure proper data management across the organization. In a federated or large-scale organization, the governance body can take on a slightly different role: it becomes responsible for defining what constitutes good data governance within the domains. Such a cultural shift also requires a mindset shift. Instead of executing all data governance activities, the team should focus on coaching and training other users. To support this shift, you should write guidelines and playbooks for all the processes that must be executed by federated teams. Here are some of the most important areas to cover:

- Defining data catalog metadata population processes
- Identifying data sources and assigning application and data ownership
- Defining policies for correct data handling according to applicable regulations, like the GDPR for handling personally identifiable information (PII)
- Defining quality control levels for data at creation and distribution (including acceptable levels of outliers), assigning data quality responsibilities, and monitoring follow-up
- Defining the granularity of data lineage and what types of applications need to deliver it
- Setting up a central classification scheme and repository for using, tagging, labeling, and securing data
- Studying the impact of new regulations on data management
- Aligning with enterprise architecture to ensure policies are deeply embedded into the architecture
- Determining what data must be mastered on a central level
- Setting data life cycle management policies, including for other information assets, such as reports and dashboards
- Defining schema identification requirements and protocol standards for common data formats, such as XML, Parquet, and JSON
- Ensuring that naming guidelines for metadata, data types, and formatting and other conventions (such as the use of snake case or camel case) are defined
- Ensuring the domain teams deliver metadata correctly
- Working on creating a culture of data awareness, including rewarding data stewards and raising awareness on ethics and the use of machine learning in certain contexts

- Defining how long data should be retained

- Monitoring and instructing users to ensure the data models are maintained correctly

- Developing methodologies and best practices for modeling data, developing ontologies, maintaining business glossaries, and so on

- Maintaining the data catalog and its metamodel, and ensuring all information assets are well described

- Identifying deviations from the data management disciplines and addressing associated risks

- Setting principles for data onboarding and consumption

- Developing other guidance, policies, and frameworks, such as for randomly auditing the SQL query logs or dealing with external data

- Guiding the organization in holding roundtable discussions about guardrails and deciding upon and implementing rules, principles, and automation

It's best to select a subset of these activities, not all of them, for your initial planning. To make the task of planning and implementing governance manageable and practical, it's important to also make conscious decisions about what *not* to do. Select your target activities based on affinity—what seems to fit together and makes sense as a first step. Consider also what must be organized based on dependencies; so, what to do in what sequence. Finally, be aware that there will be other activities, such as defining measures and review policies, that you will need to implement as you progress further in establishing your next-gen data architecture.

Making Governance Effective and Pragmatic

With the roles, framework, and processes identified, as a next step you should focus on making governance effective and pragmatic. Based on my experience, I can share the following recommendations:

Secure C-suite buy-in as soon as possible.
An important first step is securing C-suite buy-in for the goals you want to achieve. Many data governance initiatives start from the bottom up, or come after the implementation of an enterprise data platform. By establishing leadership support from the beginning, you will avoid the usual challenges around empowerment, mandate, and lack of resources.

Pair up with other large programs.
Examine whether you could align your ambitions with those of other large transformation programs. Rather than pushing yourself, you may be able to leverage initiatives that are already underway. In my previous role, the organization aligned data governance ambitions with initiatives around adhering to

external regulations. Usually these programs already have large budgets and full organizational attention.

Ensure data governance provides clear value to everyone.
Data governance done right makes tasks easier. For example, it mitigates risks by ensuring everyone understands where sensitive data is managed. It also facilitates self-service data discovery and easy data access.

Trust local teams.
In a large-scale organization, a mindset shift is required because nobody can oversee and manage all of the data. Once the boundaries are clear, and when you're confident that your domains have the skills, services, and controls they need, allow each domain to manage its data within the trust boundaries you've set.

Focus on the quality of upstream data.
If you fix quality issues at the source—that is, in the providing applications and processes that are executed close to the providing side—issues will no longer pop up in other places.

Be realistic in your ambitions and let go of the belief that all data can be "correct."
Focus on the consumers and their use cases, and determine what "good quality" means for them.

Don't see data governance as a one-time improvement.
Data governance is never finished. If you want to lower the burden, automate it; that is, make it computational.

Equip your data governance team(s) with highly skilled software engineers.
Effective governance relies in large part on automating data management tasks. For example, data products can only be published after they have been automatically validated. Similarly, rather than manually cataloging data products, services in the platform can profile for sensitive data.

Be strict on core data management principles.
The main purpose of data governance is to set a foundation. Thus, be strict on baselines and standards. A recommended approach is to start with your key principles, such as capturing data directly from the source, not allowing distribution of data you don't own, and not sharing any data without an owner. Next, consider your access models. A compute-based access model typically applies data access and permissions in the compute layer on the consuming side. This model relies on a delegated trust model: the provider admin grants access to the consumer admin, who then gives access to their consumers. The alternative is a data-centric access model, where authorization is enforced where the data lives (for example, in a data lake) against the consuming groups.

Share progress.

It's essential to show the impact of what you're doing, so work on transparency and clear communication. This may include sharing acknowledgments, presenting road maps, collecting honest feedback, and celebrating key milestones.

Measure success based on business value generated.

Showing the impact helps to retain the attention and support of top management. Consider tracking your results with metrics: for example, showing how many data quality issues were solved and what the availability of data is within the larger organization.

Find the right balance and do it piecemeal.

Adjust the level of governance to the requirements of your domains, because not all domains may suffer from the same level of regulatory pressure. If half of your data is low-risk, you don't have to put many restrictions and procedures in place around it. Focus on the critical data elements, such as customer addresses, and take it slow when scaling up. Learn by doing, and pragmatically change processes where you can!

Work on consistent communication.

Some parts of data governance are standard for all organizations, but many parts are specific to how organizations work and have organized themselves. Data governance comes with a lot of jargon; to correctly connect your teams and help them work together, consider listing out important governance terms and definitions that are frequently used. Also clearly communicate the benefits of data governance. This helps reduce resistance to change and ensures employees are involved in the process from the start.

Manage metadata in a smart way.

Many activities are centered around manually describing metadata in Excel spreadsheets. It doesn't have to be that way! Consider automatically recording metadata in your data catalog, or applying standardization on integration services so data lineage is captured more easily.

Make data governance part of your cadence for planning, execution, and coordination.

Your data governance team should see the progress and potential challenges of other teams. They should take a supportive approach. For example, if the processes of sharing or consuming data take too long, the team should make services more self-explanatory or self-service.

Make it fun.

Look for ways to create enthusiasm about governance in your organization. For example, you may be able to create new opportunities in certain job roles, or allow junior employees to practice communicating through presentations and demonstrations. Alternatively, maybe you can raise awareness and excitement through walk-in sessions, blog posts, or special rewards during your PI planning meetings.

Once you've raised the level of enthusiasm, your next task is to effectively support all of your activities. For this, your data governance team needs adequate equipment, in particular tooling and metadata repositories.

Supporting Services for Data Governance

As I've mentioned, it's important to provide transparency and trust around data. Building such trust requires the data governance team and other teams to make metadata—data about the data—available centrally via tools and platforms. The complexity here is that metadata for data governance is often scattered: it is available only in the context of a particular platform or tool.[1] So you need an overarching strategy for identifying and classifying applications, data, and data owners more precisely, and an architecture with supporting applications and repositories.

For data governance to be successful, it needs to be supported by the following applications or functions:

Data catalog
> A data catalog typically is an inventory that stores metadata such as business terms, owners, origins, lineage, labels, classifications, and so on. Modern data catalogs are often combined with many other data management and search tools, so they may include scanners or a knowledge graph for storing metadata. A large part of Chapter 9 is devoted to providing more guidance on these subjects.

Application repository
> This is a standalone central repository or IT service management system (*https://oreil.ly/sIKV-*) that keeps track of all unique applications and their application owners. Additionally, this repository can hold information about production status, vendor products, and confidentiality, integrity, and availability ratings of the application based on the controls in place. You can also use a third-party software component such as ServiceNow (*https://www.servicenow.com*) for this repository.

List of your unique data elements
> This is a standalone repository or area within your catalog that maintains an overview of all unique data, including its ownership, across the organization. Data, as described in Chapter 7, is registered on the logical level of datasets because there can be multiple data owners in a single application, and several physical datasets can originate from the same application; the

---

1 Much of Chapter 9 is dedicated to solving the metadata distribution problem.

relationship between datasets and applications, consequently, is many-to-many. The repository that tracks unique data can also keep track of the classifications of individual data elements, such as personal data and its usage purposes, enterprise data usage, and limitations on data usage.

Data contract application (DCA)

This is a standalone application that registers all data contracts between data owners, users, and consumers, including the purpose of data sharing, safeguards, conditions for modification, warranties, privacy restrictions, validity date, and so on. The DCA plays an important role in the security architecture, which will be discussed in the second part of this chapter. The DCA, as you'll learn later, acts as the Policy Administration Point (PAP) or Policy Information Point (PIP) for providing information to evaluate and issue authorization decisions. We'll talk more about these components in "Data Security" on page 241.

If you don't build a DCA but use a third-party vendor's data security application directly, you'll be tightly coupled to that specific vendor. Many security applications work only in silos or support few technologies. If you want a holistic, agnostic security view of all your data, you must decouple!

Metadata repositories

Metadata repositories are databases and associated tools that help users find and manage information about the data. You can also use a third-party software component or any homegrown solution as a metadata repository. More specific guidance for maintaining metadata is provided in Chapter 9.

Knowledge graphs

A knowledge graph is a knowledge base that uses a graph-structured data model or topology to integrate data. For data governance, this might be important to see and discover correlations and relationships. More guidance is provided in Chapter 9.

Data scanners and profiling tools

Scanners and profiling tools are needed to process and examine data to collect information such as the level of data quality, schema information, and transformation and lineage information. The more advanced data catalogs incorporate these functionalities into their default offerings, but there are also offerings dedicated to scanning and profiling.

All of these data governance–related applications or functions should work together to provide an integrated view of all of your data. You can use commercial tools or homegrown applications, and you can outsource specific parts to tools that are optimized for certain tasks.

One component that requires special attention is the DCA. In a federated architecture in which responsibilities are distributed between domains, it's harder to oversee dependencies and obtain insights on data usage. This is where data contracts come into play.

Data Contracts

A *data contract* is a formal agreement between a data provider and a data consumer about what data is allowed to be consumed for what purposes. Why do data contracts matter? They provide insights into who owns what data products, support setting standards and managing data pipelines with confidence, and provide information on what data products are being consumed, by whom, and for what. Bottom line: data contracts are essential for robust data management!

I encourage you to look at the issues of data product distribution and usage from two perspectives. First, there are technical concerns, such as data pipeline handling and mutual expectations about data stability. Second, there are business concerns, like agreeing on the purpose of data sharing, which may include usage and privacy objectives and limitations. Typically, different roles come into play for each dimension. For technical concerns, you commonly rely on application owners and data engineers. For business concerns, you commonly rely on data owners, data users, and data stewards.

Data contracts are like data delivery contracts or service contracts. They're important because when data products become popular and widely used, you need to implement versioning and manage compatibility. This is required because in a larger or distributed architecture, it's harder to oversee changes and dependencies. Applications that access or consume data from other applications always suffer from coupling, which means that there's a high degree of interdependence. Any disruptive change to the data structure, for example, could have a direct impact on other applications. In cases where many applications are coupled to each other, a cascading effect can sometimes occur. Even a small change to a single application can lead to the adjustment of many other applications at the same time. Therefore, many architects and software engineers try to avoid building coupled architectures.

Data contracts are the solution to this technical problem. A data contract guarantees interface compatibility and includes the terms of service and service level agreement (SLA). At the same time, it provides transparency for the organization. Example 8-1 shows an example of how a data contract can be implemented as a metadata record.

A data contract describes what data is allowed to be consumed. It may contain extra details about the usage (for example, whether the data is allowed to be used only for development, testing, or production) and metadata about the quality, delivery, or interface. It also might include details on uptime, allowed error rates, and availability, as well deprecation, version numbers, etc.

Example 8-1. Sample metadata record holding the information of a data contract

```json
{
  "@AgreementId": "1342",
  "contactPoint": {
    "ConsumerId": "894",
    "fn": "Marketing Department",
    "hasEmail": "mailto:email@example.com"
  },
  "ApplicationId": "201",
  "Description": "<p>This data contract captures the usage of marketing
data within the domain of HR. Usage of this data is limited to the HR department only,
as the data may contain sensitive information about employees and customers.</p>",
  "DataRequestType": "dcat:FlatFile",
  "IssuedDate": "2022-11-26",
  "StartingDate": "2022-12-01",
  "ExpirationData": null,
  "scope": [
    "DEVELOPMENT"
  ],
  "purpose": [
    "HR_ONLY"
  ],
  "dataElements": [
    "fd11d32f-4944-4bd9-a563-36d0f891e649",
    "345f0539-f3c7-4547-a2ab-cf6b66c675ce",
    "ff0e9c26-0f96-4370-8e39-7d78b27ffe88",
    "7ca735c1-20dd-43f1-a7a9-e5719340e4fa",
    "3b7c7926-7d39-4257-8029-dacc9ee22ecf"
  ],
  "ApprovalDate": "2022-11-27",
  "ApprovalFlag": true
}
```

Example 8-1 uses globally unique identifiers (GUIDs) for entities instead of using the path that defines the location of a file or data source. My motivation for using GUIDs is that data products may be duplicated and address locations may change as data is dynamically processed and organized in folders. GUIDs will solve these issues because they remain stable and are linked to the actual locations where data is physically stored.

What I see across organizations is that data contracts are often implemented as a part of a metadata-driven ingestion or data quality control framework.[2] Data contracts in such a design ensure the integrity of stable data delivery by detecting breaking

---

2 A curated list of awesome blogs, videos, tools, and other resources about data contracts can be found on AltimateAI's GitHub repo (*https://oreil.ly/pMUcF*).

changes. They can, for example, be stored as testing templates in execution of code repositories, and play an important role within the data pipeline (validating schemas, data types, file formats, etc.).

I've also seen organizations store their data contracts separately from the data product architectures; for example, in a central data contract repository or data catalog. Example 8-1 is well adapted to this approach. Storing data contracts separately usually requires more implementation work because a translation is needed between what is described in the contract and how datasets are validated within the actual data product architectures.

For a distributed architecture, you should standardize your data pipeline framework across different domains. Domains, in this approach, conform to a common way of working. They process data themselves, which means that the control and responsibility stays with the domains. However, the framework and contract metadata remain under central governance. If you're considering this model, start with the basics, like managing schema validations and data catalog information. As part of this effort, bootstrap your processes and implement controls using libraries like Great Expectations (*https://greatexpectations.io*) or dbt test (*https://oreil.ly/9ougy*) for validating technical data quality as part your data contract creation process. Next, put controls and workflows in place to allow handshakes between data providers and consumers, so, for example, domains need to sign off when a testing template is submitted as a pull request (*https://oreil.ly/mdWph*).

 Data observability refers to an organization's ability to fully understand the health of the data in its data estate. It focuses on the freshness, integrity, volume, lineage, and quality of the data, and the trends in all of these dimensions. Data contracts are expected to anchor into this by defining the patterns for the consumption and usage of data.

To continue scaling, you'll need to get observability into your data. You can do this by capturing statistics about your data pipelines. You could use the same contract repository or database for storing this information. This input about observability is needed for seeing the overall freshness, health, and status of all your pipelines.

Usage agreements

Usage agreements are an essential part of your data contracts. As discussed, they cover usage and privacy objectives and limitations. They're interface-independent and can serve as input for data security controls, providing insights into the purposes for which data can legitimately be used. These agreements may include, for example, details on what filters or security protections should be applied to the data, or restrictions on sharing consumed data or any newly created results.

Usage agreements also prevent miscommunications over data usage. Before data is shared, domains should discuss data sharing and data usage issues. When they reach a collaborative understanding, they should then document that understanding in a data sharing agreement. These agreements might also cover aspects like functional data quality, historization, data life cycle management, and further distribution. This approach of reaching a common understanding is not only important from a regulatory perspective, but also delivers value to your organization.

Attributes in your usage agreements, and your data contracts in general, should map clearly to elements from your business data catalog, which contains additional information about how data can be used. Therefore, always ensure semantic context is provided and a link is created between data attributes and business terms. This allows consumers to understand how the translation from business requirements to an actual implementation has been made. Depending on how important this is to you, you may want to consider implementing policies to ensure these relationships are respected—for example, you can only include a data product attribute in a contract if it is linked to a business term. The same policies might also apply for contextual changes, such as relationship and definition adjustments.

One last word: agreements on ethical usage and further distribution are often framed loosely because these aspects are hard to automate or enforce. However, you could implement an audit framework by periodically reviewing whether the agreements are respected.

Best practices for getting started

How should you get started with data contracts? Take it slowly. It's mostly an organizational challenge. Don't introduce too many changes in a row. Data contracts are a cultural shift; users need to become familiar with them and understand the importance of data ownership. The transition also requires finding the sweet spot between too few and too many metadata attributes. I recommend the following process for making the transition itself:

1. First and foremost, ensure that ownership is set and technical data pipelines are stable. If they're unstable and subject to unexpected and disruptive changes, none of your use cases will make it into production.

2. Put a process in place. Don't overcomplicate things. You could, for example, start with a simple form or template designed in a tool like Microsoft Forms. You should draft it in clear, concise language that is easy to understand. Accept manual processes. Limit your initial metadata requirements. Your first phase is about initiating the cultural shift and collecting requirements. You'll iterate until your metadata requirements become stable.

3. After you put your first processes in place, try to replace your manual forms with a web-based application, database, and/or message queue. During this stage,

your central data governance team will still be overseeing things. Data access will typically be coarse-grained, so standardize on containers, folders, or files. Try to utilize REST APIs for automatically provisioning data access policies or access control lists. For example, each time a data owner gives approval, a webhook (*https://oreil.ly/yJCem*) is called that triggers another function for calling the catalog, requesting the URIs, and updating the access rights.

4. Next, add automation by translating your data contracts into unit tests or data validations. So, each time a data contract is added, a post-deployment process takes place; for example, you issue an API call to a function to automatically add a testing template, or you modify the data ingestion framework in such a way that data contracts are being retrieved and used as input for schema validation.

5. Your next stage is implementing a stronger workflow for handling approvals. From this point, put your data owners or data stewards in the lead. Your central data governance team will now be overseeing from the back seat, conducting regular reviews of all the data contracts. By this stage, you should also have a data catalog up and running showing all ready-for-consumption data products. Make improvements to your data security and enforcement capabilities. Allow for finer-grained selections on columns and row filters by automatically deploying dynamic views. Consider techniques like dynamic data masking to prevent misuse. For fine-grained data access, ask your data providers to complement their data products with additional metadata for filtering. This means that during data contract creation, you'll want to ask the data providers what columns are relevant for filtering.

6. At the end of your journey, everything will be self-service and fully automated. This includes automated security enforcement and machine learning for predicting data approvals. Secure views, for example, are automatically deployed after approval.

Data contracts are a relatively new approach to data management. They're important as they provide transparency into your dependencies and data usage. Start small and focus on technical stability and standardization first. Iterate by using a lessons-learned process. Data governance is essential, but too much will cause overhead. Slowly build up and automate.

As you can see, data governance is essential for data security, which we'll discuss next. Data security requires a solid governance framework and metadata foundation to work with. If your domains don't take ownership of data and accurately describe and classify it, it will be impossible to protect your most sensitive data.

Data Security

Data security, as described in Chapter 1, covers all the activities that involve protecting data: people, processes, and technology. In particular, it's critical to keep sensitive data like PII, personal health information, banking information, and information about intellectual property out of the hands of criminals, hackers, attackers, and competitors.

The challenge is that data is volatile and, today, no longer maintained in a single monolith. It's decentralized, distributed across many systems and environments, making it harder to control what users do when they get their hands on data (for example, combining it with data from other sources and performing unethical analyses). It's also difficult to secure data without knowing its full context: HR data has a different meaning and value in the context of a reorganization than the context of organizing a company outing or celebration.

A far bigger problem is the large amount of data big companies are dealing with. Federated data can be a melting pot: diverse data sources and owners' and consumers' needs and requirements are all brought together. Individual sources and their corresponding data elements have different contexts, levels of quality, classifications, purpose bindings, owners, ratings, and so on. New sources, data products, and use cases are added all the time. Describing, governing, and protecting all this data requires an explosion of security rules and policies.

Data security within an enterprise organization is generally enforced by a dedicated security department, led by the chief information security officer (CISO). The CISO is a senior-level executive responsible for establishing and maintaining the enterprise's vision, strategy, and processes to ensure information assets and technologies are adequately protected. They work closely with the enterprise architecture and data governance representatives to ensure that the security vision and goals are correctly incorporated into the overall enterprise.

Current Siloed Approach

There's a huge gap between what most enterprises have implemented and what experts advocate. Many consultancy companies use the term *data-centric security* to emphasize that security should focus on the data itself rather than on networks, servers, or applications. However, in practice, the current security implementations focus mainly on silos—data warehouses and data lakes—because the large amounts of data available and the myriad combinations users can make mean high risks and a need for extra attention.

For API-based and event-driven architectures, the security model in many companies is implemented using different procedures, classifications, tools, and capabilities. Security in these architectures typically focuses on endpoints rather than on the data flowing through these platforms. Data classifications and surrounding context barely play a role for operational use cases. In my view, a data-centric security model should focus on trust boundaries and utilize the underlying governance metadata, so this is what we will study next.

Trust Boundaries

In a federated architecture, your domain boundaries should operate as trust boundaries (*https://oreil.ly/sRlij*). Concretely, this means that within the domain itself there is a level of trust. Thus, to a certain extent, domains can themselves decide on what security models are set, how data is internally classified, what data can be used, and by whom. This trust exists because within a domain, context is known. Everybody operating within the domain boundary can be assumed to have a good understanding of the risks and threats attached to the data that is managed there.

When moving data across domains, different rules apply because the level of trust changes. This is partly because it's harder for other domains to understand the potential risks involved when using data outside its original context. In addition, the data can be copied, manipulated, and combined with other data, out of sight of the originating domain. This could trigger a situation in which privacy risks are amplified. Therefore, it is important to manage security at the edges of your domain boundaries (interfaces to data products, APIs, and events). The recommended approach for managing trust boundaries is to perform the following set of actions:

- Implement a data classification and purpose scheme so domains know what level of protection must be provided for what data.
- Establish data contracts for data that crosses trust boundaries. This provides transparency into what data is used for what purpose and whether the level of protection that has been applied is sufficient.
- Set up monitoring and ensure that insights are provided about what data is moved across trust boundaries. This principle requires lineage to be present in your data governance or cataloging solution.
- Implement policies and controls that automatically enforce identity-based access controls, encryption of data at rest and in transit, usage of key-management services, usage of security logging and auditing services, two-factor authentication for users, and obfuscation or masking of data for unauthorized users, and so on.

Ultimately, all security controls on the edges of your trust boundaries should work consistently for all types of data distribution, based on the trust level(s) you have set. To reach such a level of maturity, your organization will require central security services, cross-domain governance, and strong guidance. Reaching a high level of control at all edges isn't easy. It requires teams and experts to consistently and correctly classify data, so you'll need a central classification scheme. In addition, you need to agree on a data usage scheme in which these classifications play a role. You will also need to implement a unified data security model that takes all of this information as input. We'll examine all of these aspects in the next sections, and then we'll make things concrete with a pragmatic example.

Data Classifications and Labels

Classifications and labels are an important aspect of data management: they are used to cluster data into relevant categories so it can be used and protected more efficiently. On a basic level, the classification process makes data easier to locate and retrieve; however, on a more advanced level, classifications are used as input for security, compliance, and regulation. Security classifications, for example, can act as input for setting restrictions on what users are allowed to see. The list of data classifications is best maintained centrally and shouldn't be too long.

 Must unstructured data, such as documents, pictures, and log files, be classified as well? Yes! You shouldn't classify only structured data. Unstructured and semistructured data can be classified using the same schemes.

Security classifications might include markers like `Personal Names`, `Social Security Number`, `Religion`, `Gender`, `Employee Information`, `Commercial Company Information`, or `Credit Card Number`. To configure autolabeling rules using these classifications, you might use labels like `Highly Confidential`, `Confidential`, `General`, and `Public`. For example, an autolabling rule might state that all data with the `Credit Card Number` classification should be automatically labeled `Highly Confidential`.

Protecting Personal Data and Compliance

The key to successfully managing personal data and user consent is combining data governance, security, and master data management. Data governance focuses on managing processes, classifications, and labels. This allows you to see what data is sensitive and should be treated with extra care. Data security focuses on restricting data access. Master data management, as you'll learn in Chapter 10, focuses on the rules around matching and identifying data. With this discipline, you must be able to uniquely identify customers and know what type of consent has been given. Complying with regulations such as the GDPR and CCPA thus isn't about focusing on any one area of data management; the road to compliance starts with an end-to-end, integrated vision. Hence, data cataloging must start at the source, rather than being a post-ETL activity.

The benefit of using labels is that your policy rules are decoupled from the data itself. If regulation forces you to take extra care of PII, for example, you don't have to relabel all your data; with a good classification scheme, restrictions are automatically inherited.

 It's not uncommon for large enterprises to acknowledge that PII protection in a highly decentralized environment is simply too complex or prone to faults. Enterprises that acknowledge this typically enforce that all extracted source data that is tagged as PII must be obfuscated, masked, encrypted, or similar.

Classifications are important because they play a role in control policies for automatically restricting data access. This becomes especially important when data is critical and has higher risks attached to it. So, for all data products, which are the main point of data access, all data elements should be classified.[3]

Data Usage Classifications

To better control data usage, security, and discoverability, consider using data usage classifications to limit data use to specific scenarios or use cases. Again, this list is best maintained centrally and shouldn't be "overclassified." If it is too long, it will be difficult for users to choose. Examples of data usage classifications are:

DATA_SCIENCE
:   For research and finding insights in data

AD_HOC_USAGE
:   For nonrepetitive work, such as creating reports on the fly

HR_ONLY
:   For work in human resources

FINANCIAL_REPORTING
:   For producing financial statements and risk reports

DQ_INVESTIGATION
:   For data quality research and investigation

Data usage classifications affect what users can see and do with the data. Imagine, for example, a situation in which you maintain a reference table that combines data usage classifications and data classifications. Such a table can be used as input for your data contracts process. HR_ONLY, in such an example, could be used to whitelist data for all

---

3 When classifying physical data—for example, rows—the classifications, or links to the classifications, are encapsulated in the data itself.

employees that belong to the human resources department, allowing them to see data that has been labeled Confidential or Highly Confidential.

Labels and classifications are essential to manage security at a larger scale. In the next section, I'll propose a unified data security framework in which they provide input for making security decisions.

Unified Data Security

The recommended approach for implementing data security is to incorporate your security requirements into your data platforms and services from the start. Successfully addressing security risks requires you to focus on two levels of control. The first level is data security controls, which include data access, data masking, data encryption, data usage monitoring, and identity providers. The second level—the infrastructure level—focuses on isolation, network encryption, firewalls, etc. For data management purposes, we are concerned only with the first level.

The most fundamental of the data security controls are the access controls. *Access* refers to the ability to view or retrieve data stored within a database or application. There are several popular data access control models for determining who has access to data, including *access control lists* (ACL), *role-based access controls* (RBAC), and *attribute-based access control* (ABAC). Let's examine these models and determine how and when to use them.

Most companies start with ACLs and RBAC. RBAC, also known as *role-based security*, is a mechanism that restricts system access to authorized users. The idea of this model, as shown in Figure 8-3, is that every user (employee) is assigned to a role with a collection of permissions and restrictions. A user can access data and execute operations only if the assigned role has the correct permissions.

The main disadvantage of RBAC is the danger of "role explosion." Within any large organization, there will be a large number of different roles, for people in different departments, subdepartments, and functions. Managing all of these roles can become a complex affair: if you don't want to use a coarse-grained role model, you'll likely end up with thousands of different roles. Another problem with RBAC is that it's static and can't take into account contextual information such as user location, time, and device information.

RBAC is often complemented with ACLs. With ACL, the permissions are directly attached to the objects you are managing. For example, Figure 8-4 shows an ACL permissions table for managing access to computing resources. It instructs the operating system which users can access an object, and which actions they can carry out. There's an entry for each user, which is linked to the security attributes of each object.

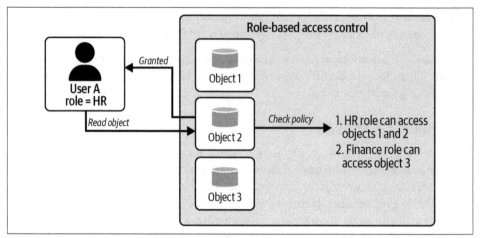

Figure 8-3. Using RBAC to restrict system access

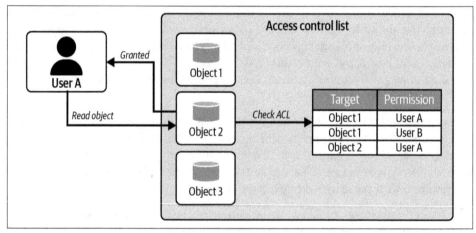

Figure 8-4. Using an ACL to determine whether a security principal (user, group, service principal, or managed identity) has permission to perform an operation

ACLs are better suited for implementing security at the individual user level and for low-level data, while RBAC better serves an organization-wide security system with overseeing administrators. An ACL can, for example, grant write access to a specific object, but it can't determine how a user might change the object.

ABAC is a more advanced security method that addresses some of the disadvantages of RBAC and ACL. Its policies combine different attributes. These policies can come from the data itself, such as classifications and metadata properties, or from the system's context and users (roles, geographical locations, device properties, and so on) and the actions to be performed on the data (read, insert, update, or delete).

Figure 8-5 shows an example of how different attributes can be combined to make a more complex decision.

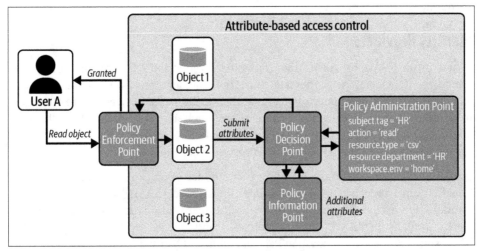

Figure 8-5. Using ABAC for access control

ABAC comes with a recommended architecture, shown in Figure 8-5, which has the following four components:

Policy Enforcement Point (PEP)
The PEP is responsible for protecting the data. It inspects the data request (query) and generates an authorization request, which is sent to the Policy Decision Point for validation and approval.

Policy Decision Point (PDP)
The PDP is the core component of ABAC. It validates incoming requests against the security policies defined on all attributes. The PDP returns an approval or rejection decision based on the policy. It then informs the PEP of its decision and the reason for approval or rejection.

Policy Information Point (PIP)
The PIP allows the PDP to use external source data, such as user attributes invoking a call to the identity provider.

Policy Administration Point (PAP)
The PAP is a repository that manages all enterprise security policies. A typical PAP also provides monitoring and logging and has a user-friendly interface.

To give a concrete example of ABAC, suppose you have sensitive HR data classified with a metadata attribute: the Employee Information tag. If a non-HR employee tries to access data with this tag, the PDP returns a rejection. Attributes can also be combined within ABAC. For instance, the HR example could be extended to take into consideration the environment from which the person tries to access the data: they might get a different response when working from home than they do in the corporate environment.

Identity Providers

When using RBAC or ABAC in a federated or distributed environment, *identity providers* (IDPs) play an important part. IDPs are external sources for retrieving attributes from the user. They offer user authentication as a service and are often used to handle sign-in processes for other systems, such as websites, CRM applications, and file servers. The best-known IDP implementations are based on either Microsoft Active Directory (AD) or OpenLDAP (*https://www.openldap.org*).

For authentication, there are currently two popular open protocols: Security Assertion Markup Language (SAML) and OpenID Connect. SAML is based on an XML standard for exchanging authorization and authentication data. OpenID Connect works similarly to SAML but is more open and is used by large companies like Microsoft, Facebook, Google, PayPal, and Yahoo. OAuth is sometimes also mentioned in this context, but it's used only for the authorization process and not for authentication. Another concept you'll hear a lot about in this space is *single sign-on* (SSO). With SSO, as the name suggests, users have to authenticate only once with a smart card or credentials such as a username and password, and can then access multiple applications without authenticating again.

Real-World Example

In this section, we'll make the security architecture concrete by discussing a solution design. Figure 8-6 is the top part of an architecture that builds upon the data product architecture that we discussed in Chapter 4. It holds all the metadata and security components that are needed for the bigger picture.

The components that you see in Figure 8-6 only represent half of the complete architecture. The other half, the bottom part, is visualized in Figure 8-7. In this design, secure access to data products is virtualized. The information about what consumers are allowed to consume comes from the upper security architecture.

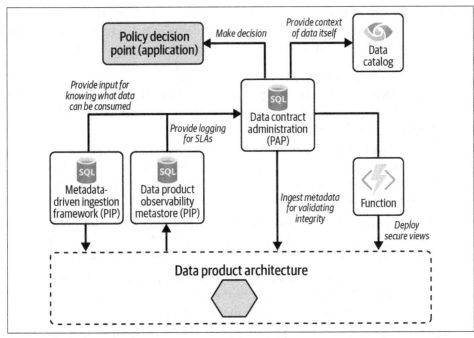

Figure 8-6. How security components work together to deliver data security at scale

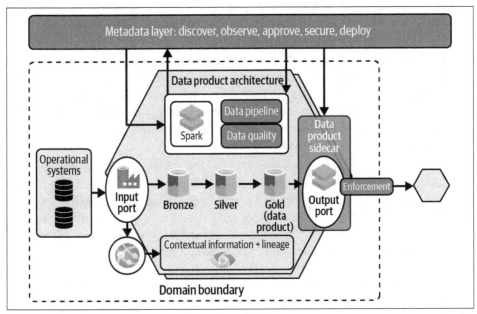

Figure 8-7. An updated data product architecture

Within Figure 8-6, each security component fulfills a critical role and is expected to work closely with the other components and underlying data product architecture. Let's take a look at how the two parts of the architecture are connected to each other:

- The data contract administration application, seen in Figure 8-6, holds all the formal agreements between data providers and data consumers about what data is allowed to be consumed for what purposes. In this architecture, this component acts as the PDP and PAP.

- The metadata-driven ingestion framework (Figure 8-6) manages the ETL process. It knows the dependencies and the order in which data must be extracted, combined, transformed, and loaded. In this architecture, it plays the role of PIP by sharing what data products are ready for consumption.

- The data product observability store (Figure 8-6) knows the health and state of all the data products within this architecture. It plays the role of PIP by providing more context. At the same time, it delivers information that is input for the SLAs.

- The data product sidecar (Figure 8-7) is an access layer that enables the enforcement of security functionality, such as the PEP. It receives its information from the PDP and PAP in the upper part of the architecture.

- The data catalog shown in Figures 8-6 and 8-7 stores additional contextual information: metadata such as business terms, lineage, labels, and classifications. In the data product architecture, it plays the role of a catalog by scanning data and collecting metadata. In the security architecture, it plays the role of a PIP by providing information about the data.

- The data pipeline (Figure 8-7) is an orchestration component with services that process the data end-to-end in the sequence described in the metadata-driven ingestion framework. It uses the DCA component and a data quality framework such as Great Expectations for detecting what breaking changes are allowed. For example, if none of the data products are subject to any data consumption, you may allow disruptive changes to happen.

- The data enforcement component (Figure 4-3) allows data to be accessed and queried. It typically also logs information about who has accessed data. If you make use of RBAC, ABAC, or ACLs, you typically use a SSO token, which you can find in your log files. This type of audit data allows you to perform analytics of analytics; i.e., determine which products are really hot, used by whom, and how. This information helps you to prioritize and rank data assets.

The security components interact closely with each other, so next I'll explain the process of data onboarding (ingestion) and consumption. As we walk through each step, I'll refer to the components and explain their role in the architecture. By the end of the next section, you'll have a good understanding of how these components work together.

Typical Security Process Flow

The first step of providing data is onboarding data and providing metadata information. During this step we expect each new dataset to be registered in the data catalog and pipelines to be designed using the metadata-driven ingestion framework. As data is moved into the data product architecture, we expect the catalog to profile and scan it. This step is also the starting point for owners to describe their data by linking business terms to the physical data. During the onboarding process, the data and its purposes should also be classified and automatically labeled.

These onboarding processes can be accelerated with the support of machine learning or profiling systems to autoclassify the data.[4] Such systems can automatically detect items like Social Security numbers, credit card numbers, customer names, and addresses. As you provide more metadata, the AI and machine learning models get smarter, accelerate the process by providing suggestions, and improve the reliability of the classifications.

It's important to preserve the security context for operational use cases as well, since this data can play a role in operational analytics. This means that local domain data, such as sensitivity labels, countries, domain ranges, and the like, must be part of the data or provided during the onboarding process. Without attaching this context to the data, it will be difficult to implement more fine-grained security rules later. After data has been classified and described, it can be certified to indicate that it is ready for usage.

The next step is data consumption, which always begins with a data contract, in which both the data owner(s) and data user agree on what data will be consumed and for what purposes, and filtering criteria. Without this agreement, data consumption shouldn't be possible.

 Data contracts apply only when users don't have access yet. If users are already permitted to see data for a specific purpose, they should be granted access automatically, and the agreement process doesn't have to be followed.

After establishing a contract, the next step is to collect information to use for making the correct decisions. This step, depending on what information you would like to use, can be more complex because it may involve multiple substeps:

---

4 An example of how the automated classification process works for Purview can be found in the Microsoft Purview documentation (*https://oreil.ly/7XvuF*).

1. Attributes from the PIPs for the consuming side are collected. PIPs provide information about users, applications, departments, groups, roles, purposes, start dates within the organization, last successful sign-on dates, and so on. All of this information will be used as input for the next series of tasks. The collection of these attributes can be abstracted and accomplished via, for example, a composite API (a component that sequentially calls other APIs).

2. Information is collected about the data itself: classifications, labels, file and container locations, production-ready status, whether data is accessed atomically or combined with other datasets, etc. For example, if you're using Microsoft Purview, you would query the REST API (*https://oreil.ly/xiCNr*) to retrieve more information about the objects the consumer is requesting.

3. The metadata of the target application(s) and consuming use case(s), which aren't seen in Figure 8-6, may be collected, such as additional ratings or classifications of the consuming application, production status, and runtime details. If, for example, the consuming application is running in a development or testing environment, you may limit the usage of the data.

4. Optionally, the surrounding metadata stores (not shown in Figure 8-6) are queried for information such as previous database access times, telemetry data, employee data or infrastructure information (on-premises or cloud).[5] For example, a data access workflow could obtain information by calling the employee management system. If that system tells the employee recently terminated the employment contract, you could decide to not grant access.

5. All of the collected information is combined and submitted to the PDP for deploying the policy.

The process described here can be seen as an advanced future state scenario in which a lot of metadata is used for making complex decisions. In the preliminary phases of designing and implementing your security architecture, I expect decisions to be far more simple and practical. For example, you might start with only labels, production or testing status, and filtering information. As you move forward, you can gradually extend this by adding more information for making more complex decisions. In the next phase, for example, insecure environments might be excluded or combinations of labels and data usage classifications might be used. Further down the road, you might consider using machine learning–based services, training a model to make recommendations or decisions instead of asking data owners or security officers to do so.

---

5 *Telemetry* is an automated communications process by which measurements and other data are collected at remote or inaccessible points and transmitted to receiving equipment for monitoring.

An alternative approach is to create security groups (by respective data owners) that have specific levels of access to data assets, which are then shared with the entitlement life cycle management engine.[6] This is often part of your IDP, which manages the multistage approval workflow, expiry settings, conditional rules for external users, etc. The entitlement engine combines multiple data asset security groups into access packages, which are presented in a catalog for consumers to discover and request. This approach effectively manages permissions regardless of the access point, as it leverages credential passthrough and forms a consumption contract.

On the solution side, things might look different. Depending on how the architecture is designed, enforcement may happen in different ways because there are different technology options and possible combinations. The PAP/PDP, for example, could be a homegrown Python and SQL application containing data contract records and business logic for making decisions and deploying secure views and/or policies, or a service provided by a commercial vendor. The design of PEPs can also vary. If your data product architecture uses, for example, Databricks SQL or Azure SQL, you could develop a small deployment framework for generating GRANT USAGE ON SCHEMA or CREATE SECURITY POLICY statements to enforce in-database row-level security (RLS) and column-level security (CLS) at runtime. The underlying service consequently will intercept all requests that pass by and validate them according to the defined policies. If the data product architecture uses a Hadoop-based platform, you could transform the PAP's policies into Apache Ranger. If you use a third-party tool, you'll have to manage the policies within that solution.

Instead of deploying views or security layers over your data, you could also choose to duplicate and de-identify data for every new use case using open source libraries or third-party tools like Privitar (*https://www.privitar.com*). A typical approach is keeping multiple (original and de-identified) versions of your data products. The de-identified ones could be generic sets for all consumers or specifically created for each consumer. The drawback of this approach is that it requires you to manage more storage.

You can use any of these approaches individually, or combine them. As long as you decouple the data sharing repository and layer of consumption, you have the flexibility to use any solution you want. You can support a variation of consumption patterns while consistently applying the same security model to all data.

---

6 The Microsoft docs (*https://oreil.ly/ocW8l*) have more information on entitlement management within Active Directory.

Let's look at a few other scenarios:

- A consumer-specific "view" or "policy" is automatically deployed by following a workflow. Based on what the contract stipulates, certain data can be hidden, filtered, masked, or scrambled. For this type of functionality, your data product architecture is expected to work together with other components. For example, an easy way to implement row-level security is to directly embed security predicates in the WHERE condition of the view.[7]

- The enforcement happens in real time, using third-party solutions. As users authenticated with SSO or applications try to access data, queries are intercepted, decisions are made, and data is returned (or not).

- For specific purposes (ad hoc reporting, data exploration), access can be granted only to specific tooling or with an expiration time. Wrangling tools, for example, can be given access to data in specific situations for only a limited time.

- Data can be duplicated and preprocessed specifically for a certain project or use case. During the processing step, data can be masked, hidden, filtered out, tokenized, or scrambled. This scenario works well for very large datasets.

After the policies are implemented and access to data has been granted, the journey continues on the consuming side, where we see applications and capabilities. The moment the consumer becomes a data provider, the entire process flow cycle, as described in this section, closes and all steps must be repeated.

The number of components, amount of metadata, and number of steps involved can be overwhelming initially, so I recommend building up your security architecture slowly. Consider the following recommendations:

Focus on security within and across domain boundaries.
With this two-way approach, data access between domains is coarse-grained and handled via contracts on data products. For example, across domains, resources are mounted via secure endpoints with read-only permissions. Then, for security within the domain itself, there's typically another pattern for restricting data access at the use case or project level. The security on this level is typically fine-grained and handled by the domain itself.

Take it slow.
Start with the basics by collecting the most important metadata and creating a limited set of classifications and only one or a few consumption patterns. As you gradually progress, extend the architecture further with more advanced capabilities and metadata. Finally, make it fully self-service to scale it up further.

---

7 If you're interested in learning how to implement row-level security in Azure Synapse Serverless SQL pools, check out Jovan Popovic's blog post (*https://oreil.ly/Gisds*) on this subject.

Automate as much as possible.
> Try to make the process of data onboarding and consumption as easy and automated as possible. At first, processes may be manual and metadata might sit in Microsoft Forms or Excel. But as you progress, try to automate whatever is possible.

Standardize authorization and data access.
> Align your security practices with your data management workflow across the enterprise to make data widely available and to simplify the process of data democratization.

Select the right tools.
> Designing a security architecture is difficult, so consider using out-of-the-box services with established (proven) patterns.

Implement guidance from the start.
> If good guidance for managing data products is not provided, it will be harder to allow fine-grained data access.

Regarding that last point, it's important to consider how you will handle ownership and manage data products when business capabilities are shared. What guidance do you need to provide to your teams? We've already discussed this in "Shared capabilities" on page 43, but there are different tricks you can apply here. One method, as seen at the top of Figure 8-8, is to physically split out data by creating multiple data products for different owners. This approach usually works best when data ownership and usage is coarse-grained—that is, when the data is linked to only a few owners, and consumers who request data typically request all the data that corresponds to one owner.

Another method, as seen at the bottom of Figure 8-8, is to encapsulate metadata for security during the data product creation process. This metadata is used for security and custom presentations, which typically require selections (dynamic virtual views) of the data. For example, when a consumer requests a data product, a WHERE clause is set for filtering out data that the consumer isn't allowed to see or use.

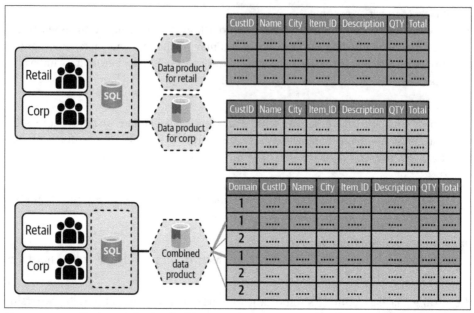

Figure 8-8. Different methods of addressing shared data ownership

The method of encapsulating metadata for security is most effective when data security is fine-grained—that is, when you have many owners and complex security scenarios to manage. To address the overhead, it is recommended to implement a data ownership delegation model to lower the burden of requiring all data owners to individually approve requests. So, for example, if a consumer requests a single data product that has 20 owners, only one data owner has to give approval.

This discussion has focused on securing data product architectures, but security doesn't end there. In the next sections, we'll examine the concerns specific to securing API- and event-based architectures.

Securing API-Based Architectures

Securing APIs, for example within SOA, is complex because communication occurs in real time. Security typically happens on two levels: at the API layer and at the API provider.

The first level of security is implemented at the API layer using API gateways, enterprise service buses, and service meshes. As seen in Figure 8-9, API consumers first have to prove their identities by calling specific authorization services. After successful identification, an identity or access token is provided (and, optionally, a refresh token), which allows API consumers to make authorized API calls using that token.[8] The API gateway, as part of the API management platform, intercepts those requests and validates the scope of access and whether the token is still valid. To periodically validate the token, it might directly query the authorization server. The API policies that are stored in the API management platform should originate from the data contract application. Either they're extracted from this application and transformed into API security policies, or the API policy decision endpoint acts as a data contract application. In this model, the API gateway is, in fact, your PEP.

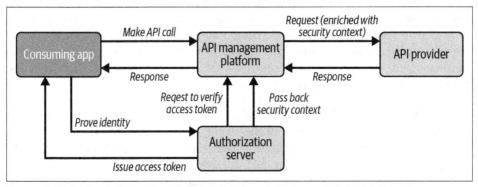

Figure 8-9. Authorization flow showing how a consumer makes API calls, after successful authentication; the authorization server in this design could be part of the API management platform or could be a third-party service

The second level of security is implemented on the data-providing side. API providers in this model use the context provided by the API consumer and API gateway to determine whether to return data, and what data to return. The API gateway may add and pass extra context (metadata) to the API provider: information about the domain, first authentication time, and so on. Some API management software providers refer to *mapping templates (https://oreil.ly/kanWm)* for passing in or retrieving additional context from other services. If your API gateway doesn't support this behavior, you could also consider building small microservices to provide this enriched context, acting as lightweight proxies. The API providers in this model might also use the data contract application as their PDP, reaching out to it to determine whether a consumer has access or not. Alternatively, they can use their local context and business rules to make decisions.

---

8 For an explanation of how authentication works with OAuth 2.0, see the guide from Apigee (*https://oreil.ly/Alm_M*).

When using a mix of API gateways and providers, variations on the described authentication model are possible. In some cases, identity providers aren't decoupled from the API gateway but are called directly. For some API calls or scopes, additional information may be obtained from other authorization endpoints, or a combination of access tokens could be required.

Cross-domain security within API management is difficult because extra context is often needed from other domains. If you access one system (for example, an order management system), how does that system know whether you're allowed to retrieve the requested information when the actual security information is stored within another system (say, a customer system)? For these types of scenarios, there are a few different approaches to consider:

- The API consumer "caches" the additional context and uses this when calling the next APIs. In the example of the customer and order management systems, the API consumer would first call the customer system, which would return the list of delegates. The next call would retrieve data using the API from the order management system, submitting the list as additional context for calling this API. This model is the preferred approach, but it only works when all domains operate within the same trust boundary.

- The API gateway knows that, for some APIs, an extra call for providing context is required. Apigee, for example, calls this a *service callout policy* (*https://oreil.ly/ Myvvm*). In this example, the API gateway calls and collects context from other domains and does some lightweight orchestration. In general, this method is more secure than the previous method because you can manipulate things on the client side; using this approach thus also depends on whether consuming domains are fully trusted or not. A benefit of this approach is that the API gateway can cache the context, so if another call is made the context doesn't have to be retrieved again. A drawback is that the API gateway might provide the wrong context when the security attributes change. So, in a dynamic environment, it's better to refresh the context with every API call that is made. Usually the domains know what approach works best for specific use cases.

- Domains use the identification token from the API consumer for retrieving additional context. The API gateway in this model acts as the go-between. In this approach, all corresponding domains must use the same identity provider. This model works only if the token isn't refreshed that regularly; it won't work if new tokens are passed back after every API call.

- The domain directly calls the other domain to retrieve the necessary context after receiving the API call. The drawback here can be a ping-pong effect of API calls going back and forth. This approach isn't wrong, but it's less preferable than using the API gateway.

Your security model preferences will vary based on what technologies you use and the level of trust that you have. I've seen some large enterprises separate the security layer from the API architecture by deploying a dedicated security product or component in the architecture as an extra layer.

Latency also influences your preferred security model. If API requests must be handled within a short time frame, the extra security layers might cause trouble because every hop in the network typically adds waiting time. Calling domains directly might be the only solution, though I generally see this more as an exception than a best practice.

A common challenge in API security is when integrated views are required and various data and integration logic must be combined. For example, multiple calls to different backend services may be needed to continuously provide data in a certain shape. In such situations a composite service, which combines several services and exposes them as a new one, can help to avoid chattiness between consumers and providers that can affect performance. For these types of services, it's important that data governance is strictly followed.

The first rule in such situations is that all the local data and security rules remain owned by the original providers. Thus, data and rules aren't allowed to be changed by the aggregator. The second rule is that aggregation services take ownership of all the overarching rules, including for any newly created data.[9] These overarching rules—for example, that a specific combination of data isn't allowed to be consumed—can be created and maintained only by the aggregation service itself because it's the only place where the data combinations are stored. The last rule is that data consumers are responsible for providing any context that the (aggregated) service provider needs to be authorized. As the overarching rules can be complex, much context might be required.

Securing Event-Driven Architectures

Policy-based access control in streaming and event-driven architectures is complex because there aren't any out-of-the-box security frameworks currently available. Kafka, for example, only supports RBAC (*https://oreil.ly/v_iKy*) and doesn't provide policy-based message filtering using combinations of attributes. So, if you want a fine-grained ABAC security model, you'll have to complement it with additional components or engineer it yourself.

---

9 Alternatively, you can store the overarching rules in the central security metadata store, which holds all the policies and attributes. The aggregation services in this setup are no longer the PAP.

One approach is to engineer a policy enforcement layer that uses microservices to read events, take the instructions from the data contract application or policy engine, and apply them. The outputted events are stored into new consumer-specific topics. In event-driven architectures, events, as they come in, are first stored in internal topics. These topics might be compacted if you want to retain the application state for longer. The next step is to bring all the security policies and related metadata to the event streaming platform. The last step is to engineer a policy-based message filtering framework, where microservices read incoming data, join it with data from the policies, filter data out, and provision consumer-specific topics with only the data consumers are allowed to see. This filtering framework can also (possibly) join data from other contexts if necessary for policy decisions: for example, retrieving the customer-servicing party for a particular financial transaction from the data product architecture.

The key takeaways of these examples are that there are many options, which are also context-sensitive. Designing and embedding security requires deep thinking about what components to use and how to apply them to your overall architecture.

Wrapping Up

Data governance can't be successful without proper data security. The opposite is true as well; the two areas are heavily intertwined.

Effective data governance is a critical success factor in building up a modern data practice. To stay compliant with regulations, it's important to define ownership and set standards for lineage, classifications, purposes, and descriptions. For these tasks, it's also key to identify all of the applications and unique (golden) sources across the organization. To make data governance scalable, you need to identify related roles and responsibilities and assign them properly. Start small and strive for quick wins. For example, start with only a small set of use cases. For each use case, data products are required. For each data product, ensure ownership is established on a data and application level. While developing the first data products, ensure your data platform team establishes a data catalog for providing transparency on the data and the usage. In addition to that, collect metadata from the very beginning. With the foundation in place, gradually adopt and professionalize DataOps practices.

Implementing data governance is mostly an organizational change, because culture can be either a massive roadblock or a catalyst. If there is no openness or willingness to change, your ambitions will fail. To overcome this, you must create excitement, energy, and momentum. I've learned over the years that transitioning is largely about communication, transparency, and gaining the support of data cheerleaders (leaders who lead by example).

For data security, it's important to create an end-to-end framework that efficiently supports the data request fulfillment process. This framework is the start of an enhanced security model for data product distribution and consumption. It must be a sensible part of your overall architecture. As you progress, slowly extend it with more metadata, classifications, labels, attributes, and so on. To scale it further, you can make it intelligent with machine learning.

In the next chapters, we'll focus on metadata management, master data management, and turning data into value.

CHAPTER 9

Democratizing Data with Metadata

Many of us have witnessed the power of OpenAI. In the future, metadata and artificial intelligence will intersect. What do you think this powerful AI will be capable of when it starts learning more about metadata? The impact could be immense. It could change the way we currently do data integration; AI models will be able to interpret language and predict and write code. AI might be able to fix data quality issues or give recommendations on how best to organize and structure your data landscape based on the lineage. Chief data officers need to prepare for these trends. As they will learn, metadata will be at the heart of it all.

In this chapter, we will look more closely at metadata's role in a modern data architecture and how it should be managed. *Metadata*, as you have learned, describes all the relevant aspects of the new architecture. It binds everything together and is key for delivering the insights, control, and efficiency large enterprises are looking for.

Metadata is complicated to manage, scattered as it is across many tools, applications, platforms, and environments. Typically, a multitude of organized metadata repositories coexist in a large data architecture. Most metadata is also tightly coupled to a specific vendor product. Because of its great volume and diversity, metadata usually needs to be properly selected, organized, and integrated before it can be managed. Part of this chapter will be dedicated to the core ingredients of a good enterprise metadata model.

A good metadata management strategy grows organically. It starts simple and small, by first identifying the most important areas. It also is supported with services and clear processes.

To get started, it's good to be aware of the different metadata categories:

Business metadata
> Describes all aspects used for governance and finding and understanding data. Some well-known examples are business terms, definitions, data ownership information, and information about data usage and origination.

Technical metadata
> Describes the structural aspects of data at design time. Some well-known examples are schema information, information about data formats and protocols, and encryption and decryption keys.

Operational metadata
> Describes processing aspects of data at runtime. Some well-known examples are process information, execution time, information about whether a process failed, and job IDs.

Social metadata
> Describes aspects of data related to its end users. Some well-known examples are use and user tracking information, data on search results, filters and clicks, viewing time, profile hits, reviews, ratings, and comments.

Metadata is also foundational for emerging design concepts, such as the data fabric and AI-supported data governance. Gartner, for example, projects a vision of using knowledge graphs with pointers to the actual data itself. This knowledge graph is complemented with an intelligent engine that uses ML for automatically creating harmonized and integrated datasets, and perhaps with data virtualization as well. In order to build such an advanced solution, you'll need to automate the collection, discovery, maintenance, and use of metadata to make it an integral part of your architecture. So, we'll also look at integration patterns in this chapter and discuss why certain metadata must be persisted centrally.

 To avoid reinventing the wheel, it's best to reuse as many integration patterns as possible.

Last but not least, we will look at data democratization and how metadata can be used to drive data governance. To facilitate this, metadata has to be ubiquitous on an enterprise level and open and accessible to everyone. It is the only central data model you will have.

Metadata Management

The concept of metadata and the principles applied for metadata management are much older, but the term *metadata*, defined as "data about data," was coined during the 1990s. During this era, many vendors jumped on the metadata bandwagon by providing tools for better managing databases' data and data models. The majority of these tools also provided forward-engineering capabilities to generate application data models automatically. In this approach, conceptual and logical application data models, which describe concepts and dependencies, are used to automatically generate physical application data models, including tables, columns, foreign key relationships, and data types. Additionally, these tools allow you to take care of operational aspects and determine what data should be active and what should be archived.

In the era of big data and alternative technologies, such as NoSQL and advanced analytics, metadata management has gotten more dynamic and diverse, with different metadata forms and shapes. With big data, we saw data catalogs gaining momentum because they enabled overseeing a lot of data. Also, the pace of change and diversity of solutions today are completely different compared to traditional architectures.

Today metadata can be found everywhere: in applications, databases, data integration technologies, master data management, cloud infrastructure, analytical services, and more. Consequently, it is also more siloed: each platform and tool may have its own database for managing metadata.

This scattering makes using metadata more difficult. In a scattered and federated environment, it is difficult to oversee where the data sits, how it moves, and what it means. Solving this problem requires you to connect metadata over different dimensions: an enterprise-wide metadata view is required.

My experience is that the process of integrating, automating, and consolidating metadata throughout the enterprise requires standardization, thoughtful choices, and carefully designed procedures. A proliferation of technologies with incompatible metadata capabilities will undermine the ambition of creating powerful data management capabilities, so tactical choices must be made to bridge the various solutions, apply automation, and decide what metadata is most relevant. I recommend focusing on three major objectives:

- Designing an enterprise metadata model as input for a metamodel implementation that represents all enterprise areas and their attributes and relationships.
- Defining the critical metadata collections and identifying the best architectural approach to collect metadata. For this, I propose a new architecture: a metalake.
- Democratizing and delivering the value of metadata through knowledge graphs and self-service capabilities, such as catalogs and data marketplace portals.

In the following sections, I will discuss each of these objectives in more detail.

The Enterprise Metadata Model

Metadata management typically grows slowly. It should be supported with a proper blueprint, clear processes, and the right selection of building blocks. Your metadata blueprint is an integrated and unified model that works across all data management disciplines and technologies. The key here is not to focus on a narrow catalog or commercial metadata solution, but to look at the broader picture and identify core entities within your enterprise metadata model.

I'm not asking you to build an enterprise database model, but to think about what binds your organization together. Ask yourself what business metadata is critical. What technical metadata is essential for interoperability? What makes up your domains, and how do you keep track of what applications they use? What processes and streams capture the data? Where are the applications and database models or schemas created and maintained? What information do teams need to deliver centrally to allow the data governance department to do its work correctly? After you have answered these questions, you need to map out the content life cycle for each of the metadata areas and determine all of the dependencies. What you will end up with is a vendor-agnostic, unified metadata model that connects many entities, such as organizational units, domains, business processes, technology components, data products, and so on.

DataOps Has a Strong Relationship with Metadata

DataOps is an advanced and collaborative data management practice focused on improving the efficiency of communication, integration, and automation of data flows between teams across an organization. It is also about everyone "speaking the same language" and agreeing on what the data is and is not. Metadata provides these semantics and ensures a broad understanding of what data means. Thus, a good DataOps practice comes with a good set of metadata management standards.

For building the metadata model itself, I recommend initially keeping things abstract and not introducing too much change and complexity quickly. Start with the basics: domains, lists of applications, authoritative data sources (golden sources), database and schema metadata, data ownership, lineage, and security. By slowly extending the scope, you can control your metadata management. It's important to work on coherence and make sure all the metadata can be integrated.

Practical Example of a Metamodel

For your metadata management, I encourage you to implement a metamodel using a data governance solution.[1] You can think of this as a blueprint or a map, using relationships and reference points to make it easier to navigate. It tells you about how your data is grouped, organized, and mapped to other areas; for example, how your data is used in business processes, what projects are impacted by the data, and ultimately how the data fits into the day-to-day of your business. To conclude, metamodels are important artifacts because they help you to add rich business context to your data catalog and manage it.

For a simple example of a metamodel, let's consider the customer management domain at Oceanic Airlines, discussed in Chapter 2. Imagine that we have cataloged two physical datasets after scanning our data sources. Assume that we want to manage this cataloged data by connecting it to concepts like processes, departments, lines of business, data owners, and data products. How would this work?

Figure 9-1 shows an example of a metamodel created with Microsoft Purview; it's simply a diagram or map that shows what metadata areas you could focus on. The metamodel is built from logical entities and the relationships between them.

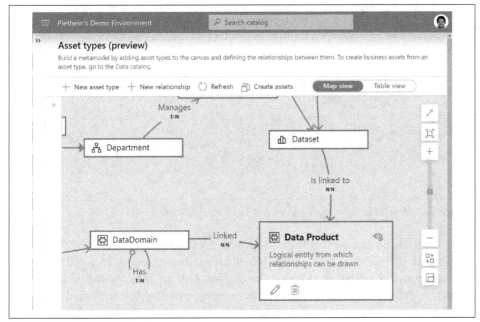

Figure 9-1. How Microsoft Purview manages a metamodel

---

1 A *metamodel* is a model that manages a set of models. A *semantic model*, which describes the basic meaning of items and the relationships among them within a model, is usually a strong starting point for a metamodel.

In the screenshot, you see that a data product is defined as a logical entity. You also see that the data product has relationships to other entities: a data domain and (physical) dataset.

Let's make this more tangible by showing how you could use this map to curate metadata. Figure 9-2 shows an example of how logical entities are instantiated and used in practice. Here, we've used the blueprint to instantiate a "customer dataset" asset. This entity inherits all the properties of a data product, so you must provide a name, description, data owner, and so on. Next, you define its relationships to other entities, using the map as a guide.

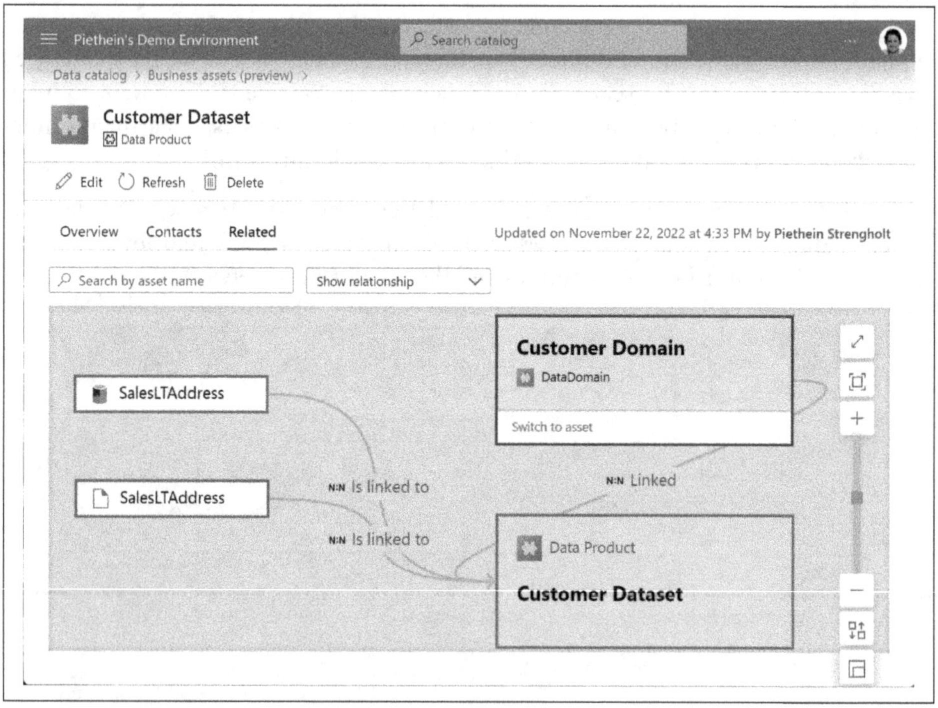

Figure 9-2. How Microsoft Purview visualizes a business entity

In Figure 9-2, you can see that the customer dataset entity is related to multiple items: a customer domain business entity (based on the logical entity of a data domain) and two physical representations of the dataset. One of these is stored in Parquet format, and the other in CSV format. Once you record all of this information in your metamodel, everyone will be able to tell that that there is a customer domain and a customer dataset, and that there are two physical representations of that same data.

In this example, you learned that relationships are derived from the design of the metamodel. If you want to add more relationships to the design, you can add more lines. The examples shown here were relatively simple, but mature metamodels are often very large. They could span across many data management and other areas and cover many items and relationships, and they can be enriched with external content as well.

A metamodel can be seen as an implementation of your enterprise metadata model. You can use that model as a starting point, but the actual implementation of a metamodel in a data governance solution might be different. For example, it might include only a subset of the full set of requirements that you defined on a conceptual level, or the tool you're using might impose constraints that require you to adapt your metamodel in certain ways. In the next sections, we'll take a closer look at some of the foundational elements of the metadata model.

Data Domains and Data Products

At the heart of your enterprise metamodel, there are data domains and data products. Figure 9-3 shows what this might look like, using the definition of a data product from Chapter 4. In that chapter, you learned that data products are logical entities and represent the most significant type of value that needs to be managed and governed. They can (as you saw in the previous sections) be linked to (physical) data objects, as well as applications, processes, owners, business terms, terms of usage, and so on.

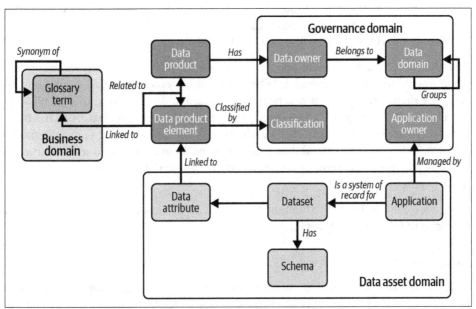

Figure 9-3. A metamodel design for data products

To allow this information to be searchable and tracked, I recommend building and maintaining the metamodel and its corresponding metadata in a data catalog.

Data domains are the boundaries in which your data is managed. You should align these with your value streams and business capabilities. Data, processes, people, and technology come together inside these entities, so just like data products, data domains typically have many relationships to other entities.

The recommended approach for managing data products is to first define a data product as a logical entity in the metamodel. You may want to extend or relate this to another entity called a *data product element*, as shown in Figure 9-3. Data product elements are the linking pins to the glossary terms and technical data attributes, which are often directly linked. So, this is another abstraction for providing flexibility. Considering that business terms and data attributes are often directly linked, how do you design and implement these elements? There are two common approaches.

You could argue that whenever a data product is linked to a glossary term, and that glossary term has a relationship to a data attribute, the term represents a "data product element." In this case, a feature is needed to quickly filter and search on these elements in the catalog. So, you quickly want to see the difference between what business terms are only about sharing context, and what glossary terms contain relationships and thus behave like data product elements (linking pins).

The alternative approach would be to create another logical entity called "data product element" in your metamodel. When doing so, I recommend to configure that entity in such a way that no description is needed and a relationship to a physical attribute is always required. The description in this case is inherited from the business term to which you connect it to. The benefit of implementing your metamodel this way is that you can extend data product elements to be linked to more entities as well. So, this approach allows for richer context creation. At the same time, it causes more overhead to manage.

Next, we'll look at how the different types of data models (conceptual, logical, and physical) fit into your metadata model.

Data Models

Data models require special attention because ordering and grouping these logically is a difficult exercise. Not only are there different types/levels of models, but within each level there are models with different degrees of maturity, depth, and complexity. In addition to that, there are relationships between the models in any given level, and also between models on different levels. So, before we get to best practices, let's take another look at the different types of data models and how to extract metadata from them.

Conceptual data models

At the highest level are the *conceptual data models*,[2] which might be designed as folksonomies (*https://oreil.ly/MuBUC*), ontologies (*https://oreil.ly/HLye3*), or taxonomies (*https://oreil.ly/qeYLv*). They summarize critical business concepts and convey the meaning and purpose of data from a business standpoint. You can keep these abstract, but my recommendation is to enrich all business terms with definitions, attributes, and dependencies. The definitions should be domain-specific, accounting for both the data providers' and consumers' bounded contexts and helping the organization better understand what the data means in a particular context.

A conceptual data model or glossary can also include and capture concepts that are used to make the context clearer, but don't play a direct role (yet) in the application or database design. It may also include concepts that represent future requirements, but haven't yet found their way into the actual design. It's a good idea to make your teams aware of these aspects so they don't leave out useful terms.

Conceptual data models often take the form of user-generated glossaries, but there are no rules for their size and representation. They can be abstract and high-level or detailed, carefully describing attributes, dependencies, relationships, and definitions. A conceptual data model or glossary isn't limited to describing a single domain; it can span across several domains and thus touch upon countless applications and multiple databases.

From a domain point of view, multiple applications can work together to accomplish a specific business need. This means that the relationship between a conceptual data model or glossary and data attributes is generally one-to-many. Exceptions to this rule are shared business capabilities and/or shared information domains, such as master data management and enterprise-wide context; for these, the relationships between glossaries and data attributes are usually many-to-many and also spanning across domains.

---

2 An alternative name for a conceptual data model is a *business data model*. You may also see these referred to as *domain*, *domain object*, or *analysis object models*.

Why Conceptual Data Models Are Often Missing

Conceptual data models are often missing for several reasons. One reason is that conceptual models are frequently created implicitly—for example, as a sketch on a whiteboard or in a document—but are not digitally stored. Conceptual models are also often confused with other data models. Many business users and IT professionals are not familiar with them. Others perceive conceptual data modeling as too abstract or difficult. People with expertise and deep knowledge in conceptual modeling are rare.

Capturing these models is also difficult because of the lack of good, easy-to-use tools for recording them and mapping them to all of your applications. Most tools cover only a narrow range of technologies. Protégé (*https://oreil.ly/uFm9Y*) is a popular open source tool for building conceptual data models using OWL. Its main drawback is that it's fairly complex to use without adequate training.

Another reason why conceptual data models are often absent is that people question the added value of creating them. Within Agile development processes, or under time pressure, I have seen people decide not to capture any implicit thoughts or concepts at all. In such situations, business users, developers, and engineers take shortcuts to deliver the application on time.

You have different options for structuring the business terms and definitions in your glossary. For example, you might create individual glossaries aligned with your business domains and/or perhaps use parent/child hierarchical structures. This logical segmentation is useful when the same term has different meanings across domains or teams, or when you want to give management control of the glossary to experts in separate areas. It can be helpful to introduce naming standards or term templates to ensure consistency and capture additional information about your business metadata. Between the glossary terms there can also be relationships, such as *acronyms, related terms*, and *synonyms*. Defining these relationships helps avoid confusion, and identifying synonyms can allow you to weed out duplicate terms and standardize on just one, lowering management overhead.

One thing conceptual data models make clear is that knowledge overlaps. This is to be expected because contextual domains may overlap, span across other domains, or be managed with the scope of a larger domain. The organization at this conceptual level is consequently very different from how we manage and look at the solution space, where artifacts (applications, databases, files, folders, tables, and so on) are tangible. To design those solution artifacts, we use logical and physical data models. On these lower levels, we also tend to make the boundaries more strict.

Logical data models

One level below conceptual data models are the *logical data models*.[3] These models, which are where we start to see solution designs, logically evolve from the conceptual models. Here, the abstract business terms are translated into entities and attributes, and relationships are captured. It's sometimes possible to retroactively recover this type of metadata because the translations from conceptual to logical designs can be retrieved from data modeling tools such as SqlDBM (*https://sqldbm.com*) or erwin Data Modeler (*https://oreil.ly/Je4P3*).

Physical data models

At the lowest level are the *physical data models*: schemas that specify exactly what data lives inside which databases, applications, etc. There are three ways to populate your data catalog with information about your physical data models:

- You can use connectors (or agents) that scan your applications, databases, reports, and so on and automatically upload the metadata into the catalog.
- You can manually extract metadata from data modeling tools or frameworks, then upload or ingest it into the catalog using APIs.
- You can manually document the information (i.e., provide the metadata) within the catalog itself.

Security, integrity, and performance requirements play important roles in the design of database schemas. On a logical level, you might define two objects (as logical tables), but for performance reasons all the attributes of these two objects might be stored in the same (physical) table. The physical database design can therefore be quite different from the logical model. This also means that the same logical application data model can be used to create completely different implementations of the physical design. For example, you could use the same logical model to implement a transactional system or a reporting system, but each would use its own physical design.

---

3 Logical application and database design is the first concrete step toward your selected technology, which means that your technology choice significantly affects design. When you're choosing relational databases, the logical model will generally contain database tables, columns, and keys; for XML documents, the model will contain XML elements, attributes, and references.

Limitations and best practices

The dilemma with all of these models and the relationships between them is that not all tools cover the entire space of services and database types yet. Most catalogs provide scanners that do metadata discovery and allow you to reverse engineer the physical models into the logical models and eventually the conceptual models. Linking business terms to technical attributes in this way allows you to find your data faster, and by extending this approach with analytics, like machine learning, you can better predict what users would like to see or discover value hidden in the data. However, the drawback is that these scanners don't cover all solutions.

The same issue with coverage applies for data modeling tools. At the time of this writing, no database modeling tool supports all databases.[4] Additionally, automatic forward engineering works only for some database types.

Given these limitations, I recommend standardizing on the services, database types, scanners, and data modeling tools you use. If extracting metadata is difficult or impossible with your data sources, store higher-level or abstracted versions of the physical data models in your data catalog using your central metamodel. This gives teams at least some insights into what metadata is managed.

Another approach to collecting metadata about your data models is *crowdsourcing*, which uses the wisdom of the crowd to scale up the process of collecting missing information through easy-to-use, intuitive tooling. This inclusive approach provides a single point of entry for everyone who works with data to supply information about that data. Crowdsourcing can be useful for linking, annotating, and providing additional contextual information, such as descriptions, ratings, comments, and so on.

The approaches of scanning, exporting, and crowdsourcing metadata can be combined and blended. The bottom-up method of scanning, harvesting, and generating initial conceptual models, for example, can be complemented by letting data and application owners make manual improvements to finalize the end results.

The main benefit of capturing application and database metadata is that business terms and their translations to the underlying database designs are made clear to the organization. This should allow technical teams to quickly assess and react to new requirements and solve issues around the data. It also allows them to reuse existing knowledge and helps in data migration and integration projects.

In addition, linking all the metadata from data modeling and design allows for intelligent integration and consumption. If business metadata is linked to technical metadata, you know where the physical data objects and their data attributes are stored. This enables you to automatically extract this data, combine and integrate it,

---

4 DBMS Tools (*https://oreil.ly/Bzjd5*) maintains a comprehensive list of these tools and what databases they work with.

and serve it out to consumers. This approach is also known as *ontology-based data integration* (*https://oreil.ly/9_YyJ*).

 If data modeling metadata is obsolete, your data fabric ambitions will fail. Lack of accurate metadata makes automated or intelligent data integration impossible because important information is missing about the data's meaning, the translation of business concepts, and the physical representation, availability, and addressability of the data.

Data Lineage

Lineage information is about data's origins and where it moves over time. This is critical knowledge because it provides visibility into application dependencies and how data flows through the information supply chain. It also allows for debugging or providing insights into transformation logic. Based on the relationships, statistics, and variations you detect, you could also potentially use lineage to determine the impact that data quality in the source system has on different data consumers.

To capture lineage, you can apply the same export approaches you used with the data models. The scanners that come with data catalogs often provide this behavior out of the box: they crawl and automatically extract lineage at an attribute level, including transformation details. You can also collect lineage while running and executing code; for example, while your Spark notebooks are running, you can capture this information using APIs or a software development kit (SDK). Alternatively, you can provide lineage manually, perhaps uploading it from another source.

Lineage often plays a key role in metadata management and data governance. It is therefore important to set principles and criteria for how lineage must be captured. If, for example, a team uses an exotic ETL tool or programming language, they might need to invest in customized functionality to bring the lineage over to a catalog or the repository in which lineage metadata is stored.

Other Metadata Areas

Let's look at some additional types of metadata that might bring value:

Application metadata
> For your IT processes and to support the development of your applications, you have an IT management system that maintains a complete list of all the unique applications throughout your organization. This information may be relevant for your users as it provides insights on application ownership, technologies used, operational incidents, and so on.

Collaborative metadata

Social metadata, delivered via collaboration, can add a great deal of value. By making data visible, sharing knowledge, and allowing users to collaborate, you can establish a community. Examples of collaborative metadata include feedback forms, ratings, votes, bookmarks, and comments.

Data quality metadata

Metadata about data quality is a prerequisite for many key business processes and analytical models. It is measured along different data quality dimensions, such as accuracy, currency, and completeness. These metrics and scores are typically linked to the attributes of the monitored physical data attributes.

Business architecture metadata

To contextualize data, it is important to link metadata to your business architecture. You can do this through business capabilities, organizational structures such as divisions and departments, processes, applications, and generic application functions. This information will enable you to correlate data with domain-driven design models and identify what data sits behind what processes.

Technology metadata

Technology metadata includes all metadata you want to link to related technologies: server platforms, applications, data flows, data stores, infrastructure, and so on. Having this information on the relationships between technical platforms and business capabilities helps the IT department see the impact of maintenance, version and vendor management, and issue management on data management as the company goes through system upgrades and changes.

Interface metadata

Interface metadata includes interface designs, version numbers, lineage, delivery patterns, schedules, and so forth. The availability of this metadata helps your developers and data engineers know how interfaces work, what data is available, and what interesting trends are sitting behind each interface. Interface metadata also lets them test and validate compatibility, which ensures that data consumers can safely subscribe.

BI and ML metadata

The last area I want to mention is the metadata that comes with business intelligence and machine learning services: reporting metadata, model management metadata, and so on. This metadata also might include lineage, showing the movement of data through a series of jobs or small transformations from sources to reports, or information on what datasets different models are trained on. Capturing this information offers insight into what granular data was used for individual reported measurements and figures.

Metadata and its management, as you can see, can bring a lot of value to your organization. The more efficiently you manage it, the more insights metadata will yield. It can help you lower costs by speeding up development time and decreasing maintenance. It can also help with compliance and ensuring the security of the overall architecture. Organizing metadata is a difficult task; now, let's look at how metadata lakes can help.

The Metalake Architecture

If you want to be successful with data management, you need to have a metadata lake, or *metalake*: a unified repository that stores and manages all kinds of metadata, which can be used to deliver insights for data management. The metalake doesn't just allow business users to see what data is available. It's also what enables the chief data officer to bring data management to the next level. It's what allows the data management department to oversee data discovery, lineage, data usage, data quality, data observability, and so on. Let's take a look at some of the key architectural components of the metalake.

Role of the Catalog

One of the critical components of a metalake architecture is a data catalog. Simply put, a data catalog is a repository or inventory in which a collection of metadata is managed.[5] A data catalog is often combined with data management and search services. It enables data analysts and other users to easily find the data they need. It may also provide information to evaluate the fitness of data for intended and future use cases.

The Enterprise Data Catalog by Ole Olesen-Bagneux (O'Reilly) is a must-read for anyone planning to implement a data catalog.

The problem, however, is that data catalogs often fall short, for various reasons. First, they lack capabilities for automated control and proactive enforcement. Second, they're often missing essential integrations with other metadata collection services, or robust capabilities for intelligently discovering and ingesting metadata by scanning other sources. This leads to situations in which users need to do all the heavy lifting of manual metadata entry, and also risks the metadata becoming outdated or invalid. And finally, catalogs promote how the vendor sees data management. This view may

---

5 For a discussion of best practices for Microsoft Purview and a federated way of working, see my blog post (*https://oreil.ly/cR1hh*).

not match your own because how organizations do data governance largely depends on how they are organized internally. Requirements on data governance are typically very company-specific and differ widely.

 Populating data catalogs is often a complex undertaking. The patterns you need for this are the same ones we discussed in Chapters 4, 5, and 6.

Given the limitations of data catalogs, how should you approach them? I recommend looking at a data catalog from a broad perspective. Position it as a component in your metadata management architecture, and complement it with other services to address its weaknesses. Leverage its strengths and the features you like, but don't try to fit yourself into the vendor's vision. This is easier said than done, and it may be possible only for large-scale enterprises, which have the resources for additional investment to effectively address the shortcomings of their chosen product. Smaller enterprises may not be able to go the extra mile, so some level of conformance may be required. You may need to adjust your processes or way of working to fully realize the potential of your data catalog. Here are some best practices to keep in mind:

- Start by defining a metadata strategy by listing out what metadata you want to manage now and in the future. Identify the high-priority activities and standardize the relationships between your metadata objects. Also, align your data governance roles with the key activities, authorization model, and tasks that must be performed within the catalog.

- For a domain-oriented way of working, clearly scope, delegate the ownership, and align your business and technical metadata with your data domains. Technical metadata is used to organize data assets and sources. You can cluster this metadata, set a boundary, and align it with a particular domain. This means that technical metadata from source systems and data products that are managed by a particular domain team is clustered together and managed by that team. You should do the same for your business metadata: create individual glossaries or hierarchy structures within your glossary and align these with your domains. In addition, ask your domains to take responsibility for linking glossary terms and technical attributes. This creates transparency about data ownership and improves your data semantics.

- Always start with aligning data ownership. As an enterprise architect, I helped establish a principle that the workflow for onboarding new data must always start with defining an owner. This avoids data being shared without clear ownership. You can introduce similar principles for semantic discovery; don't allow data products to be published or shared if linkage to glossary terms is obsolete.

- Create special entries for enterprise data and master data management. It's important to know what data falls under master data management. This includes consensus for the business terminology of the data that is subject to MDM and the relationships to domain data. Accordingly, you'll want to agree on the business rules and policies that will be enforced for the management of "golden source data."
- Define and implement metadata life cycle management policies. Metadata management isn't a one-time activity, so develop a process that will support your organization as your metadata collection grows.
- Be strict and consistent about labels and classifications. If you plan to use these within processes for automatic data enforcement and security, you want to remain in control of the labels and classifications used by your domains.
- Pay attention to lineage. This is especially difficult because interoperability between tools and services is often missing. Therefore, it is recommended to make consistent choices about what transformation services you offer to your teams.
- Strike a balance between scanning all data and only relevant data. Scanning all data will result in overwhelming complexity with no clear view of what matters and what doesn't.

Metadata management and the successful implementation and correct use of a data catalog are difficult tasks. Consider a top-down approach by bringing attention to the importance of these activities. Clearly communicate your ambition, objectives, progress, milestones, and roadblocks. Create excitement about your vision of data management, and get buy-in from others. This will make users more likely to help ensure that metadata is complete and of high quality. Such metadata can provide the foundation for advanced services such as search, maintenance, and automated delivery—which brings us to the second key component of the metalake architecture, the knowledge graph.

Role of the Knowledge Graph

Knowledge graphs are gaining more and more traction as a key enabler of data management. A knowledge graph represents a collection of real-world concepts and relationships. It integrates and links data from different sources and represents that data as a network of connected entities. This network structure is particularly useful for navigating, searching, and answering complex queries. The way objects and resources can be linked together is similar to how the World Wide Web works: hypertext links can link anything to anything. A hyperlink can refer to another page, a specific section of a web page, a picture, or even a file. Search engines, as they observe hyperlinks, can easily navigate through all of these resources through their relationships.

Knowledge graphs have great potential. In addition to addressing the shortcomings of today's data catalogs, when complemented with AI they become futuristic data management technologies.

Technologies and standards

In 2000, Tim Berners-Lee, one of the inventors of the World Wide Web, published an article building on the idea that anything can be linked. By extending the current internet standard with a semantic web framework (*https://oreil.ly/d0LYh*), any data can be shared and reused across any application, enterprise, and community boundaries.[6] A variety of technologies enable the encoding of semantics with data, such as:

Resource Description Framework (RDF)
: RDF is a technology framework for representing information about resources in a graph form. It allows data to be distributed and decentralized, but at the same time it can be used to query and glue data together using the HTTP protocol. RDF's data model is a schemaless design with collections of triples, which can easily be extended and represented.

Web Ontology Language (OWL)
: OWL is a specification that adds ontological capabilities to RDF. It defines precisely what you need to write with RDF in order to have a valid ontology. OWL also provides useful expressions and annotations for bringing data models into the real world. It's considered a conceptual modeling language, but since it links and interrelates datasets, it is also a logical data model. One interesting thing about OWL itself is that it can have an RDF representation, thus allowing the meaning of the data to become part of the dataset it describes.

SPARQL Protocol and RDF Query Language (SPARQL)
: SPARQL (*https://oreil.ly/5eHVY*) is the query language used to retrieve and manipulate data stored in RDF. It can join together queries across federated data sources, so multimodel graph databases can be incorporated to support multiple data models against a single, integrated backend.

Shapes Constraint Language (SHACL)
: SHACL is a language for describing and validating RDF graphs. With SHACL, you can take a shapes graph and data graph as input and validate the two against each other.

Simple Knowledge Organization System (SKOS)
: SKOS is a common data model for sharing and linking knowledge organization systems via the web. It can be used to define knowledge organization

---

6 *Semantic web* refers to the W3C's vision of a web of linked data. Semantic web technologies (*https://oreil.ly/kkJv3*) enable people to create data stores on the web, build vocabularies, and write rules for handling data.

systems such as thesauri,[7] classification schemes, subject heading systems, and taxonomies.

The semantic web standards are the new de facto standards for ontology-based interoperability and content publication on the web. Big technology companies such as Meta, Google, Microsoft, and Amazon have adopted and applied their principles and methodology. The beauty of this is that same set of semantic web standards can also be applied within data management, and, more specifically, metadata management.

Through a combination of ontology-based management capabilities, you can create an open and enterprise-wide metadata-driven knowledge graph. This is essentially a database that represents and combines all of the organization's (domain) knowledge and relationships. It is a collection of references to everything that has been described within your enterprise metadata model. This repository can contain as much relevant metadata as you can collect and can be enriched with contextual and semantic information.

The amazing part of the vision here is that you can also connect your knowledge graph straight to your data or metadata (depending on how you see it). This will allow you to either populate and create graphs automatically or find corresponding data based on the ontology you define. Querying and combining distributed data works, as long you stick to the industry standards like RDF, OWL, and SPARQL. Using this approach you can see all the data-related information, such as semantics, origin, lineage, data life cycle phases, ownership, and relevant regulations, all linked together in one place for deep analysis. The more you add and connect, the stronger your knowledge graph becomes.

Companies like Cambridge Semantics (*https://oreil.ly/p6Pqg*) are already working on the vision of combining knowledge graphs of metadata and data. They collect and analyze all forms of metadata, convert this information, and build a data integration backbone. In the next section, I'll make this tangible by providing an example.

Data fabric example

A *data fabric* is an emerging approach for managing data using a network-based and metadata-driven architecture. The metadata in this architecture is meant to be flexible, reusable, discoverable, intelligent, and augmented. If you're considering building a data fabric, it's worth evaluating Anzo (*https://oreil.ly/alkGe*), a platform that combines a knowledge graph, virtualization engine, and reporting solution. The platform fits into the vision of building an integrated layer (fabric) of data. It uses Graphmarts, which are collections of (physical) datasets that can be connected, shared, discovered, and enhanced collaboratively. For the discovery and design of data, the platform

---

7 A *thesaurus* is a reference that lists words in groups of synonyms and related concepts.

utilizes metadata by scanning. After scanning, it asks data experts and data engineers to provide additional information and correlate entities by creating relationships. After the Graphmarts are created, users can add Data Layers to their Graphmarts for data cleansing, transformation, linking, and access control, dynamically enhancing the in-memory graph in an iterative manner.

Figure 9-4 shows how Graphmarts and Data Layers are managed. The neat part is that you can map metadata and sources into layers and build another series of layers on top of this. For example, your first layers could be "source layers" that directly take your sources and metadata as input. The metadata for building your first layers could come from ontologies (OWL files) you provide, or metadata that is discovered by scanning. Your second layers expand the first layers by connecting entities and making improvements using SPARQL. These are the Data Layers. Then, you could add another series of layers for making projections that are specifically designed for data consumers. These layers are also called Data Layers, but they're specially designed for consumers using semantic layers. Between all of the layers, there are relationships. The recipes that describe the sequence of transformation steps that are applied are stored as ontologies in the RDF format. They include references to other ontologies describing the contents of each layer.

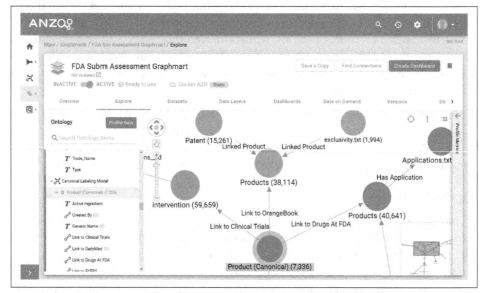

Figure 9-4. A screenshot of how Anzo visualizes and connects entities within a graph: the models represent datasets that you can execute queries against

The advanced aspect of this vision is that you can also set up knowledge graphs in a distributed model, with some parts maintained by domains and another (central) part maintained on a central or enterprise level. This central part forms the core of your model. Of course, when you implement a central model, it's important to set enterprise-level standards for the most important metadata objects and how they relate to each other.

When you implement a distributed design, your domains can extend the central metadata model without compromising the core model. For example, a marketing domain team might add their own domain-specific entities or properties to this model for the context and data they need. They might even make their models publicly available for other users or consumers. Everything can easily be extended, combined, and queried together, as long the underlying data repositories are accessible and the relationships to the resource (data) locations are embedded.

Data fabric for metadata management

You can expand the vision of using the semantic web standards for metadata management even further, and link it all the way to your enterprise metamodel. Your metamodel then becomes a semantic layer that sits on top of your knowledge graph, in which all your important metadata is stored. You can use this semantic layer for navigating, searching, and answering complex queries. In other words, you can query your metadata just the way you would query your regular data using a knowledge graph. With this approach, for example, central data privacy classifications can be linked to conceptual terms, and since you have the underlying links to the application data endpoints, you know what data attributes are sensitive.

The knowledge graph, seen as a giant semantic web of entities and their attributes, allows you to find the closest-matching entities based on semantic similarities between them. You can also allow domains to extend their domain-specific knowledge graphs with domain-specific vocabularies, taxonomies, or ontologies, as shown in Figure 9-4. Although the ontology-based approach is difficult to implement, it's impact can be huge: it can greatly improve the overall consistency of the data landscape and boost data consumption and productivity; it can completely change the way users interact with complex data representations; it may automatically generate ontologies, classifications, graph relationships, or embeddings for natural language processing, recommendation, and search algorithms. So, it is important to prepare yourself for this data fabric development.

The technologies behind the data fabric utilize the same open standards that drive the web. Internal knowledge and the meaning associated with data thus becomes accessible to everyone. Big tech companies often integrate this technology with artificial intelligence, machine learning, and NLP. You can even connect this vision to the disciplines of data integration or data security: for example, you could integrate and transform data automatically based on the semantic context and relationships provided, or dynamically change data access based on process descriptions documented in one of the knowledge graphs.

A data fabric, as an intelligent and metadata driven–architecture, can be a great solution for managing metadata at scale. When using a knowledge graph–based approach for metadata management, I recommend taking it step by step. Don't try to create enormous charts with all connections that only a small group of technical people will understand. Build it up slowly, and make the model accessible for business users, too, so everybody benefits from new insights. In the end state, you can apply advanced algorithms and additional tools to the knowledge graphs to enable intelligent data consumption, improve overall quality, and detect hidden patterns.

Metalake solution design

For designing a knowledge graph architecture, consider mirroring the patterns that we discussed in earlier chapters. Metadata, just like regular data, often needs to have its quality validated and be cleansed and integrated with other metadata before it can land in your knowledge graph for metadata management purposes. To get started quickly, reuse blueprints and services from your data product architecture. Figure 9-5 clearly shows the overlap with some of the patterns from Chapter 4. Layered on top of these are several services from the API architecture for real-time communication between frontend services and the underlying services in which metadata is stored.

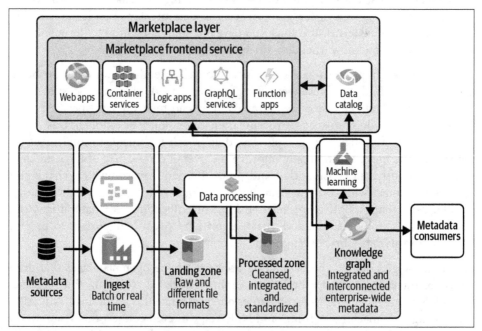

Figure 9-5. A metalake solution design showing how a knowledge graph can be used to fuel a data marketplace—the marketplace frontend services are there to visualize end-to-end data management insights

The relationship between your data catalog and knowledge graph is strong; the majority of the metadata is managed by your data catalog. The difference between these two is that your knowledge graph is more flexible, easier to adapt, and broader: it covers a wider range of metadata and can integrate metadata from many different places. The data catalog, on the other hand, is scoped to finding and searching for data for the purposes of data use and data management.

 I expect future-generation data catalogs to look different. At some point, data catalogs will become open and interoperable knowledge graph platforms with many surrounding services for visualization, workflow management, integration, and so on.

Once you've successfully designed your knowledge graph and started to use it for managing your data management metadata, you can also use it to monitor the maturity of your enterprise architecture. For example, using the business capability model for Oceanic Airlines from Chapter 2, Figure 9-6 shows how you might indicate the data management maturity level of each business capability within your organization.

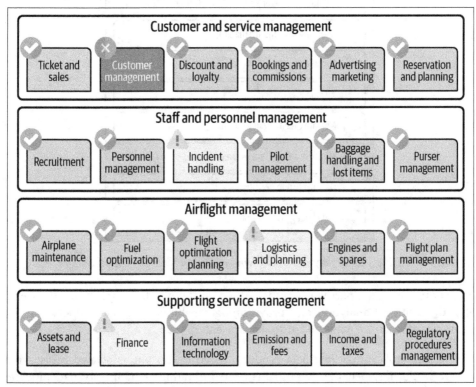

Figure 9-6. Business capability model showing the maturity of each business capability through the lens of data management

If something is wrong, you can drill down to see the number of datasets, data quality issues, and consumers. Figure 9-7 shows what a report about the domain's health status could like like. These statistics are just examples; the more metadata you have, the more insights you can provide. The information that is retrieved to show such a visualization could come from different places; metadata can come from your catalog, knowledge graph, other metadata repositories, or a combination of these.

Your knowledge graph has great potential for providing insights into your architecture, but the story shouldn't end there. Knowledge graphs are powerful solutions for building data marketplaces. A marketplace, as shown at the top of Figure 9-5, is typically a thin orchestration layer with an appealing look and feel. It serves as a one-stop shop for data usage and a central hub for data governance within the organization. It uses the stores in which metadata is kept: your catalog, knowledge graph, and any other relevant metadata repositories. You collect this metadata by making API calls to, for example, your catalog and/or knowledge graph.

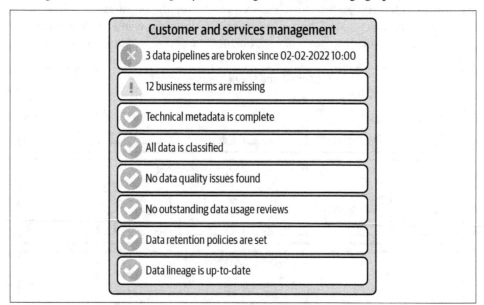

Figure 9-7. Business capability report showing characteristics for data management

Depending on how smart you want to make your knowledge graph, you can extend it with additional analytical and provisioning capabilities too. Let me share a few examples of what I've witnessed at some large enterprises:

- A marketplace may rate data products based on certain associated measurable KPIs. For instance, the sum of KPIs related to ratings, data quality, data pipeline success rates, data freshness, and usage statistics may give hints about what data products are good candidates to be used as input for preparation for data analysis by data consumers.

- A marketplace may automatically conduct data product incident analyses and proactively notify data consumers when they might be impacted.

- A marketplace may contain features to automatically create and publish data contracts for customers through a self-carrier channel.

- A marketplace may integrate with reporting or development environments (such as Jupyter Notebook) for better data exploration.

- A marketplace may use machine learning for proposing data quality rules and schema metadata suggestions for newly onboarded data products.

- A marketplace may be able to make intuitive queries that can be resolved through a synthesis of multiple data sources. Potentially, it may have the capability to invoke data virtualization or transformation engines for transforming and aggregating data.

- A marketplace may contain a search engine for quickly processing full-text searches.

- A marketplace may enforce data not being shared when certain metadata is missing. For example, if no linkages between business terms and technical attributes exist, data may not be visible to outside consumers.

- A marketplace may become a reward system, motivating domains and users to actively participate.

- A marketplace may contain features for quickly discovering data; for example, showing the top 100 records of a dataset.

Future data marketplaces are likely to be a combination of many products. They may begin as a catalog of data products, but are expected to be extended over time with more tools and services. Data marketplaces are also likely to go through various maturity cycles as they grow. With respect to that, what best practices can we observe? Here are a few suggestions:

- Follow a step-by step approach, starting with a few use cases and metadata sources and slowly scaling to other data domains and metadata areas.

- Bidirectionally integrate your data marketplace, knowledge graph, and data catalog. For example, you might create a data contract using your data catalog, but do data access permission management in your data product architectures. This will require you to closely integrate several metadata components.

- Promote metadata enrichment by all parties. Consider rewarding teams with extra budgets.

- Define a collaborative governance model based on roles and data domains, with clear responsibilities and functions for all stakeholders.

- Define a metamodel that manages all knowledge and context of your organization's data. This metadata should be closely aligned with the model that is being used in your catalog.

- Create dashboards, metrics, and alerts for monitoring metadata quality. Develop feedback loops for improving metadata quality at the source.

As you can see, successfully building a data marketplace is a major challenge in terms of platform creation, organization, and processes. However, it will deliver a large number of benefits with regard to achieving the goals defined in your data strategy.

Wrapping Up

If data is fuel for business users, then metadata is the data needed by chief data officers. With metadata, CDOs can oversee and gain insights into the overall health and status of the organization's data management capabilities and take it to the heights of efficiency.

Metadata, as you have discovered, binds everything together. Validating the integrity and quality of the data, routing it to or replicating it in a new location, transforming the data, and knowing its meaning—all of these rely on metadata. Metadata management isn't just about big data, business intelligence, and analytics. It's also linked to application integration, service orientation, microservices, and DevOps, including continued integration and deployment.

You've also learned that metadata must be combined with analytics to continuously improve your data management capabilities. By using a knowledge graph and machine learning, you can detect new patterns and relationships between data points. With the right set of services, you can make better suggestions to model your data, improve data quality, and automatically classify data. This intelligence is the missing piece of the data mesh. So, your next-gen architecture is a hybrid: both data mesh and data fabric.

Metadata is also essential for democratizing data through self-service portals. To drive consumption, you should introduce a data marketplace through which users can intuitively explore accessible data. You can launch your data marketplace with only a few data products available, then expand it as your architecture grows by onboarding more domains. Consider enriching your data marketplace architecture with additional services, like virtualization for querying and processing data products directly. This allows for a richer experience and will attract more users. Ultimately, your data marketplace is also connected. It not only promotes the value of data, but is the looking glass for overseeing the entire enterprise.

Building a data marketplace is not only about metadata. It's also about structure, culture, and people. You need to give users trust, provide training, and work on awareness. These cultural aspects require less rigid governance, but the magnitude of these activities should not be underestimated. When your users are correctly trained, they become valuable resources: they each own or use a specific part of the data landscape, which they carefully maintain and optimize; they help each other out and increase one another's effectiveness.

In the next chapter, we'll discuss master data management. You'll learn that some enterprise consistency will be placed back into the architecture by mastering, curating, and republishing data.

CHAPTER 10

Modern Master Data Management

In this book's first edition, I offered the following advice about data and master data management (MDM): "If it's fast and fluid, break it apart into smaller pieces and leave it up to the domains. If it's stable and it truly matters, consider using MDM." Three years later, I stand by this recommendation. Why? Because in a heavily distributed environment, applications are often intertwined. In previous chapters, we discussed the scale at which enterprises need to manage and distribute data. Large organizations typically have a multitude of domains, each taking ownership of its data assets and responsibility for sharing reusable data products with data consumers. This federation increases speed, but it's a concern for several reasons:

- Domains tend to take care of only their own data products and not how to work with other products, possibly making it difficult for consumers to combine data from multiple domains.

- If each domain is building its own data transformation code, then there will be much duplication of effort, which makes the architecture costly and ineffective.

- Having multiple domains that have aggregates or copies of data from other domains for performance reasons leads to data duplication and increased complexity.

- There may be inconsistencies in contexts between domains, and therefore variance in the levels of data quality.

To address the challenges of data reusability and consistency, we need to add the discipline of MDM to the architecture, and ensure we fix data quality and inconsistency issues at the root of our source systems. MDM, as described in Chapter 1, is about managing and distributing critical data to ensure consistency, quality, and reliability. This is important because inconsistent or incorrect data can result in damaged credibility and decreased revenues and profits. Other trends driving the demand for MDM are security, fraud detection, and regulations such as the GDPR and the CCPA. Inefficiencies in managing master data can result in failures to detect fraud or penalties from regulators.

 It's easy to fall into the trap of enterprise data unification: widening your scope and mastering too much data requires more effort to integrate, govern, and coordinate data dramatically. Use metadata to decide what to include. Analyzing lineage, data models, and data contracts can reveal overlap and common ares of interest between domains and thus determine which data should be subject to MDM. In general, data elements that are used within only a single domain shouldn't be within MDM's scope. Data elements shared by numerous domains, however, are candidates.

Before demonstrating how to apply MDM within a large ecosystem, it is important to say that MDM can't—or shouldn't—be solved with technologies that primarily focus on data integration (ETL). It's considerably more involved than that. A modern MDM stack comprises many aspects, including the following:

- Data quality management, such as detection handling, correction handling, and follow-up management
- Automated match and merge rule management for handling data duplication
- Location/localization handling for managing geographic limitations and implications
- Data enrichment management for supplementing missing or incomplete data
- Consent management, such as data legislation and usage management
- Data governance management, such as workflow and life cycle management for the approval process and decisions made on data quality, rules, localization, data access, and so on
- Data source management and integration features, such as updating your source system data with newly created MDM records

Demystifying Master Data Management

Most organizations have systems that share data elements with commonalities. Take "customer" and "product,"[1] for example: chances are high that multiple versions of the same master data are stored in different parts of the organization, across many

---

1 In practice, you'll find numerous data elements (for example, "customer") don't even have unique and coherent identifiers that can easily be stitched together. MDM can be a solution for this problem as well.

applications and systems. Such overlap isn't only inefficient but can result in inconsistencies as well. The customer's name might be spelled differently; addresses can differ; each customer might have their own unique ID number in each system. Each copy of the data can belong to a different department or domain. If customers' data changes or needs to be combined, how will you recognize who the same customers are, despite these differences? This is where MDM comes in. MDM focuses on detecting and resolving data inconsistencies by distributing mastered versions of data across applications and systems.

MDM can be implemented in many different ways using different approaches and scopes. In the following sections, we'll look at some possible implementation styles and data integration options and then move on to designing an MDM solution.

Master Data Management Styles

To manage your master and reference data successfully, you need to design and implement an MDM solution. Lyn Robison, writing for Gartner (*https://oreil.ly/Pki76*), identifies four MDM styles: consolidation, registry, centralized, and coexistence (see Figure 10-1).

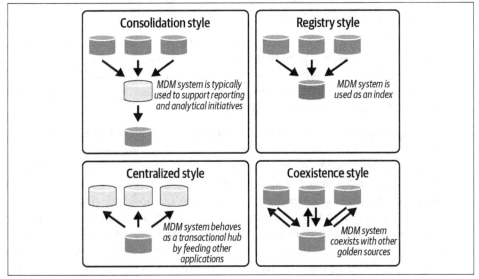

Figure 10-1. An abstract comparison of the four master data management implementation styles from Gartner

Let's take a closer look at each of these:

Consolidation style

The *consolidation* style has a great deal of overlap with data warehousing: it consolidates master data and other data into a single repository or hub, called the *master data store* or *MDM hub*. The hub uses data integration patterns to continuously pull together master data from the operational systems to improve quality and manage governance. Data from this consolidated repository is available for consumption by downstream applications. This style is typically implemented for analytics, business intelligence (BI), and reporting. No effort is made to clean up or improve data in the golden source systems. Improvements made to the data are limited to the hub, so only consuming applications benefit.

Registry style

The easiest MDM style to implement is the *registry* or *repository* style. The registry is typically a simple cross-reference table that provides direct insights into objects that are deduplicated and what relationships have been found between them. It uses an internal reference system and local identifiers (such as customer identifiers) to link back to the original data sources.

This style has no impact on the golden source applications. Each source system remains in control of its own data and remains the golden source. Since there's no distribution of data from the registry back to the source systems, there's also no direct impact on data quality.

Centralized style

In the *centralized* style, the master data store serves as a central repository for master data for all operational and analytical systems. It collects, links, cleans, matches, and enriches data, then immediately publishes the enhanced data back to the respective (transactional) source systems.

The biggest concern about this style is that it requires intrusion into the golden source systems for two-way synchronization: applications need to conform to use the master data repository as their backend. This conformity pattern can be difficult to implement because application designs can't always be changed. Off-the-shelf products, for example, usually can't be modified. Another concern is tight coupling: if you want to change the centralized repository, for whatever reason, you're forced to change all the other systems too. Although commercial MDM vendors will tell you that this is the best approach for well-managed and governed master data, I advise you to seriously consider any of the other approaches.

Coexistence style

The *coexistence* style is used in situations where the master data can't be used centrally and must be distributed in multiple locations throughout the enterprise. In this style, improvements find their way back to the original systems, so updates are performed within the golden source systems. Coexistence is the most complex implementation style because complex data integration patterns must be implemented for distribution and to ensure data consistency in the golden source systems and master data store.

These four implementation styles aren't mutually exclusive. You can start, for example, with the registry style and move to coexistence later. You can also use different styles for different datasets. You might choose to manage a reporting structure with the consolidated style but customer data with coexistence. When implementing a style, you can also blend different product implementations. It's important to note that the implementation style shouldn't be driven by technology, but rather by your organizational and data needs. That said, not all MDM vendors allow you to switch between or combine the different styles easily. You have to be cautious about which vendor you choose and consider which style(s) you might want to adopt.

Data Integration

Data integration is a foundational piece of enabling MDM. Many MDM implementations must support both batch and real-time processing; in transactional systems processing typically happens in real time, while analytical systems usually focus on batches for larger quantities of data. MDM must rest on the same foundation we've used so far for distributing and integrating data. In this model, MDM simultaneously plays the role of data consumer and provider by collecting data from and distributing it to sources.

When distributing MDM data, you must balance between consistency of the data and latency. Depending on the situation you're dealing with, different implementation and integration designs are possible.

If the use cases are operational or require low latency, use APIs or events. An approach for microservices is to use state stores: instead of moving millions of records at once, you use an event-driven architecture to expose the MDM records as a streaming database to consuming applications. In this way, the microservices of a domain can be a conglomerate of services developed by the domain and a read-oriented microservice that is responsible for the MDM data.

 Using MDM for critical and time-sensitive operational paths can be complex. For example, if an order management system receives an order and looks for a customer in the MDM system, you need to ensure that the critical matching and merging process happens within milliseconds.

One option for implementing an MDM state store is using a NoSQL database, which is constantly injected with data from the source systems. Within the database, the state store keeps track of what newly created data can be linked to global identification numbers. To streamline this process and improve the quality, you can extend the state store with machine learning capabilities. Having an MDM state store that holds the full transaction log of all events (for example, creates, updates, deletes) provides the ability to replay entire backlogs of data. In general, this simplifies managing the inevitable changes in data models because you're working with a paradigm that allows you to replay all the data if needed, without the involvement of the source systems to play a role. Having said that, it's important not to mix roles and responsibilities, and it may be better to keep this transaction log separate from your MDM solution (while ensuring that your MDM platform can work with an event streaming way of thinking).

For use cases that can tolerate higher latency, you can distribute master data using your data product architecture. However, it's important to not make point-to-point connections between the MDM hub and providing and consuming applications. If you do this, there's a risk of data inconsistency. Data consumers, for example, might get new records delivered from the MDM hub directly, while data products aren't yet up-to-date and may not reflect the data used within the MDM hub. If the MDM hub always uses the data products, you'll never have these inconsistencies, so a good principle is to feed your MDM environment with the same data products your consumers are using for their analytical workloads.

Designing a Master Data Management Solution

The process of implementing MDM starts with identifying what unique and trustworthy data is created and maintained in what applications and systems. The golden datasets, from the golden source systems, are the basis. Since data is stored differently in each application, it's important to understand each context and what business rules, formats, and reference ranges impact the master data there.

The next step is designing an MDM solution that harmonizes the data and makes it consistent. You can either go for a vendor-provided solution, or design one yourself. Some popular vendors in the MDM space are CluedIn (*https://www.cluedin.com*), Profisee (*https://profisee.com*), Informatica (*https://oreil.ly/yA4qx*), and Tamr (*https://www.tamr.com*).

The design and implementation of MDM has a strong relationship with data modeling and data integration: identifying overlapping data attributes, harmonizing and modeling the data through ETL processes into proper data models is a vital part of the overall design of the MDM solution. Depending on the style and solution type you choose, the amount of data modeling and data integration work involved can vary, as well as the integration patterns and architectures. The coexistence style, for example, relies more on real-time processing and uses API-based and event-driven architectures, while a consolidated approach can be engineered using only batch data from your data product architecture(s).

You'll need to establish governance, making sure data owners and application owners are in agreement on the following items:

- What regulations must be applied (for example, certain laws don't allow different customer datasets to be combined)
- The scope of data that will be mastered
- Rules for cleaning, matching, merging, linking, and consolidation[2]
- For what data usage classifications (see "Data Usage Classifications" on page 244) the central master data store can be used as an authoritative source and for what situations data consumers must fall back on their local (original) source systems
- Which data quality rules and processes to implement
- Whether improvements should be delivered back to the original source systems, and if so how quickly and with what data integration techniques (expect variations and combinations of batches, APIs, and streaming)
- Who owns the newly created data (domain teams or a central team)
- Which users are authorized to approve or reject proposed changes
- Master data definitions, which should be stored in central metadata repositories such as the data catalog

Once you've completed these steps, you can start to strategize about how to distribute data back to the original source systems and other applications.

Domain-Oriented Master Data Management

Although many MDM solutions can manage both reference data and master data, I recommend clearly delineating between how to manage these two. *Reference data* is data used to define, classify, organize, group, or categorize other data (or value hierarchies, like relationships between product and geographic hierarchies). *Master data*, by contrast, is the core data that is absolutely essential for the enterprise. Each type is typically managed differently and comes with its own methods of data distribution.

Reference Data

One approach for achieving data consistency between domains is asking your domains, when distributing data products, to conform themselves to centrally managed reference data. Currency codes, country codes, and product codes are common

---

2 Enterprises rarely get the rules for matching and merging right the first time. You'll also overfit and underfit with merging and linking. Having an agile MDM system that allows you to iterate on your rules is important.

examples of reference data that should be provided. This data can be published, for example, in a master data store or central repository. When any of your domains distribute data products to other domains, they should use the identifiers from the enterprise reference data to classify the data. The mapping of local data to enterprise data allows other domains to quickly recognize master data within data products.

 Asking domains to conform their data products to enterprise reference data sounds like a contradiction to the data mesh approach. To some degree this might be true, but if regulation forces us to be consistent on certain data dimensions, then master data management is the only way to properly achieve this.

Of course, if domains are to map local reference data to centrally managed reference data, they need to know exactly what should be mapped to what—for example, if alpha-2 codes (e.g., US) and numeric values (e.g., 840) for country codes should always be mapped to the standard alpha-3 codes (e.g., USA).[3]

When asking your domains to conform their data products to enterprise reference data, there are different approaches you can follow. One option is to provide central services so domains can discover, understand, select, and incorporate enterprise reference values when building data products. For example, you might have a data catalog that references a central storage account in which all reference data is hosted. With this approach, domains perform the mapping activities themselves, using synchronized copies of enterprise reference data to look up the reference values before distributing any data products. This integration process can be anywhere from fully automated to manual.

An alternative is to offer central MDM services so domains can manage the local-to-enterprise mapping within the MDM solution. In this case, each time a data product is published, a postprocessing activity will run to check for inconsistencies and enrich the data product with enterprise reference data. This approach might take more work to implement up front, but it removes the need to build solutions for this within all of the respective domains. It also guarantees better quality because the mappings are validated on a central level.

You can use both approaches to adding reference data to data products side by side. That is, some domains might do the mapping themselves, while other domains rely on centrally managed services. In this case, a central governance body should oversee reference data management across the enterprise to ensure the goals of standardization, quality, and operational efficiency are met.

---

3 It's worth mentioning that many of these reference codes can be automatically rectified, even if they are in different formats, using external services. Many programming languages have this capability built in as well.

Master Data

For master data, the approaches to data distribution and integration are different because the results may flow in different directions.

Master identification numbers

The first important aspect of master data is master identification numbers,[4] which link master data and data from your domains together. These data elements are critical for tracking down what data has been mastered and what belongs together. Identifying unique data and assigning master identifiers can only be done centrally, not locally within systems. It requires having the master data from the different systems come together in an MDM solution. Figure 10-2 shows how this works in practice.

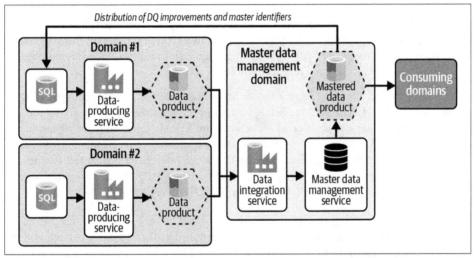

Figure 10-2. Solution design for mastering and distributing data via an MDM

Identifying and maintaining these relationships is important not only for knowing what data has been mastered, but also what data can be quickly linked to other data. If local (domain) keys in an operational system change, the only element that binds everything together will be the master identifier, so you should also build feedback loops from your MDM solution to your local domains. One option is for domains to maintain the relationships between local identifiers and master identifiers in a lookup table, which may be stored within the MDM solution itself. For golden sources, you

---

4 The *master identification number*, or *master identifier*, is one of the extended attributes that MDM has created. It ensures that records are unique by assigning unique identifiers and, most importantly, by documenting the relationships between matched records.

might want to implement a principle of routing master identification numbers back to the underlying domain.

Application Keys Versus Surrogate Keys

Data engineers have two choices for unique identifiers: you can use a unique, existing business identifier or application key, or a unique system-generated surrogate key that is immutable and will never be duplicated. The benefit of using a surrogate key is that it has no semantic meaning. MDM assigns a surrogate key to every master record to help you recognize groups of master data.

When using application keys, you have to remember that a key that is unique in the source system may not be unique across all systems. For example, take a system that uses seed identity keys starting from 1 and going up. You might say this is a bad practice—clearly, if there are other systems in the organization that use the same approach, the identifiers will not be unique across systems—but there are many systems that do actually work like this! Using a random GUID removes this problem. Thus, a business identifier by itself is often not enough to uniquely identify an object when we're bringing data together from multiple systems.

Now imagine the following situation: you ingest data from an operational application into your MDM system, and the MDM system generates a new random GUID for it. Then, someone decides to wipe all data from the MDM system and ingest the data again. A new GUID would be generated for each record. What happens if the data that was in the system was already being used and referenced out in the business? MDM can address this problem by using *deterministic* GUIDs, where the same input data from the same location will yield the same GUID every time.

When distributing master identifiers, it's recommended that you not extrapolate the MDM master identifiers to all source systems, which can create consistency issues between domains. Thus, only applications or systems that are subject to master data management should obtain the master identifiers from the hub. Systems that aren't subject to MDM should use their own local (domain) identifiers.

MDM domains and data products

When integrating, cleansing, and harmonizing data and storing it in a master data store, you generally create new MDM domains. These domains create uniform sets of data for certain subject areas. Well-known examples are customers, products, geographical locations, finance and risk data, and employee data. Master data from these MDM domains is expected to find its way (back) to other domains. It's distributed as data products, in the usual manner (as described in Chapter 4). A general recommendation is to distinguish regular data products from master data products because master data products use regular data products as input for master data management. You could do this, for example, by using a data catalog.

Note that you might not need to distribute master data products to all domains. You might have a set of domains within the boundaries of a certain scope that need to conform to using master data, while domains outside that scope don't.

Domain-level MDM

When you look for overlapping data, you'll likely discover various degrees of overlap. Some data is generic and spans many domains. Other data might span only two or three domains. You can draw distinctions about the amount of data overlap and its importance by implementing *domain-level MDM*. To do this, you create partial views of your master data within specific scopes. To distinguish the importance and amount of overlap, I recommend using the following classifications:

Enterprise data
> Data with enterprise-wide scope and applicability. It may be used across several domains, all domains, or even outside the enterprise. Enterprise data includes both master and reference data, and its consistency is important.

Domain data
> Data that is shared by some, but not all, domains. It's important for the overlapping domains to manage but has no enterprise importance, nor does it have any regulatory importance. Domain data is typically managed and maintained within a few domains and not on a global level.

Local data
> Data that is used only within a single local domain or system. It isn't shared or used by any other domains.

Figure 10-3 shows an example of managing master data within the boundaries of a domain. As you can see, the overlap with a data product is significant. Instead of only using ETL, MDM and ETL are used for creating new data products.

With an approach like this, you can support your domains by providing MDM services to them on an as-a-service basis. We'll look at this next.

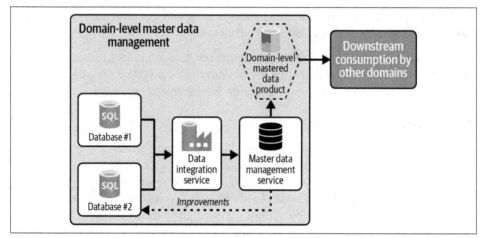

Figure 10-3. Mastering and distributing data within the domain itself (this form of MDM is aligned with domain data, while the previous example you saw is aligned with enterprise data)

MDM and Data Quality as a Service

To successfully implement MDM within your enterprise and domains, I recommend offering MDM capabilities to the domains as a service. MDM solutions are often complex and can be hard to implement. Abstracting away the infrastructure and providing MDM services to your domains in this way can simplify usage tremendously. If you're using a central solution, I recommend segregating the domains (or groups of domains) from one another. If all master and reference tables are stored centrally, you can distinguish them using, for example, a catalog and metadata, and classify which datasets are enterprise and which are domain data.

The same applies for data quality services, such as profiling, matching, standardization, and validation functionality. With this model, quality measures and controls become transparent, and domains don't have to implement these solutions themselves. A recommendation that applies here is to make it part of your data pipeline solution. So, bake it into your data product architecture as a standard service or component.

Master and reference data management are ways of achieving higher levels of consistency and reuse in your organization, but there are different approaches as well. In the next section, I'll discuss how these approaches may overlap in integration and data distribution, as seen in MDM.

MDM and Data Curation

Master data management overlaps with the discipline of *data curation*: the process of collecting data from diverse sources and integrating it so that it becomes more valuable than its independent parts. We've already touched upon the creation of new data in Chapter 2 when discussing constructor domains, which are data-consuming domains that also act as providers by creating and distributing new data products. This can be seen as a form of data curation.

Data curation removes repeatable integration work from other teams, which can be important for enterprises. Within large organizations this process is typically combined with DataOps, a methodology to create and deliver automated, integrated, and trusted data pipelines. Although data curation overlaps with MDM, it's important to clearly show the differences and formulate some strong principles around each of them. In the next sections, I'll highlight some different approaches to creating and managing curated data.

 There's a tremendous amount of overlap between DataOps and MDM, but they target different personas (data engineers for Data-Ops and data stewards for MDM). The goal of DataOps is to build automated pipelines that can solve data quality problems with code. MDM offers an operational flow that involves a human when an issue is identified that cannot (or maybe shouldn't) be managed in or automated with code.

Both MDM and curated data creation aim to deliver value and make data consumers' lives easier. They share techniques like ETL, data cleansing, data science, and metadata management (capturing lineage, describing data models, etc.).

As you've learned, at its core MDM consists of the processes used to collect, link, cleanse, integrate, match, enrich, and distribute (master) data. During these processes, duplicates are typically removed and inconsistencies in the data are corrected. MDM also has a strong focus on entity consolidation (creating one entity out of several similar or identical entities) and cluster reduction (creating a single golden record). The results MDM produces are authoritative sources of master and reference data. Unique data is typically detected centrally and the output persisted in a new physical location, since it includes many improvements. Most importantly, *no new data is created using a different context*. Facts, such as quantitative information, remain in their own context, although improvements are made for correctness and consistency.

MDM in Relation to Data Warehouses and Lakehouses

In the previous paragraph, I mentioned "authoritative sources." You might be wondering what it is that makes the results produced through MDM authoritative, versus, say, the Gold layer in your data lakehouse or the dimension tables in your data warehouse. The answer is that the MDM system contains the golden records, together with their lineage and all the history of how they got to that point and came to be. The Gold layer and dimension table only store the output of the golden records from the MDM system itself. Which brings us to another question: does your MDM system write directly to your dimension table or Gold layer? The answer should be no! Your MDM system should feed into a source that the data warehouse team can use to populate the dimension tables, and it should play an interim role between the Silver and Gold layers in the classic "medallion" setup (*https://oreil.ly/KEKop*) in modern lakehouses. In the Gold layer, data tends to be organized in consumption-ready "project-specific" databases; MDM data provides input for this layer.

Data curation is different from MDM because it doesn't explicitly state whether existing data will be modified or new data created. That means the semantic context of the data can be changed. Data curation isn't explicit about whether data is persisted or created on the fly. For example, curated data could be delivered from a database view based on a query that runs on one or more database tables, or generated by code executed at runtime. The entire data curation process can also be metadata-driven, meaning you generate curated data using metadata. This implies a strong relationship with metadata management because a large part of these activities involves organizing metadata (schema, table, and column information, queries, joins, and filters, etc.).

Let's look at a few different approaches for enforcing consistency across the enterprise. Each has its pros and cons.

Knowledge Exchange

One way to achieve more semantic consistency is to exchange knowledge. With this approach, you can share knowledge between domains in several ways. Information about the data can be delivered along with the data itself, by providing an extra metadata file or encapsulating the metadata into the data. Alternatively, you could maintain the information in a central repository, such as a data catalog. The metadata could contain information about specific data entities, including their locations, annotations, attributes, relationships, and semantic meanings. If entities are equivalent, that can be made clear using labels or annotations. This should make information exchange easier.

The process of building up knowledge, as you learned in Chapter 9, can be accelerated in different ways. Data experts typically work with subject matter or domain experts to describe data. Another approach is crowdsourcing: inviting communities of users or the public to provide context. Scanners and annotation tools may be used as well; these typically use algorithms to detect duplicates, classify or rate data, and predict what data belongs together.

Integrated Views

Integrated views are predefined queries that re-create data, using the same SQL statements, at execution time. This approach to ensuring consistency is common in both MDM and EDW architectures. Integrated views are sometimes also called *virtual tables*, because it feels like you're querying a table, but in fact it's the query that is saved under the view.

The difference from the previous approach (providing semantic consistency through metadata) is that views can contain business logic. They can even create or generate new data elements. These changes aren't only syntactic translations; they could be context transformations as well. Another difference is that data can be duplicated: views can be materialized, meaning that the results are copied and persisted. This is especially useful for improving query performance.

Views can also be combined with metadata. They can, for example, be generated from metadata and automatically change when the metadata changes.

Reusable Components and Integration Logic

Another way of facilitating data collaboration and reusability is *code sharing*. Here, it's not the curated data that is shared but the underlying code (templates, snippets, and scripts) used to generate the outputs. This code is stored in a central and open repository, including versioning, allowing DevOps teams to contribute and improve upon what has been published.

The benefit of this model is that business logic is applied only within domains, which allows teams to alter and optimize this logic as they see fit. In addition, the outputs regenerated as improvements from the community find their way to the central code repository. One drawback of this model is consistency, since allowing teams to modify the code can make comparing results between teams more difficult.

Republishing Data Through Integration Hubs

Several database vendors advocate that data curation can be done by encapsulating the original sources. Domain teams, in this approach, extract and load data into an integration platform, and then republish or distribute it. During this process, the semantic context can be changed, so transformations and enhancements can be applied to existing datasets. New datasets can be created as well.

Although this model of trusting certain domains appears elegant, it involves several risks and challenges:

- Traceability and versioning, so that you know what happens with the data, are a concern. To mitigate the risks of a lack of transparency, ask data curators to catalog their acquisitions, as well as the sequences of actions and transformations they apply to the data. This metadata should be published centrally.

- Data quality and governance issues could arise. Having the data fixed in a hub introduces the risk that improvements will never find their way back to the original golden source systems. This would prevent transactional and operational processes from benefiting from improvements to the data. There's also potential for ownership concerns because the original data ownership is obfuscated through new data ownership.

- Operational systems may be extended with new functionality and application components via the hub, meaning that the transitional integrity of the processes and the data spans across both the operational system and the hub. Ensuring transactional consistency becomes more difficult because data not only is spread further but is also optimized to fit the needs of other use cases and consumers. When not designed correctly, differences can arise, hierarchical dependencies between the hub and operational system(s) can be created, and services can pop up that encapsulate data from both the transitional system and the hub. The end result can be a tightly coupled architecture.

Providing enterprise-side semantic consistency through republishing data in this way works only if there are clearly defined standards for data models, lineage, and documentation; data cleansing rules; and data governance processes that determine if data is captured and distributed back to the platform. In the next section, we'll look at an alternative approach: using aggregates.

Republishing Data Through Aggregates

MDM activities (such as collecting, cleansing, integrating, and harmonizing data) overlap with the activities of aggregate domains that create curated data for sharing with other domains. When attempting to address the overlap by clustering activities and assigning responsibilities to domains, it's good to pay attention to the collaboration models between domains. Let's use an example to make this clear.

Suppose you have three use cases in which the data requirements overlap. Different collaboration patterns, as shown in Figure 10-4, can be applied within and across the different teams.

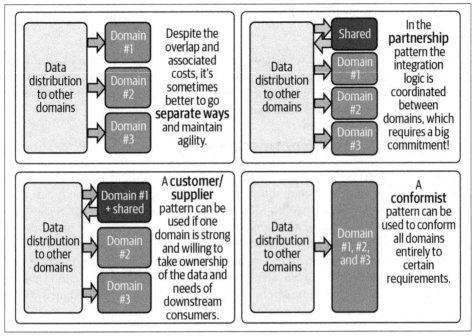

Figure 10-4. Different collaboration patterns for domains with shared data needs

Let's explore the different approaches:

- The *separate ways* pattern can be used when a high degree of flexibility and agility are required. It can also be a valid choice when little or nothing is shared from a modeling perspective, limiting reusability, and the cost of duplication is acceptable.

- Teams can use a *partnership* pattern to accommodate the shared development needs of all parties when there's a large amount of overlap. All teams must be willing to cooperate and respect each other's needs. A significant commitment is required of all the teams because none will be able to change the shared logic freely. Data engineering teams, in this approach, are both data consumers and providers: they capture, extract, and load the data into data stores, and republish or distribute it.

- A *customer/supplier* pattern can be used if one team is willing to take ownership of the data and needs of downstream consumers. The drawback of this pattern is the possibility of conflicting concerns, forcing downstream teams to negotiate deliverables and schedule priorities.

- A *conformist* pattern can be used to conform all domains entirely to all requirements. This pattern can be a valid choice when the integration work is extremely complex, when (distributed) coordination isn't desired, or when vendor packages are used.

The patterns discussed in this section are especially important when there's significant overlap in the data integration or harmonization needs between domains. In these cases, it can help to separate out generic, repeatable, integration logic and distribute it back as a newly created data product (an aggregate).

Data Governance Recommendations

As mentioned previously, there's a lot of overlap between MDM and data curation. However, there are also important differences, so from a governance standpoint, they should be managed separately. With MDM, data is typically adjusted for consistency reasons. MDM isn't supposed to change the meaning and create new data, so data users and governing bodies can always follow a trail back to the data owners and the original golden source systems. Data curation, on the other hand, can result in new data ownership because it can involve creating or deriving new data from existing data. Data curation is thus more strongly aligned with domains and executed within them.

The various approaches to creating curated data have a strong relationship with data democratization, which we discussed in Chapter 9. A federated approach shifts away from central data management teams and toward decentralized teams. Making transparent what integration logic has been applied, and allowing teams to distribute data back to other teams, can greatly improve and refine the quality and interpretation of data, leading to enhanced decision making. However, for delegation and determining scopes, a central authority is required to oversee the overall management of data.

Users can only make correct decisions if the data they use is consistent and correct. With MDM, you ensure data consistency and quality on the enterprise level.

That said, it's important to find the correct balance. Having too many areas of master data or reference values leads to too much cross-domain alignment. Having no enterprise data at all makes it impossible to compare any results. Therefore, consider the opening sentences of this chapter: if data is fast and fluid, break it apart into smaller pieces and leave it up to the domains. But if data is stable and it truly matters, consider using MDM. For gaining insights into what truly matters, your data lineage helps: it points to the assets you have that are already being utilized and that are in the critical paths of usage. Most importantly, you need to take an Agile approach to master data, recognizing that these assets may span across many domains, and that the assets themselves and the domains they fall into may change over time. This results in the realization that trying to predefine exactly what your MDM information model will look like will typically result in much rework as your data estate evolves.

A practical way to begin using MDM in a balanced manner is to implement a repository. This is the simplest way to manage your organization's master data. With a repository, you don't need to adjust your domain systems to learn what data is low quality or needs to be aligned. With a repository helping you gain that information, you can deliver value more quickly.

Another recommendation is to align your processes and governance once you've come to an agreement with your domains. Consider making data contracts specifically for MDM, holding agreements on timelines and reviews by all involved domains. Also make sure you work on your metadata. Catalog your master data so domains can easily recognize which data is subject to master data management. Also, secure lineage showing how this data flows through your data pipelines.

As you progress further, when your metadata is of high quality, consider using machine learning to predict where the overlap will be and what data you should manage on an enterprise level. Models can learn and predict what data is important. I haven't seen any companies reaching this stage yet, but to me this would be the highest possible level of maturity.

Wrapping Up

The importance of master data management is obvious: users can only make good decisions if the data they use is consistent and correct. MDM ensures consistency and quality on the enterprise level—two areas so heavily intertwined that many solutions make a point of targeting both. It addresses the concerns of usability and efficiency in several ways:

By adding master data products
> This ensures enterprise-wide consistency and avoids having multiple domains build their own data transformation logic for harmonization and data quality. You can apply master data creation on different levels: on an enterprise level for when data truly matters and spans across the entire organization, and on the domain level for when data is shared between some, but not all, domains. These scopes can sometimes overlap; for example, some domains might use domain-level and enterprise-level master data products.

By introducing reference data for data product creation
> This approach requires your domains to conform themselves to centrally managed reference data, but addresses the concerns of interpreting local reference data and combining data.

By allowing domains to play the role of domain aggregates
> Although data curation can be used to transform data into a new context, a better approach to managing repeatable integration logic is by distributing and sharing this as a newly created data product.

A practical way to begin implementing MDM in your organization is to start with the simplest implementation style: registry. With this style, you can quickly deliver value by learning what data needs to be aligned or is of bad quality without adjusting any operational systems.

The next step should be to set a clear scope. Don't fall into the trap of enterprise data unification by selecting *all* data. Start with a subject that adds value for the organization, such as customers, contracts, organizational units, or products. Only select the most important fields to master. The number of attributes should be in the tens, not the hundreds. After you've come to an agreement, align the processes and governance. Make your agreements on timelines and reviews clear to everyone. Work on the metadata, too, so master data is cataloged, and users know what data elements from what source systems are candidates, and how these elements flow through the data pipelines.

The last step, which is the ultimate goal, is to achieve coexistence, where improvements flow directly back to the original source systems. This step is the most difficult because it requires many changes to the architecture. Source systems need to be capable of handling corrections and improvements to master data from the master data store. These changes need to be distributed accordingly, using the patterns of the integration architecture.

We also discussed improving data consistency across the enterprise through curated data creation. For this, an effective communication model and data governance are important. When data reuse is promoted, the organization becomes more effective. This is why many companies look to community-based approaches, open data models, and data marketplaces (discussed in Chapter 9). Now we're going to get back in our helicopter and investigate how integrated data plays a role when turning data into value. Be aware that the next chapter will be a bumpy ride with lots of context-switching; we'll fly up and down, and out and in. So, fasten your seatbelt and put your chair in the upright position. Happy travels!

CHAPTER 11

Turning Data into Value

In this chapter, we'll discuss most people's favorite part of data management: turning data into value with intelligent services, such as business intelligence and advanced analytics. We'll do this by focusing more on the consuming side of the architecture, while keeping in mind everything we've already covered about the data-providing side of the architecture. You learned that it takes a village to make data available in a safe and controlled way, with proper governance and security.

Let me immediately put my cards on the table: on the consuming side, use cases often need data to be combined from different domains and data products. This interaction is complex on both the technical and organizational levels. Therefore, I advocate for managing consumer-focused data differently from data products. The core concern here is bringing data together and combining it for different business use cases. It's about turning data into value and using services that may be specific to the use case at hand. So, a large part of this chapter will be devoted to this topic.

The data-consuming side is also the most complex part of the architecture because each business problem has its own unique context and requirements. A large variety of tools, disciplines, roles, and activities are expected on the consuming side, which makes standardization difficult.

Business requirements always come first. Turning data into insights or actions requires understanding how information flows and using that knowledge to identify business opportunities. Use cases may start as one-off projects, but ideally you'll develop maintainable solutions based on your key data that deliver constant value for the organization. Depending on your business requirements, you might use different techniques, tools, and frameworks.

You'll also need to consider nonfunctional requirements. It takes many different database technologies to accommodate a large variety of complex use cases. Depending on the use case in question, you might pick one or several of these. Additionally, there are variations in the types and velocities of transformations you make to your data, optimizations for parallelization, and consumption patterns, all of which affect your end result. Finally, there are different business intelligence and machine learning patterns for delivering business value (actionable insights), which are complex and consist of many components. We'll look at all of these topics in this chapter.

To address all of these challenges, I suggest creating standardized, reusable patterns and building blocks. This approach is similar to how data product architectures are managed. However, for consuming data, you need to define different patterns, set principles for managing self-service data and managed data, and get clarity on considerations for selecting data stores, building pipelines, and using business intelligence and machine learning services. The consuming architecture we unpack in this chapter is built upon the data foundation discussed in Chapter 2 and works with the governance model discussed in Chapter 8.

The Challenges of Turning Data into Value

I've seen it happen all too many times: in the absence of specific analytical capabilities and with the need for greater speed, business users start to purchase and deploy their own tools themselves. They create point-to-point interfaces and hook analytical tools up directly to data warehouses and operational systems. They also begin to extract, transform, and load data directly into their self-managed business environments. As new use cases and opportunities pop up, more and more of these tools are brought in to solve just one problem, without regard to related issues. The inevitable result: the architecture becomes complex, expensive, and difficult to manage.

To avoid business users steering your data management architecture into chaos, you need to create controlled environments that integrate deeply with the underlying data management services and support the federated model of many business domains, while also addressing the needs of different audiences and user groups in a *self-supported* manner. We'll explore how this works—but first, let's recap what we've covered and the part of the architecture we'll be concentrating on here.

So far, we've mostly been focusing on making data ready and available for consumption. In Chapter 4, we discussed the design and management of data products. In the chapters that followed, we continued to explore the distribution and management of data by delving into areas such as API and event management, metadata, master data management, governance, and security. All of these topics fall into the realm of the data providers, on the left side of the architecture depicted in Figure 11-1.

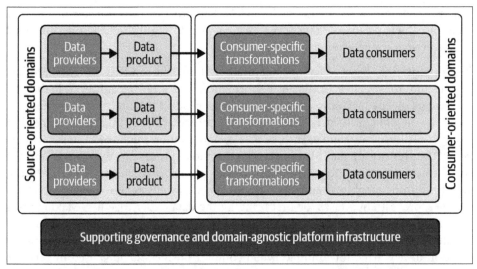

Figure 11-1. Decentralized collaboration of data providers and data consumers

On the right side of the architecture in Figure 11-1 are the consumer-aligned domains. As you learned in Chapter 2, these domains consume the data supplied by the providing domains, transforming it as needed to fit their business requirements. Consumer-aligned domains are unique contexts. Therefore, this consumer-specific transformation step is *always* required. The data consumers are the experts on their own use cases, so they're responsible for this step; they set the requirements and know what data must be integrated for what business (analytical) purpose. How do they go about this?

Data consumption, and the transformation that comes with it, often starts with duplication of the data. However, this isn't always necessary. Indeed, in a large architecture, you want to limit the number of copies of the same data because maintaining them can be costly and difficult. Security is a concern, and data may change or become outdated. Therefore, as a consumer, your first consideration should be whether you can use data products from data providers directly, without copying or persisting them.

Data products, as described in Chapter 4, are designed to serve out large volumes of immutable data repeatedly to consumers. Because of their underlying performance and access patterns, they can be used for directly retrieving data at the query time (e.g., for reporting, ad hoc analysis, analytics, or self-service activities). In a direct data consumption pattern, data is read but no new data is created. Consuming applications use the data products directly as their sources, perhaps performing some lightweight integration tasks based on mappings between similar data elements. They may change the context and temporarily create new data, but they don't require these results to be stored elsewhere. The benefit of this direct usage model is that it doesn't require creating new (complex) data models. You don't extract, transform, and load data into a new database. Transformations happen on the fly, but these results don't need a permanent new home.

To support this direct read consumption pattern, the underlying data product architecture must deliver sufficient performance. The problem, however, is that the consumers' needs may surpass what your data product architecture can offer. For example, the amount of data that needs to be processed may exceed what the data product platform can handle. In such a case, one solution might be to incrementally bring the (historical) data over to a new location, process it, and preoptimize it for later consumption. You may also run into problems when multiple data products need to be combined and harmonized. This typically requires many structural changes, orchestrating tasks, or first bringing the data closer together. Making users wait until all of these tasks are finished before presenting the data to them will negatively affect the user experience. In other cases, there's a clear need for the creation of new data; for example, when complex business logic is used to generate new business insights. To preserve these results for later analysis, you need to retain this information somewhere. Rather than using data products directly, in such cases you will need to use a different data consumption pattern: creating domain data stores.

Domain Data Stores

Newly created data should be managed the same way as data products are managed by domains, which raises two questions. First, how should we refer to the architecture in which the newly created data is managed? Some practitioners use the terms *data applications* and *analytical applications*, but to me, these terms could mean anything; they merely describe the architecture in which data products are consumed and integrated. For example, an analytical application could be any type of business application.

The second question is how to refer to this newly created data. Some people use the term *data products* for datasets created on the consuming side of the architecture as well, but I find that usage misleading. As we've seen, data products have certain universal characteristics: they inherit the ubiquitous language from the underlying providing domain; they remain stable and compatible after creation; they're decoupled from the application; they're designed for intensive readability. These characteristics contrast with how consumer-aligned domains in general operate. Data that has been transformed for a specific use case is tightly coupled to that use case: it doesn't necessarily have to be stable, and it should take on the structure and shape that best complement the requirements of the use case. Its design may vary depending on the specifics of the supporting system(s) and database technology in use (row-oriented database, time series database, columnar store, etc.).[1]

 Some organizations use the term *consumer-aligned data products* for data that specifically targets unique business needs. This term might work, as long as you strictly define the scope and purpose of this data. However, in casual usage it's likely to be shortened to just "data products," leading to confusion as the distinction is lost.

In conclusion, building and serving data products is unlike consuming and integrating data for business use cases. There might be some overlap in the services and techniques used, but the underlying concerns are different. Providing data—creating data products—is about serving data to others. It requires adhering to set principles to guarantee stable, easy, and safe consumption. Consuming data is about utilizing data for value creation. It involves data-driven decision making, which may require many extra tools and services. The consumed and transformed data might become a candidate for data product creation, but this doesn't mean that turning data into value is the same as managing data as a product.

To facilitate the management of that data and the related services and business use case application(s), I propose a new building block: *domain data stores* (DDSs). As with data products in Chapter 4, I advocate for approaching the management of the data and corresponding architecture (technology services) from two perspectives. The technology viewpoint addresses the underlying solution architecture needed for consuming, integrating, and using data. At this level, you'll find ETL, BI, ML, and other services, as well as products such as databases. Second, the data viewpoint addresses the consumed and newly created data. On this level, you may classify data as one of the following:

Copied data
Data with the same semantics as the original data product data, although it might have gone through some technical or structural changes.[2]

Integrated data
Data that has been consumed, combined, and transformed into a new context.[3] It has been specifically designed for the consuming use case.

---

1 *Polyglot persistence* is the term used to describe solutions that use a mix of data storage technologies.

2 In my previous role, I used the terms *syntactic* and *semantical* data changes. Syntactic data changes don't change the meaning of the data, although it might be presented differently. Semantical data changes change the context and thus the meaning.

3 Some engineers in the field use the term *cooked data* to make it clear that the data has been processed.

(Newly created) data product data
>   Integrated data that will be made available to other domains to consume. This data is similar to data product data, and therefore follows all the principles discussed in Chapter 4 for managing data as a product. The difference with data products from the consumer side is that this data has already gone through the structural changes we described, and it is being shared after going through all of those steps.

 You could use your metamodel to classify data and set principles for each type. For example, for newly created data, lineage always must be present.

Correctly classifying data is important because different principles apply to each type. For example, integrated data should never be directly shared with other domains as it is tightly coupled to the underlying use case. Needless to say, any disruptive change will directly impact data consumers. As a result, when such data must be shared with other domains, it first must become a new data product.

For managing the consumption side as a whole—both technology and data—I propose using DDSs. As shown in Figure 11-2, DDSs are similar to data product stores. Their role is to store and manage the newly created data that is needed for facilitating the consumer's use case.

DDSs importing and storing data, as domain C in Figure 11-2 shows, is necessary only in cases where consumers can't use data products from other domains directly. The underlying technology for domains is selected by use case, based on cost, agility, knowledge, and skills, as well as nontechnical requirements such as performance, reliability, data structure, data access, and integration patterns.

DDSs are architectures on their own. Just like data product architectures, DDSs are typically offered as blueprints that you can use to quickly spin up environments for domain teams. The blueprint may deploy a set of services you can use for data analytics and data science. It might also include ETL services, scheduling tools, CI/CD services, and so on. Any services your teams don't require should be explicitly disabled.

It is important to understand that a DDS can play the roles of data consumer and data provider at the same time. In such a situation, the DDS, in the role of consumer, consumes, integrates, and transforms the consumed data into newly integrated data. As provider, it provides the newly created data products to other data consumers. This process is shown in Figure 11-3.

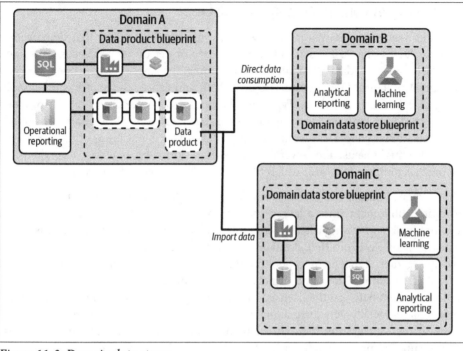

Figure 11-2. Domain data stores

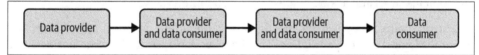

Figure 11-3. A consumer can become a provider, which can result in a chain of data consumption and further distribution

It is essential to classify applications as either a golden source (see "Golden Sources" on page 26) or a DDS, because doing so makes accountability for and the origins of unique and authentic data explicit. It also guarantees that data remains unique and unchanged throughout the entire chain of distribution. Note that an application can sometimes be both, depending on the role it is playing. For example, you can classify an application as a DDS when it consumes data from other domains, but if that same application generates new data, then it will play the role of a golden source for the newly created data.

When consuming, combining, integrating, and distributing data, you need to make certain decisions about the size and scope of your DDS. We'll explore these aspects in the next section.

Granularity of Consumer-Aligned Use Cases

To avoid having too many or too few DDSs, you need to ensure that demarcation lines for DDSs are clearly set and each use case or set of use cases consumes and integrates only the data it requires. Determining the appropriate scope, size, and placement of logical DDS boundaries is difficult and causes challenges when distributing data between domains. Typically, the bounded contexts are subject-oriented and aligned with both business capabilities and value streams. Preferably, the boundaries of a domain and DDS would be aligned, but this is not always the case: a very large DDS might be used for several use cases (i.e., domains), or a large domain might encompass multiple DDSs for different use cases of that same domain.

Thus, when defining the logical boundaries of a domain, there could be value in grouping subdomains into a larger domain, and then decomposing the DDS design to simplify data modeling activities and internal data distribution within a larger context. For example, if multiple domains within the boundaries of a value stream work closely together, it may help to pool them together logically within the boundaries of a DDS architecture. The same principle might apply for use cases that require data to be consistent between themselves. Decomposing domains when possible is equally important, especially when the domain is large or when subdomains require generic —repeatable—integration logic. In such situations, it could help to create a generic subdomain that provides integration logic in a way that allows other subdomains to standardize and benefit from it.[4] A ground rule is to keep the shared model between subdomains small and always aligned on the ubiquitous language.

When designing analytical architectures, the important task is to think carefully about the logical role of your DDSs. This involves consideration of both business and technical granularity:

- Start with a top-down decomposition of the business concerns: an analysis of the highest-level functional context, scope (that is, boundary context), and activities. These must be divided into smaller functional areas, use cases, and business objectives. This exercise requires good business knowledge and expertise on how to efficiently divide business processes, domains, functions, etc. The best practice is to use your business capabilities as a reference model and look for common terminology (ubiquitous language) and overlapping data requirements, such as shared integration logic.

- Next, consider your technical goals and how to achieve them. These include reusability, flexibility (easy adaptation to frequent functional changes),

---

4 Domain-driven design uses the term *shared kernel* to indicate that part of the domain model is shared between different teams or subdomains. The shared kernel integration strategy reduces duplication and overhead.

performance, security, and scalability. The key point is making the right trade-offs. Two business domains might use the same data, but if their technical requirements conflict, it might be better to separate the concerns. For example, if one business task needs to intensively aggregate data and another only quickly selects individual records, it may be preferable to separate them, even if they use the same data. Similarly, if one use case requires updating the data structures daily while the other expects them to remain stable for at least a quarter, you should consider separating them.

The story doesn't end there, however. For example, as mentioned previously, you'll also need to think about data reusability concerns. The same integrated data might be needed for multiple use cases. Organizing data internally within a business boundary can become more complex when a domain is larger and composed of several (overlapping) subdomains. The DDS in this situation can become a conglomerate of different domain zones: some zones are shared between multiple subdomains, while other zones are exclusively mapped to one domain. Let me try to make this concrete with an example using the medallion architecture. For a large domain, you could plot a boundary around the various zones of one DDS. Within this DDS, the first two zones (Bronze and Silver) can be shared between multiple subdomains, so tasks such as cleansing, correcting, and building up historical data are performed in common for all subdomains. For the transformations in the third zone (Gold), the story becomes more complex because data is required to be specific for each subdomain or use case. So, there will be pipelines that are shared and pipelines that are specific to one use case. This entire chain of data, including all of the pipelines, belongs together and thus can be seen as one giant DDS implementation.[5]

The idea of building a common integration model and then introducing specific selections and designs for consumers isn't new. Layering is a core concept of data warehousing. The difference with DDSs, when applying layering for a larger domain, is the clear scope. In DDSs, the boundaries are clearly set: rather than integrating all data, you only select and consume data for a specific business purpose.

Properly guiding the consuming side is one of the key requirements for successfully implementing a federated architecture. If no architecture guidance is provided to your domain teams, you risk seeing overlapping and repeated activities across multiple domains, with different solutions to the same integration challenges that occur

---

5 A similar layering can be observed in data product development and the establishment of (providing) domain boundaries, as discussed in Chapter 4. However, there is a clear difference between data product architecture and DDS architecture. Within data product architectures, there's a strong source system alignment. Within DDSs, you don't see this alignment, as the integration activities typically span across multiple sources.

when combining data. Therefore, I recommend managing the consuming side jointly with your data product and master data management activities.

DDSs Versus Data Products

The goal of data products is providing data. DDSs have the opposite goal: consuming data and turning it into value. They're about making business decisions, supported by functions such as reporting and machine learning services. The data that is consumed by DDSs also differs from the data that is typically managed by data product architectures. Data in DDSs has been structured and optimized for the use case at hand. Each business problem is unique and may involve different target user groups, different business requirements, and different nonfunctional requirements.

DDSs may have some overlap with data products when it comes to distributing newly created data, however. We've already discussed that DDSs can play the role of data consumer, provider, or sometimes both. That is, DDSs may share newly created insights and data with other applications. To facilitate this, you need to carefully consider how to align the data providing and consuming sides of your architecture. As you can see in Figure 11-4, there are two design patterns you can choose from:

- Domain A uses one architecture to solely consume and use data and another for data product development.

- Domain B uses a combined architecture that supports both data value creation and data product development.

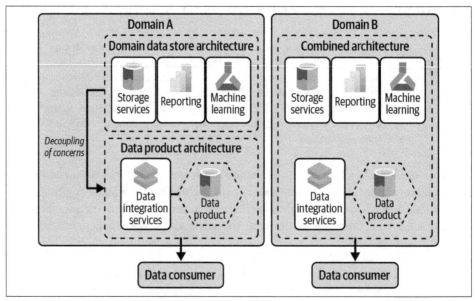

Figure 11-4. DDSs and data products can be managed together or independently

If DDSs are designed to solely consume and use data for analytical use cases, a separate architecture must be used for sharing newly created data (i.e., when building new data products). The DDS architecture, in this scenario, requires another blueprint with a new set of services. The motivation for managing your DDS with two separate blueprints is to decouple the concerns of using and sharing data. With this option, the inner architecture of the analytical use case is isolated from the architecture in which data products are being created and shared.

If DDSs are designed to include data product architectures, the same architecture can be used for consuming and sharing newly created data directly with other consumers. If you design your blueprints like this, there will be synergy in terms of the underlying services that are used for data consumption and sharing. For example, you can use the same ETL framework or share compute resources for transforming data for the two objectives of consuming and sharing newly created data. On the other hand, it will be harder to recognize data copies and newly created data because both are managed within the same architecture. So, there's a coupling risk that needs to be mitigated, for example, by using a metamodel (discussed in Chapter 9).

Your blueprint designs will thus be heavily influenced by the choice you make about whether DDSs and data products are managed together or independently from one another. In addition, your blueprints may differ based on what you need to offer for the activities involved in turning data into value. Analytical use cases are unique and may require different services. For example, a use case that only utilizes reporting services requires a different blueprint than a use case that utilizes machine learning capabilities.

For the data that is managed inside a DDS itself, I recommend distinguishing between data product data and integrated data with a few basic principles. Integrated data, as you've learned, is data that has been consumed, combined, and transformed into a new context. The input and original data originated elsewhere, so lineage is a bigger concern because it shows all the dependencies with other domains. Data ownership works differently, too, because the accountability for data creation and quality lies outside the domain of integration. Thus, distributing integrated data requires approval from the owner(s) of the original data. The same applies for copied data: the origins are elsewhere, so you'll need to track its lineage. You will also need to manage overlapping integration concerns with care: introduce master data management, or consider using any of the aggregation patterns discussed in Chapter 10.

The principles of scoping and decoupling apply to BI and analytical services too. If, for example, one domain wants to expose its analytical models to another domain, they must be decoupled using proper integration patterns. The same coupling concerns apply to newly created data. Distributing integrated data creates new dependencies, so consider breaking down the data into small, highly focused pieces that each solve only one specific problem. Limit the shared domain model to a bare minimum. Don't create a distributed monolith that all teams rely on; require the scope to be set clearly. If data is subject to intensive reuse, it has to become part of the master data management discipline, as discussed in Chapter 10.

Best Practices

The biggest problem with delivering value on an enterprise scale is that use cases are highly diverse and scattered throughout the organization. They all try to address various aspects of solving a business problem, targeting different audiences. Use case scenarios are wide-ranging, and a large variety of data stores and services are needed to facilitate them. For example, one use case may require data that arrives at a fast pace for stream analytics, while another use case may require slowly arriving historical data for reporting. Others may focus on process mining, image recognition, or artificial intelligence. Some use cases are descriptive or diagnostic and only look back to the past, while others are predictive or prescriptive and peek into the future. As the demands of data consumers continue to diversify, it's impossible to enforce a common way of working and a generic solution design for all use cases. However, there are some best practices that can always be followed with regard to business requirements, the target audience and operating model, nonfunctional requirements such as databases and tools, and data pipelines and data models. We'll examine each in this section.

Business Requirements

Your starting point should always be your business requirements. Your use cases will mostly depend on the concerns and the opportunities that business teams see. There could be, for example, projects that add new revenue to the organization by monetizing insights, increasing customer satisfaction, or gaining competitive advantage by getting insights into market trends. Other use cases, for example, might be centered around risk, finance, cost reduction, sentiment analysis, cohort and tracking analysis, and increased operational efficiency with process mining and better insights. Some other use cases just want more accurate data to make better and more predictable business decisions. For all of your business use cases, the recommended approach is to make a long-term business plan. So, look at the long-term value-add. Don't end up in a situation where you're solving ad hoc problems with one-off solutions.

Carefully consider the need for any new services; they might be expensive and hard to maintain, control, secure, etc. If a new service is truly needed, enable it and evaluate the usage before enabling any additional services. In all cases, pay attention to overlapping services.

Implementing use cases is a challenging task in terms of analysis and required resources. To prepare, have brainstorming meetings with your business teams, then organize and cluster all of the output. Creating a business model canvas (*https:// oreil.ly/49ZSJ*) can be a good way to highlight what business use cases potentially unlock what value using what tools and services. You might want to extend this information with the required stakeholders, needed data sources, connections to any existing use cases, actors and interactions involved, and timelines and success criteria for implementation.

Your business requirements will also determine the amount of data you need to obtain. For example, if you want to develop a machine learning algorithm based on data with many fluctuations and high variability, you'll probably need much more data than you would for a simple model with low variability.[6]

After you've analyzed your business requirements, you'll need to ensure that your objectives and goals are well defined, detailed, and complete. Understanding them is the foundation for your solution and requires you to clarify what business problems need to be solved, what data sources are required, what solutions need to be operational, what data processing must be performed (in real time or offline), what the integrity and criticality requirements are, and whether the outcome is subject to reuse by other domains.

Target Audience and Operating Model

An important next step for working out your analytical use case is to determine who you need and what their responsibilities should be. There are many roles related to turning data into value. These can be defined in many ways, and also can be easily misunderstood. Therefore, it's a general best practice to make these roles part of your data governance framework (see "The Governance Framework" on page 224). Here are some suggestions for how you might define the different personas:

Domain owner
> Higher-level decision maker, typically a product owner or business representative, who collaborates with business users on requirements and governance teams on data management policies, processes, and requirements, as described in Chapter 8.

---

6 Within machine learning, there's a common principle that more data beats clever algorithms (*https://oreil.ly/ ntW42*).

Application owner
> Responsible for the application or technical solution design, including all development, security, and application and data maintenance activities.

Analysts or subject matter experts (SMEs)
> Responsible for defining business requirements, what data is used for, who may access it, and how the data is shared with others. Collaborate with the domain owner and other data owners as needed and support the business in its use of data. Data analysts or SMEs are typically referred to as "power users" because they know how to analyze data with tools but aren't necessarily data scientists or business intelligence experts.

Data engineers
> Responsible for collecting, integrating, and enriching data. Data engineers have an important role, enabling the data analysts and data scientists to do their work properly. They maintain data pipelines and often work with languages like SQL and Python.

Data scientists
> Statisticians, usually with a background in computer science or mathematics. Data scientists are experienced with algorithms, machine learning, and deep learning. They are usually familiar with the business and follow market trends. Their end goal is to find patterns and correlations and make predictions based on the data. They often work with languages like Python, Scala, R, and Java.

Report builder
> Responsible for designing and building reports and dashboards for other users. A report builder typically has superior business intelligence skills.

Depending on the size and complexity of the business problem, some or all of these roles will be working together in a cross-functional (domain) team. The optimal size of such a team is often considered to be the size of a DevOps team: between 5 and 10 people. Creating small, independent teams doesn't mean that they can't share talent, but it should be clearly defined where responsibilities lie. Having small teams focusing on clearly defined and scoped targets enables scaling, as many teams can advance different aspects of the business simultaneously. All team members must have a good understanding of the business challenge, corresponding solution, and required data.

Nonfunctional Requirements

Nonfunctional requirements can make or break the success of a software system or product. These include cost, scalability and performance, latency, ease of maintenance, consistency, security and governance, write and read characteristics, data volume, variety, and velocity, and so on. Each will guide you in a certain direction.

The central question is often what type of database technology or data store should be used. Selecting the optimal data store depends on many criteria. There's no silver bullet. It's sometimes also a matter of taste and experience. The following questions are worth considering:

- How is your data structured? Structure influences preprocessing steps, type of cleansing performed, modeling steps, type of storage, and more. Failing to understand this from the beginning will result in wasted time and an incorrect outcome.

- Are your queries predictable? This can make a significant difference to your implementation. If the queries are predicted, you can optimize with caches, indexes, or preoptimized data, for example.

- What types of queries are you using? Simple lookups, aggregations, joins, mathematical operations, text search, geographic search, other complex operations? Relational databases, for example, are usually better at joins.

- What are the requirements for current, historical, and archived data? Does all data need to be retained?

- How do you want to balance between optimizing for integrity versus performance? For example, must your application design enforce strong consistency, or is eventual consistency good enough? If integrity is important, RDBMSs typically enforce consistency better.

- What trade-offs can you make with regard to prioritizing reads, ingestion, or integrity? Different data models have different characteristics. A Data Vault, for example, is flexible in its design and can handle parallel loads; however, reading the data is more performance-intensive.

- What kinds of operations will your database be doing? Certain types of operations are likely to be more dominant. Distributed filesystems are well suited for appends but not for (random access) inserts. Relational databases, on the other hand, excel at these.

- What volumes of data will be coming in and going out, and at what velocities? Some NoSQL databases perform badly with batch data ingestion. For high-speed data ingestion (messaging and streaming), normalized data models and ACID consistency models may decrease performance because of integrity and locking controls.

- What data access protocols do you need? Some databases are only accessible via SQL, ODBC/JDBC, or native drivers, while others only allow access via RESTful APIs.

- How much flexibility will you need to adapt or change the data structure? NoSQL databases can handle changing data structures well since they can be schemaless.

- How much scalability and elasticity will you require? Some systems support dynamic horizontal scaling.

- What are the database dialects and languages that are supported? Are your engineers already familiar with these? How difficult are they to learn?

- Does your vendor require specific storage solutions? The vendor's requirements might limit your choices.

Other considerations include costs, open source standards, features, integration with other components, security (such as access control), privacy, data governance, and ease of development and maintenance.

Consider how many and what types of data stores you want to offer to your organization. You might want to define a common set of reusable database technologies and patterns, as part of your blueprints, to ensure you best use the strengths of each data store. For example, mission-critical and transitional applications might only be allowed to go with strong consistency models, or business intelligence and reporting might only be allowed with stores that provide fast SQL access. Strive to offer a comprehensive list of choices, but limit the overlap! You don't want to end up with dozens of different database technologies.

Additionally, align your database choices with other tools and services. For example, some ETL frameworks work better with some types of databases than others. Also take these considerations into account when developing blueprints. Finally, you might want to vary between different cloud environments. You'll probably end up with a list of several technology services that will facilitate most use cases. Consider developing a flowchart or decision tree for supporting your teams in making the right decisions.

Data Pipelines and Data Models

Another important step in turning data into value is engineering a data pipeline that selects data and brings it all together in the target solution. The key point here is that all the data is already immutably persisted in data product stores, so there's not always the need to make an extra copy. This means you either obtain data directly on your regular schedule or wait for the data provider to tell you when you can start processing. When data is pulled over, a data transformation is typically required because you're moving data from one context into another. For this context transformation, you need ETL tooling (which we'll discuss in a moment).

For real-time ingestion, the pipeline works differently because you need to include a way to capture and store real-time messages. You can choose to store incoming messages in a folder or database for further processing. Another option is to use a buffer or extra application component, or use the integration capabilities of the streaming platform, which allow you to analyze, manipulate, and distribute messages. For more on this topic, revisit Chapter 6.

Note that many variations are possible, depending on your use case requirements. For example, for later analysis it's better to retain data by storing it as it's ingested, before transforming it or applying target semantics. For faster processing, you might combine ETL batch and stream processing. For handling different users' needs, you can also use a polyglot design that incorporates different data storage technologies. Again, look at your use case requirements, and make conscious choices.

Building a data pipeline is the most complex part of the entire project. Start small and keep it flexible. Most project failures happen when engineers try to "boil the ocean" and model all of the data at once. Another common mistake is immediately jumping into the technology and starting to write code before thinking through your requirements. Before you start building, carefully consider all of the functional and nonfunctional requirements, and address the fundamental questions. Are there reusable tasks? What is the best order for processing all the data? Are there dependencies, or can some processing steps be completed at the same time? How will the data be queried?

 Data scientists like to refer to what they call the "80/20 rule": 80% of a data scientist's valuable time is spent on finding, cleansing, and organizing data, leaving only 20% for actual development. There's no single algorithm that uses raw data and gives you the best model.

I recommend assembling your data pipelines as a series of isolated, immutable transformations that can be reused and combined easily. Input, transformation logic, and output in this case must be clearly separated from each other. For reproducible output data, I recommend versioning all pipelines. For better performance that takes advantage of the elasticity of modern infrastructure, you might want to engineer your pipelines to run in parallel. When it comes to complex data transformation and processing, it's sometimes a better option to use in-memory distributed processing engines like Apache Spark. Another consideration is to write your transformation logic in templates or a high-level programming language within a development-friendly ecosystem. This approach can be supported with best practices for writing and sharing good code.

SQL Versus NoSQL Pipelines

SQL pipelines, in general, handle and execute complex queries much better, but also require a better understanding of the relationships between tables. A SQL pipeline, therefore, might require more validation steps and transformation and update logic, because data must be parsed into the right (restrictive) structure.

NoSQL pipelines, on the other hand, can be simpler and more flexible. They can create data immediately and dynamically without defining structures. They're also more easily scalable, and queries often run faster since they don't involve joining many tables. Data can be more easily replicated horizontally, but querying and integrating it can be more difficult.

For data quality you can rely in part on the validations in the data products, but this doesn't mean there are no extra validations required in the pipelines. Consumers' viewpoints on data quality vary, so pipelines need to be extended to address common ETL issues, which typically involve constraints, completeness, correctness, and cleanliness. Additionally, security and privacy concerns must be handled with care. So, extra steps are expected before importing and processing your data.

Additionally, I recommend categorizing all your ETL tools and frameworks in a unified portfolio, coupled with best practices and considerations. Provide flexibility, but standardize by limiting the options. For example, GUI- or template-based frameworks can be best used when data movements and transformations are somewhat straightforward. Programming-oriented languages, on the other hand, may be best suited for situations that require complex transformations or machine learning.

Finally, the entire pipeline must be set up to provide metadata for lineage, so it's possible to trace and understand what data is mutated in what way at each specific step in the pipeline. This requires transparent back-pointers to, for example, your data products. File and event names, business keys, source system identifiers, and the like must be made available in central tools to ensure the correctness and completeness of all transformation steps. You might want to use a data catalog to stitch all of the integration architectures together. I also recommend formulating strict principles when teams build data pipelines, for example, determining under what conditions the lineage must be delivered centrally. These lineage requirements may also put constraints on the ETL tools you offer, because not all ETL tools perfectly integrate with all lineage solutions.

Scoping the Role Your DDSs Play

Persisting data for downstream consumption can happen for various reasons. Let me first provide some examples, and then I'll share some best practices for DDSs:

Analytical data stores

Analytical data stores, or file stores, should be used for integrating and combining data for analytical workloads, such as machine learning. Their purpose is to provide high-quality data for accurate model development. Data in analytical data stores is typically flattened and denormalized.

Reporting stores

Reporting stores are used for business intelligence or dimensional reporting. Data is typically modeled into facts (measurements) and dimensions for another context. The most popular and easiest design choice is a star (*https://oreil.ly/ NQQGM*) or 3NF schema (*https://oreil.ly/3jVoZ*).

Aggregate stores

As discussed in Chapter 10, when domains have overlapping data requirements it can be preferable to cluster some of the business logic and create a new, aggregate data product for the domains to use. Aggregate data stores are also a good design option when a domain can be decomposed into several subdomains and the data requirements overlap heavily.

Third-party or SaaS solutions

Some of your use cases might sit outside the logical boundaries of your architecture. For these situations, you will need connectors and a store for extracting and prepping the data before serving it to the external consumers

Operational consumers

Operational consumers are like OLTP systems, with a subtle difference: they don't just create data, but also consume and integrate data from other domains.

Data warehouses or data lakes

Consumers might require data warehouses or data lake services when they need to combine and integrate larger amounts of (historical) data from other domains into a common format that is easier to work with.

For all your use cases, standardize on what tools and services you would like to offer to your different domain teams. Consider aligning your blueprints for supporting different scenarios. For example, an aggregate store that only distributes newly created data doesn't require any business intelligence or machine learning services. Such a scenario can be best facilitated with a simpler blueprint that only contains some lightweight integration services. Scoping data stores and aligning on what blueprints your teams can choose from helps to reduce the overall complexity. For a federated approach, aim to always use a generic blueprint as a starting point. That is, each time a domain wants to consume data or build a use case, choose a generic blueprint, adjust it (as minimally as possible) to suit the domain's requirements, and deploy it.

For your blueprints, also consider aligning with your data product architectures, because the overlap is significant. For example, you might want to standardize on the services you choose from the modern data stack or the layering applied when using data lake services. Additionally, standardize on the software development aspects, including automation of code deployment, orchestration, and what frameworks, libraries, and tools users can deploy. Finally, you'll want to standardize on different aspects of data modeling and design, such as grains,[7] naming standards, materialization, permissions, data normalization techniques, and so on. A typical approach for organizing all this is to use inner sourcing or set up a central center of expertise.[8]

 Have you noticed how many times I've used the word *standardize*? A transition toward a federated architecture starts with setting standards.

Different data stores manage and organize their data internally in different ways. One common strategy is to separate (either logically or physically) the concerns of ingesting, cleansing, curating, harmonizing, serving, and so on. Within modern data stores or data lake services, this could involve various zones using different storage techniques, such as folders, buckets, databases, and the like. Zones also allow you to segregate concerns or purposes, so one store can be used for use case consumption and another can be used for data product maintenance and distribution. For all stores and zones, the scope must be very clear. They shouldn't span across multiple bounded contexts. Each domain operates within its own boundary, within which it will consume, integrate, and create new data. Again, consider making the zoning part of your blueprint designs.

---

7 The *grain* of a relation defines what each row represents in the relation. In a table like `products`, the grain might be a single product, so every product is in its own row, with exactly one row per product. By ensuring that your grains are clear, you specify exactly what a table record contains. This gives users insight into what data can be combined.

8 Nick Tune talks about inner sourcing in his blog post (*https://oreil.ly/TY1xA*) on how to better manage and eliminate cross-team dependencies.

Inmon Versus Kimball Versus Data Vault

What data modeling technique should you use on the consuming side when designing data warehouses or data lakes? Well, it very much depends on the characteristics and requirements of your solution. For cloud-based data warehouses, I generally prefer wide, nested, denormalized tables because such a design better utilizes the infrastructure provided by the cloud vendors. Furthermore, with such tables you avoid expensive computational joins and shuffling of data between compute nodes,[9] which can make your queries run slowly. On the flip side, if you have complex integration challenges, then a design such as a Data Vault could be more appropriate. For example, if many of your sources use the same business concepts, which are related and need to be integrated together, then you can separate concerns more easily with hubs, links, and satellites. In addition, a Data Vault has the benefit of decreasing dependencies between tables during the load process and simplifying the ingestion process by applying only inserts, which load faster than updates or merges. Bottom line: each domain should select a data modeling methodology that best matches its use case requirements.[10]

Although all data-driven decision solutions are expected to be designed specifically for each use case, you may notice that BI tools and ML services are common denominators. In the next sections, we'll take a closer look at each of these.

Business Intelligence

Business intelligence tools help businesses take a more structured look at data while providing deep interpretations. They allow for decision making via interactive access to and analysis of data. For BI tools such as reporting and dashboarding services, there are some extra considerations to weigh to ensure you're delivering the right value to the business.

Semantic Layers

The most fundamental question is whether you want to abstract your DDS with a semantic layer to present the available data to users in an understandable way for easy and consistent use. *Semantic layers* are business representations of data that help end users access data autonomously using common business terms. They are typically part of a reporting service and built and maintained by BI developers and

---

9 A *shuffle* occurs when a part of a distributed table is moved to a different node during query execution. More information on this can be found in the Azure docs (*https://oreil.ly/QtiCa*).

10 Christian Kaul maintains an extensive list of resources on data modeling (*https://oreil.ly/HYde3*).

business users. Using a semantic layer for business intelligence and other forms of data consumption has many benefits:

- Semantic layers make it easy for users to query the data and make the right combinations. Typically users don't have to worry about making the joins. The relationships are predefined and help everyone make the right combinations, avoiding incorrect calculations or interpretations. Fields are consistently named, formatted, and configured. For example, an amount can be automatically summed, or a date field can be used for time-oriented calculations.

- Data in semantic layers is optimized (preintegrated, aggregated, and cached) for consumption to improve overall performance. This results in a much better and quicker user experience.

- The underlying data store is decoupled, which means that changes to its data structure won't necessarily affect all reports and dashboards immediately.

- Semantic layers can have extra features, such as versioning, row-level security, and monitoring.

- A semantic layer can be built using a technology called *data virtualization*. This hides the technical implementation details from the consumers.

Semantic layers can be used to facilitate different kinds of data integration scenarios. They can be directly used by domains for data models that already align to specific analytical use cases. Domains can also use them as input for other semantic models: so one domain uses a semantic layer from another domain as input for its own semantic layer. In this case, the semantic models often need some tweaking, or are combined with data from another domain. To conclude: a semantic layer can be used to generate curated data, which means the semantic context of the data could change. This can mean that the ownership of data changes as well.

Most BI tools allow you to build semantic layers in two different ways. The first option is to use the proprietary in-memory or caching model. With this model, data from the underlying data store is transferred to the caching layer (refreshed) on a schedule. This often results in the data being duplicated; there's extra data latency because the underlying data store can be more up-to-date than the caching layer.

The second option is to utilize the underlying data store. In this model, queries are passed on to the underlying data source, so the semantic layer is only a metadata layer that directly federates the queries. This option is better for real-time and operational reporting because the database is updated within seconds, meaning there's less latency. The drawback is that data must be modeled and optimized for the reporting structure, typically a dimensional data model.

Semantic layers do have drawbacks and must be used with caution. For simple reports and predictable queries, it isn't essential to add the overhead of an extra layer. Another problem is that advanced tools can easily pick up and hold lots of data, which eventually makes the semantic layer costly. Another complicating factor is managing the overlap between reports and underlying (shared) data models that may combine the same data from different sources. As your landscape grows, so does the complexity of your reports, and the number of relationships to shared datasets grows. Set clear boundaries and align them with your capabilities. Only use shared (or composite) models if they are stable and truly matter.

The challenge of building semantic layers and reporting solutions is that you need to be clear about what insights you want to extract from the data. You need to know your business questions, organizational goals, and data sources up front. In many cases you'll first want to evaluate, explore, and discover what actionable patterns can be extracted from the data. This is why self-service data discovery and data preparation tools are so popular.

Self-Service Tools and Data

Self-service capabilities such as data discovery, preparation, and visualization tools aim to accelerate the process of deriving value from data by providing easy-to-use, intuitive self-service functions for exploring, combining, cleaning, transforming, and visualizing data. The rationale behind data preparation is that the data becomes more user-friendly and can be more easily used for reporting and analytics—i.e., it's more suitable for further processing and analysis. Data analysts and scientists can perform these activities themselves without requiring any programming or complex IT skills.[11] Some BI and data analysis tools come with machine learning algorithms to recommend or even automate and accelerate data preparation.

Some people use the terms *data discovery* and *data exploration* interchangeably, but they aren't identical. *Data discovery* is the broader term used to describe the iterative process of searching for data in a data catalog, and then finding patterns and trends in data. It's usually the first step before performing a data analysis. *Data exploration* is about getting a further-reaching, deeper understanding of what's inside the data and what its characteristics are.

Empowering data professionals to turn data into value themselves influences your architecture design and blueprints because data management and end-user tools need to be integrated and accessible. Data professionals are segmented based on their skills and required tools. This segmentation and focus on self-service affects standardization. If dozens of tools are available, it will be hard to integrate and apply automation.

---

11 Sean Kandel et al. wrote an interesting scientific paper (*https://oreil.ly/G2X7z*) on a data preparation tool called Wrangler.

Successfully implementing self-service capabilities thus requires trimming down the number of business intelligence and analytical tools with overlapping features and aiming for standardized solutions that meet the enterprise's specific needs. It also requires you to clearly distinguish between managed and self-service data:

- Managed data is for ongoing business needs, and thus by nature stable, automated, and standardized. It must meet all your data governance criteria.
- Self-service data is for ad hoc and one-off analyses and thus temporary by nature.

Self-service processes typically start with trying to understand what is in the data, what possible relationships there are, and how the data may be used for different business purposes. By manually analyzing, combining, and adjusting the data, you can validate a general hypothesis. These activities can also include experimenting with the data. Once the outcomes of your discovery and exploration activities are clear, it's time to operationalize the value, which means building a properly managed data pipeline (model and ETL) in a managed (production) environment with real data. Self-service can also be used to help business users looking to answer a single, specific business question quickly. This is known as an ad hoc analysis.

Between self-service activities and managed production workloads there must always be a proper handover from business users to data engineers. Self-service is often achieved through the creation of a semantic layer or a project that is run by only business users. This means IT is removed as the middleman; it allows business users to drive their own analysis. In that respect, IT's role should be focused on delivering the self-service capabilities as a platform. The data in this environment could be temporary and should be allowed to leave only under strict conditions. Self-service activities can also be managed with policies. I see a lot of organizations that provision lightweight, trimmed-down discovery environments, within which end users cannot orchestrate data pipelines or use Spark.

 To prevent users from copying data and storing results locally, provision self-service capabilities into a (temporary) workspace layer (in addition to Bronze, Silver, and Gold) for the purpose of self-service discovery. Some organizations even allow data in workspace layers to be discovered by other domains; however, by virtue of being in a workspace layer, it is marked as noncertified. This approach enables power users in the organization to quickly discover and share insights without having to go through all the validations, formal approval, documentation, etc.

Managed data, unlike self-service data, can be offloaded directly into self-service environments. The opposite (moving self-service data into managed environments) is forbidden, because managed data is never allowed to depend on human intervention.

The transition between self-service and IT-managed environments should be smooth. Users who maintain IT should work closely with those using the self-service exploration environment. An engineer, for example, might examine the self-service effort and even help build some sample ETL scripts, which are first tested in the self-service environment and eventually find their way to the managed environment.

Business intelligence, which includes managed and self-service data, powers decision making; however, it's important to find the right balance for your organization's needs. There's no one-size-fits-all solution, so consider following some generic best practices.

Best Practices

To ensure you get the maximum value out of your business intelligence investments, consider the following key actions:

- Make purposeful decisions about your BI strategy. Decide on the ideal balance of self-service BI, managed self-service BI, and enterprise BI.[12] Align the ownership and management of these models with your domains.

- Develop playbooks and design patterns for helping your users. For example, what is the best approach for loading data into BI tools? Should reports directly load data into a reporting environment, or should a database be created first, and all reports connect to that? As there are no fixed answers and many design decisions to make, consider writing playbooks: sets of rules or suggestions that are considered to be most suitable given a particular situation.

- Consider setting up a center of excellence (COE): a central team that's responsible for defining company-wide standard processes, training, guidelines, best practices, support, and much more. Talk to stakeholders in different business domains to understand which practices are currently working well and which practices aren't working well for data-driven decision making.

- Use different maturity levels for guiding the conditions in which business intelligence can be used. Level 1, for example, focuses on use cases that are new, undocumented, and without any process discipline. For this level, there can be few formal processes in place. Level 2 focuses on use cases that are repeatable or managed. A governance model must be in place and all users should be certified. Level 3 is for critical use cases that deliver much business value. On this level, automation and monitoring must be in place.

- Develop a champions network of recognized experts that continually build and share their knowledge with other people within the organization.

---

12 Microsoft describes the three primary strategies for how business intelligence content can be owned and managed in the Power BI documentation (*https://oreil.ly/GXt4r*).

- Require domains to provide a sample report of the data that they're providing. Not only does this mean the datasets and connections to use cases are made available within the BI layer so consumers can discover and request access to it, but by seeing a dashboard, users can quickly get an idea of what the data means, how it's joined, etc.

Business intelligence is a way to create a holistic view of all your relevant business data. At the same time, business intelligence is often about looking backward, attempting to figure out why something has happened. It may involve analytics, but for really predicting what will happen next and making automated decisions, we need to look at advanced analytics.

Advanced Analytics (MLOps)

Machine learning, artificial intelligence, and *cognitive computing* are trending buzzwords. They all overlap and complement each other. Artificial intelligence is the umbrella term for when machines work "intelligently" and perform tasks that are normally done by humans. Machine learning is a subfield of artificial intelligence, which is broadly defined as the capability of a machine to learn to mimic intelligent behavior. For example, a machine learning model can predict the probability of you clicking on a link or buying something based on past behavior. Cognitive computing is another subfield of artificial intelligence; it places more emphasis on how the human brain works and can be used, for example, to translate speech to text or recognize and classify items in images.

While these services are getting easier to use for training and developing accurate models, deploying them into production—especially at scale—is a major challenge.[13] The reasons for this include:

- Models strongly depend on data pipelines. Using offline data from the data preparation environment is easy, but in production everything must be automated: data quality must be guaranteed, models must be automatically retrained and deployed, and human approvals must be required to validate accuracy after using fresh data.

- Many models are built in an isolated data science sandbox environment, without scalability in mind. Different frameworks, languages, libraries pulled from the internet, and custom code are often all mixed and combined. With an organizational structure with different teams and no proper handover, it's difficult to integrate everything in production.

---

13 Google researchers D. Sculley et al. have written a paper (*https://oreil.ly/6MaH-*) that describes the hidden technical debt in machine learning systems. Typically, only a small fraction of a real-world ML system is composed of ML code. The required surrounding infrastructure is often vast and complex.

- Managing models in production is a different ball game because in production everything needs to be continuously monitored, evaluated, and audited. When making real-time decisions, you need to guarantee the scoring efficiency, accuracy, and precision. You don't want to end up in a situation where two days later you find out that all your customers got a free promotion.

To overcome the challenges of managing analytical services, new practices for collaboration and communication have emerged.

Machine learning is difficult to manage at scale. The ML life cycle consists of many complex tasks, including data collection, data preparation, model training, model deployment, model monitoring, and explainability. It also requires collaboration between various user groups: business users, data engineers, application developers, machine learning experts, and platform engineers. A framework for a way of working, often called *MLOps* (a compound of "machine learning" and "operations"), can help organizations to streamline the process of deploying machine learning models to production and then maintaining and monitoring them.

MLOps tackles the collaboration and communication between data scientists and operations professionals to help manage the production ML life cycle. It overlaps with DevOps, although deploying software in production is fundamentally different from deploying analytical models into production. This is because software, in general, is static, whereas ML data is constantly refreshed. This means analytical models must be constantly retrained, recalibrated, and redeployed using the latest data.

A good MLOps process can be perfectly aligned with a federated way of working and thus nicely positioned within a data mesh architecture. It enables you to operate at scale by using a standard process for managing the activities end-to-end. Such a framework is also helpful because each phase within the process may involve several complex stages. To help you manage ML end-to-end, I'm going to lay out an MLOps reference process, which I'll discuss more intensively over the following sections. Figure 11-5 shows the entire life cycle of a machine learning project. Each phase has different stages, and each stage has multiple steps.

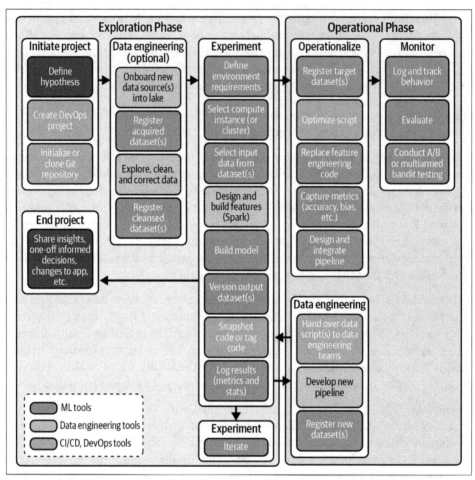

Figure 11-5. Recommended MLOps process for managing machine learning projects end-to-end

Starting at the left of Figure 11-5 with the exploration phase, we initiate a project and get clarity on the business requirements. Next, we iterate, testing different algorithms and parameters. This often requires data engineering activities for feature creation.[14] After we've demonstrated the project's value, we might enter a new phase: deploying the model into a production system. This phase is sometimes called *productionizing* or *operationalization*.[15] This is the most complex part of the process; it involves many activities and requires an automated machine learning pipeline for managing all the

---

14 *Feature creation* or *feature engineering* is a machine learning technique that leverages data to create new variables that aren't in the training set.

15 Some data scientists abbreviate operationalization as "o16n."

steps, from data collection to data validation, model training, model validation, and model deployment.

Depending on your specific use case, your machine learning project might look different. For example, you might train, evaluate, and deploy multiple models in the same pipeline, or your project might be a one-off analysis, where analytical insights are shared with the business but no models are deployed in production. Your starting point may vary too; for example, if data isn't already available, you first must go through the steps of data collection and onboarding.

To help you better understand what MLOps is about, I'm going to discuss each step in detail. While doing so, I'll share best practices and describe the deliverables from each stage. At the end, I'll discuss some variations and exceptions.

Initiating a Project

The first phase of the MLOps project (the "initiate process" step in Figure 11-5) is devoted to understanding your business requirements and data needs, and planning the implementation and development work to be carried out in subsequent stages. It sets the foundation for the later stages. You start by defining your business objectives and formulating your success criteria, which define under what conditions you will move on to the next phase. For collaboration between team members, I recommend using DevOps tooling. For example, you could use a kanban board (*https://oreil.ly/CNibQ*) to manage and track your activities throughout the life cycle of your project. One of these activities might be to identify your data sources and determine whether data products already have been developed.

A good practice when starting a machine learning project is to create a new code repository in which all (future) artifacts will be stored and managed. A general best practice is to segment use cases from one another, so each time you create a new ML project, you should create a new repository. To do this efficiently, consider standardizing on a code template—this will allow for code reuse, and decrease the ramp-up time at project start or when a new team member joins the project.

When you initiate a new project, you typically produce several artifacts:

- A project document or wiki covering the business requirements, success criteria, ethical dilemmas, etc.
- A list of data sources and additional requirements that must be applied
- A team board, which holds the initial activities
- A new code repository using templates to ramp up the project development

These artifacts help your project team to track progress. They also help to share insights for other future projects. Once the business objectives are clear, you enter the next phase: experimentation and tracking.

Experimentation and Tracking

After you've defined your goals and ambitions and set up your project, it's time for experimentation. During this process, I recommend tracking all of your experiment results. Thus, each time you train and run a model, you should capture all the parameters, metrics, algorithms, and other artifacts, as well as the output. This enables you to do the following:

- Gather and organize all the elements needed to conduct the experiment.
- Reproduce any results using saved experiment data.
- Log iterative improvements across time, data, frameworks, models, users, etc.
- Prove to regulators how your models were developed, what algorithms were chosen, and what datasets were used as input.

For experiment tracking, there are many tools to choose from. A popular framework is MLFlow (*https://mlflow.org*); it's free and open source and is used by many large vendors, including AWS, Databricks, Google, and Microsoft.

When performing experiments, the first step is to determine what compute infrastructure and environment you need.[16] A general best practice is to start fresh, using a clean development environment. Keep track of everything you do in each experiment, versioning and capturing all your inputs and outputs to ensure reproducibility. Pay close attention to all data engineering activities. Some of these may be generic steps and will also apply for other use cases. Finally, you'll need to determine the implementation integration pattern to use for your project in the production environment. This should be one of the following:

Model as an API
In this approach, the model is deployed as a web service so it can be used by other applications and processes. An API call has to be made in order to get predictions from the model.

Model as batches in/out
In this approach, the model works with batches of input and outputs minibatches or batches of predictions. Chunks or subsets of the data with labels

---

16 *Environments* are an encapsulation of the environment where your machine learning training happens. They typically specify the Python packages, environment variables, and software settings around your training and scoring scripts. They also specify runtimes for languages and tools like Python, Spark, and Docker.

are used for training, predicting, and making recommendations. The input and output typically consists of a set of files (e.g., CSVs or Parquet files).

Model as stream

In this approach, the model interacts reactively with a data stream, where the data segments arrive in increments. If extra data is needed, the model can be allowed to read the DDS's database directly. The model can generate and publish new events as well.

During the experimentation phase of your project, it's common to have manual processes. Your goal is to confirm your hypothesis by validating your assumptions. At the end of this stage, the project might end as a one-off exercise, where the learnings are shared. Alternatively, you might see sustainable business value. In this case, your next step will be to continuously deliver value. You'll do this by automating the entire process of data collection, data validation, model training, model validation, and deployment. You'll learn more about this after we've discussed the data engineering activities.

By the end of the experimentation stage, you'll have several new deliverables. These may include:

- A project document covering the outcome and criteria for model operationalization. This document also contains a model report: for each model that's tried, a standard, template-based report that provides details on the experiment is produced.

- New objects in the analytical workspace:[17] environments, models, datasets, and experiments, including all logging and metrics.

- A feature report: a document that contains pointers to the code used to generate new features. You may want to classify what code is generic and can be used for other use cases, what features are trained on potentially personal sensitive data, etc.[18]

- An updated code repository or code templates for new projects.

- A list of other improvements that can be made (e.g., adjustments to environments or new compute infrastructure options).

---

17 A *workspace* is the top-level resource in which your artifacts are managed.

18 *Features* are the columns of data in your input data. For example, if you're trying to predict someone's age, your input features might be things like height and hair color. The *label* is the final output: 12 years, 78 years, and so on.

Data Engineering

During experimentation and model development, you may have encountered data quality issues or missing data. It's important to report any such issues back to the source system or data owners, because you don't want to see these problems pop up in other places. Another recommendation is to develop data pipelines that automate the process of using data products to retrain models in production. For this, you may want to implement some controls for data drift detection (decreasing model performance) and schema changes. Once you're done, and your data pipeline is built, you should register your newly created dataset as an official artifact in your machine learning environment. This accelerates model development and takes away the pain of dealing with configuration, such as folder locations and user credentials.

Another part of the data engineering phase is developing a feature store. A *feature store* is a centralized repository where you standardize the definition, storage, and features for model training and deployment.[19] This has a few important benefits:

- It makes the process of creating features much more streamlined and efficient, because developers can discover and reuse features, instead of re-creating the same or similar ones.

- It reduces costs by lowering complexity and improving performance. For example, suppose you have a feature that is computationally expensive and is used in multiple machine learning projects. Rather than using a transform function and storing the transformed feature in multiple training datasets, it's much more efficient and maintainable to store it in a shared repository. The same applies when preprocessing or building features takes a long time, or when features are time-dependent or depend on other features.

New deliverables added to the list of artifacts after you've finished the data engineering phase may include:

- An updated solution design. This is a diagram or description of your architecture, including sources, data pipeline(s), integration patterns, and so on.

- New or updated data pipelines for data collection and cleansing.

- An updated code repository that contains all the production-ready artifacts.

- A record of data quality issues or gaps that are reported back to data owners.

---

19 As described in my blog post "Feature Stores and Data Mesh" (*https://oreil.ly/rNRxe*), I'm no big fan of centralized or shared stores: they add unnecessary complexity to your architecture.

Model Operationalization

For rapid and reliable deployments in production, you need to automate the entire end-to-end process using a machine learning pipeline. This part is often the hardest, as it involves many additional steps and adds constraints for integrating with your production application(s). Let's look at a few of those steps:

- Replace all hardcoded command-line statements, file locations, user credentials, and so on with parameters and arguments.

- Remove all generic data engineering steps, handing them off to the data engineering team to embed into the data product pipelines.

- Implement continuous and automatic testing, training, and deployment for both data and models.

- Create unit and integration tests for your inference endpoints for enhanced debugging and accelerated time to deployment.

- Add statements for collecting additional metrics: features, model accuracy, visuals, record counts, and so on.

- Implement A/B or shadow testing, and validate bias and accuracy before deploying into production.

- Share lessons learned and best practices with other teams or team members.

- Integrate the model with the rest of your applications. For example, you may need to create a composite service for combining and integrating data from different places.

- Consider using frameworks for interoperability and environment migration, for example, using standards such as ONNX (*https://oreil.ly/T40p4*). This allows developers to host the output in a number of environments, stacks, and programming languages. It even allows groups of developers to combine ML models using different ML frameworks.

- Add information about the model itself to a central model catalog. For example, you should note whether any discriminating features are used or if personally identifiable data was used for training.

Rather than having data scientists spend a lot of their time and effort setting up environments, I recommend defining standard environments, languages, and libraries that allow data scientists to work efficiently. Another recommendation is to design your runtime platforms to always be stateless. They preferably won't persist data over the long term, although they can create temporary data or hold reference data. Any data that they must use should come from input folders and be written back to output folders. This is important because it means you can easily replace models without moving or migrating any data.

At the end of this stage, your list of artifacts will be even longer. New deliverables may include:

- Updated workspace objects: models, pipelines, metrics, new datasets, and so on
- An updated code repository that contains all production artifacts
- A status dashboard that displays model and system health and key metrics
- A final modeling report with deployment details
- A final solution architecture document
- New or updated data pipelines for data collection and cleansing
- Adjustments to other applications for integrating with the machine learning application
- Updated code templates
- A final project document

Exceptions

As you can see, MLOps is a complex process. To further complicate matters, there are several factors that might cause variations to your generic architecture. For example:

- Pipelines can be engineered to require manual approval after retraining or to stop automatically when data quality reaches a specific threshold.
- Model retraining can be triggered in several ways: a new release process for an updated model, a business event, new data coming in, by hand, etc. The model deployment pipeline can also be tightly coupled with the data engineering pipeline, so the model is automatically retrained and deployed when new data comes in.
- The design and structure of the DDS can vary based on your requirements. You might want to use a polyglot database design to validate different data structures and read patterns.
- To monitor bias, fairness, and the quality of your models, you can capture the output and automatically check for anomalous results. Multiple models can run simultaneously in this situation.
- Explainability might require you to version and tag all training data and models automatically.
- The output of models can be served back in many different ways, including via batches that include multiple scoring results in one set, via events that are generated by analyzing other events, or via API endpoints (i.e., request/response web services).

- Unstructured data can make the architecture look different. You might want to use external or cognitive services, or share data with external parties.

- Models may be deployed and running in different environments. To have an end-to-end oversight, you may need to add an extra central metadata repository to log, store, display, organize, compare, and query all metadata generated during the machine learning processes.

- Not all cognitive services can be trained or easily customized. For example, OpenAI's ChatGPT comes as is; there's no way to change how the service behaves. This means that it might be difficult to detect bias or monitor the service over time. Consider putting principles in place about what types of cognitive services are allowed or require approval.

- You might need to implement complex composite services or read stores for first collecting and aggregating data, before making any API calls to the model itself.

As you can imagine, these factors largely depend on the business requirements of the models and how they are consumed by or integrated into other downstream processes. There will always be exceptions and differences in the details of how analytical models are implemented, but the generic architecture, with all of its best practices, will help you to be much more scalable.

Wrapping Up

Turning data into value is difficult. However, you've seen that by taking data management and automation seriously, you can democratize data usage at large. In this chapter, we focused on the data-consuming side of the architecture. We looked at different patterns of consumption (direct, or through domain data stores), and we walked through best practices for building DDSs. We learned to smash silos and keep dependencies between DDSs to a minimum by analyzing both functional and nonfunctional requirements. We also touched upon self-service and managed data activities and the principles that support them. Finally, we examined business intelligence and machine learning, the common denominators in most data-driven decision solutions. As you saw, with good processes in place, you can manage these activities end-to-end.

You also learned that to achieve a faster time to value, it's important to remove manual effort for tasks like versioning, analytics monitoring, and deploying. This requires a different culture that goes way beyond the traditional data modeling. Your data architects will need to become well-trained and experienced software engineers. It also requires that automation is embraced broadly. The following best practices will help:

- Guide your teams in how to manage overlapping concerns. Pay attention to setting boundaries: if they're too fine-grained, this can lead to overlap and repeated activities; if they're too coarse-grained, you can end up with too many coupling points.

- Align analytical consumption patterns with your landing zones. Develop blueprints for implementing standard and reusable functionality. Align these blueprints with your playbooks and best practices. Make concise choices about aligning your data-providing capabilities with your data-consuming capabilities.

- Set up a data modeling community within your organization for guiding your teams and ensuring data is transformed in line with your company standards.

- Pay attention to the providing side and the consuming side. On the consumer side, you generally see heavy diversification in the way data is used. This contrasts with the providing side, which can be more easily standardized. When combining these two concerns in situations where data consumers are also data providers, you risk tight coupling when analytical solutions are classified as data products. Therefore, I advocate to strictly separate data usage from data distribution by using two type of blueprints: one for data product creation and another for turning data into value.

- Plan the alignment of your configurations, workspaces, and domains. A workspace is the top-level resource in which analytical services, such as machine learning, are managed. From a manageability standpoint, it's important to map out how these workspaces are aligned with your activities. For example, you may have a workspace per team, with each team getting its own workspace instance. The benefit of such an alignment is that everything is managed within one place. Team members can easily access, explore, and reuse results. Alternatively, you might have one workspace per project. The benefit of this approach is that you manage costs at the project level and segregate conflicting (security) concerns. However, the discovery and reuse of assets might be more difficult because assets are spread across multiple workspace instances. Another consideration is that the management overhead becomes larger when more workspaces are used.

- Work closely with your infrastructure and networking team on how linked services and networks are integrated. For example, certain endpoints or linked services may require the network or DNS records to be changed by the central infrastructure team. A recommendation for this is to apply automation rather than using a ticket system: listen for cloud-based events, trigger workflows, invoke functions, and apply policies.

- Use code repositories to decouple generic blueprint templates from actual implementations. For example, each team might have its own repository in which they manage parameters for different environments, customizations, and so on. At a higher level, implement a policy-driven governance framework to prevent noncompliance by either restricting resources from being created or modifying settings to make resources compliant.

Following these recommendations will make your architecture more cost-efficient and interoperable. It will also help you manage your data in a more consistent way. We're almost at the end of our trip, but now we're going to get back in our helicopter one last time and pick up some speed. In this final part of the journey, we'll combine everything we've learned so far by putting theory into practice. May the skies treat you well!

CHAPTER 12

Putting Theory into Practice

Here we are at the final chapter. But don't be sad—we're going to make things real! In this chapter, we're going to walk through a pragmatic example of implementing a modern data architecture, step by step. Along the way, I'll summarize the various topics discussed throughout the book and explain how to convert theory into a practical approach, outlining the overall plan, stages, and sequence in which to implement the various capabilities you'll need to get up and running.

We'll begin with a short reflection on your data journey, and whether you should start with a centralized or decentralized approach. Then we'll go through the phases of implementing a data architecture, from setting the strategic direction, to laying the foundation, to professionalizing your capabilities. We'll discuss the importance of a data-driven culture to ensuring the success of your project, including governance and a DataOps way of working, then look at the role enterprise architects must play. Finally, I'll close out the chapter with some last words.

A Brief Reflection on Your Data Journey

The goal of this book is to support you on your data journey. But before you jump on the bandwagon, ensure you have a data strategy in place. Whether you're starting small or have a large set of use cases to implement, without a plan, as you learned in Chapter 1, you're doomed to fail. I see countless enterprises fail because they're unable to bring everybody onboard or to articulate their strategy; because they don't include business users or lack support from senior leadership. I can't emphasize this enough, but before you start implementing any change, ensure you have a balcony view and a clear map guiding you in the right direction.

After establishing a vision that clearly articulates your ambition and the path ahead of you, it's time to enter the next phase. Your next steps are about communicating your vision, building the right team, optimizing your architecture, making execution plans, defining processes, and selecting use cases. Again, it's important to get everybody aligned and committed to your objectives. During the initial stages of development, start small with the implementation, but at the same time keep the big picture in mind because your target state architecture must be inclusive for all use cases. You'll need data governance capabilities for implementing roles, processes, policies, procedures, and standards to govern your most critical data. You'll need master data and data quality management capabilities for ensuring consistency and trust. You need metadata for tracking lineage, capturing business context, and linking to physical data. You need integration and analytical services for building data products and turning data into value. The recommended approach for achieving all these objectives is to look holistically at the building blocks you need. These building blocks will remain stable throughout your journey, while the underlying technologies will change over the years to come.

After you've identified your critical ingredients, you must secure top-down commitment. In addition, communicate and engage with your business stakeholders: create awareness and excitement. Make sure your intended approach, business objectives, and goals are clear and well understood throughout the organization. Begin to identify strategic initiatives and business use cases. A good approach is to get started by compiling a short list of use cases with the greatest potential for impact. Ensure each use case is aligned with your data strategy, as well as your business strategy. For each use case, the value to your organization should be clear. Next, do a technical complexity assessment so you can prioritize your data projects. Benchmark the feasibility for each use case in terms of complexity, financial costs, commercial added value, risks, and operational manageability. After that, select the best candidates to start with. Begin with the low-hanging fruit: your first use case shouldn't be too difficult to implement, but at the same time should deliver enough value to justify the work. It should set an example for the rest of the organization. The rest of the use cases will come later.

Centralized or Decentralized?

After you've prepared for the potential challenges and identified your first workloads, it's time to get started with the actual implementation. At this point, you also need to make a decision about whether a more centralized or decentralized approach is suitable.

If your company has a lower level of data management maturity, a centralized approach in the beginning is more appropriate. Why? A complex transformation requires a cultural shift, upskilling, building mature self-service capabilities, breaking down silos and political boundaries, and sharing knowledge. The complexity of these activities shouldn't be underestimated. So, if your organization doesn't have the maturity or scale yet to tackle them, consider centralization over decentralization. As you progress in your journey, onboard more use cases, and enhance your data management and self-service capabilities, allow federation to happen next to centralization.

If your company already has a high level of data management maturity or is decentrally organized, then you can begin with a more decentralized approach to data management. However, to align your decentralized teams, you will need to set standards and principles and make technology choices for shared capabilities. These activities need to happen at a central level and require superb leaders and good architects. I'll come back to these points toward the end of this chapter, when discussing the role of enterprise architects.

Besides the starting point, there are other aspects to take into consideration with regard to centralization and decentralization. First, you should determine your goals for the end of your journey. If your intended end state is a decentralized architecture, but you've decided to start centrally, the engineers building the architecture should be aware of this from the beginning. With the longer-term vision in mind, engineers can make capabilities more loosely coupled, allowing for easier decentralization at a later point in time. Second, you should determine which capabilities you intend to remain under central control and which ones you plan to decentralize later. Making this clear up front will save a lot of arguments and political infighting on the way forward.

Making It Real

After you've articulated your data strategy and ambitions at an organizational level, your next activities are aimed at making things real! My recommendation here, based on my experiences and success stories from customers, is to use a phased approach and start small: build a hypothesis for value-add, begin with only one or a limited number of use cases, get some experience with what building data products is like, put principles in place and address operational inefficiencies, and determine what "just enough" governance means for your organization.

Note that the discussion here follows the "happy path." So, it doesn't represent a nasty multiheaded complex beast with many tails. Nor does it go too deep into highly context-specific subjects. My aim is to describe the main stages of a general data journey to give you an idea of what to expect.

Opportunistic Phase: Set Strategic Direction

For onboarding your first domains, it's not essential to map out all your business capabilities, delineate your data domains, and align them with the organizational structure. Instead, your goals during this phase are centered around learning how concepts work and can be translated into practice. For this purpose, I recommend selecting a fairly simple use case with one or two source systems as a starting point. You'll use these sources as input for data product development, then serve these data products directly to consumers for turning data into value. You don't need to focus on data value creation capabilities yet, though; those will come later. For now, you should concentrate on the source system side of your new architecture.

This first phase is about figuring out what mindset your teams need to have for taking data ownership and building the first series of data products. During this stage, the central team watches over other teams, coaching and delivering expertise while the domain teams write data pipelines, debug problems, and fix data quality issues at the source. All teams need to work closely together during this phase to get an understanding of the shared needs because many collective decisions must be made about storage services, ETL tools, security, the data catalog, and so on.

Your first steps in this phase will be as follows:

- Select the first use case and identify a business team that is a good candidate to be the starting team for building the first data products. Preferably, this business team would have all the engineering skills necessary to develop the first deliverables. If not, the data platform team can assist the business team.
- Define a project that has a clear but limited scope, and preferably can be finished in a few months. Set up a small program board with senior representatives for the needed top-down support and coordination.
- Identify (potential) members for your data platform team, who are dedicated to the overall process. This team will be available to assist the domain team, which will be responsible for building the first data pipelines for producing data products.

From a data architecture point of view, I encourage you to start with only one landing zone and one data management landing zone. As mentioned in "Landing Zone Topologies: Managing Solution Spaces" on page 78, all the major cloud providers supply blueprints for these. Best practices and recommendations are discussed in Chapter 3. Next, provision only the services that are needed for capturing and storing, transforming, and cataloging data. Put aside what you don't need, and focus on what's essential.

For your solution design, consider adopting a lakehouse architecture. While this design initially might look like centralization, it brings many benefits: it's a proven, common, and well-understood pattern, it's easy to set up, and it simplifies management of the infrastructure. Figure 12-1 shows an example of how the architecture might look in the beginning. It's a small architecture, designed for a single domain.

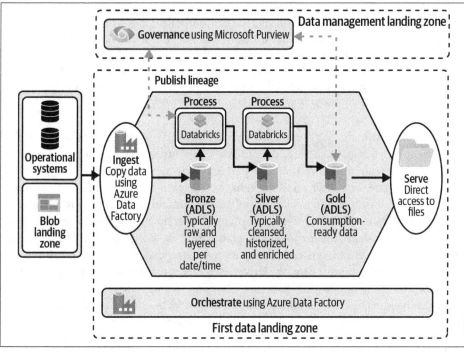

Figure 12-1. Initial lakehouse architecture

When you're just starting your journey, the architecture only uses a few essential services. During the initial phase, data engineers from the domain engage with members of the data platform team. Together, they determine the scope and analyze what services are needed for building the first data products.

The intent of this design is to create a foundation for building data products at scale, supporting the objectives of data ownership and self-service with computational data governance. The first domain team, the product owner, and the data engineers, work closely together to make the data available. They start by extracting data from the source systems and ingesting it into the Bronze layer. For this, the team uses integration services offered by the central platform team. Next, they select the relevant data and transform it into several user-friendly datasets, for example using notebooks or data transformation services. During these activities, the data may pass through additional layers: Silver for intermediate data; Gold for functionally cohesive and consumable data. After all the transformations are performed, the data catalog scans all the data. Optionally, it may also scan the integration services for lineage. The configuration for scanning happens on a central level, so it's handled by the central platform team or data governance team. The final step is to make the data available. After that, other teams can use this data as input for their analytical use cases.

Although the three-layer design in Figure 12-1 is common and well known, there is still much discussion about the scope, purpose, and best practices for each of these layers. I've also observed that there's a huge difference between theory and practice. If you want to learn more about how the layering of your data architecture can be best implemented, I encourage you to read my blog post on the medallion architecture (*https://oreil.ly/-rx5m*).

Do not underestimate the complexity of organizing your catalog. When you start implementing your data catalog, do not scan all your sources or domains at once. Instead, only scan domains that are part of your new ecosystem. Onboard one domain at a time, one after another. What you'll learn in practice is that the alignment between business domains and application domains depends on whether business capabilities are shared or used exclusively. To set up a good structure, first divide and group your data sources and data platform(s) in a logical way. The key point here is that every asset from each data source or application can only be stored in a single location within your catalog. This means that, on a technical level, you need to relate data assets to application domains. Then, on this application domain level, you align the responsibilities, assigning administrator, data source admin, and curator roles to the respective people who manage databases, applications, data products, data pipelines, and other services. Next, you'll need to perform the same grouping and ordering activities for information that describes the meaning of data, applications, and domains in a business sense. Identify your business domains by studying business capabilities and finding people who work together on common business goals. Assign glossary owner and data steward roles for managing metadata such as descriptions and glossary terms. Finally, align your application and business domains, asking the domain users to create relationships between metadata that is managed on an application domain level and metadata that is managed on a business domain level.

Here's where things should stand after you've implemented the initial architecture and shared your first data products as input for your analytical use case(s):

- There is a central operating model. Your platform and governance teams are in the lead for setting standards and making technology choices.

- Configuration of data pipelines is done by the central team. In parallel, this team coaches and trains other teams.

- Data products may be perceived as too raw or technical when guidance on data modeling is missing. Allow this to happen, but require iteration and improvements before new consumers are onboarded.

- Data pipelines are typically manually triggered or run at fixed intervals.

- Source system–aligned domain teams must register their data products in a central catalog. They are responsible for maintaining the metadata, such as definitions, and making sure it's accurate and up-to-date. For these activities, they require help from the central team.

- Your teams use a single landing zone and single set of resources.

- Data lineage is either obsolete or lives in islands.

- Your data catalog isn't yet open for domains to publish and maintain metadata on a self-service basis. The information that has been published is limited. However, this doesn't mean that your teams aren't held accountable for quality, even if it's somewhat manual, or via a middleman/central data steward.

- Services for interactively querying the data are nascent or still absent. Instead, consuming domains duplicate data into their own environments. Because of this, permissions for data consumers and users are usually manually assigned. Data access during the initial stage of building the architecture is typically coarse-grained, on a service, container, or folder level.

- The quality of the templates and the amount of hardening that is required and performed to protect and secure the architecture may vary across different teams, contractors, etc.

During this initial phase, your capabilities won't have a high degree of maturity. It's also likely that you'll have many manual processes, which you'll need to automate or make self-service as you progress to the next stages. Metadata also becomes more important during the next stages, because what worked in Excel will no longer work on a larger scale.

Building a large data platform puts a lot of pressure on your central IT or cloud department, so you'll need to build up your platform and data management capabilities and get buy-in from these parts of the organization before moving on to the next stage. Consider consulting Chapter 7 for best practices.

After you've implemented your first use case, working from the bottom up, it's time to conquer the hearts and minds of your first (business) stakeholders by showing your results to the rest of the organization. Don't be shy about showcasing your success and demonstrating the added value and the benefits of using data. These activities shouldn't be underestimated. They are essential for securing a top-down commitment from the higher-level executives. As you progress further, your program should become a role model that empowers you to decommission and clean up legacy data management platforms or systems, and stop similar kinds of projects that don't align with the new data management strategy. With all this accomplished, you're ready to collect new use case requirements for the second phase.

Transformation Phase: Lay Out the Foundation

After you deliver your first use case(s) into production, it's all about scaling up, adding more data domains and refining your architecture. At this stage, it's important to have the full picture of your landscape sharp. Thus, by now your business capabilities should be clear, including the alignment with people, processes, and technology. You should know which domains own which applications, and what they are responsible for. You should also know what new use cases can be served by what potential new data products (for more on this topic, or a refresher on how to identify your business domains, consider consulting Chapter 2). Additionally, during this phase, you will work on budgeting plans, road maps, added value for the business, and operating models. These activities are important as you gradually scale up.

 Processes matter, but these shouldn't lead to bureaucracy. Instead, focus on your use cases and the corresponding delivered results. Delivering value at scale requires a continuous loop of attention, reflection, and adaption.

With the high-level target state in mind, your next steps are about defining what domain and landing zone topologies are best suited to your organization. For any topology that we discussed in Chapter 3, I recommend you harmonize blueprints that include services for processing, storing, and cataloging data; publishing metadata; enforcing policies; and so on. Next, you should study data traffic flows between domains. Based on your analysis, you'll need to make several design decisions. For example, if many domains require data from many other domains, then a highly decentralized or fine-grained domain topology is not recommended, as it leads to complexity and management overhead. In that situation, a governed topology that uses a centralized location for managing shared data products is usually a better option. If the amount of data flowing between domains varies significantly, you could also implement a hybrid approach of centrally managed and peer-to-peer distributed data. In that case, you should make choices about how you will manage data products within databases and storage account services between and within domains. Consider consulting "Organizing data products" on page 83 for some best practices.

After your first domains have been onboarded, it's time to consider the lessons learned from the initial phase. You will probably find that your domain teams want to be more proficient and self-supporting. Your first data products weren't that complicated: you took incoming raw data, fed it through a few data pipelines, and turned it into more accessible data for consumers. The difficulty arises when you must do this repeatedly and in a governed and controlled manner. For this, you need to add automation and more advanced capabilities to your data product development process. For example, you might want to add a data quality framework for validating schemas and data quality, or set a standard for ETL services that your domains must adhere to when building new data products. Instead of writing more notebooks or using one-off, nonreusable solutions, you'll need to provide blueprints and patterns for implementing this standard functionality.

Figure 12-2 illustrates how the architecture might look during this next stage. In this updated architecture, you can see that real-time data ingestion capabilities, a metadata-driven framework, a logging database, and virtualized access have been added.

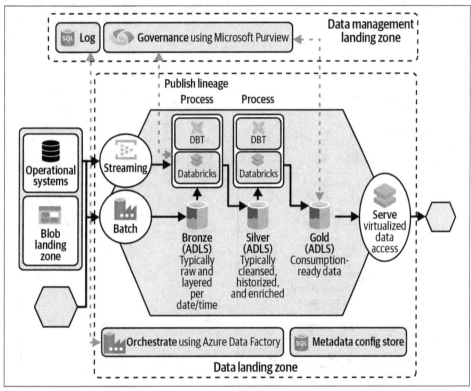

Figure 12-2. Updated lakehouse architecture

Next, you'll need to make similar improvements to your data pipelines. The most efficient way to scale and have flexibility is to use parameterized, metadata-driven pipelines. So, instead of reengineering and manually creating new pipelines (with their own data sources, selections, transformations, and output) using hardcoded values, you can create a common and configurable pipeline that will retrieve the configuration at runtime from, for example, a database or code repository. Your parameterized workflows will thus use metadata inputs and conditions provided by your domain teams. The role of the central platform team is to provide all these capabilities using an as-a-service model by making everything part of your infrastructure blueprints.

You might also observe that your domain teams are looking for more proactive cooperation between teams. They don't want to rely on the central platform team(s) as a middleman passing messages back and forth between providers and consumers, for example, when a new consumer wants to consume a provider's data, or when a provider has data quality issues or will be delivering its data late. Instead, the platform team should implement central monitoring services and a control framework that enables action-oriented interaction between providers and consumers. For instance, you may want to add a central logging store, or a good monitoring service that detects issues and proactively notifies users using alert rules, notifications, or events. An example of a multidomain architecture can be seen in Figure 12-3.

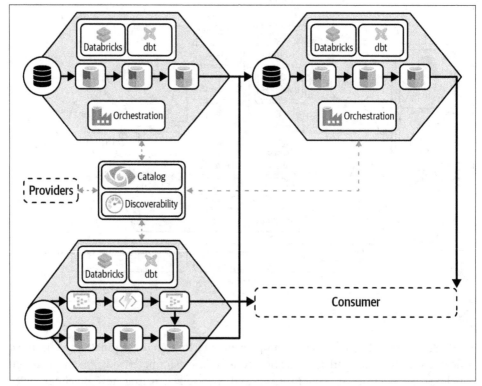

Figure 12-3. To support the addition of new domains, complement your architecture with standardized services for data observability, data quality, data transformation, and automation

The recommended approach when adding domains is to focus on the source system side of your architecture for a while, before scaling up the consuming side. Why? Typically, there are many more data consumers than data providers. In addition, consumer-oriented analytical services are complex and draw a lot of attention. It is therefore essential to guarantee stable and scalable delivery of new data products before you add large numbers of consumers. If you shift your focus to the consuming side too quickly, you risk seeing all your teams trying to fix the same data engineering problems again and again. This can cause your entire organization to lose trust in the architecture, undermining your data ambitions. So, for every step you make, make sure you're adding business value, while at the same time not losing trust from the business in the effectiveness of the data platform.

 In my previous role, we introduced three unique and complementary strategic themes to direct execution:

- Golden source management, which focuses on ensuring ownership, addressing data quality issues, and closing data gaps
- Data marketplace management, which focuses on facilitating data product creation, data sharing, and data monetization
- Turning data into value management, which focuses on empowering everyone to make autonomous and intelligent data-driven decisions

By gradually maturing all three themes at the same time, we reduced the number of bottlenecks between teams, which contributed to a high degree of business satisfaction.

After you've made data product development more efficient, implement the first set of computational data governance controls. For example, don't allow data to be shared without first linking it to a data owner. For this, you'll need to use workflows that are provided by your data governance solution. The goal of this exercise is to put guardrails in place, allowing your domain teams to be more self-supporting without unknowingly causing themselves harm. The role of the central team during this phase changes. They oversee what help is needed and may step in when required. Thus, instead of executing all data governance–related activities themselves, the central team trains, coaches, and guides other teams. In addition, this is the point where the central team needs to start thinking, "Control is good; trust is better." Platform policies and audit reports act as automated declarative guardrails.

A consideration when scaling up further is whether to enable different data ingestion patterns and options based on the needs of your teams. For example, rather than batch loading data on a daily basis, you might offer event-driven or CDC services to ingest data faster, or you might allow landing areas to be used in which intermediate data can be staged before it lands in a data product architecture. This might be required for external data sources or legacy systems as well.

Here's where things should stand at the end of this stage:

- The new governance and operating models, as discussed in Chapter 8, are defined. These include new roles and responsibilities.

- Dashboards have been created to show how well your domains and their corresponding metadata are represented.

- Domain teams own the data life cycle, from start to end (from the applications that create the original data to the data products that are consumed by other teams). They own all the data models, and determine what data is suitable for sharing with others.

- Domain teams use DataOps best practices for managing their data products. This could, for example, mean that each team uses its own individual Git repository, from which they provision their CI/CD and data pipelines through code. (There is more guidance on this in "Data-Driven Culture" on page 365.)

- Data product development is supported with tooling and data modeling best practices. Guidance (such as standards for identifiers, reference data, layering and structuring data in separate tables for providing coarse-grained security) is published in wikis for better collaboration.

- Development teams have visibility into pipelines and how they impact downstream consumers. Developers are supported by data quality services, which proactively alert users when problems occur.

- Manual processes and pipelines are replaced with templates and services. Instead of hardcoding locations and parameters, developers store their information as source code in version control. These repositories may include other artifacts as well, such as test and deployment scripts, libraries/packages, configuration information, and so on.

- Additional ingestion patterns have been added, such as real-time or event-driven ingestion.

- Data access policies, which specify who can access what data products, are stored as code or configurations. At this stage, still expect your central team to be in full control of provisioning data access.

- You still use one single landing zone. There's limited variation in the services you offer. All domain teams use the same blueprint configuration(s).

- There's a consistent metamodel that uses a data product and data domain. This metamodel is managed in a data governance service and ensures that all domain teams know what data products are owned by what domains.

While onboarding new use cases and domains into your architecture, it's likely that you will run into migration or legacy scenarios. For example, you may encounter situations in which consumers demand historical data from several years back. When building up your new data product architecture, you'll learn that historical data is only available from the moment you onboarded your first data products into the new architecture. So, if you need historical data from before the onboarding period, you'll have a gap. To solve this problem, make an extract or one-off copy of the historical data from your other environment(s). For example, if your data warehouse retains data from the past seven years, you can use that data to build a legacy data product, then combine that legacy data product with incoming data that feeds into the new architecture. This will give your domains the full picture. Note that combining historical data with new data isn't always that easy, however; you'll often need to match fields, delete duplicates, clean the data, or write business logic.

When scaling up further, you'll need to interconnect domains by enabling them to exchange or directly share data products. For this, you need to set interoperability standards and implement query services. Consider popular file formats such as Parquet or Delta, and (serverless) SQL services to allow other domains to access and browse the data products.

Optimization Phase: Professionalize Your Capabilities

After the foundation has been established, it's time to iterate on prioritized business use cases and further professionalize your capabilities. One of the key objectives for this stage is to carry over all the supporting activities from the central team to your domain teams. Look for inefficiencies, and try to solve these with self-service and automation. To strengthen your organization, guide your teams so they become more efficient in managing their data and corresponding data pipelines. Allow them to self-onboard and self-subscribe to data products. Deploy services that allow for self-registration and maintenance of metadata. For example, deploy APIs that can be easily integrated with the CI/CD processes of your domains.

For the next iteration of your architecture, you will focus on real-time data processing, consumption-readiness, security, MDM, and distribution of curated data. Try to standardize the consuming side of your architecture with blueprints and services. Remember that data usage is diverse: many variations are possible. To remain in control, gradually expand by launching one new service at a time. For each new service, evaluate the need before handing it out to your domains. Figure 12-4 shows an example of an updated design.

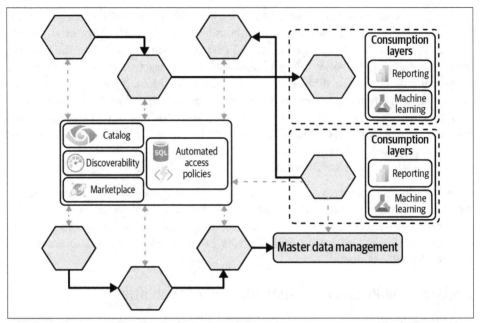

Figure 12-4. As the adoption of your architecture grows, new services will be added

One key thing about the solution architecture is that many of the services don't yet support a federated way of working. Your central team must focus on closing these gaps by integrating services and delivering self-service and automation capabilities. They are the ones to arbitrate between deviation, tools, and technical requirements. They own all choices related to programming frameworks, ETL services, and storage-related services.

For managing data reusability concerns and consistency, look for data products that have the highest levels of usage. What you've most likely encountered is multiple domains complaining about data that is too hard to integrate and combine with data from other domains. So, look for repetitive harmonization and quality improvement activities that are being performed across teams. If you see many of these overlapping activities, the data products in question might be candidates for master data management. Alternatively, you can separate out generic (repeatable) integration logic and ask one data product team to take ownership of the data using a customer/supplier model. Consult Chapter 10 for recommended approaches.

As part of the data sharing experience, your data product teams should be able to describe which data products can be used for which purposes. Domains should be able to manage, in close collaboration with the central governance team, data access controls on data they own. Unfortunately, at the time of writing, I'm not aware of any out-of-the-box solutions that will give your teams a great experience. If you want to support your teams with easy-to-follow workflow processes and automated creation of policies, consider building a small data contract framework yourself that deploys consumer-oriented (secure) views using a workflow process. This framework may include pointers to business semantics, as well data quality and service level agreements. For more guidance, see Chapter 8.

At the end of this stage, here's where things should stand:

- Your architecture supports different patterns for data distribution and application integration. Preferably, guidance for data products, APIs, and events would be aligned.

- New data domains can be onboarded quickly via automation and provisioning through Infrastructure as Code.

- Standards on classifications and labels have been formalized, guidance and playbooks have been created, and teams are trained.

- Techniques such as natural language processing and machine learning are applied to support domains with metadata management.

- Governance and access control policies are automated. For this, consider setting up a small workflow, an application, and programmatic access APIs for registration.

- Data usage and processes for turning data into value are standardized. Updated blueprint templates are offered to your domain teams, from which they can choose what to use for individual use cases.

- Master data management services have been added to your architecture for ensuring end-to-end and cross-domain consistency.

- Interaction between stakeholders is optimized through data governance bodies. Teams come together on a periodic basis for triage and overall planning.

- Data products have multiple endpoints, also known as *output ports*, to cater for a large variety of use cases.

- Extra landing zones have been added for situations in which domain teams have contrasting requirements.

When scaling up further, it is important to have your structures for data governance clear. So, you need to move away from poorly defined data roles to a clear structure with well-aligned processes. Depending on your organization's size, you may have multiple governing bodies and data product teams that interact. Figure 12-5 shows an example of how this interaction could work.

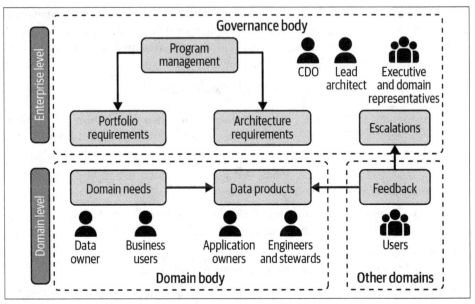

Figure 12-5. An example of how different data governance bodies and domain teams can work together

At the top, your governance bodies manage strategic oversight, working together to further the enterprise's vision and goals. Thus, decisions on high-level designs, road maps, and large programs have a huge dependency on the new architecture. In these bodies you usually expect representation from the chief data officer, lead architects, senior domain owners, and other executive management members.

At the bottom, your domain teams are grouped together in domain bodies for managing use cases and dependencies, onboarding new data, and reworking issues. While doing this, they might receive feedback and requirements from other teams. Thus, between all bodies there is interaction. For example, one domain team might require mediation from another domain team or a strategic decision from the program management team.

After you've worked out your governance structures and set up your meeting cadence for synchronizing and coordinating the planning and feedback loops, it's time for the icing on the cake: intelligent data fabric and data marketplace capabilities. Here, as you learned in Chapter 9, there are also spaces to fill in, so you'll either need to wait, conform, or address gaps yourself with homegrown application components.

Data-Driven Culture

While iterating and iterating, you'll start to see that you also need a data-driven culture. It's critically important that you make business users part of all discussions. They should see the value, drive the need for data product creation, take ownership, and adhere to core standards. This shift requires a lot of campaigning, and putting your foot down when things go in the wrong direction. If data owners don't describe or correctly classify their data, don't allow it to be shared. If data quality drops below a certain threshold, block its distribution. Control and guide the organization while remaining open to feedback and making improvements.

The same cultural shift is needed for your engineering community. The data-as-a-product mindset requires data management and software development to be brought closer together. This necessitates DevOps practices and methodologies, such as versioning, IaC, automation, and quality testing. Let's zoom into this in a little more detail.

DataOps

For your data product teams to be successful, they need to get familiar with the iterative process of developing, building, testing, deploying, operating, and monitoring. This is where "DevOps for Data" (DataOps) comes in. A well-organized data team requires engineers and developers to embrace at least the following responsibilities:

- Organize work using Agile sprints and a backlog in which feedback can be incorporated by other teams.
- Manage artifacts, such as data pipelines, code, configuration, schema metadata, and documentation, in a code repository.
- Automatically test and build all components using isolated environments before they are deployed into production.
- Monitor data pipelines for quality and breaking changes.
- Provide continuous feedback between teams to drive improvements.
- Reduce inefficiencies by adding automation.
- Use templates and code snippets for improving time to market.

The benefit of the DataOps way of working is that it encourages greater team autonomy, while promoting flexibility. Multiple teams can work in parallel without affecting each other, as long as they each focus on their own project.

Efficient and isolated workflows are an essential component of a successful DataOps practice. For these workflows, the responsibilities of a data team typically boil down to maintaining two different orchestrators. The first orchestrator is a data pipeline, which focuses on the coordination of data-related process steps. In the context of building data products or use cases, it converts the raw input data into meaningful information, thus delivering value to the business. The processes related to managing data pipelines are generally owned by the data engineers of the respective domain teams. Depending on the design, a data pipeline can be a long sequence with many steps. Figure 12-6 shows an example of what this might look like in practice.

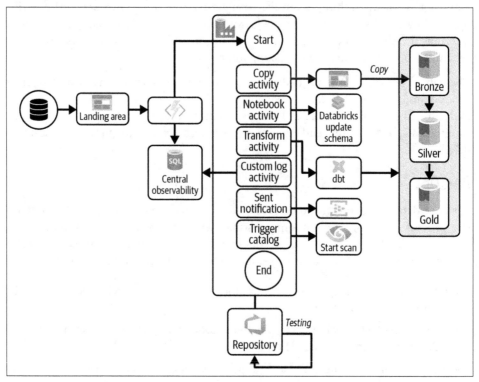

Figure 12-6. DataOps in practice: an example of how a data pipeline stitches several activities together

Here's a breakdown of the steps in this data pipeline from end to end:

1. Collect data. This step is usually automatically triggered whenever new data is ingested into the data landing area. For example, in Figure 12-6, a function invokes the data pipeline to run. This same function also submits a record to the central observability store.

2. Validate the source location.

3. Copy the source data from the intermediate landing area to the Bronze layer.

4. Trigger a notebook to update schemas and external tables using the latest location where data is stored.

5. Trigger a batch job that invokes the execution of all data quality and data transformation activities.

6. Update the record in the central observability store to indicate that processing is complete (or has failed).

7. Inform data consumers that processing is complete or has failed.

8. If processing was successful, trigger the central data catalog.

There are many factors to consider and questions to answer when designing data pipelines. For example, will data be pushed into a landing area, or is it pulled by accessing a database? Is a third-party service needed for capturing data changes? Are there specific security needs that require structuring the data differently for different consumers? Depending on the specific requirements, your pipelines will look different from other pipelines and the example shown here. When building data pipelines, you'll also find that some steps are specific while others are generic and easier to standardize with common components. For example, monitoring the progress and logging the status is a generic step, visible in Figure 12-6. A best practice is to standardize all these generic steps between teams (e.g., with common components or functions).

At the bottom of Figure 12-6, you see a code repository in which all artifacts are managed. The repository maintains the configuration and code for executing the entire sequence, end to end. It also plays a vital role for the second orchestrator: the CI/CD pipeline, responsible for coordinating the steps that are needed to deliver a new version of software (and infrastructure). In the context of managing a data platform, this orchestrator moves the platform configuration, schema information, and data pipeline code from one environment to another. For CI/CD pipelines you typically see more standardization between teams, in terms of how they work and how artifacts are deployed into production.

A common best practice for managing data engineering workloads is to give each team its own code repository and configure it using three different branches: development, testing, and production. Teams can then follow the classic Git workflow cycle for development:

1. Developers and engineers develop individual features in a feature branch and validate using unit tests (e.g., implemented notebooks or templates).

2. When the developers are satisfied with their results, they create a pull request from the feature branch to the main developer or collaboration branch. After this, the proposed changes can be reviewed by peers.

3. After a pull request is approved, changes are merged in the main development branch. Usually the CI/CD pipeline will run another series of integration and unit tests to validate that everything still works as expected.

4. When the team has validated the results, it can promote everything to test, where the new features can be tested by customers and/or end users.

5. If no additional changes are needed and all tests are green, an approval for production can be given. After that, the CI/CD process automatically releases all updated data pipelines and configuration to production.

Figure 12-7 shows how you could implement this approach.

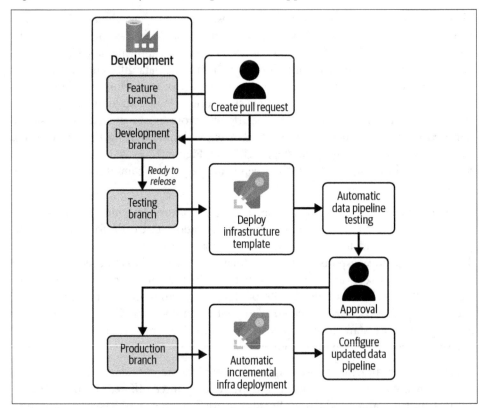

Figure 12-7. DataOps in practice: an example of how a CI/CD process promotes everything from development to testing and production

The CI/CD approach can be particularly useful when striving for complete isolation between development, testing, and production activities. A general best practice is to set up multiple workspaces and align them to the different code branches. In this setup, the infrastructure template(s) for provisioning these workspaces will be maintained within the team's code repository. Another part of this best practice is to set up policies for ensuring that the environments that are deployed by the domain teams will comply with the organization's standards. This approach minimizes potential interference and is typically favored in higher-security environments. At the same time, the innovation work and ad hoc activities are decoupled, as the dev environments typically have more relaxed policy controls.

Depending on how you set up your CI/CD process, environments can also be provisioned on the fly. For example, instead of keeping your testing environment always on, you can choose to provision new testing environments on demand. When all tests are completed and everything works as expected, you can run a cleanup activity to decommission all the infrastructure.

This shift to DataOps is mostly a cultural one. For this transition, you need a central team that takes the lead for setting standards and developing configuration templates and blueprints. This same team is also responsible for setting up coaching, creating training materials, organizing walk-in sessions, and so on. Don't underestimate the weight of these activities; they can require additional staffing.

Governance and Literacy

A data-driven culture means you must work on governance. For this, clearly define your roles and activities. Use a RACI model, as discussed in Chapter 8, for making clear where the responsibilities and accountabilities lie. Next, clearly describe practical instructions for how to manage data. Capture everything in a data governance framework. Pay attention to data literacy, too, because not all leaders within your organization will see the value of data or know how to best communicate using concepts from data management. Make it fun, and create enthusiasm.

All of these changes, in addition to the architectural changes, are significant. Enterprise architecture plays an important part in aligning all of these activities. We'll look at that next.

The Role of Enterprise Architects

As you progress through your data journey, the role of enterprise architects in your organization will change as much as the architecture itself. We've already discussed some aspects of this in Chapter 7. Enterprise architects must be seen as leaders who can guide development teams through the implementation of future-state architectures. They must be pragmatic and realistic, yet lay out the vision and inspire everyone to follow. They must breathe technology and excel in different areas, such as security, cloud infrastructure, software architecture, integration, and data management. Enterprise architects must also have a very deep understanding of business boundaries and know how to decouple them using modern integration patterns and business architecture.

This profile—strategist, deeply skilled engineer, custodian, inspiring leader—is far from the traditional stereotype of an architect as someone who thinks only in terms of static objects and diagrams, and usually sits deep down in an IT department or high in the ivory tower. In this new era, establishing an enterprise architecture practice requires different role profiles and focus areas. Let's see what other changes we might expect.

Blueprints and Diagrams

Enterprise architects traditionally delivered their artifacts as formalized models or Visio diagrams. This craft is no longer scalable in the era of dynamic, large enterprises. In modern practice, models, blueprints, and diagrams should be constructed from the underlying metamodel, using a code repository tool. This repository should be frequently updated with data modeling and design information, cost information, lineage, new application registration, ownership registration, and so on. On top of the repository there should be a layer visualizing what the modern enterprise looks like: its designs, business capabilities, domains, applications, data products, and so on.

Modern Skills

The core skills of enterprise architects are changing. Whereas traditionally architects have been considered content experts, in the new era architects are expected to be leaders in problem solving, design thinking, and creativity.

This shift from expert to problem solver requires both leadership and innovation, as is typically seen in expensive strategy consultancy firms. It also requires different frameworks and techniques, such as design thinking, prototyping, business-model canvas modeling, mind maps, and UX design, to name a few. Try to set realistic goals, and manage business users' expectations carefully.

Listening and communication skills are also crucial for the modern architect. Don't overload your business stakeholders with architecture-specific jargon. Try to be—or find people who are—assertive, open-minded, empathetic, and pragmatic. Finally, be prescriptive. Product owners and engineers often need to be guided, as they cannot oversee everything.

Control and Governance

Your enterprise architecture practice must find a balance between longer-term objectives and practicality. This need is contributing to the demise of enterprise architecture frameworks (such as the Open Group Architecture Framework's TOGAF standard)[1] because their logic of formalizing longstanding, static future states doesn't

---

1 In his book *The Practice of Enterprise Architecture: A Modern Approach to Business and IT Alignment* (SK Publishing), Svyatoslav Kotusev openly challenges the idea of enterprise architecture as a logical framework. Instead, he suggests an enterprise architecture practice that is based not on logical assumptions but empirical observations of how it is actually performed and works.

fit well into the new world of DevOps and DataOps. Yes, you need to paint the big picture, but you also need to be comfortable letting go of the "policing" mindset. A modern enterprise architect should become a community leader, taking the initiative to define minimum viable products, organizing design and whiteboard sessions, and discussing and translating customer needs. Leave the details to the teams, but be an authoritative expert when things go wrong.

Last Words

Future-generation enterprise data landscapes will be organized in completely new ways. Data, as you've learned throughout this book, will be much more distributed in the years to come—and so will data ownership. Enterprises need to learn how best to balance the imperatives of centralization and decentralization. This change, as you will soon start to experience for yourself, requires trial and error, and a new vision of data management.

Although the term *enterprise architecture* has negative associations for some, I strongly believe this function is critical for effecting large-scale change. Enterprise architecture is founded in working from an initial idea through to final implementation. There will always be a need to sketch a vision, design an abstract concept, make a strategy, create energy, and support teams in delivering on that vision. The same applies for implementing data management at scale. The process of building a data architecture at large, after all, starts with seeing the value of data.

A last word of advice: don't be nervous, flying is the safest form of travel! There's plenty of fun to be discovered in the wonderful world of data. We're only getting started.

Index

business users, 225

C

Cambridge Analytica, 11
Cambridge Semantics, 281
canonical data models, 154-155
canonical models, 155
capability maps, 37-38
    capability instances, 42
    domain-oriented data management, 56
catalogs, 76
    (see also data catalogs)
    data governance, 234
    data requests, 76
    initial implementation considerations, 354
    lineage metadata, 114
    metamodel searching, 270
CDC, event generation, 181
centers of excellence (COEs), 335
central data repositories, 298
    semantic consistency, 304
central distribution, data products, 66-68
centralization, 3, 8
    disadvantages, 14
    domains, selecting topologies, 77-78
centralized (MDM style), 294
centralized platforms, 8
CEP (complex event processing), 179
    compared to ESP, 183
ChatGPT, 8
chief data officer, 224
chief information security officer (CISO), 241
CI/CD (continuous integration/continuous
    delivery), DataOps process, 367-369
CISO (chief information security officer), 241
client libraries, application-generated events,
    180
cloud
    data processing advantages, 128
    efficiency considerations, 10-11
cloud adoption frameworks, 78-80
cloud computing services, FaaS, 162
cluster reduction, 303
coarse-grained and partially governed domain
    topology, 73
coarse-grained domain topology, 71
code sharing, data curation, 305
COEs (centers of excellence), 335
coexistence (MDM style), 294

collaboration
    challenges, 13
    data governance teams, 227
    data monetization, 28
    domains, 46
collaboration patterns, shared data, 306
collaborative metadata, 276
command sourcing, 189
command stores, 189
common driveway pattern, 62
complex event processing (CEP) (see CEP
    (complex event processing))
complicated subsystem teams, 219, 221
composite services, APIs, 160-161
conceptual application data model, 208-210
conceptual data models, 271-272
conformist pattern (data sharing), 307
consolidation (MDM style), 294
constructor domains, 47
consumer-aligned data products, 315
consumer-aligned domains, 27, 46
consumer-aligned landing zone topology,
    87-88
control planes, 162
control zones, 80
core subdomains, 33
CQRS data product design pattern, 104-107
cross-domain interoperability, 202-203
cross-domain security, 258-259
cross-functional teams
    data governance, 226
    size considerations, 324
crowdsourcing, metamodels, 274
CRUD database operations, 146
customer experience management, 166
customer/supplier pattern (data sharing), 307

D

dashboards compared to reports, 17
data
    applications, 314
    classification, 243-244
        DDSs, 315-316
    consistency, 297
    consumers, 27-28
        application logic filtering, 53
        data optimization for, 54
    consumption, 56, 313
        DDSs, 315-317

About the Author

Piethein Strengholt works as the chief data officer for Microsoft Netherlands. In this exciting role, he acts as a counterpart to CDO executives at large enterprises and is a driving force in growing the community and creating alignment with the product group. Piethein is also a prolific blogger and regularly speaks about the latest trends in data management, including the data mesh concept, data governance, and strategy at scale. He lives in the Netherlands with his family.

Colophon

The animal on the cover of *Data Management at Scale* is a European green lizard (*Lacerta viridis*), which can be found across southeast Europe. European green lizards gravitate toward dense hedges and shrubs where they can catch insects and small invertebrates and easily venture out into the sun.

European green lizards have bluish scales on their throats that are especially pronounced in the males. They sometimes eat fruit, bird eggs, smaller lizards, and mice. The lizards can grow to be 16 inches long, with the tail making up two-thirds of that length. If a predator has a European green lizard by the tail, it can detach its tail to escape and regrow it later.

These lizards have a classification status of Least Concern. Many of the animals on O'Reilly covers are endangered; all of them are important to the world.

The cover illustration is by Karen Montgomery, based on a black-and-white engraving from *Encyclopedie D'Histoire Naturelle*. The cover fonts are Gilroy Semibold and Guardian Sans. The text font is Adobe Minion Pro, the heading font is Adobe Myriad Condensed, and the code font is Dalton Maag's Ubuntu Mono.

O'REILLY®

Learn from experts.
Become one yourself.

Books | Live online courses
Instant answers | Virtual events
Videos | Interactive learning

Get started at oreilly.com.

Printed in the USA
CPSIA information can be obtained
at www.ICGtesting.com
JSHW051806290424
62133JS00012B/292

9 781098 138868